AMERICAN
FOREIGN POLICY

AMERICAN FOREIGN POLICY

The Twentieth Century in Documents

Gary A. Donaldson
Xavier University of Louisiana

New York   San Francisco   Boston
London   Toronto   Sydney   Tokyo   Singapore   Madrid
Mexico City   Munich   Paris   Cape Town   Hong Kong   Montreal

Vice President and Publisher: Priscilla McGeehon
Acquisitions Editor: Ashley Dodge
Executive Marketing Manager: Sue Westmoreland
Supplements Editor: Kristi Olson
Media Editor: Patrick McCarthy
Production Manager: Joseph Vella
Project Coordination, Photo Research, Text Design, and
    Electronic Page Makeup: Shepherd Incorporated
Cover Design Manager: Nancy Danahy
Cover Designer: Keithley and Associates, Inc.
Cover Photo: © Getty Images/PhotoDisc, Inc.
Manufacturing Buyer: Roy Pickering
Printer and Binder: Hamilton Printing Company
Cover Printer: The Lehigh Press

Library of Congress Cataloging-in-Publication Data

American foreign policy : the twentieth century in documents / [compiled by] Gary Donaldson.
        p. cm.
    Includes bibliographical references.
    ISBN 0-321-10506-0
    1. United States—Foreign relations—20th century—Sources.   I. Donaldson, Gary.

    E744 .A5326 2002
    327.73'009'04—dc21

                                                    2002070223

Please visit our website at http://www.ablongman.com

ISBN 0-321-10506-0

1 2 3 4 5 6 7 8 9 10—HT—05 04 03 02

CONTENTS

Preface xi

CHAPTER 1
The New Imperialism, 1898–1914   1

1.1   Carl Schurz Opposes Expansion After the Spanish-American War,
      January 1899   3
1.2   Albert Beveridge Supports Imperialism Before the U.S. Senate,
      January 1900   9
1.3   The Philippine War, A Suffragist's View   11
1.4   The Open Door Note to Germany, September 1899   14
1.5   J. P. Gordy, "The Ethics of the Panama Case"   17
1.6   Theodore Roosevelt Responds to His Critics, *An Autobiography*, 1916   20
1.7   The Roosevelt Corollary to the Monroe Doctrine, December 6, 1904   24
1.8   Secretary of State Philander Knox and U.S. Private Investments in China,
      November 6, 1909   26
1.9   President William Howard Taft Defends Dollar Diplomacy,
      December 3, 1912   27
1.10 President Woodrow Wilson's Address to Congress on the Crisis
      in Mexico, April 20, 1914   30

CHAPTER 2
War and Peace, 1914–1920   32

2.1   President Woodrow Wilson's Appeal for Neutrality, August 19, 1914   34
2.2   Secretary of State William Jennings Bryan's Note Protesting the Sinking
      of the *Lusitania*, May 13, 1915   35
2.3   The *Sussex* Pledge, May 4, 1916   37
2.4   The Zimmermann Note from the German Foreign Secretary,
      Arthur Zimmermann, to the German Ambassador to Mexico,
      January 16, 1917   40
2.5   Do the People Want War? *The New Republic*, March 3, 1917   41
2.6   President Woodrow Wilson's War Message to Congress, April 2, 1917   42
2.7   Wilson's Fourteen Points, Delivered to a Joint Session of Congress,
      January 8, 1918   46
2.8   President Woodrow Wilson's Statement to the Senate Foreign
      Relations Committee, August 19, 1919   52

2.9　Senator William E. Borah's Speech Before the Senate in Opposition
to Ratification of the League, November 19, 1919　　　　54

CHAPTER 3

The Interwar Period and Preparing
for War, 1920–1939　59

3.1　Five-Power Treaty, February 6, 1922　　　　61
3.2　President Herbert Hoover's Disarmament Proposal, Delivered
to the League of Nations, June 22, 1932　　　　62
3.3　Letter from Joseph C. Grew, Ambassador to Japan, to Secretary of State
Cordell Hull, May 11, 1933　　　　65
3.4　The Consul General at Berlin (George Messersmith) to the
Undersecretary of State, June 26, 1933　　　　66
3.5　H. C. Engelbrecht and F. C. Hanighen, *Merchants of Death*, 1934　　　　68
3.6　The Hirota Government's National Foreign Policies (Reported
to Emperor Hirohito, August 15, 1936)　　　　73
3.7　President Franklin Roosevelt's Address Before the Pan-American
Conference for the Maintenance of Peace, Buenos Aires, Argentina,
December 1, 1936　　　　76
3.8　Neutrality Act of 1937, May 1, 1937　　　　80
3.9　*The London Times* Reports Prime Minister Neville Chamberlain's
Return from Munich, September 30, 1938　　　　82

CHAPTER 4

U.S. Foreign Policy and World War II　86

4.1　President Franklin Roosevelt's Fireside Chat on the Dangers
of Nazi Domination of Europe, December 29, 1940　　　　88
4.2　Charles Lindbergh, "We Cannot Win This War for England,"
May 1941　　　　91
4.3　The Atlantic Charter, August 14, 1941　　　　93
4.4　FDR Responds to the *Greer* Incident, September 11, 1941　　　　94
4.5　Memorandum Handed by the Japanese Ambassador (Nomura)
to the Secretary of State at 2:20 P.M., December 7, 1941　　　　98
4.6　FDR's War Message to Congress, December 8, 1941　　　　102
4.7　The Yalta Conference Accords, February 1945　　　　105
4.8　Henry Stimson Explains Why the Bomb Was Necessary　　　　108
4.9　Was the Bomb Necessary?　　　　112

CHAPTER 5
Origins of the Cold War, 1945–1952   115

5.1	President Harry S. Truman's Statement on the Fundamentals of American Foreign Policy, October 27, 1945	117
5.2	Henry Wallace's Madison Square Garden Speech, September 12, 1946	118
5.3	The Novikov Letter, September 1946	123
5.4	The Truman Doctrine, March 12, 1947	127
5.5	Secretary of State George Marshall's Report to the Senate Committee on Foreign Affairs, January 8, 1948	130
5.6	"X" and Containment. George Kennan, "The Sources of Soviet Conduct"	136
5.7	Walter Lippmann Responds to "Mr. X"	142
5.8	Declaration of the Founding of the Cominform, September 1947	148
5.9	National Security Council Paper #68, April 1950	152
5.10	Truman's Decision to Enter the War in Korea, June 1950	160

CHAPTER 6
New Look: U.S. Foreign Policy in the Age of Eisenhower   162

6.1	Secretary of State John Foster Dulles, "The Threat of a Red Asia," March 29, 1954	164
6.2	Secretary of State John Foster Dulles' Strategy of Massive Retaliation, January 12, 1954	167
6.3	Hans Morgenthau's Response to Dulles	169
6.4	Secretary of State John Foster Dulles Explains Events in Guatemala, June 30, 1954	173
6.5	E. Howard Hunt Explains Events in Guatemala	175
6.6	President Dwight Eisenhower's Speech in the Aftermath of the Suez Crisis and the Soviet Invasion of Hungary, January 5, 1957	178
6.7	Sputnik and the Space Race, *Newsweek,* October 14, 1957	182
6.8	Speech by Fidel Castro at the UN General Assembly, September 26, 1960	186
6.9	U.S. Response to Castro's Speech, October 14, 1960	192
6.10	Eisenhower's Farewell Address, January 18, 1961	194

CHAPTER 7
Kennedy, Johnson, and an American Tragedy, 1961–1968   197

7.1	Dean Rusk Recalls the Bay of Pigs Incident, April 17, 1961	200
7.2	E. Howard Hunt Recalls the Bay of Pigs Invasion	202

7.3   President John Kennedy Addresses the Nation on the Cuban
      Missile Crisis, October 22, 1962   204
7.4   President John Kennedy, *Ich bin ein Berliner,* Berlin, West Germany,
      June 26, 1963   207
7.5   President Lyndon Johnson's Message to Congress on the Tonkin
      Gulf Incident, August 5, 1964   209
7.6   President Lyndon Johnson's Speech, "Peace Without Conquest,"
      at Johns Hopkins University, April 7, 1965   211
7.7   Senator J. William Fulbright on the Johnson Administration's
      Foreign Policy in Vietnam, May 1966   215
7.8   "Beyond Vietnam: A Time to Break Silence." Martin Luther King, Jr.
      Opposes the War, April 4, 1967   217
7.9   Vo Nguyen Giap on Neo-colonialism and the American War   225
7.10 Robert McNamara's Memoir of U.S. Involvement in Vietnam   228
7.11 Mr. McNamara's Other War: A Vietnam Veteran Responds   230

CHAPTER 8

From Nixon to Carter, 1969–1981   233

8.1   President Richard Nixon on the Vietnamization of the War,
      November 3, 1969   235
8.2   Senator George McGovern and the "Cruel Hoax" of Vietnamization,
      February 4, 1970   240
8.3   CIA Operating Guidance Cable on Coup Plotting in Chile,
      October 16, 1970   243
8.4   "UN Seats Peking and Expels Taipei," *New York Times,*
      October 26, 1971   245
8.5   The Shanghai Communique, February 27, 1972   246
8.6   Secretary of State Henry Kissinger, Détente, and the Grand Design.
      Speech Before Senate Foreign Relations Committee, September 1974 250
8.7   President Jimmy Carter on Human Rights as Foreign Policy.
      Commencement Address at University of Notre Dame,
      May 22, 1977   257
8.8   President Jimmy Carter Announces the Camp David Accords,
      September 18, 1978   258
8.9   *Time's* Report of the Iranian Hostage Crisis, November 19, 1979 262

CHAPTER 9

The Reagan Era, the Gulf War, and the New World Order   266

9.1   President Ronald Reagan's "Evil Empire" Speech, March 8, 1983   269
9.2   President Ronald Reagan's "Star Wars" Speech, March 23, 1983   272
9.3   Senator Christopher J. Dodd's Opposition to Ronald Reagan's Central
      American Policy, April 28, 1983   276

9.4   Pat Buchanan, "How the Gulf Crisis Is Rupturing the Right,"
       August 1990   279
9.5   Congressman Stephen Solarz, "The Stakes in the Gulf," January 1991   280
9.6   President George H. W. Bush, "The Challenge of Building Peace:
       A Renewal of History," September 23, 1991   285
9.7   U.S. Department of State, Country Reports on Human Rights
       Practices for 1996   287
9.8   China Responds, *China Daily*, March 5, 1997   290
9.9   Secretary of State Madeline Albright on the Legacy of the Marshall
       Plan, Harvard Commencement Address, June 5, 1977   294
9.10   President Bill Clinton, "Remarks by the President on Foreign Policy,"
       San Francisco, February 26, 1999   299
9.11   President George W. Bush, September 11, 2001 Evening Address
       to the Nation   303

PREFACE

The purpose of foreign policy is not to provide an outlet for our own sentiments of hope or indignation; it is to shape real events in a real world.
— John Fitzgerald Kennedy

Among the many topics and areas of study in U.S. history, the nation's foreign policy is quite possibly the most contentious. Nearly every event in the nation's foreign policy history has its many detractors, its various critics, its opposing viewpoints. At times there seems to be as many schools of thought as there are foreign policy historians. Some members of other disciplines might see this sort of dissent as a problem, an inability to get at the truth, a fractious environment that finds no answers. But in history such variations of opinion and interpretation make for interesting and exciting study—an almost continuously opened window on world events, past and present. U.S. foreign policy is a rich field. It produces a never-ending mountain of research and writing that tries to explain the nature of the nation, its place in history and the world.

The question is, then, how best to study it. One way is through the study of documents, the original sources of text, those pieces of information that have forged the decisions that have shaped the nation's foreign policy. For the historian, this is where history begins. It is from these types of original sources that historians form their opinions, build and document their arguments, and devise their various schools of thought.

For young historians, however, the classroom use of documents has a different purpose. Documents greatly enhance other forms of teaching. They can supplement class lectures, additional readings, and narrative texts. They show students the origins of the decision-making process, the origins of national policy, and even the origins of those historical viewpoints and opposing viewpoints. For historians and students alike, historical documents are the headwaters of a great river.

U.S. foreign policy (like the foreign policy of all nations) was established in its treaties, the speeches of its leaders, and through various international communiqués. But in the United States national policy has also been molded by various opinions and dissenting opinions inside and outside the government, by documents that reflect the opposing side in international conflicts, and even by various documents that reflect the foreign policies of other nations and national leaders. Possibly it would not be surprising that documents originally having nothing to do with the United States also later impacted the United States greatly. For instance, few would oppose the argument that the Munich Accords between Great Britain and Nazi Germany in 1938 had a tremendous influence on postwar U.S. foreign policy. To make that point, in 1990, in response to Saddam Hussein's invasion of Kuwait, President

George H. W. Bush insisted, "No more Munichs." Necessarily, there are included here a large number of speeches, treaties, and communiqués. But there are also opinions, dissenting opinions, international viewpoints, and documents between other nations that later changed the course of U.S. foreign policy and American history.

It is important for students studying these documents to see that U.S. foreign policy (as a topic of history or as the events themselves in history) does not stand alone. History is inexorably interconnected. Foreign policy cannot be understood without an intense study of the political and even the social background of the events. To ask, "how did the American people perceive the events?" is always an important question. There can be, for instance, no real understanding of the Vietnam War without an understanding of the political decisions being made in Washington or the powerful pressures on the government from certain sectors of American society during the war years. Diplomacy was only part of the decision-making processes. The same can be said of most events: the acquisition of the Philippines, the decision to enter World War I, the playing out of events during the Cold War—and on and on. America is a democracy. The American people, through their own voices or through the voices of their elected representatives, will have a say in events. It should be recognized that it is a part of American history—a part that holds greater importance in the United States than in most other nations of the world. Again, U.S. foreign policy does not stand alone.

*   *   *

Twentieth-century U.S. foreign policy was dynamic. The nation made its way from continentalism to imperialism, back to a post–World War I cautious isolationism, and then to a post–World War II internationalism. By the end of the century, America had become a global entity, with interests in nearly every corner of the world. The twentieth century had become (as Walter Lippmann once predicted it would become) the American century. That seemed to tout America's greatness, not only in its military might, but also in its economic power and even in the strength of its social structures and cultural identities that seemed to spring up in every corner of the world. That you could buy a Coke in deepest Africa or stay at a Holiday Inn in Urumqi in northwestern China seemed to show the power of everything American. Unfortunately, not all of those interests and cultural icons were welcomed. And as the century closed, the United States has been forced to grapple with accusations of being a global policeman, a cultural imperialist, and even a hegemonic power to be feared. It was the American century, but the results of that have not always been good in the eyes of the rest of the world—or even in the eyes of some Americans.

Another important theme in the history of U.S. foreign policy has been the conflict, throughout the century, between the nation's internationalists and those who would take a more cautious approach toward diplomacy. It has often divided the nation, divided the government, and even divided historians. That argument, that difference of opinion, has largely shaped the nation's foreign policy—shaped the way Washington has, through the century, dealt with the world. It is an exciting topic of study that has engaged some of the nation's greatest minds and leaders. It is one of the real defining topics in twentieth-century American history.

I would like to thank my family for their support in the production of this book. I would like to thank Xavier University for continually supporting my work over the years. And I would also like to thank the following reviewers for their help in putting this material together: Mark Bradley, University of Wisconsin–Milwaukee; Walter Burdick, Elmhurst College; Mary Byrnes, Wofford College; Kenton Clymer, University of Texas at El Paso; Betty Dessants, Florida State University; Larry G. Gerber, Auburn University; Martin Haas, Adelphi University; Joe Heim, California University of Pennsylvania; Marry Ann Heiss, Kent State University; Joan Hoff, Ohio University; Karen Jacobsen, Regis College/Tufts University; Lorraine Lees, Old Dominion University; Judy Barrett Litoff, Bryant College; James I. Matray, New Mexico State University; Martin Menke, Rivier College; William Howard Moore, University of Wyoming; David Painter, Georgetown University; Noel Pugach, University of New Mexico; Travis Ricketts, Bryan College; Nick Sarantakes, Texas A&M University–Commerce; Thomas A. Schwartz, Vanderbilt University; E. Timothy Smith, Barry University; Kevin Smith, Ball State University; Tom Spencer, Northwest Missouri State University; Michael Tarver, McNeese State University; Patricia Wallace, Baylor University; Edward Wehrle, East Illinois University; and Tom Zeiler, University of Colorado.

Gary A. Donaldson
New Orleans

CHAPTER 1

The New Imperialism, 1898–1914

1.1 Carl Schurz Opposes Expansion After the Spanish-American War, January 1899

1.2 Albert Beveridge Supports Imperialism Before the U.S. Senate, January 1900

1.3 The Philippine War, A Suffragist's View

1.4 The Open Door Note to Germany, September 1899

1.5 J. P. Gordy, "The Ethics of the Panama Case"

1.6 Theodore Roosevelt Responds to His Critics, *An Autobiography,* 1916

1.7 The Roosevelt Corollary to the Monroe Doctrine, December 6, 1904

1.8 Secretary of State Philander Knox and U.S. Private Investments in China, November 6, 1909

1.9 President William Howard Taft Defends Dollar Diplomacy, December 3, 1912

1.10 President Woodrow Wilson's Address to Congress on the Crisis in Mexico, April 20, 1914

1898–1914 Timeline

Date	Year	Event
April 20, 1898	1898	US declares war on Spain
January 1899	1899	Carl Schurz opposes expansion
September 1899	1900	Open Door Note to Germany
January 1900	1901	Albert Beveridge supports expansion
September 1901	1902	Theodore Roosevelt becomes president
December 6, 1904	1903	Roosevelt Corollary to the Monroe Doctrine
March 1909	1904	William Howard Taft becomes president
November 6, 1909	1905	Knox on US investments in China
December 3, 1912	1906	Taft defends Dollar Diplomacy
February 1913	1907	Vitoriano Huerta takes control in Mexico
March 1913	1908	Woodrow Wilson becomes president
April 9, 1914	1909	Tampico incident
April 20, 1914	1910	Wilson's address on the crisis in Mexico
August 15, 1914	1911	Panama Canal opens
	1912	
	1913	
	1914	

1.1 **Carl Schurz Opposes Expansion After the Spanish-American War, January 1899**

1.2 **Albert Beveridge Supports Imperialism Before the U.S. Senate, January 1900**

The Spanish-American War was a significant turning point in American foreign policy. The remnants of the crumbled Spanish empire, both in America and Asia, lay at the feet of the victorious United States. A debate immediately grew over the wisdom of becoming an imperial power, a role that many Americans believed was inconsistent with their history. The debate was engaged poignantly in the Senate. Few were concerned with the fate of Cuba. The big questions concerned the Philippines. How should the U.S. deal with that former Spanish colony?

While the debate raged in Congress, anti-imperialist leagues formed throughout the nation with the largest and most important being in Boston. There, such august figures as Grover Cleveland, Carl Schurz, John Sherman, Samuel Gompers, Andrew Carnegie, Charles Francis Adams, William James, William Dean Howells, Jane Addams, Lincoln Steffens, and Mark Twain headed the membership list. These great figures had little in common with each other, and just as varied were their motives. Some opposed annexation because they believed in the right of the Filipinos to govern themselves, while others feared racial contamination if the Filipinos became Americans, and still others like Samuel Gompers worried that Filipinos would take jobs from American workers.

The main argument against the annexation of the Philippines, however, was the basic belief that the United States simply did not have the right to govern people without their consent. To do so, they argued, violated the primary principle of American democracy. Citing many lessons of history, these anti-imperialists insisted that to rule by tyranny abroad would bring tyrannical rule home to the American people. The members of the Anti-Imperialist League of Boston wrote the following into their platform: "We maintain that governments derive their just powers from the consent of the governed. We insist that the subjugation of any people is 'criminal aggression' and open disloyalty to the distinctive principles of our Government."

Carl Schurz was a primary figure in the anti-imperialist movement. Forced to leave Germany because of his participation in the revolution of 1848, Schurz came to America in 1852. He served as a brigadier general in the Union army, was elected to the Senate, and served as Secretary of the Interior in the Hayes administration. Here, in *Document 1.1*, Schurz argues that imperialism is immoral and historically un-American. He also attacks the widely held belief that imperialism was necessary for the growth of the American economy.

On the other side of the argument were the imperialists, the advocates of annexation. Among them were businessmen who argued convincingly that the Philippines would open Asian markets to U.S. products, thus boosting the U.S. economy. Military men like Alfred Thayer Mahan and Theodore Roosevelt pointed out that a large navy stationed in the Philippines could protect U.S. commercial shipping in the eastern

Pacific. The press was also avidly expansionist. *The Literary Digest* listed 84 major American newspapers that supported annexation. Protestant clergymen supported annexation; they chafed at the bit to Christianize the Filipinos—ignoring that a large part of the population was already Catholic. These imperialists argued for manifest destiny, claimed that the Constitution set no limits on expansion, and insisted that they had no plans to rule by tyranny. "We come as ministerial angels, not as despots," declared a pro-annexationist senator from Minnesota.

By the time the Paris treaty came up for a vote in the Senate on February 6, 1899, the nation was in a frenzy over the issue—but it was also in an expansionist mood. Most observers expected a close vote that would transcend party lines. However, William Jennings Bryan, an important spokesman for the anti-annexationists and the titular head of the Democratic party, persuaded several Democratic senators to support annexation because, he said, the 1900 presidential election (in which Bryan expected to run on an anti-imperialist platform) would be a referendum on the Senate vote. It was a mistake. Bryan's advice swayed enough anti-imperialists to ratify the treaty in a close vote of 57 to 27. Ratified, the treaty became law and the Philippines were annexed. Bryan then lost the election. The forces of anti-imperialism, it seemed, had come to the aid of imperialism.

The vote in Washington did not take into account the Filipinos, who had come to the conclusion that post-war independence for Cuba also meant independence for the Philippines. The exiled leader of the Filipino resistance movement against Spain, Emilio Aguinaldo, was under the impression that the United States had promised Philippine independence. The Filipino force under Aguinaldo's command was formidable, ardently nationalist, and not surprisingly unwilling to accept a second colonial ruler. In February 1899 fighting broke out between the nationalists and the Americans, followed by three and one-half years of ugly guerrilla warfare.

Document 1.2 is a speech delivered in the Senate in January 1900 by Indiana Senator Albert Beveridge on the topic of imperialism. One of the great advocates of expansionism at the turn of the century, Beveridge spoke of America's manifest destiny, the promise of the great China market, the importance of the Pacific to the future of American trade, and of the future of God's chosen people. As he spoke the Filipino resistance was waging a revolt against U.S. occupation of the Philippines.

....

DOCUMENT 1.1

CARL SCHURZ OPPOSES EXPANSION AFTER THE SPANISH-AMERICAN WAR, JANUARY 1899

If ever, it behooves the American people to think and act with calm deliberations, for the character and future of the republic and the welfare of its people now living and yet to be born are in unprecedented jeopardy. To form a candid judgment of what this republic has been, what it may become, and what it ought to be, let us first recall to our minds its condition before the recent Spanish War.

Our government was, in the words of Abraham Lincoln, "the government of the people, by the people, and for the people." It was the

SOURCE: Carl Schurz, *American Imperialism: The Convocation Address Delivered on the Occasion of the Twenty-Seventh Convocation of the University of Chicago, January 4, 1899* (Boston: Dana Estes and Company, 1899), 3–31.

noblest ambition of all true Americans to carry this democratic government to the highest degree of perfection in justice, in probity, in assured peace, in the security of human rights, in progressive civilization; to solve the problem of popular self-government on the grandest scale, and thus to make this republic the example and guiding star of mankind.

We had invited the oppressed of all nations to find shelter here, and to enjoy with us the blessings of free institutions. They came by the millions. Some were not so welcome as others, but under the assimilating force of American life in our temperate climate, which stimulates the working energies, nurses the spirit of orderly freedom, and thus favors the growth of democracies, they became good Americans, most in the first, all in the following generations. And so with all the blood-crossings caused by the motley immigration, we became a substantially homogeneous people, united by common political beliefs and ideas, by common interests, laws, and aspirations,—in one word, a nation. Indeed, we were not without our difficulties and embarrassments, but only one of them, the race antagonism between the Negroes and the whites, especially where the Negroes live in mass, presents a problem which so far has baffled all efforts at practical solution in harmony with the spirit of our free institutions, and thus threatens complications of grave character.

We glorified in the marvelous growth of our population, wealth, power, and civilization, and in the incalculable richness of the resources of our country, a country capable of harboring three times our present population, and of immeasurable further material development. Our commerce with the world abroad, although we had no colonies, and but a small navy, spread with unprecedented rapidity, capturing one foreign market after another, not only for the products of our farms, but also for many of those manufacturing industries, with prospect of indefinite extension.

Peace reigned within our borders, and there was not the faintest shadow of danger of for-

According to this cartoon, Dewey's taking of Manila surprised the European monarchs and thrust the United States onto the world stage. *Courtesy of BoondocksNet.com*

eign attack. Our voice, whenever we chose to speak in the councils of nations, was listened to with respect, even the mightiest sea-power on occasion yielded to us a deference far beyond its habit in its intercourse with others. We were considered ultimately invincible, if not invulnerable, in our continental stronghold. It is our boast, not that we possessed great and costly armies and navies, but that we did not need any. This exceptional blessing was our pride, as it was the envy of the world. We looked down with pitying sympathy on other nations which submissively groaned under the burden of constantly increasing armaments, and we praised our good fortune for having saved us from so wretched a fate.

Such was our condition, such our beliefs and ideals, such our ambition and our pride, but a short year ago. . . .

Then came the Spanish War. A few vigorous blows laid the feeble enemy helpless at our feet.

The whole scene seemed to have suddenly changed. According to the solemn proclamation of our government, the war had been undertaken solely for the liberation of Cuba, as a war of humanity and not of conquest. But our easy victories had put conquest within our reach, and when our armies occupied foreign territory, a loud demand arose that, pledge or no pledge to the contrary, the conquests should be kept, even the Philippines on the other side of the globe, and that as to Cuba herself, independence would only be a provisional formality. Why not? was the cry. Has not the career of the republic almost from its very beginning been one of territorial expansion? Has it not acquired Louisiana, Florida, Texas, the vast countries that came to us through the Mexican War, and Alaska, and has it not digested them well? Were not those acquisitions much larger than those now in contemplation? If the republic could digest the old, why not the new? What is the difference?

Only look with an unclouded eye, and you will soon discover differences enough, warning you to beware. There are five of decisive importance.

1. All the former acquisitions were on this continent, and, excepting Alaska, contiguous to our borders.
2. They were situated, not in the tropical, but in the temperate zone, where democratic institutions thrive, and where our people could migrate in mass.
3. They were but very thinly peopled,—in fact, without any population that would have been in the way of new settlement.
4. They could be organized as territories in the usual manner, with the exception that they would presently come into the Union as self-governing States, with populations substantially homogeneous to our own.
5. They did not require a material increase of our army or navy, either for their subjection to our rule, or for their defense against any probable foreign attack that might be provoked by being in our possession.

Acquisitions of that nature we might, since the slavery trouble has been allayed, make indefinitely without in any dangerous degree imperilling our great experiment of democratic institutions on the grandest scale; without putting the peace of the republic in jeopardy, and without depriving us of the inestimable privilege of comparative unarmed security on a compact continent which may, indeed, by an enterprising enemy, be scratched on its edges, but is, with a people like ours, virtually impregnable. Even of our far-away Alaska it can be said that, although at present a possession of doubtful value, it is at least mainly on this continent, and may at some future time, when the inhabitants of the British possessions happily wish to unite with us, be within our uninterrupted boundaries.

Compare now with our old acquisitions as to all these important points those at present in view. They are not continental, not contiguous to our present domain but beyond the seas, the Philippines many thousand miles distant from our coast. They are all situated in the tropics, where people of the northern races, such as the Anglo-Saxons, or, generally speaking, people of Germanic blood, have never migrated in mass to stay; and they are more or less densely populated, parts of them as densely as Massachusetts, their populations consisting almost exclusively of races to whom the tropical climate is congenial,—Spanish Creoles, mixed with Negroes in the West Indies, and Malays, Tagals, Filipinos, Chinese, Japanese, Negritos, and various more or less barbarous tribes in the Philippines. . . .

The scheme of Americanizing our "new possessions" in that sense is therefore absolutely hopeless. The immutable forces of nature are against it. Whatever we may do for their improvement, the people of the Spanish Antilles [Philippines] will remain in overwhelming numerical predominance . . . some of them quite clever in their way, but the vast majority utterly alien to us, not only in origin and language, but in habits, traditions, ways of thinking, principles, ambitions,—in short, in most things that are of the greatest importance in human intercourse and especially in political cooperation. And under the influence of their tropical climate they will prove incapable of becoming assimilated to the Anglo-Saxon. They would, therefore, remain in the population of this republic a hopelessly heterogeneous element,—in some respects more hopeless even than the colored people now living among us.

What, then, shall we do with such populations? Shall we, according, not indeed to the letter, but to the evident spirit of our constitution, organize those countries as territories with a view to their eventual admission as States? If they become States on an equal footing with the other States they will not only be permitted to govern themselves as to their home concerns, but they will take part in governing the whole republic, in governing us, by sending Senators and Representatives to our Congress to help make our laws, and by voting for President and Vice-President to give our national government its executive. The prospect of the consequences which would follow the admission of the Spanish Creoles and the Negroes of the West India Islands [Cuba and Puerto Rico], and of the Malays and Tagals of the Philippines, to participation in the conduct of our government is so alarming that you instinctively pause before taking the step.

But this may be avoided, it is said, by governing the new possessions as mere dependencies, or subject provinces. I will waive the constitutional question and merely point out that this would be a most serious departure from the rule that governed our former acquisitions, which are so frequently quoted as precedents. It is useless to speak of the District of Columbia and Alaska as proof that we have done such things before and can do them again. Every candid mind will at once admit the vast difference between those cases and the permanent establishment of substantially arbitrary government, over large territories with many millions of inhabitants, and with a prospect of their being many more of the same kind, if we once launch out on a ca-

reer of conquest. The question is not merely whether we can do such things, but whether, having the public good at heart, we should do them.

If we adopt such a system, then we shall, for the first time since the abolition of slavery, again have two kinds of Americans: Americans of the first class, who enjoy the privilege of taking part in the government in accordance with our old constitutional principles, and Americans of the second class, who are to be ruled in a substantially arbitrary fashion by the Americans of the first class, through congressional legislation and the action of the national executive,—not to speak of individual "masters" arrogating to themselves powers beyond law.

This will be a difference no better—nay, rather somewhat worse—than that which a century and a quarter ago still existed between Englishmen of the first and Englishmen of the second class, the first represented by King George and the British Parliament, and the second by the American colonists. The difference called forth that great paean of human liberty, the Declaration of Independence,—a document which, I regret to say, seems, owing to the intoxication of conquest, to have lost much of its charm among some of our fellow citizens. Its fundamental principle was that "governments derived their just powers from the consent of the governed." We are now told that we have never fully lived up to that principle, and that, therefore, in our new policy we may cast it aside altogether. But I say to you that, if we are true believers in democratic government, it is our duty to move in the direction toward the full realization of that principle, and not in the direction away from it. If you tell me that we cannot govern the people of those new possessions in accordance with that principle, then I answer that this is a good reason why this democracy should not attempt to govern them at all.

If we do, we shall transform the government of the people, for the people, and by the people, for which Abraham Lincoln lived, into a government of one part of the people, the strong, over another part, the weak. Such an abandonment of a fundamental principle as a permanent policy may at first seem to bear only upon more or less distant dependencies, but it can hardly fail in its ultimate effects to disturb the rule of the same principle in the conduct of democratic government at home. And I warn the American people that a democracy cannot so deny its faith as to the vital conditions of its being, it cannot long play the king over subject populations, without creating within itself ways of thinking and habits of action most dangerous to its own vitality,— most dangerous especially to those classes of society which are the least powerful in the assertion, and the most helpless in the defense of their rights. Let the poor and the men who earn their bread by the labor of their hands pause and consider well before they give their assent to a policy so deliberately forgetful of the equality of rights. . . .

The cry suddenly raised that this great country has become too small for us is too ridiculous to demand an answer, in view of the fact that our present population may be tripled and still have ample elbow-room, with resources to support many more. But we are told that our industries are gasping for breath; that we are suffering from overproduction; that our products must have new outlets, and that we need colonies and dependencies the world over to give us more markets. More markets? Certainly. But do we, civilized beings, indulge in the absurd and barbarous notion that we must own the countries with which we wish to trade? Here are our official reports before us, telling us that of late years our export trade has grown enormously, not only of farm products, but of the products of our manufacturing industries; in fact, that "our sales of manufactured goods have continued to extend with a facility and promptitude of results which have excited the serious concern of countries that, for generations, had not only controlled the home markets, but had practically monopolized certain lines of trade in their hands."

There is a distinguished Englishman, the Right Hon. Charles T. Richie, President of the Board of Trade, telling a British Chamber of Commerce that "we [Great Britain] are being rapidly overhauled in exports by other nations, especially the United States and Germany," their exports fast advancing, while British exports are declining. What? Great Britain, the greatest colonial power in the world, losing in competition with two nations, one of which had, so far, no colonies or dependencies at all, and the other none of any commercial importance? What does this mean? It means that, as proved by the United States and Germany, colonies are not necessary for the expansion of trade, and that, as proved by Great Britain, colonies do not protect a nation against a loss of trade. Our trade expands, without colonies or big navies, because we produce certain goods better and in proportion cheaper than other people do. British trade declines, in spite of immense dependencies and the strongest navy, because it does not successfully compete with us in that respect. Trade follows, not the flag, but the best goods for the price. Expansion of export trade and new markets! We do not need foreign conquests to get them, for we have them, and are getting them more and more in rapidly increasing growth.

"But the Pacific Ocean," we are mysteriously told, "will be the great commercial battle-field of the future, and we must quickly use the present opportunity to secure our position on it. The visible presence of great power is necessary for us to get our share of the trade of China. Therefore, we must have the Philippines." Well, the China trade is worth having, although for a time out of sight the Atlantic Ocean will be an infinitely more important battle-field of commerce than the Pacific, and one European customer is worth more than twenty or thirty Asiatics. But does the trade of China really require that we should have the Philippines and make a great display of power to get our share? Read the consular reports, and you will find that in many places in China our trade is rapidly gaining, while some British trade is declining, and that while Great Britain has on hand the greatest display of power imaginable and we have none. And in order to increase our trade there, our consuls advise us to improve our commercial methods, saying nothing of the necessity of establishing a base of naval operations, and of our appearing there with war-ships and heavy guns. Trade is developed, not by the best guns, but by the best merchants. But why do other nations prepare to fight for the Chinese trade? Other nations have done many foolish things which we have been, and I hope will remain, wise enough not to imitate. If it should come to fighting for Chinese customers, the powers engaged in that fight are not likely to find out that they pay too high a price for what can be gained, and that at last the peaceful and active neutral will have the best bargain. At any rate, to launch into all the embroilments of an imperialistic policy by annexing the Philippines in order to snatch something more of the Chinese trade would be for us the foolishest game of all. . . .

The American flag, we are told, whenever once raised, must never be hauled down. Certainly, every patriotic citizen will always be ready, if need be, to fight and to die under his flag, wherever it may wave in justice, and for the best interests of the country. But I say to you, woe to the republic if it should ever be without citizens patriotic and brave enough to defy the demagogues' cry, and to haul down the flag wherever it may be raised not in justice, and not for the best interests of the country. Such a republic would not last long.

But, they tell us, we have been living in a state of contemptible isolation which must be broken so that we may feel and conduct ourselves "as a full-grown member of the family of nations." What is that so-called isolation? Is it commercial? Last year our foreign trade amounted to nearly two thousand million dollars, and is rapidly growing. Is that commercial isolation? Or are we politically isolated? Remember our history. Who was it that early in this century broke up the piracy of the Barbary States? Who was it that took a leading part in delivering the world's commerce of the Danish

Sound dues? Who was it that first opened Japan to communication with the Western world? And what power has in this century made more valuable contributions to international law than the United States? Do you call that contemptible isolation? It is true, we did not meddle much with foreign affairs that did not concern us. But if the circle of our interests widens, and we wish to meddle more, must we have the Philippines in order to feel and conduct ourselves as a member of the family of nations . . . ?

Thus we shall be their best friends without being their foreign rulers. We shall have done our duty to them, to ourselves, and to the world. However imperfect their governments may still remain, they will at least be their own, and they will not with their disorders and corruptions contaminate our institutions, the integrity of which is not only to ourselves, but to liberty-loving mankind, the most important concern of all. We may then await the result with generous patience,—with the same patience with which for many years we witnessed the revolutionary disorders of Mexico on our very borders, without any thought of taking her government into our own hands.

Ask yourselves whether a policy like this will not raise the American people to a level of moral greatness never before attained! If this democracy, after all the intoxication of triumph in war, conscientiously remembers its professions and pledges, and soberly reflects on its duties to itself and others, and then deliberately resists the temptation of conquest, it will achieve the grandest triumph of the democratic idea that history knows of. It will give the government of, for, and by the people a prestige it never before possessed. It will render the cause of civilization throughout the world a service without parallel. It will put its detractors to shame, and its voice will be heard in the council of nations with more sincere respect and more deference than ever. The American people, having given proof of their strength and also of their honesty and wisdom, will stand infinitely mightier before the world than any number of subjugated vassals could make them. Are not here our best interests both moral and material? Is not this genuine glory? Is not this true patriotism?

DOCUMENT 1.2

ALBERT BEVERIDGE SUPPORTS IMPERIALISM BEFORE THE U.S. SENATE, JANUARY 1900

The Philippines are ours forever, "territory belonging to the United States," as the constitution calls them. And just beyond the Philippines are China's illimitable markets. We will not retreat from either. We will not repudiate our duty in the archipelago. We will not abandon our opportunity in the Orient. We will not renounce our part in the mission of our race, trustee, under God, of the civilization of the world. And we will move forward to our work, not howling out regrets like slaves whipped to their burdens, but with gratitude for a task worthy of our strength, and thanksgiving to Almighty God that He has marked us as His chosen people, henceforth to lead in the regeneration of the world.

This island empire is the last land left in all the oceans. If it should prove a mistake to abandon it, the blunder once made would be irretrievable. If it proves a mistake to hold it, the error can be corrected when we will. Every other progressive nation stands ready to relieve us.

But to hold it will be no mistake. Our largest trade henceforth must be with Asia. The Pacific is our ocean. More and more Europe will manufacture the most it needs, secure from its colonies the most it consumes. Where shall we turn for customers for our surplus? Geography answers the question. China is our natural customer. She is nearer to us than to England, Germany, or Russia, the commercial powers of the

present and the future. They have moved nearer to China by securing permanent bases on her borders. The Philippines give us a base at the door of all the East. . . .

And the Pacific is the ocean of the commerce of the future. Most future wars will be conflicts for commerce. The power that rules the Pacific, therefore, is the power that rules the world. And, with the Philippines, that power is and will forever be the American Republic. . . .

No; the oceans are not limitations of the power which the Constitution expressly gives Congress to govern all territory the nation may acquire. The Constitution declares that "Congress shall have the power to dispose of and make all needful rules and regulations respecting the territory belonging to the United States." Not the Northwest Territory only; not Louisiana or Florida only; not territory on this continent only, but any territory belonging to the nation. The founders of the nation were not provincial. Theirs was the geography of the world. They were soldiers as well as landsmen, and they knew that where our ships should go our flag might follow. They had the logic of progress, and they knew that the republic they were planting must, in obedience to the laws of our expanding race, necessarily develop into the greater Republic which the world beholds to-day, and into the still mightier Republic which the world will finally acknowledge as the arbiter, under God, of the destinies of mankind. And so our fathers wrote into the Constitution these words of growth, of expansion, of empire, if you will, unlimited by geography or climate or by anything but the vitality and possibilities of the American people: "Congress shall have power to dispose of and make all needful rules and regulations respecting the territory belonging to the United States. . . . "

God has not been preparing the English-speaking and Teutonic peoples for a thousand years for nothing but vain and idle self-contemplation and self-admiration. No! He has not made us the master organizers of the world to establish a system where chaos reigns.

SOURCE: *Cong. Globe,* 56th Cong. 1st sess. (1900), XXXIII, 704–12.

He has given us the spirit of progress to overwhelm the forces of reaction throughout the earth. He has made us adept in government that we may administer government among savage and senile peoples. Were it not for such a force as this the world would relapse into barbarism and night. And of all our race He has marked the American people as His chosen nation to finally lead in the regeneration of the world. This is the divine mission of America, and it holds for us all the profit, all the glory, all the happiness possible to man. We are trustees of the world's progress, guardians of its righteous peace. The judgment of the Master is upon us: "Ye have been faithful over a few things; I will make you ruler over many things."

What will history say of us? Shall it say that we renounced that holy trust, left the savage to his base condition, the wilderness to the reign of waste, deserted duty, abandoned glory, forgot our sordid profit even, because we feared our strength and read the charter of our powers with the doubter's eye and the quibbler's mind? Shall it say that, called by events to captain and command the proudest, ablest, purest race of history in history's noblest work, we declined that great commission? Our fathers would not have had it so. No! They founded no paralytic government, incapable of the simplest acts of administration. They planted no sluggard people, passive while the world's work calls them. They established no reactionary nation. . . .

Blind indeed is he who sees not the hand of God in events so vast, so harmonious, so benign. Reactionary indeed is the mind that perceives not that this vital people is the strongest of the saving forces of the world; that our place, therefore, is as the head of the construction and redeeming nations of the earth; and that to stand aside while events march on is a surrender of our interests, a betrayal of our duty as blind as it is base.

1.3   The Philippine War, A Suffragist's View

It took two years and 125,000 troops to suppress the Filipino Insurrection and bring the Philippines under U.S. control. Over 7,000 U.S. soldiers died in the conflict, along with an estimated 200,000 Philippine civilians. It was a fierce, ruthless, guerrilla war fought thousands of miles away for American colonial interests in Asia. The anti-imperialists continued their drumbeat against the nation's subjection of a people against their will.

The *Woman's Journal* was a primary publication of the suffragist movement at the turn of the century. *Document 1.3* is a short article from the *Journal* by a woman who sees a direct relationship between America's actions in the Philippines and the unwillingness of the nation's politicians to give women the right to vote. Her answer to the problem of America's overseas aggressions is clear. The writer, Lida Calvert Obenchain, was not from Boston, Philadelphia, or New York, the hotbeds of the suffragist movement, but from a small town in southern Kentucky.

DOCUMENT 1.3

THE PHILIPPINE WAR, A SUFFRAGIST'S VIEW

In an article entitled "The Sin Against Light," in *The Public* of May 20 [1899], Henry De Forest Baldwin accuses the United States of deserting its "political ideals," and then looks around to find the reasons for "our new and revolutionary policy." He suggests that "our policy respecting the negro in the South, our protective tariff, our pension legislation, and the great mass of special legislation for private gain at the public expense," have led us into a war of conquest and the repudiation of those principles on which our government is supposed to be founded. This explanation is very far-fetched and unsatisfactory. The Philippine war is a perfectly natural and logical event, and it seems strange to hear intelligent people wondering over the spectacle of "the greatest republic on earth trying to wrest from these little islands the sacred right of self-government."

This government of ours is not a republic. It does not derive its just powers from the consent of the governed. Taxation without representation exists today just as in the days of '76. American women, except in a few favored States, are governed without their consent and taxed without representation, and it is the most logical thing in the world that a nation which disfranchises its women should enter upon a career of conquest and injustice, of which this present war is only a foretaste. An English paper, *The Manchester Guardian*, thinks it rather odd that the United States does not "apply the 'golden rule' of its own Constitution to the problem of the Philippines." Not at all. The United States has never applied the "golden rule" of its own Constitution to its own prob-

lems, and why should it be expected to apply it to the problems of other nations? The strange thing is not that we are trying to rob the Filipinos of the right of self-government. It would be inexplicably strange if we were not doing this very thing. Justice, like charity, must begin at home, and it would be the height of unreasonableness to expect a nation to render justice to a foreign people when it denies justice to its own women. We are fond of saying that if women were enfranchised, war would be an impossibility. This is capable of two constructions. The one that most readily occurs to the mind is that the votes of peace-loving women would over-balance the votes of belligerent men, but there is a nobler meaning still. Wars will cease when women are enfranchised, not because the votes and the influence of women will set aside the votes and the influence of men, but because the sentiment of justice in man that will lead to woman's enfranchisement will forever prevent him from wronging either a nation or an individual. I like to think that the reforms we hope for, when women are admitted to citizenship, will be brought about not by women working against men, but by the evolution of the sentiment of justice in the souls of both.

I cannot understand how any suffragist can uphold this Administration in the matter of the Philippine war. Every argument that is used to defend our injustice to the Filipinos has been worn threadbare in the defense of injustice to women. I am sick of hearing over and over again of "our duty" to the Filipinos and their "incapacity for self-government" and the necessity laid upon us of "protecting" them from foreign aggression and domestic strife. It is the same old story of "chivalry" and "mercy" being proffered where nothing but justice is asked.

It is the flimsiest of arguments to say that the Filipinos are not ready for self-government. Any people that can fight for liberty as the Filipinos have been fighting for it, may safely be left to carve out their own destiny. . . .

SOURCE: Lida Calvert Obenchain, "The Philippine War," *The Woman's Journal* 30 (June 3, 1899).

While some are trying to find out the cause of the war, others are more interested in its results. "Oh, what is it all for?" was the agonized inquiry of a mother whose son died recently in the Philippines. It is a hard question. But looking forward from the standpoint of a suffragist I seem to see that one of the things it may be "for" is this: It may teach women that they have not all the rights they want, that politics are not out of woman's sphere, and that a government from which woman's *direct* influence and actual presence are excluded is an unspeakably barbarous thing.

Women are familiar with the record of the hunger, starvation, sickness, and death thrust upon our soldiers by an incompetent commissary department and medical department. If any woman can read even one page of this sickening report, and then declare that she has no desire to vote, no interest in the affairs of government, she represents a type of "womanliness" that I have no desire either to understand or to emulate. In the political crisis of today, women have more at stake than they have ever had before. Imperialism! Expansionism! If women realized what these words mean to them, politics would be the theme of every tongue and thought. And if such a moral awakening could come to women as a result of the Philippine war, one could almost cease to regret that unhallowed strife.

Admiral Dewey, it is said, estimates that it will be two years before the Philippine Islands are perfectly subdued. This means the death of fifteen thousand American soldiers a year. Women of America, mothers, wives, sisters! Can you look at that statement, can you read the daily list of casualties in the newspapers, can you think of the Nebraska volunteers appealing for relief, can you look at this shameful war in any of its phases, and then say you do not want to vote? If you can, you may have the face and form of a woman, but the heart of motherhood or wifehood or sisterhood does not beat in your breasts.

1.4 The Open Door Note to Germany, September 1899

The prize in the Philippines was more than a colony in the South China Sea. For many imperialists, particularly those with financial interests, the primary objective was the vast China market with its potential to absorb tremendous amounts of U.S. agricultural and industrial products. In fact, the U.S. involvement in the Pacific, and later in Panama, was at least partly motivated by the need for a speedy passage to China. It was a dream that American businessmen had long dreamt: a half billion consumers demanding millions of dollars worth of American products. In reality, China was poor, barely above the subsistence level in most parts of the nation, and genuinely lacking any real desire for western products. But the prospect of the China market continued to keep American businessmen panting after the hope of supplying a demand with such enormous economic potential.

Protestant missionaries in the U.S. as well saw the Philippines as a market for their own product of Christianity, even though Spanish Catholic missionaries had been working in the Philippines for nearly four hundred years. These missionaries, however, also wanted to use the Philippines as a jumping-off station for further inroads into the seemingly religious vacuum of what was considered "pagan" China.

By the turn of the century, China lay prostrate before the imperialist Western powers and their Asian partner, Japan. The Qing dynasty could not maintain its own territorial integrity and that was a signal for the West to begin carving their own "spheres of influence," as they were called, from China proper. England had maintained such a sphere in Hong Kong since 1842. In 1898 Germany carved out a large sphere on the Shandong Peninsula, Russia demanded and got the Liaodong Peninsula, and France (already well placed in Indochina) had come to control a large section of Guangzhou Bay between Hong Kong and the old Portuguese colony of Macao. As a result of its 1895 victory over China, Japan controlled Formosa and the Pescadores Islands, but it undoubtedly had its eye on the mineral rich regions of Korea and Manchuria.

During the Spanish-American War, England twice proposed a joint Anglo-American resolution to maintain China's commercial status and to allow equal commercial opportunities throughout China. Washington, generally more interested in its war in Cuba than in commercial concerns in East Asia, ignored both proposals. After the war and the acquisition of the Philippines, however, U.S. interests in the Ear East changed dramatically, and the idea of a China held wide open to international trade was now very much to U.S. advantage. But as the Western powers began to carve up sections of China, American interests seemed threatened if these nations imposed old mercantile standards and denied U.S. trade within their areas of control. In addition, there were rumors that Russia, France, and Germany might try to exclude U.S. and British trade from East Asia by reducing China to a system of tributary provinces. Such a plan would deny the United States commercial access to much of East Asia and make the U.S. efforts in the Philippines nearly worthless.

Then Britain grabbed Wei-Hai-Wei at the north end of the Shandong Peninsula, and it appeared that the United States might be shut out in China. With little recourse, Secretary of State John Hay, in September 1899, fell back on the British plan proposed the year before and sent what became known as the "Open Door Notes" to Germany, England, and Russia, and later to France, Japan and Italy. The notes asked that commercial equality for all nations be preserved within the spheres of influence in China. *Document 1.4* is the note sent by Hay to the German foreign secretary. All the notes were generally similar. The responses from the various nations were evasive and vague at best. Most nations, however, insisted that they had no intention of closing the Chinese ports under their control, while backing away from any specific acceptance of Hay's open door policy. Most nations did agree to accept Hay's proposal contingent upon the approval of the other nations in China.

Hay announced on March 20, 1900 that the United States would "therefore consider the assent given to the open-door principle as final and definitive." None of the nations objected; to do so would have been an admission of intentions to close off trade, and no nation was willing to admit that. International open trade continued to be an important aspect of U.S. foreign policy through the twentieth century.

Among the Chinese, these blatant power grabs by the West (and Japan) had become intolerable, and anti-foreign sentiment in China began to grow strong near the turn of the century. Several anti-Western organizations emerged here, and some turned to violence. One group, the Yehequan (or "The Righteous and Harmonious Fists," better known in the West as the "Boxers") obtained the quiet aid of the Chinese government and began a campaign of terror intent on removing Western influence from China. Carrying with them little more than the mystical claim of invincibility against Western bullets, the Boxers in June 1900, laid siege to the foreign compound in Beijing. An international expedition comprised of British, German, Russian, and Japanese forces lifted the siege. Hay and others in Washington concluded that the European powers and Japan might use the incident to overthrow the Qing government (which had clearly supported the rebellion) and further divide China. Such a prospect added to the fears that the U.S. might be squeezed out of the China trade, and again Washington was forced to act. To protect its interests in China, the United States sent 2,500 troops from the Philippines to join the international contingent of 15,000 troops headed to Beijing. Then Hay used the situation to issue a second set of Open Door notes—designed to clarify and bolster the first. These notes, sent to the several powers in July and known as the "open door corollary," insisted that China's territorial integrity be maintained.

The Open Door notes are important not for what they accomplished in China at the turn of the century, but because they became one part of the foundation of the United States foreign policy in the twentieth century. In fact, such principles had always been basic to U.S. foreign policy. Colonial powers that denied their colonies the right to trade with the United States could hurt U.S. commerce. As long as the world's imperial powers allowed the United States an open door to trade, the U.S. did not need its own colonial system; it could compete on an equal footing. The Open Door policy of maintaining China's political integrity and keeping its doors open to trade shaped American diplomacy in China and East Asia at least until mid-century.

....

DOCUMENT 1.4

THE OPEN DOOR NOTE TO GERMANY, SEPTEMBER 1899

At the time when the Government of the United States was informed by that of Germany that it had leased from His Majesty the Emperor of China the port of Kiao-chao and the adjacent territory in the province of Shantung, assurances were given to the ambassador of the United States at Berlin by the Imperial German minister for foreign affairs that the rights and privileges insured by treaties with China to citizens of the United States would not thereby suffer or be in anywise impaired within the area over which Germany had thus obtained control.

More recently, however, the British Government recognized by a formal agreement with Germany the exclusive right of the latter country to enjoy in said leased area and the contiguous "sphere of influence or interest" certain privileges, more especially those relating to railroads and mining enterprises; but as the exact nature and extent of the rights thus recognized have not been clearly defined, it is possible that serious conflicts of interest may at any time arise not only between British and German subjects within said area, but that the interests of our citizens may also be jeopardized thereby.

Earnestly desirous to remove any cause of irritation and to insure at the same time to the commerce of all nations in China the undoubted benefits which should accrue from a formal recognition by the various powers claiming "spheres of interest" that they shall enjoy perfect equality of treatment for their commerce and navigation within such "spheres," the Government of the United States would be pleased to see His German Majesty's Government give formal assurances, and lend its cooperation in securing like assurances from the other interested powers, that each, within its respective sphere of whatever influence—

First. Will in no way interfere with any treaty port or any vested interest within any

SOURCE: *Papers Relating to the Foreign Relations of the United States, 1899* (1901), 129–30.

so-called "sphere of influence" or leased territory it may have in China.

Second. That the Chinese treaty tariff of the time being shall apply to all merchandise landed or shipped to all such ports as are within said "sphere of interest" (unless they be "free ports"), no matter to what nationality it may belong, and that duties so leviable shall be collected by the Chinese Government.

Third. That it will levy no higher harbor dues on vessels of another nationality frequenting any port in such "sphere" than shall be levied on vessels of its own nationality, and no higher railroad charges over lines built, controlled, or operated within its "sphere" on merchandise belonging to citizens or subjects of other nationalities transported through such "sphere" than shall be levied on similar merchandise belonging to its own nationals transported over equal distances.

The liberal policy pursued by His Imperial German Majesty in declaring Kiao-chao a free port and in aiding the Chinese Government in the establishment there of a customhouse are so clearly in line with the proposition which this Government is anxious to see recognized that it entertains the strongest hope that Germany will give its acceptance and hearty support.

The recent ukase of His Majesty the Emperor of Russia declaring the port of Ta-lien-wan open during the whole of the lease under which it is held from China to the merchant ships of all nations, coupled with the categorical assurances made to this Government by His Imperial Majesty's representative at this capital at the time and since repeated to me by the present Russian ambassador, seem to insure the support of the Emperor to the proposed measure. Our ambassador at the Court of St. Petersburg has in consequence been instructed to submit it to the Russian Government and to request their early consideration of it. A copy of my instructions on the subject to Mr. Tower is herewith enclosed for your confidential information.

The commercial interests of Great Britain and Japan will be so clearly served by the desired declaration of intentions, and the views of the Governments of these countries as to the desirability of the adoption of measures insuring the benefits of equality of treatment of all foreign trade throughout China are so similar to those entertained by the United States, that their acceptance of the propositions herein outlined and their cooperation in advocating their adoption by the other powers can be confidently expected. . . .

In view of the present favorable conditions, you are instructed to submit the above considerations to His Imperial German Majesty's Minister for Foreign Affairs, and to request his early consideration on the subject.

1.5 J. P. Gordy, "The Ethics of the Panama Case"
1.6 Theodore Roosevelt Responds to His Critics, *An Autobiography*, 1916

On September 6, 1901 President William McKinley was shot in Buffalo. Six days later Theodore Roosevelt became president. Probably the nation's most ardent and vocal imperialist when he took office, Roosevelt was young, aggressive and confident. He personified many characteristics of the United States itself at the turn of the century. His foreign policy was aggressive, represented in the press and in numerous political cartoons by the "big stick," a reference to a west African proverb that

Roosevelt repeated often before he became president: "Walk softly and carry a big stick, and you will go far." It best describes his foreign policy.

Possibly the best example of Roosevelt's "big stick" policies was his acquisition of the rights to build a canal across the Isthmus of Panama. In early 1903 the U.S. and Colombia signed the Hay-Herran Treaty giving the U.S. the rights to build the canal across Panama, Colombia's most northern province. The U.S. would pay an initial amount of $10 million and an annual fee of $250,000. In March the U.S. Senate ratified the treaty, but the Colombian legislature balked, insisting on an additional $10 million to seal the deal. In August, Colombia rejected the treaty. The act infuriated Roosevelt, who called the Colombians "contemptible little creatures," and complained that "you could no more make an agreement with the Colombian rulers than you could nail currant jelly to the wall."

On October 10, Roosevelt met in Washington with Philippe Bunau-Varilla, a French engineer living in Panama. Bunau-Varilla would be Roosevelt's revolutionary. On November 3, the American warship *Nashville* arrived at Colon (on the Pacific side of the isthmus) and the revolution began. The next day, Colombian troops came ashore at Colon. But with U.S. support for Bunau-Varilla's revolutionaries apparent, the Colombian force departed rather than risk an engagement with the Americans. The next day, Secretary of State Hay recognized the sovereign state of Panama. Its president was Philippe Bunau-Varilla. Within two weeks, the Hay–Bunau-Varilla Treaty was signed between the U.S. and Panama. It allowed the United States to build, operate, and fortify a canal across Panama. Construction began in mid-1904 and was completed ten years later.

These events left a bad taste in the mouths of the nation's anti-imperialists. They saw Roosevelt's actions as heavy-handed imperialism, the bullying of a weak nation to further American interests. J. P. Gordy, a nationally recognized philosopher and academic, took Roosevelt to task for his actions in Panama in an article in *The Forum* magazine (*Document 1.5*). His concerns about the events in Panama echo many of the same concerns expressed by Carl Schurz and other anti-imperialists at the turn of the century.

In 1911, Roosevelt reportedly said: "I took the Canal Zone and let Congress debate, and while the debate goes on the Canal does also." In his autobiography in 1916, Roosevelt expressed much the same sentiments as he tried to explain why he made the decisions in 1903 that led to American control of the canal. An excerpt from his *Autobiography*, published in 1913, is *Document 1.6*. John Milton Cooper has written about these statements that they have "the overwrought quality that Roosevelt's language usually assumed when he was unsure of his moral ground."

In 1922, following Roosevelt's death, the United States paid $25 million to Colombia to make amends for the events of 1903. The American press could not resist calling it "canalimony."

DOCUMENT 1.5

J. P. GORDY, "THE ETHICS OF THE PANAMA CASE"

In June, 1902, a law was passed authorizing the President to make a treaty with Colombia for the building of a canal across the Isthmus of Panama, and providing that, in the event of failure to make such a treaty after the lapse of a reasonable time, recourse should be had to Nicaragua. In accordance with this law, a treaty was framed, ratified by our Senate and submitted to the Congress of Colombia. That Congress rejected it, and a few days later (November 3, 1903) the people of Panama revolted against Colombia and proclaimed their independence. On the 6th of the same month we acknowledged the *de facto* government, on the 13th the independence, of Panama, and on the 18th we negotiated a treaty with the new Republic providing for the construction of a canal and guaranteeing the independence of the new-born state. This treaty has since been ratified by the Senate and is now a part of the law of the land. The independence of Panama and the guarantee of its independence by our Government are accomplished facts. Discussion cannot change them. But it is eminently fitting that, as a self-governing people, we should carefully inquire whether we have observed the principles of justice in those dealings with Colombia to which Panama owes its existence as an independent state.

When the President received the new minister from Panama, he made a short speech in which he said: "It is fitting that we should do so [acknowledge the independence of Panama] as we did nearly a century ago, when the Latin peoples of America proclaimed the right of popular government, and it is equally fitting that the United States should now, as then, be

For many Americans, Roosevelt's negotiations with Colombia for a canal across the isthmus at Panama were little more than stern encounter with a barely legitimate nation. *Courtesy of BoondocksNet.com*

the first to stretch out the hand of fellowship . . . toward the new-born state."

No one needs to be told that there is the sharpest contrast between our attitude toward the South American Republics nearly a century ago and our attitude toward the new Republic of Panama; . . . we did not forcibly intervene in behalf of the former; while we have so intervened in behalf of the latter; and most important of all, our pecuniary interest in the independence of the South American Republics was as nothing when compared with our pecuniary interest in the independence of Panama. The consideration of this latter fact cannot but raise the doubt whether it would not have been more fitting in the United States to have been the last rather than the first of the great Powers of the world to recognize the independence of Panama.

Nor will this doubt be removed by a study of the official correspondence in relation to the affair. On November 6, Secretary *[of State]** Hay, in telegraphing to Mr. *[A. M.]* Beaupre',

---

SOURCE: J. P. Gordy, "The Ethics of the Panama Case," *The Forum*, XXXVI (July–September, 1904), 115–24.

*Italicized brackets added here. All other brackets and italics are included in the original text.

our minister to Colombia, that we had acknowledged the *de facto* government of Panama, made this statement: "He [the President] holds that he is bound not merely by *treaty obligations* but by the *interests of civilization* to see that the peaceable traffic of the world across the Isthmus of Panama shall no longer be disturbed by a succession of unnecessary and wasteful wars." On November 11 he sent another telegram, in which he said: "It is not thought desirable to permit landing of Colombian troops in the Isthmus, as such a course would precipitate civil war, and disturb for an indefinite period the free transit which we are pledged to protect." In accordance with this policy, telegrams were sent, on November 3, to the commander of the "Nashville" at Colon, ordering him to make every effort "to prevent *[Colombian]* government troops from proceeding to Panama, or taking any action which would lead to bloodshed." In a word, the Government of the United States stepped in between Colombia and the Panama insurgents, on the ground that we were required by the interests of civilization and the obligations of treaty to prevent any steps that would lead to civil war.

The appeal to civilization can be quickly disposed of. Perhaps the Governments of England and France were of the opinion, in the time of the Civil War, that the interests of civilization required them to interpose in behalf of the South; but no American needs to be told that such intervention would have been a flagrant violation of our rights. If any nation has a right to do anything whatever in the interests of what it pleases to consider the interests of civilization, international law is at an end, and we are back again in the Middle Ages.

Strange as it may seem, there are indications that President Roosevelt regards it as a settled principle that the United States has a right arbitrarily to interfere in the affairs of the South American states whenever, in the judgment of the American Government, the interests of civilization will thereby be promoted. In a recent

letter to Mr. *[Secretary of War, Elihu]* Root read at the Cuban birthday dinner, the President wrote the following remarkable paragraph:

> If a nation shows that it knows how to act with decency in industrial and political matters, if it keeps order and pays its obligations, *then* – [italics not in the original] – it need fear no interference from the United States. Brutal wrongdoing or an impotence which results in a general loosening of the ties of civilized society may finally require intervention by some civilized nation, and in the Western Hemisphere the United States cannot ignore its duty; but it remains true that our interests and those of our Southern neighbors are in reality identical. All that we ask is that they shall govern themselves well and be prosperous and orderly.

A more dangerous doctrine than this, one which, if generally carried out, would be more certain to result in "a general loosening of ties of civilized society" it would be difficult to conceive. If the President expected to hold his office for a long life, or if he were sure that his successors would have the same infallible judgment as to the circumstances justifying our interference, and the same capacity to rise above the temptation to interfere for selfish purposes which he evidently imputes to himself, his position would not be so amazing. But does he not see that if strong nations, in their dealings with weak ones, get in the habit of setting aside the restraints of international law for what they consider good reasons, they will be sure to set them aside for reasons that are not good? . . .

Suppose there grew on the Isthmus of Panama some vegetable absolutely necessary to the rest of the world and found nowhere else, would Colombia have had the right to forbid its exportation? Such an attempt in such a case would certainly justify the nations of the world in asserting and acting upon the same principle which is acted upon by all civilized communities in relation to individuals, the principle of *eminent domain*. As a state or community can appropriate to a necessary public use the property of an individual whether he is willing or not—reasonable compensation being made—so the nations of the world could justly appropriate to the use of civilization any property imperatively necessary to promote the general interest of humanity.

But however true this principle may be, its application in international affairs is attended with such extraordinary difficulties that a nation anxious above all things to be just, a nation that believes the interests of civilization will be most surely promoted by a scrupulous regard for the rights of weaker states, will resort to it only when nothing else is possible. For (1) who is to decide whether the property of a nation is so urgently required by the interests of "collective civilization" as to justify a stronger Power in appropriating it? And (2) who is to say what constitutes a reasonable compensation? In the analogous case there is a legally constituted tribunal composed of disinterested persons to answer both questions. The laws have so safeguarded the rights of the individual as to give every reasonable guarantee that he shall not be imposed upon. But where is the international tribunal to which a weak state can appeal for the protection of its rights?

The absence of such a tribunal makes it peculiarly difficult for the United States to justly apply the principle of international eminent domain in its dealings with Colombia. This country, the one country in the world with the greatest interest in an isthmian canal, arrogates to itself the right to decide whether such a canal is so necessary to civilization as to justify setting aside the ordinary principles of international law! And the country with such an interest at stake assumes to decide whether the conditions upon which Colombia will agree to the building of a canal are reasonable! . . .

Now the Monroe Doctrine is a doctrine which we have forced upon the world. Because of the principle that underlies it, we have said in effect that we will permit no European nation to build the canal. As nature gives to the owner of the Isthmus a monopoly of the territory through which the canal is to be built, so our Monroe Doctrine has given to us a practical monopoly of the right to build the canal. Only one nation—ignoring Nicaragua—could

authorize the building of the canal; only one nation could be permitted to build it. Colombia's monopoly naturally tempted her to try to extort unjust concessions from this country. Our monopoly naturally tempted us to use our power to demand unreasonable concessions from Colombia. If the United States had a right to say that Colombia's rejection of the treaty was unreasonable, Colombia certainly had an equal right to say that the provisions of the treaty were improper.

President Roosevelt, indeed, is perfectly sure that the terms offered to Colombia were not only just but generous. Perhaps they were. But does he not know that in any event he would be likely to think so? Has history taught anything more clearly than that when a civilized nation comes in contact with one of "imperfect social development," the rights of the latter are likely violated? . . . Surely until a ruler regards himself as having attained to infallibility he will hesitate to make his judgment of a nation's deserts a criterion of absolute justice. . . .

The President and Mr. Root make a number of irrelevant arguments to justify the action of the Government. The President says, for example, that the course of the Administration saved great suffering, waste of life, and destruction of property. Perhaps so. But is he quite sure that he has not established a precedent that may lead to a far greater loss of life than he has averted? And may one nation interfere in the internal affairs of another whenever it thinks such interference will avert suffering and loss of life?

Mr. Root calls attention to the fact that the rights of Panama as a sovereign state were usurped by Colombia in 1885, and that the people of the Isthmus have three times since risen in rebellion against their oppressors. Before these facts can be shown to have any bearing upon the question, the ex-Secretary of War must prove that similar acts of usurpation confer upon outside Powers the right to interfere. Is he willing to undertake that? It is currently supposed that the methods by which England has acquired her title to many parts of her vast colonial empire will not bear investigation; but

is Mr. Root willing to say that in case of rebellion by an English colony, whose rights
had been invaded—the Boers of Africa, for
example—any outside Power would have the
right to interfere? In truth, a very poor argument will do if backed by sufficient force; and
an argument that seems entirely valid when
used against a weak Power of "imperfect social
development" would seem ridiculously inadequate if urged to justify similar action in case of
a really great Power.

Criticism is cheap, it may be replied. If the
course of the Administration was wrong what
was its proper course? The Government should
have rigidly refrained from interfering, without
the authority of Congress, with the attempts of
Colombia to put down the rebellion of
Panama. If Colombia had succeeded in reestab-
lishing her control over Panama, then the just
alternatives before the Government were the
selection of the Nicaraguan route or the submission of the question—say to The Hague
Tribunal—whether we had not a right to dig
the canal through Panama in spite of Colombia, and, if so, on what conditions.

DOCUMENT 1.6

THEODORE ROOSEVELT RESPONDS TO HIS CRITICS, *AN AUTOBIOGRAPHY,* 1916

By far the most important action I took in
foreign affairs during the time I was President related to the Panama Canal. Here again
there was much accusation about my having
acted in an "unconstitutional" manner—a
position which can be upheld only if Jefferson's action in acquiring Louisiana be also
treated as unconstitutional; and at different
stages of the affair believers in the do-nothing
policy denounced me as having "usurped
authority"—which meant that when nobody

SOURCE: Theodore Roosevelt, *An Autobiography* (New
York: Macmillan, 1913), 526–42.

else could or would exercise efficient authority, I exercised it.

During the nearly four hundred years that
had elapsed since Balboa crossed the Isthmus,
there had been a good deal of talk about building an Isthmus canal, and there had been various discussions of the subject and negotiations
about it in Washington for the previous half
century. So far it had all resulted merely in conversation; and the time had come when unless
somebody was prepared to act with decision
we would have to resign ourselves to at least
half a century of further conversation. . . .

We had again and again been forced to intervene to protect the [railroad] across the Isthmus, and the intervention was frequently at the
request of Colombia herself. The effort to build
a canal by private capital had been made under
[French canal builder Ferdinand] De Lesseps
and had resulted in lamentable failure. Every
serious proposal to build the canal in such manner had been abandoned. The United States had
repeatedly announced that we would not permit it to be built or controlled by any old-world
government. Colombia was utterly impotent to
build it herself. Under these circumstances it
had become a matter of imperative obligation
that we should build it ourselves without further delay.

I took final action in 1903. During the preceding fifty-three years the Governments of
New Granada and of its successor, Colombia,
had been in a constant state of flux; and the
State of Panama had sometimes been treated
as almost independent, in loose Federal league,
and sometimes as the mere property of the
Government at Bogota; and there had been in-
numerable appeals to arms, sometimes for inadequate reasons. . . . In short, the experience of over half a century had shown
Colombia to be utterly incapable of keeping
order on the Isthmus. Only the active interference of the United States had enabled her to
preserve so much as a semblance of sovereignty. Had it not been for the exercise by the
United States of the police power in her interest, her connection with the Isthmus would

have been sundered long before it was. In 1856, in 1860, in 1873, in 1885, in 1901, and again in 1902, sailors and marines from United States warships were forced to land in order to patrol the Isthmus, to protect life and property, and to see that the transit across the Isthmus was kept open. In 1861, in 1862, in 1885, and in 1900, the Colombian Government asked that the United States Government would land troops to protect Colombian interests and maintain order on the Isthmus. The people of Panama during the preceding twenty years had three times sought to establish their independence by revolution or secession—in 1885, in 1895, and in 1899. . . .

Meanwhile, Colombia was under a dictatorship. In 1898 M. A. Sanclamente was elected President, and J. M. Maroquin Vice-President, of the Republic of Colombia. On July 31, 1900, the Vice-President, Maroquin, executed a "coup d'etat" by seizing the person of the President, Sanclamente, and imprisoning him at a place a few miles out of Bogota. Maroquin thereupon declared himself possessed of the executive power because of "the absence of the president"—a delightful touch of unconscious humor. He then issued a decree that public order was disturbed, and, upon that ground, assumed to himself legislative power under another provision of the constitution; that is, having himself disturbed the public order, he alleged the disturbance as a justification for seizing absolute power. Thenceforth Maroquin, without the aid of any legislative body, ruled as a dictator, combining the supreme executive, legislative, civil, and military authorities, in the so-called Republic of Colombia. The "absence" of Sanclamente from the capital became permanent by his death in prison in the year 1902. When the people of Panama declared their independence in November 1903, no Congress had sat in Colombia since the year 1898, except the special Congress called by Maroquin to reject the [Hay-Herran] canal treaty, and which did reject it by a unanimous vote, and adjourned without legislating on any other subject. The constitution of 1886 had

taken away from Panama the power of self-government and vested it in Colombia. The *coup d'etat* of Maroquin took away from Colombia herself the power of government and vested it in an irresponsible dictator.

Consideration of the above facts ought to be enough to show any human being that we were not dealing with normal conditions on the Isthmus and in Colombia. We were dealing with the government of an irresponsible alien dictator, and with a condition of affairs on the Isthmus itself which was marked by one uninterrupted series of outbreaks and revolutions. As for the "consent of the governed" theory, that absolutely justified our action; the people on the Isthmus were the "governed"; they were governed by Colombia, without their consent, and they unanimously repudiated the Colombian government, and demanded that the United States build the canal. . . .

When, in August, 1903, I became convinced that Colombia intended to repudiate the [Hay-Herran] treaty made the preceding January, under cover of securing its rejection by the Colombian Legislature, I began carefully to consider what should be done. By my direction Secretary Hay, personally and through the Minister at Bogota, repeatedly warned Colombia that grave consequences might follow her rejection of the treaty. The possibility of ratification did not wholly pass away until the close of the session of the Colombian Congress on the last day of October. There would then be two possibilities. One was that Panama would remain quiet. In that case I was prepared to recommend to Congress that we should at once occupy the Isthmus anyhow, and proceed to dig the canal; and I had drawn out a draft of my message to this effect. But from the information I received, I deemed it likely that there would be a revolution in Panama as soon as the Colombian Congress adjourned without ratifying the treaty, for the entire population of Panama felt that the immediate building of the canal was of vital concern to their well-being. Correspondents of the different newspapers on the Isthmus had sent to their respective papers widely published forecasts indicating that there would be a revolution in such event.

Moreover, on October 16, at the request of Lieutenant-General Young, Captain Humphrey and Lieutenant Murphy, two army officers who had returned from the Isthmus, saw me and told me that there would unquestionably be a revolution on the Isthmus, that the people were unanimous in their criticism of the Bogota Government and their disgust over the failure of that Government to ratify the treaty; and that the revolution would probably take place immediately after adjournment of the Colombian Congress. They did not believe that it would be before October 20, but they were confident that it would certainly come at the end of October or immediately afterwards, when the Colombian Congress had adjourned. Accordingly, I directed the Navy Department to station various ships within easy reach of the Isthmus, to be ready to act in the event of need arising.

These ships were barely in time. On November 3, the revolution occurred. Practically everybody on the Isthmus, including all the Colombian troops that were already stationed there, joined in the revolution, and there was no bloodshed. But on that same day four hundred new Colombian troops were landed at Colon. Fortunately, the gunboat *Nashville,* under Commander Hubbard, reached Colon almost immediately afterward, and when the commander of the Colombian forces threatened the lives and property of the American citizens, including women and children, in Colon, Commander Hubbard landed a few score sailors and marines to protect them. By a mixture of firmness and tact he not only prevented any assault on our citizens, but persuaded the Colombian commander to reembark his troops for Cartagena. On the Pacific side a Colombian gunboat shelled the City of Panama, with the result of killing one Chinaman—the only life lost in the whole affair.

No one connected with the American Government had any part in preparing, inciting, or encouraging the revolution, and except for the reports of our military and naval officers, which I forwarded to Congress, no one connected with the Government had any previous knowledge concerning the proposed revolution, except such as was accessible to any person who read the newspapers and kept abreast of current questions and current affairs. By the unanimous action of its people, and without the firing of a shot, the state of Panama declared themselves an independent republic. The time for hesitation on our part had passed. . . .

I recognized Panama forthwith on behalf of the United States, and practically all the countries of the world immediately followed suit. The State Department immediately negotiated a canal treaty with the new Republic. One of the foremost men in securing the independence of Panama, and the treaty which authorized the United States forthwith to build the canal, was M. Philippe Bunau-Varilla, and eminent French engineer formally associated with De Lesseps and then living on the Isthmus; his services to civilization were notable, and deserve the fullest recognition.

From the beginning to the end of our course was straight-forward and in absolute accord with the highest of standards of international morality. Criticism of it can come only from misinformation, or else from a sentimentality which represents both mental weakness and a moral twist. To have acted otherwise than I did would have been on my part betrayal of the interests of the United States, indifference to the interests of Panama, and recreancy to the interests of the world at large. Colombia had forfeited every claim to consideration; indeed, this is not stating the case strongly enough: she had so acted that yielding to her would have meant on our part that culpable form of weakness which stands on a level with wickedness. As for me personally, if I had hesitated to act, and had not in advance discounted the clamor of those Americans who had made a fetish of disloyalty to their country, I should have esteemed myself as deserving a place in Dante's inferno beside the faint-hearted cleric who was guilty of "il gran rifiuto." The facts I have given above are mere bald statements from the record. . . .

There had been a no less universal feeling that it was our duty to the world to provide this transit in the shape of a canal. . . . Colombia was then under a one-man government, a dictatorship, founded on usurpation of absolute and irresponsible power. She eagerly pressed us to enter into an agreement with her, as long as there was any chance of our going to the alternative route through Nicaragua. When she thought we were committed, she refused to fulfill the agreement, with the avowed hope of seizing the French company's property for nothing and thereby holding us up. This was a bit of pure bandit morality. It would have achieved its purpose had I possessed as weak moral fiber as those of my critics who announced that I ought to have confined my action to feeble scolding and temporizing until the opportunity for action passed. I did not lift my finger to incite the revolutionists. The right simile to use is totally different. I simply ceased to stamp out the different revolutionary fuses that were already burning. When Colombia committed flagrant wrong against us, I considered it no part of my duty to aid and abet her in her wrongdoing at our expense, and also at the expense of Panama, of the French company, and of the world generally. There had been fifty years of continuous bloodshed and civil strife in Panama; because of my action Panama has now known ten years of such peace and prosperity as she never before saw during the four centuries of her existence—for in Panama, as in Cuba and Santo Domingo, it was the action of the American people, against the outcries of the professed apostles of peace, which alone brought peace. We gave to the people of Panama self-government, and freed them from subjection to alien oppressors. We did our best to get Colom-

bia to let us treat her with more than generous justice; we exercised patience to beyond the verge of proper forbearance. . . . Colombia was solely responsible for her own humiliation; and she did not then, and has not now, one shadow of claim upon us, moral or legal; all the wrong that was done was done by her. If, as representing the American people, I had not acted precisely as I did, I would have been an unfaithful or incompetent representative; and inaction at that crisis would have meant not only indefinite delay in building the canal, but also practical admission on our part that we were not fit to play the part on the Isthmus which we had arrogated to ourselves. I acted on my own responsibility in the Panama matter. . . .

I deeply regretted, and now deeply regret, the fact that the Colombian Government rendered it imperative for me to take the action I took; but I had no alternative, consistent with the full performance of my duty to my own people, and to the nations of mankind. . . . If Brazil, or Argentine, or Chile, had been in possession of the Isthmus, doubtless the canal would have been build under the governmental control of the nation thus controlling the Isthmus, with the hearty acquiescence of the United States and of all other powers. But in the actual fact the canal would not have been build at all save for the actions I took. If men chose to say that it would have been better not to build it, than to build it as the result of such action, their position, although foolish, is compatible with belief in their wrongheaded sincerity. But it is hypocrisy, alike odious and contemptible, for any man to say both that we ought to have built the canal and that we ought not to have acted in the way we did act.

1.7 The Roosevelt Corollary to the Monroe Doctrine, December 6, 1904

In 1823 the Monroe Doctrine made it clear that the United States would not tolerate further colonization of the Western Hemisphere. By 1900, however, a number of weak, poverty-stricken Latin American countries had borrowed heavily from the European powers and were now unable to repay the loans. Roosevelt feared that the creditor nations of Europe might use the situation to intervene in the affairs of Latin America—as they had done in similar instances in Asia and Africa. Such a situation might also allow the European nations to build naval bases on the Caribbean islands or in Central America, thus inhibiting U.S. control of the soon-to-be-built Panama Canal.

Germany was one of the greatest fears. Organized as a world power only since 1871, Germany had become aggressive in world affairs in what seemed an attempt to catch up with the major imperialist nations like Britain and France. By the turn of the century, it was widely rumored that Germany wanted naval bases in the New World. In 1904 a situation in Latin America seemed to invite European intervention. A series of violent revolutions in the Dominican Republic caused the government there to default on its debts to several European countries—most prominently Germany. When German intervention seemed imminent, Roosevelt responded by seizing the Dominican Republic's customs houses. Over the next thirty-six years, the United States government collected duties and paid off the Dominican debt.

This incident seemed to make clear to Roosevelt what the European powers had been insisting for years: If the United States, through the Monroe Doctrine, was going to maintain itself as the protector of the Western Hemisphere, it must also take on the obligation of maintaining peace within the region. On December 6, 1904, Roosevelt presented to Congress his plan for dealing with the Dominican Republic. This statement, known as the Roosevelt Corollary to the Monroe Doctrine (*Document 1.7*), marks the beginning of the realization that the United States must do more than simply dominate the economies of Latin America. The Roosevelt Corollary thus became the American justification for future intervention into the affairs of Latin America.

....

DOCUMENT 1.7

THE ROOSEVELT COROLLARY TO THE MONROE DOCTRINE, DECEMBER 6, 1904

It is not true that the United States feels any land hunger or entertains any projects as regards the other nations of the Western Hemisphere save such as are for their welfare. All that this country desires is to see the neighboring countries stable, orderly, and prosperous. Any country whose people conduct themselves well can count upon our hearty friendship. If a nation shows that it knows how to act with reasonable efficiency and decency in social and political matters, if it keeps order and pays its obligations, it need fear no interference from the United States. Chronic wrongdoing, or an

SOURCE: *Cong. Rec.* 58th Cong. 3d sess., XXXIX, 19.

impotence which results in a general loosening of the ties of civilized society, may in America, as elsewhere, ultimately require intervention by some civilized nation, and in the Western Hemisphere the adherence of the United States to the Monroe Doctrine may force the United States, however reluctantly, in flagrant cases of such wrongdoing or impotence, to the exercise of an international police power. . . . Our interests and those of our southern neighbors are in reality identical. They have great natural riches, and if within their borders the reign of law and justice obtains, prosperity is sure to come to them. While they thus obey the primary laws of civilized society they may rest as-sured that they will be treated by us in a spirit of cordial and helpful sympathy. We would interfere with them only in the last resort, and then only if it became evident that their inability or unwillingness to do justice at home and abroad had violated the rights of the United States or had invited foreign aggression to the detriment of the entire body of American nations. It is a mere truism to say that every nation, whether in America or anywhere else, which desires to maintain its freedom, its independence, must ultimately realized that the right of such independence can not be separated from the responsibility of making good use of it.

1.8   Secretary of State Philander Knox and U.S. Private Investments in China, November 6, 1909

1.9   President William Howard Taft Defends Dollar Diplomacy, December 3, 1912

Roosevelt's successor in the White House, William Howard Taft, had served the Roosevelt administration as governor-general in the Philippines and then as plenipotentiary in Cuba and Korea. Taft was a conservative with considerable ties to big business and finance. As president he seemed to realize the difficulty of maintaining colonies by force of arms (as had been done in the Philippines against the insurrection there) and began looking to the finances of America's private investors to influence nations without actually maintaining colonies. This policy became known as Dollar Diplomacy.

In Central America the goals of Dollar Diplomacy were the same as Roosevelt's Big Stick diplomacy: to maintain stability there, which would, in turn, thwart European intervention—and to protect the Panama Canal, then under construction. The plan had the additional advantage of making profits for American investors. When Nicaragua defaulted on its foreign debt in 1911, Taft arranged for American bankers to reorganize that country's finances, control its customs houses, and repay the debt. Nicaragua, however, did not stabilize. Efforts to establish similar situations in Honduras, Guatemala, and Costa Rica all failed when the Senate refused to endorse the plans. In Haiti, however, U.S. lenders took over the assets of the National Bank of Haiti, which resulted in removing all European financial concerns from that nation's economy.

In China, Dollar Diplomacy manifested itself a bit differently. There the Taft administration lobbied a consortium of international investors to allow U.S. bankers to join in
a deal to build railroads in the Yangtze River Valley. In *Document 1.8* Taft's secretary
of state, Philander Knox, suggests Dollar Diplomacy to Great Britain as a way of financing the Chinchow-Aigun Railroad in Manchuria. But in 1913 the new president,
Woodrow Wilson, who opposed the concept of Dollar Diplomacy, pulled the plug on
the entire plan by announcing that the United States would not protect private investments in East Asia. The bankers quickly withdrew their support from the consortium
and Dollar Diplomacy in China came to an end.

Many Americans came to view Dollar Diplomacy as an alternative to imperialism,
at least that type of imperialism defined as occupying and governing foreign lands.
Those questions raised by the anti-imperialists and the problems associated with occupation and control of colonies may have, by the end of the Roosevelt administration,
produced a change of heart in the nation and thus a change of policy in Washington.
The occupation and governing of foreign areas was simply not in the American
character—a character that had been born out of the concepts of popular sovereignty
and the absolute will of the people. Economic imperialism—the domination of other
economies in the world for the benefit of the American market—had, however,
brought little criticism or concern from the American people.

Dollar Diplomacy disappeared from the language of American foreign policy after
the Taft administration, but private U.S. investment overseas would continue to be an
important part of the American economy, while allowing the United States to influence
worldwide events with considerable force.

Document 1.9 is President Taft's defense of Dollar Diplomacy. It is part of his annual
message to Congress, delivered on December 3, 1912, just one month after he finished
a distant third in the election that year. He would be in office for another three months.

....

DOCUMENT 1.8

SECRETARY OF STATE PHILANDER KNOX AND U.S. PRIVATE INVESTMENTS IN CHINA, NOVEMBER 6, 1909

Now that there has been signed and ratified
by an unpublished imperial decree an
agreement by which the American and British
interests are to cooperate in the financing and
construction of the Chinchow-Tsitihar-Aigun
Railroad, the Government of the United States
is prepared cordially to cooperate with His Britannic Majesty's Government in diplomatically
supporting and facilitating this enterprise, so

SOURCE: *Papers Relating to the Foreign Relations of the
United States, 1910* (1915), 234–35.

important alike to the progress and to the commercial development of China. The Government of the United States would be disposed to
favor ultimate participation to a proper extent
on the part of other interested powers whose
inclusion might be agreeable to China and
which are known to support the principle of
equality of commercial opportunity and the
maintenance of the integrity of the Chinese
Empire. However, before the further elaboration of the actual arrangement, the Government of the United States asks His Britannic
Majesty's Government to give their consideration to the following alternative and more comprehensive projects: First, perhaps the most effective way to preserve the undisturbed enjoyment
by China of all political rights in Manchuria
and to promote the development of those
Provinces under a practical application of the

policy of the open door and equal commercial opportunity would be to bring the Manchurian highways, the railroads, under an economic, scientific, and impartial administration by some plan vesting in China the ownership of the railroads through funds furnished for that purpose by the interested parties willing to participate. Such loans should be for a period ample to make it reasonably certain that it could be met within the time fixed and should be upon such terms as would make it attractive to bankers and investors.

The Government of the United States has some reason to hope that such a plan might meet favorable consideration on the part of Russia and has reason to believe that American financial participation would be forthcoming. Second, should this suggestion not be found feasible in its entirety, then the desired end would be approximated, if not attained, by Great Britain and the United States diplomatically supporting the Chinchow-Aigun arrangement and inviting the interested parties friendly to complete commercial neutralization of Manchuria to participate in the financing and construction of that line and of such additional lines as future commercial development may demand, and at the same time to supply funds for the purchase by China of such of the existing lines as might be offered for inclusion in this system. The Government of the United States hopes that the principle involved in the foregoing suggestions may commend itself to His Britannic Majesty's Government.

SOURCE: *Cong. Rec.* 62 Cong., 3rd sess., XLIX, 13–14.

DOCUMENT 1.9

PRESIDENT WILLIAM HOWARD TAFT DEFENDS DOLLAR DIPLOMACY, DECEMBER 3, 1912

The diplomacy of the present administration has sought to respond to modern ideas of commercial intercourse. This policy has been characterized as substituting dollars for bullets. It is one that appeals alike to idealistic humanitarian sentiments, to the dictates of sound policy and strategy, and to legitimate commercial claims. It is an effort frankly directed to the increase of American trade upon the axiomatic principle that the Government of the United States shall extend all proper support to every legitimate and beneficial American enterprise abroad. How great have been the results of this diplomacy, coupled with the maximum and minimum provision of the tariff law, will be seen by some consideration of the wonderful increase in the export trade of the United States. Because modern diplomacy is commercial, there has been a disposition in some quarters to attribute to it none but materialistic aims. How strikingly erroneous is such an impression may be seen from a study of the results by which the diplomacy of the United States can be judged. . . .

In Central America the aim has been to help such countries as Nicaragua and Honduras to help themselves. They are the immediate beneficiaries. The national benefit to the United States is twofold. First, it is obvious that the Monroe Doctrine is more vital in the neighborhood of the Panama Canal and the zone of the Caribbean than anywhere else. There, too, the maintenance of that doctrine falls most heavily upon the United States. It is therefore essential that the countries within that sphere shall be removed from the jeopardy involved by heavy foreign debt and chaotic national finances and from the ever-present danger of international complications due to disorder at home. Hence the United States has been glad to encourage and support American bankers who were willing to lend a helping hand to the financial rehabilitation of such countries because this financial rehabilitation and the protection of their customhouses from being the prey of would-be dictators would remove at one stroke the menace of foreign creditors and the menace of revolutionary disorder.

The second advantage of the United States is one affecting chiefly all the southern and Gulf ports and the business and industry of the South. The Republics of Central America and the Caribbean possess great natural wealth. They need only a measure of stability and the means of financial regeneration to enter upon an era of peace and prosperity, bringing profit and happiness to themselves and at the same time creating conditions sure to lead to a flourishing interchange of trade with this country.

I wish to call your special attention to the recent occurrences in Nicaragua, for I believe the terrible events recorded there during the revolution of the past summer—the useless loss of life, the devastation of property, the bombardment of defenseless cities, the killing and wounding of women and children, the torturing of noncombatants to exact contributions, and the suffering of thousands of human beings—might have been averted had the Department of State, through approval of the loan convention by the Senate, been permitted to carry out its now well-developed policy of encouraging the extending of financial aid to weak Central American States with the primary objects of avoiding just such revolutions by assisting those Republics to rehabilitate their finances, to establish their currency on a stable basis, to remove the customhouses from the danger of revolutions by arranging for their secure administration, and to establish reliable banks. . . .

If this Government is really to preserve to the American people that free opportunity in foreign markets which will soon be indispensable to our prosperity, even greater efforts must be made. Otherwise the American merchant, manufacturer, and exporter will find many a field in which American trade should logically predominate preempted through the more energetic efforts of other governments and other commercial nations. . . .

America can not take its proper place in the most important fields for its commercial activity and enterprise unless we have a merchant marine. American commerce and enterprise can not be effectively fostered in those fields unless we have good American banks in the countries referred to. We need American newspapers in those countries and proper means for public information about them. We need to assure the permanency of a trained foreign service. We need legislation enabling the members of the foreign service to be systematically brought into direct contact with the industrial, manufacturing, and exporting interests of this country in order that American business men may enter the foreign field with a clear perception of the exact conditions to be dealt with and the officers themselves may prosecute their work with a clear idea of what American industrial and manufacturing interests require.

1.10   President Woodrow Wilson's Address to Congress on the Crisis in Mexico, April 20, 1914

For the new president, Woodrow Wilson, imperialism was born neither from Roosevelt's Big Stick, nor Taft's Dollar Diplomacy. In fact, Wilson thought little about foreign policy issues at all. Just after his election he remarked to a friend, "It would be an irony of fate if my administration had to deal chiefly with foreign affairs." Foreign affairs did, however, occupy much of Wilson's presidency, and the policy reflected the man. Drawing possibly on his Presbyterian background, or his moral convictions associated with progressivism, or both, Wilson developed a foreign policy based on moralism. He believed strongly that the American culture had developed a special moral base. "The force of America," he once asserted, "is the force of moral principle . . . there is nothing else that she loves, and there is nothing else for which she will contend." This American system of constitutional democracy, Wilson believed, was so morally right that the United States had a predestined obligation to carry it to the entire world. "Every nation," he said, "needs to be drawn into the tutelage of America." While it was a common belief at the time that democracy was reserved for only the chosen few, (those capable of dealing with the nuances of the system, specifically white Anglos and Protestants) Wilson believed that all people, from Mexican peasants to Chinese peasants, would either accept the American system or they could be taught to accept it. "When properly directed," he said, "there is no people not fitted for self-government." From there, Wilson jumped to the conclusion that one day the world would accept American-style democracy, and only then would there be world peace. These convictions would turn Wilson-the-moral-crusader into Wilson-the-interventionist; he would make the world safe for democracy. William Jennings Bryan, Wilson's secretary of state and another moralist, shared most of these beliefs.

At the turn of the century, Wilson had been an ardent imperialist, writing often on the subject, even becoming an admirer and acquaintance of Theodore Roosevelt. But by 1912, he had come to see imperialism as exploitive, in fact, immoral. But his desire to export the American system made him essentially nothing less than an imperialist. Wilson's rhetoric may have been different, but the results were essentially the same, particularly in Latin America. Wilson was determined that the United States should dominate the Caribbean, complete the canal, and protect it. He sent troops into Haiti in 1915, and then again in 1918 to put down revolts. The troops remained there for the next 20 years. He sent troops into the Dominican Republic, and he kept them in Nicaragua. He concluded the purchase of the Virgin Islands from Denmark in 1917, and U.S. influence in Cuba remained strong. Wilson's policy toward the Philippines changed only in that his goal there was to teach the Filipinos to become good democrats. It was in Mexico, however, where Wilson most revealed his moralistic view of foreign policy as it co-existed with the Roosevelt-like policy of intervention. The problems there began in 1910 when a liberal revolution led by Francisco Madero overthrew the dictator Porfirio Diaz. The Madero administration had wedded itself to a series of reforms that included destroying the landed aristocracy, the Church, and foreign business interests in Mexico. The result was a counterrevolution that ended in Madero's murder, orchestrated by his chief general, Victoriano Huerta. The foreign investment community applauded the new conservative government that pledged to protect foreign investments, and most European nations immediately recognized the new Huerta government. But despite pressure from America's investment bankers to support Huerta, Wilson regarded the Mexican president as illegitimate, a murderer, a subverter of the will of the Mexican people, and he refused to recognize his government. By this action, Wilson became the first American president to use non-recognition as a diplomatic tactic.

Following Huerta's takeover, a group of anti-Huertistas calling themselves Constitutionalists pledged to overthrow the Huerta government and replace it with a democratically elected constitutional government. Venustdano Carranza led the rebels, and their strength increased in the months following the Huerta coup. Through the summer of

1913, Wilson tried to mediate between the supporters of Huerta and Carranza, but to no avail. The interference was neither asked for nor wanted by either side, but that was of little consequence to Wilson who seemed intent on interfering in Mexico's affairs.

In October 1913, Huerta abandoned all pretense of moderation and declared himself dictator, much to the distress of the Wilson administration. Wilson responded by throwing U.S. support to Carranza, insisting only that he hold elections once he took the seat of government. Carranza refused, making it clear that he did not want U.S. assistance, and that he would oppose any U.S. intervention in the Mexican revolution. Wilson then concluded that neither Huerta nor Carranza represented the people of Mexico, and that the United States government should intervene.

That opportunity came in Tampico in April 1914. A Huertista colonel arrested a group of U.S. sailors from the *USS Dolphin* when they landed their skiff in an unauthorized zone. The Huertista government released the sailors immediately and apologized to the commander of the U.S. squadron, then at anchor off Veracruz. The squadron commander, however, demanded a twenty-one-gun salute to the American flag in addition to the apology. Huerta agreed, but only if the U.S. warships would salute the Mexican flag in return. The Americans refused. Finally, when the Mexican salute did not come, Wilson issued an ultimatum: salute the flag or prepare for intervention. On April 20 he went before Congress (*Document 1.10*) and accused the Huerta government of insulting the American flag, and asked for permission to use force. Before Congress could act, however, news reached Washington that a German ship, laden with weapons for the Huerta government, was steaming toward Veracruz. The next morning, rather than allow the ship to dock and supply Huerta's army, Wilson ordered intervention. In the fighting that followed, 145 soldiers on both sides were killed. In late 1914 the Constitutionalists took Mexico City and Huerta resigned. It seemed that Wilson had what he wanted, although Carranza continued to resist assistance from the Wilson government. Stability, however, did not come to Mexico. Immediately, the Constitutionalist government split and the country again fell into civil war that led to further U.S. intervention.

....

DOCUMENT 1.10

PRESIDENT WOODROW WILSON'S ADDRESS TO CONGRESS ON THE CRISIS IN MEXICO, APRIL 20, 1914

It is my duty to call your attention to a situation which has arisen in our dealings with General Victoriano Huerta at Mexico City which calls for action, and to ask your advice and cooperation in acting upon it. On the 9th of April a paymaster of the *U.S.S. Dolphin* landed at the Iturbide Bridge landing at Tampico with a whaleboat and boat's crew to take off certain supplies needed by his ship, and while engaged in loading the boat was arrested by an officer and squad of men of the army of General *Huerta.* . . . Admiral [Henry T.] Mayo [of the *Dolphin*] regarded the arrest as so serious an affront that he was not satisfied with the apologies offered, but demanded that the flag of the United States be saluted with special ceremony by the military commander of the port.

SOURCE: *Papers Relating to the Foreign Relations of the United States, 1914* (1918), 474.

The incident can not be regarded as a trivial one, especially as two of the men arrested were taken from the boat itself—that is to say, from the territory of the United States—but had it stood by itself it might have been attributed to the ignorance or arrogance of a single officer. Unfortunately, it was not an isolated case. A series of incidents have recently occurred which can not but create the impression that the representatives of General Huerta were willing to go out of their way to show disregard for the dignity and rights of this Government and felt perfectly safe in doing what they pleased, making free to show in many ways their irritation and contempt. . . .

The manifest danger of such a situation was that such offenses might grow from bad to worse until something happened of so gross and intolerable a sort as to lead directly and inevitably to armed conflict. It was necessary that the apologies of General Huerta and his representatives should go much further, that they should be such as to attract the attention of the whole population to their significance, and such as to impress upon General Huerta himself the necessity of seeing to it that no further occasion for explanations and professed regrets should arise. I, therefore, felt it my duty to sustain Admiral Mayo in the whole of his demand and to insist that the flag of the United States should be saluted in such a way as to indicate a new spirit and attitude on the part of the Huertistas.

Such a salute, General Huerta has refused, and I have come to ask your approval and support in the course I now propose to pursue.

This Government can, I earnestly hope, in no circumstances be forced into war with the people of Mexico.

Mexico is torn by civil strife. If we are to accept the tests of its own constitution, it has no government. General Huerta has set his power up in the City of Mexico, such as it is, without right and by methods for which there can be no justification. Only part of the country is under his control. If armed conflict should unhappily come as a result of his attitude of personal re-

sentment toward this Government, we should be fighting only General Huerta and those who adhere to him and give him their support, and our object would be only to restore to the people of the distracted Republic the opportunity to set up again their own laws and their own government.

But I earnestly hope that war is not now in question. I believe I speak for the American people when I say that we do not desire to control in any degree the affairs of our sister Republic. Our feeling for the people of Mexico is one of deep and genuine friendship, and every thing that we have so far done or refrained from doing has proceeded from our desire to help them, not to hinder or embarrass them. We would not wish even to exercise the good offices of friendship without their welcome and consent. The people of Mexico are entitled to settle their own domestic affairs in their own way, and we sincerely desire to respect their right. The present situation need have none of the grave implications of interference if we deal with it promptly, firmly, and wisely.

No doubt I could do what is necessary in the circumstances to enforce respect for our Government without recourse to the Congress, and yet not exceed my constitutional powers as President; but I do not wish to act in a manner possibly of so grave consequence except in close conference and cooperation with both the Senate and House. I, therefore, come to ask your approval that I should use the armed forces of the United States in such ways and to such an extent as may be necessary to obtain from General Huerta and his adherents the fullest recognition of the rights and dignity of the United States, even amidst the distressing conditions now unhappily obtaining in Mexico.

There can be in what we do no thought of aggression or of selfish aggrandizement. We seek to maintain the dignity and authority of the United States only because we wish always to keep our great influence unimpaired for the uses of liberty, both in the United States and wherever else it may be employed for the benefit of mankind.

CHAPTER 2

War and Peace, 1914–1920

2.1 President Woodrow Wilson's Appeal for Neutrality, August 19, 1914
2.2 Secretary of State William Jennings Bryan's Note Protesting the Sinking of the *Lusitania,* May 13, 1915
2.3 The *Sussex* Pledge, May 4, 1916
2.4 The Zimmermann Note from the German Foreign Secretary, Arthur Zimmermann, to the German Ambassador to Mexico, January 16, 1917
2.5 Do the People Want War? *The New Republic,* March 3, 1917
2.6 President Woodrow Wilson's War Message to Congress, April 2, 1917
2.7 Wilson's Fourteen Points, Delivered to a Joint Session of Congress, January 8, 1918
2.8 President Woodrow Wilson's Statement to the Senate Foreign Relations Committee, August 19, 1919
2.9 Senator William E. Borah's Speech Before the Senate in Opposition to Ratification of the League of Nations, November 19, 1919

1914–1919 Timeline

August 1914	1914	War begins in Europe
August 19, 1914		Wilson's appeal for neutrality
May 7, 1915		*Lusitania* sunk
May 13, 1915	1915	Bryan protests the sinking of the *Lusitania*
May 4, 1916		*Sussex* Pledge
November 1916		Wilson elected to second term
January 16, 1917	1916	Zimmermann Note
March 3, 1917		"Do the People Want War?"
April 2, 1917		Wilson's War message
November 1917	1917	Bolshevik takeover in Russia
January 8, 1918		Wilson's Fourteen Points
November 11, 1918		Armistice
January–May 1919	1918	Versailles conference
August 1919		Wilson's statement to the Senate Foreign Relations Committee
October 1919		Wilson suffers stroke
November 19, 1919	1919	Borah's speech in the Senate

2.1   **President Woodrow Wilson's Appeal for Neutrality, August 19, 1914**
2.2   **Secretary of State William Jennings Bryan's Note Protesting the Sinking of the *Lusitania*, May 13, 1915**
2.3   **The *Sussex* Pledge, May 4, 1916**

The dawn of the twentieth century seemed to bring hope that the age of wars, at least major wars, was at an end, that reason and treaties would replace the need for military force. To most observers, cool-headed diplomats would maintain the peace by mediating the incidents and conflicts of the era. These incidents included several colonial conflicts around the world, several Balkan wars, and even the assassination of Archduke Franz Ferdinand in Sarajevo in June 1914. Consequently, when the European powers began their Great War in August 1914, Americans were exasperated by their brethrens' inability to find a peaceful solution to the conflict. One advantage of being an American, it seemed, was being at peace. "We never appreciated so keenly as now," wrote a midwestern editor, "the foresight exercised by our forefathers in emigrating from Europe." Immediately after the war in Europe began, President Woodrow Wilson declared American neutrality. That message is *Document 2.1.*

America, however, was slowly and surely drawn into the European conflict. One point of contention was Wilson's insistence, from the war's very beginning, that U.S. cargo ships be allowed to travel freely on the high seas, something that neither Germany nor England could allow. Both nations refused Wilson's concept of neutral rights, but it was England more than Germany that interfered with U.S. shipping. England's violations of maritime law led mostly to searches, confiscations, and warnings—little more than an inconvenience to U.S. ships attempting to trade with Germany. Germany, however, resorted to submarine warfare in the face of the indomitable British navy. The rules of naval warfare required that commercial vessels be stopped and their cargoes be inspected for contraband before being seized or sunk. German submarines, however, were simply too small and too vulnerable above the surface to comply with that law. In addition, British merchant ships were often armed and prepared to fire on and even ram the thin-skinned German submarines if given the chance. By early 1915 it became clear to the Germans that if they did not impose a shoot-on-sight-hit-and-run strategy that their submarine warfare in the North Atlantic would be ineffective. In February, the German government announced that it was establishing a war zone around the British Isles, and that its submarines would sink all ships within it. Wilson responded immediately that the German government would be held to "a strict accountability" for the loss of American lives. In March, the British steamer *Falaba* was sunk and one of its passengers, Leon Thrasher, became the first American casualty of the war. While Wilson agonized over how to handle the situation, a German submarine sank the British passenger liner *Lusitania* on May 7. Twelve hundred people were killed in the attack; 128 were Americans. It was the first of several incidents that would move the United States closer to war on the Allied side.

Secretary of State William Jennings Bryan, an outspoken pacifist, believed that the American passengers had entered the war zone at their own risk, and that a belligerent response from Washington could only propel the United States and Germany toward war. However, he reluctantly signed the note to the German government protesting the incident (*Document 2.2*). When Germany's response was not satisfactory, Wilson insisted on a more strongly worded note, sent on June 9, demanding that Germany abandon submarine warfare altogether. Bryan, rather than sign the second note, resigned from the administration and joined the peace movement. A third note threatened to break diplomatic relations if the Germans continued to attack passenger ships.

The German government secretly ordered its submarine captains to avoid sinking passenger liners in the future, but on August 15 the *Arabic*, a British liner bound for New York, was sunk without warning, killing two Americans. Germany, believing that a U.S. declaration of war was imminent, issued a statement on September 1, known as the *Arabic* Pledge, in which they promised that neither passenger liners nor merchant ships would be sunk without warning and without making provisions for the safety of the passengers and crew.

The incidents brought war cries from the American press and from belligerents like Theodore Roosevelt. But more importantly, many Americans saw these acts as little more than terrorism and cowardice, and the Germans began to fit more clearly into the role of a national enemy. The situation, however, cooled down during the next months. Then on March 25, 1916 a German submarine torpedoed an unarmed French freighter, the *Sussex*. Eighty passengers were killed and wounded in the attack, including several Americans who were severely injured. Several members of Wilson's cabinet insisted that the United States break diplomatic relations with Germany over the incident, but the president instead only threatened to break relations if Germany did not end its submarine warfare against passenger and merchant ships. Germany relented with the *Sussex* Pledge of May 4, 1916 (*Document 2.3*).

···

DOCUMENT 2.1

PRESIDENT WOODROW WILSON'S APPEAL FOR NEUTRALITY, AUGUST 19, 1914

My fellow countrymen. I suppose that every thoughtful man in America has asked himself during these last troubled weeks, what influence the European war may exert upon the United States, and I take the liberty of addressing a few words to you in order to point out that it is entirely within our own choice what its effects upon us will be and to urge very

SOURCE: Woodrow Wilson, *Message to Congress*, 63rd Cong., 2d Sess., Senate Doc. No. 566, 1914, 3–4.

earnestly upon you the sort of speech and conduct which will best safeguard the Nation against distress and disaster.

The effect of the war upon the United States will depend upon what American citizens say and do. Every man who really loves America will act and speak in the true spirit of neutrality, which is the spirit of impartiality and fairness and friendliness to all concerned. The spirit of the nation in this critical matter will be determined largely by what individuals and society and those gathered in public meetings do and say, upon what newspapers and magazines contain, upon what ministers utter in their pulpits, and men proclaim as their opinions upon the street.

The people of the United States are drawn from many nations, and chiefly from the nations now at war. It is natural and inevitable that there should be the utmost variety of sympathy and desire among them with regard to the issues and circumstances of the conflict. Some will wish one nation, others another, to succeed in the momentous struggle. It will be easy to excite passion and difficult to allay it. Those responsible for exciting it will assume a heavy responsibility, responsibility for no less a thing than that the people of the United States, whose love of their country and whose loyalty to its government should unite them as Americans all, bound in honor and affection to think first of her and her interests, may be divided in camps of hostile opinion, hot against each other, involved in the war itself in impulse and opinion if not in action.

Such divisions amongst us would be fatal to our peace of mind and might seriously stand in the way of the proper performance of our duty as the one great nation at peace, the one people holding itself ready to play a part of impartial mediation and speak the counsels of peace and accommodation, not as a partisan, but as a friend.

I venture, therefore, my fellow countrymen, to speak a solemn word of warning to you against that deepest, most subtle, most essential breach of neutrality which may spring out of partisanship, out of passionately taking sides. The United States must be neutral in fact, as well as in name, during these days that are to try men's souls. We must be impartial in thought, as well as action, must put a curb upon our sentiments, as well as upon every transaction that might be construed as a preference of one party to the struggle before another.

My thought is of America. I am speaking, I feel sure, the earnest wish and purpose of every thoughtful American that this great country of ours, which is, of course, the first in our thoughts and in our hearts, should show herself in this time of peculiar trial a Nation fit beyond others to exhibit the fine poise of undisturbed judgment, the dignity of self-control, the efficiency of dispassionate action; a Nation that neither sits in judgment of others nor is disturbed in her own counsels and which keeps herself fit and free to do what is honest and truly serviceable for the peace of the world.

Shall we not resolve to put upon ourselves the restraints which will bring to our people the happiness and the great and lasting influence for peace we covet for them.

DOCUMENT 2.2

SECRETARY OF STATE WILLIAM JENNINGS BRYAN'S NOTE PROTESTING THE SINKING OF THE *LUSITANIA*, MAY 13, 1915

In view of the recent acts of the German authorities in violation of American rights on the high seas which culminated in the torpedoing and the sinking of the British steamship *Lusitania* on May 7th, 1915, by which over 100 American citizens lost their lives, it is clearly wise and desirable that the Government of the United States and the Imperial German Government should come to a clear and full understanding as to the grave situation which has resulted.

The sinking of the British passenger steamer *Falaba* by a German submarine on March 28, through which Leon C. Thrasher, an American citizen, was drowned; the attack on April 28 on the American vessel *Cushing* by a German aeroplane; the torpedoing on May 1 of the American vessel *Gulflight* by a German submarine, as a result of which two or more American citizens met their death; and, finally, the torpedoing and sinking of the steamship *Lusitania*, constitute a series of events which the Government of the United States has observed with growing concern, distress, and amazement. . . .

The Government of the United States has been apprised that the Imperial German Government considered themselves to be obliged by the extraordinary circumstances of the present war and the measures adopted by their

---

SOURCE: *Foreign Relations of the United States, 1915* (1929), supplement, 393.

adversaries in seeking to cut Germany off from all commerce, to adopt methods of retaliation which go much beyond the ordinary methods of warfare at sea, in the proclamation of a war zone from which they have warned neutral ships to keep away. This government has already taken occasion to inform the Imperial German Government that it cannot admit the adoption of such measures or such a warning of danger to operate as in any degree an abbreviation of the rights of American shipmasters or of American citizens bound on lawful errands as passengers on merchant ships of belligerent nationality; and that it must hold the Imperial Government to a strict accountability for any infringement of those rights, intentional or incidental. It does not understand the Imperial German Government to question those rights. It assumes, on the contrary, that the Imperial Government accept, as of course, the rule that the lives of non-combatants, whether they be of neutral citizenship or citizens of one of those nations at war, can not lawfully or rightfully be put in jeopardy by the capture or destruction of an armed merchantman, and recognize also, as all other nations do, the obligation to take the usual precaution of visit and search to ascertain whether a suspected merchantman is in fact carrying contraband of war under the neutral flag.

The Government of the United States, therefore, desires to call the attention of the Imperial German Government with the utmost earnestness to the fact that the objection of their present method of attack against the trade of their enemies lies in the practical impossibility of employing submarines in the destruction of commerce without disregarding those rules of fairness, reason, justice, and humanity which all modern opinion regards as imperative. It is practically impossible for the officers of a submarine to visit a merchantman at sea and examine her papers and cargo. It is practically impossible for them to make a prize of her; and, if they can not put a prize crew on board of her, they can not sink her without leaving her crew and all on board her to the mercy of the sea in her small boats. These facts it is un-

derstood the Imperial German Government frankly admit. We are informed that, in the instances of which we have spoken, time enough for even the last poor measure of safety was not given, and in at least two cases cited, not so much as a warning was received. Manifestly submarines can not be used against merchantmen, as the last few weeks have shown, without an inevitable violation of many sacred principles of justice and humanity.

American citizens act within their indisputable rights in taking their ships and in traveling wherever their legitimate business calls them upon the high seas, and exercise those rights in what should be the well-justified confidence that their lives will not be endangered by acts done in clear violation of universally acknowledged international obligations, and certainly in the confidence that their own Government will sustain them in the exercise of their rights. . . .

Long acquainted as this Government has been with the character of the Imperial German Government and with the high principles of equity by which they have in the past been actuated and guided, the Government of the United States can not believe that the commanders of the vessels which committed these acts of lawlessness did so except under a misapprehension of the orders issued by the Imperial German naval authorities. It takes it for granted that, at least within the practical possibilities of every such case, the commanders even of submarines were expected to do nothing that would involve the lives of non-combatants or the safety of neutral ships. . . . It confidently expects, therefore, that the Imperial German Government will disavow the acts of which the Government of the United States complains, that they will make reparation so far as reparation is possible for injuries which are without measure, and that they will take immediate steps to prevent the recurrence of anything so obviously subversive of the principles of warfare for which the Imperial German Government have in the past so wisely and so firmly contended.

The Government and the people of the United States look to the Imperial German

Government for just, prompt, and enlightened action in this vital matter with the greater confidence because the United States and Germany are bound together not only by special ties of friendship but also by the explicit stipulations of the treaty of 1828 between the United States and the Kingdom of Prussia.

Expressions of regret and offers of reparation in case of the destruction of neutral ships sunk by mistake, while they may satisfy international obligations, if no loss of life results, can not justify or excuse a practice the natural and necessary effect of which is to subject neutral nations and neutral persons to new and immeasurable risks.

The Imperial German Government will not expect the Government of the United States to omit any word or any act necessary to the performance of its sacred duty of maintaining the rights of the United States and its citizens and of safeguarding their free exercise and enjoyment.

DOCUMENT 2.3

THE *SUSSEX* PLEDGE, MAY 4, 1916

As the German Government has repeatedly declared, it can not dispense with the use of the submarine weapon in the conduct of warfare against enemy trade. The Government, however, has now decided to make a further concession in adapting the methods of submarine warfare to the interests of the neutrals; in reaching this decision the German Government has been actuated by considerations which are above the level of the disputed question. . . .

For, in answer to the appeal made by the United States Government on behalf of the sacred principles of humanity and international law, the German Government must repeat once more with all emphasis that it was not the German but the British Government which, ignoring all the accepted rules of international law, has extended this terrible war to the lives and property of non-combatants, having no regard whatever for the interests and rights of the neutrals and non-combatants that through this method of warfare have been seriously injured.

In self-defense against the illegal conduct of British warfare, while fighting a bitter struggle for her national existence, Germany had to resort to the hard but effective weapon of submarine warfare. As matters stand, the German Government can not but reiterate its regret that the sentiments of humanity which the Government of the United States extends with such fervor to the unhappy victims of submarine warfare are not extended with the same warmth of feeling to the many millions of women and children who, according to the avowed intentions of the British Government, shall be starved and who, by their sufferings, shall force the victorious armies of the central powers into ignominious capitulation. . . . It will therefore be understood that the appeal made by the Government of the United States to the sentiments of humanity and to the principles of international law can not, under the circumstances, meet with the same hearty response from the German people which such an appeal is otherwise always certain to find there. If the German Government, nevertheless, has resolved to go the utmost limits of concessions, it has not alone been guided by the friendship connecting the two great nations for over a hundred years, but it also has thought of the great doom which threatens the entire civilized world should this cruel and sanguinary war be extended and prolonged.

The German Government, conscious of Germany's strength, has twice within the last few months announced before the world its readiness to make peace on a basis safeguarding Germany's vital interests, thus indicating that it is not Germany's fault if peace is still withheld from the nations of Europe.

The German Government feels all the more justified to declare that the responsibility could not be borne before the forum of mankind and history if, after 21 months' duration of the war,

SOURCE: *Foreign Relations of the United States, 1916* (1929), supplement, 259–60.

the submarine question under discussion between the German Government and the Government of the United States were to take a turn seriously threatening the maintenance of peace between the two nations.

As far as it lies with the German Government, it wishes to prevent things from taking such a course. The German Government, moreover, is prepared to do its utmost to confine the operations of the war for the rest of its duration to the fighting forces of the belligerents, thereby also insuring the freedom of the seas, a principle upon which the German Government believes, now as before, to be in agreement with the Government of the United States.

The German Government, guided by this idea, notifies the Government of the United States that the German naval forces have received the following orders: In accordance with the general principles of visit and search and destruction of merchant vessels recognized by international laws, such vessels, both within and without the area declared as naval war zone, shall not be sunk without warning and without saving human lives, unless these ships attempt to escape or offer resistance.

But neutrals can not expect that Germany, forced to fight for her existence, shall for the sake of neutral interests, restrict the use of an effective weapon if her enemy is permitted to continue to apply at will methods of warfare violating the rules of international law. Such a demand would be incompatible with the character of neutrality, and the German Government is convinced that the Government of the United States does not think of making such a demand, knowing that the government of the United States has repeatedly declared that it is determined to restore the principle of the freedom of the seas, from whatever quarter it is violated.

Accordingly, the German Government is confident that, in consequence of the new orders issued to its naval forces, the Government of the United States will now also consider all impediments removed which may have been in the way of a mutual cooperation towards the restoration of the freedom of the seas during the war as suggested in the note of July 23, 1915, and it does not doubt that the Government of the United States will now demand and insist that the British Government shall forthwith observe the rules of international law universally recognized before the war as they are laid down in the notes presented by the Government of the United States to the British Government on December 28, 1914, and November 5, 1915. Should the steps taken by the Government of the United States not attain the object it desires, to have the laws of humanity followed by all belligerent nations, the German Government would then be facing a new situation, in which it must reserve itself complete liberty of decision.

2.4 The Zimmermann Note from the German Foreign Secretary, Arthur Zimmermann, to the German Ambassador to Mexico, January 16, 1917

2.5 Do the People Want War? *The New Republic*, March 3, 1917

2.6 President Woodrow Wilson's War Message to Congress, April 2, 1917

Woodrow Wilson's decision to take the nation to war in the spring of 1917 was a complicated one. It was more than submarines, and more than the right of Americans to sail the waters of the world unencumbered. Wilson had clearly decided that for the United States to have a say in the events of the post-war, to in fact take a seat at the peace table, it would have to be a combatant. Wilson hoped to establish a new world order, to advance democracy and the Open Door, and even to outlaw revolution and aggression. He had come to believe, as the events of early 1917 unfolded, that to gain an American-fashioned peace, the United States would have to go to war.

There were, however, a number of specific incidents that pushed Wilson to call for a declaration of war against the Central Powers on April 2, 1917. In January, in hopes of scoring a quick knockout punch against the Allies before the United States could enter in any significant way, Germany announced that it would repudiate the *Sussex* Pledge and embark on a policy of unrestricted submarine warfare. Four days after that announcement Wilson told a joint session of Congress that he had broken diplomatic relations with Germany. On February 26 he asked Congress for the power to arm merchant ships, but a few Midwestern isolationists blocked the president's request. He armed the vessels anyway. A few days later, the Zimmermann Note broke in the press. This short message (*Document 2.4*) from the German foreign secretary Arthur Zimmermann to the German ambassador to Mexico, proposed an alliance between Germany and Mexico in the event of a war between Germany and the United States. In exchange, the note continued, Germany would help Mexico recover the "lost territories" of Texas, Arizona and New Mexico. The British had released the note to Wilson on February 24 hoping to draw the United States into the war. Wilson then released it to the press on March 1 in an effort to convince Congress that merchant vessels should be armed. But the impact of the note was much greater. It exploded onto the front pages of the national press, and it went a long way toward pushing the United States closer to war; it was an emotionally charged issue that aroused the average American and further demonized Germany. Also in March, the Russian Czar abdicated and the provisional government was formed in St. Petersburg promising democracy and a further prosecution of the war in the east. To many Americans, including Wilson, America could now join the war of the democracies against the autocracies. It was a moral issue.

Despite Germany's actions the American peace movement remained alive and well. In March 1917, just as much of the nation was anticipating war, the anti-war group Committee for Democratic Control published a statement in *The New Republic* affirming a common refrain that it was American industry that had the most to gain by the nation's involvement in the European war (*Document 2.5*). It was the titans of Wall Street, they argued in the advertisement, and not the American people, who wanted war.

German submarines had sunk five American merchant vessels during the first weeks of March, and on March 20 Wilson polled his cabinet and received a unanimous endorsement for a declaration of war. The president met a joint session of Congress on April 2 to deliver his war message. It is *Document 2.6*.

DOCUMENT 2.4

THE ZIMMERMANN NOTE FROM GERMAN FOREIGN SECRETARY, ARTHUR ZIMMERMANN, TO THE GERMAN AMBASSADOR TO MEXICO, JANUARY 16, 1917

We intend to begin . . . unrestricted submarine warfare. We shall endeavor in spite of this to keep the United States of America neutral. In the event of this not succeeding,

SOURCE: *Foreign Relations of the United States, 1917* (1931), supplement, 147–48.

we make Mexico a proposal of alliance on the following basis: Make war together, make peace together, generous financial support and an understanding on our part that Mexico is to reconquer the lost territory of Texas, New Mexico and Arizona. You will inform the President [of Mexico] of the above most secretly as soon as the outbreak of war with the United States of America is certain and add the suggestion that he should, on his own initiative, invite Japan to immediate adherence and at the same time mediate between Japan and ourselves. Please call the President's attention to the fact that the ruthless employment of our submarines now offers the prospect of compelling England in a few months to make peace.

The Zimmermann Note infuriated Americans. Pro-German elements in the US insisted the note was a British hoax. It was not. *Courtesy of BoondocksNet.com*

DOCUMENT 2.5

DO THE PEOPLE WANT WAR? *THE NEW REPUBLIC,* MARCH 3, 1917

In the second week of February the American Union Against Militarism sent out 100,000 return postal cards, asking people whether they wanted to go to war to enforce our rights of commerce in the war-zone declared by Germany. These cards went to all kinds of people in city and country, from two registration lists supplied by Congressmen themselves. The recipients were asked to mail their answers to their congressmen. We are informed that the result, based on returns to thirty congressmen from widely scattered parts of the country, was a heavy vote for peace. The average was six to one against war. The lowest vote against war in any district was four to one, the highest eleven to one. The people do not want this country to go to war.

Who does want the country to go to war?

The following quotation from the weekly letter of a Baltimore firm, a member of the New York Stock Exchange, may shed some light on the question:

"Regarding war as inevitable, Wall Street believes that it would be preferable to this uncertainty about the actual date of its commencement. Canada and Japan are at war and are more prosperous than ever before. . . .

The popular view is that stocks would have a quick, sharp reaction immediately upon outbreak of hostilities and that then they would enjoy an old-fashioned bull market such as followed the outbreak of war with Spain in 1898. . . .

The advent of peace would force a readjustment of commodity prices and would probably mean a postponement of new enterprises. As peace negotiations would be long drawn out, the period of waiting and uncertainty for business would be long. If the United States does not go to war it is nevertheless good opinion that the preparedness program will compensate in good measure for the loss of the stimulus of actual war."

In other words, Wall Street's first choice is war, and its second, a great preparedness program. In the last two and a half years, Wall Street has sold two and a half thousand million dollars worth of war supplies to the Allies. But the Allies are now, to a large extent, making their own supplies, and Wall Street must find a new market. War with Germany would be the surest means of selling these products to the United States government. War is, indeed, "preferable," but a great preparedness campaign is the next best bet. They must sell here what they can no longer sell over there. Someone must take up the White Man's Burden.

Wall Street charges that the "peace campaign" in the United States, being a hint to Germany that we do not want to fight, is an invitation to her to sink our ships. The opposite is true. Germany has no fear of our military participation in the war. Germany realizes, as do the statesmen of the Allies themselves, that, for the present, our entrance into the war would not materially aid the Entente. But Germany does fear three things when she considers the possibility of war with us: (1) Losing the influence of a great, unembittered neutral nation in the peace negotiations; (2) losing the friendship of the only rich power that can help her, financially and industrially, in the reconstruction period, to which she already looks forward with dread; and (3) losing the friendship of millions of German-Americans who, though loyal to the United States, have a legitimate affection for the nation of their birth, which would be largely destroyed by war between the two countries. In short, the more real our friendship appears to Germany at this time, the more unwilling will she be to forfeit it through ruthless submarine aggressions.

The forces in the United States that represent money power, and the great newspapers which these forces control, are urging the country to war in the name of national honor. We say there is no defense of national honor in going to war with a nation that is down, even if that

SOURCE: *The New Republic*, March 3, 1917.

nation, in its frantic efforts to get up, has committed aggressions that are barbarous and unwarranted, though not primarily directed against us. Germany's armies are outnumbered and surrounded by a ring of steel, her warships and transports cannot sail in any one of the seven seas. Submarines cannot carry troops. If today there was no one on the American continent except children with toy bows and arrows, it is doubtful whether Germany could land a single regiment on our soil. Does any grown man seriously maintain that going to war with Germany under such circumstances will vindicate the honor of the United States?

Wall Street is loud in its denunciation of a popular referendum before war is declared.

And yet, if there is any one thing in the world that the people themselves have a right to decide, it is whether there shall be peace or war. Congress has the constitutional power to declare war, but if war comes it will not be Congress that will do the fighting. The editors will not do the fighting; nor will our bellicose lawyers, bankers, stock brokers and other prominent citizens, who mess at Delmonico's, bivouac in club windows, and are at all times willing to give to their country's service the last full measure of conversation. No, the people themselves will do the fighting, and they will pay the bill. In death, in suffering, in sorrow, and in taxes to the third and fourth generations, the people who fight will pay. And therefore, we say that the people themselves should speak before Congress is permitted to declare war.

Abraham Lincoln said, "I am for the people,— the people of the whole nation—doing just as they please in all matters which concern the whole nation." We say with Lincoln that "The people are the rightful masters of both Congresses and Courts." We say with James Bryce that "A state . . . is no wiser, no more righteous than the human beings of which it consists."

The people may be against war, or they may be for it, but whether they are for or against it, they have a right to decide, and no man and no

condition of the world's affairs can take that right from them.

AMOS PINCHOT
RANDOLPH S. BOURNE
MAX EASTMAN
WINTHROP D. LANE
Committee for Democratic Control

DOCUMENT 2.6

PRESIDENT WOODROW WILSON'S WAR MESSAGE TO CONGRESS, APRIL 2, 1917

I have called the Congress into extraordinary session because there are serious, very serious, choices of policy to be made, and made immediately, which it was neither right nor constitutionally permissible that I should assume the responsibility of making.

On the third of February last I officially laid before you the extraordinary announcement of the Imperial German Government that on and after the first day of February it was its purpose to put aside all restraints of law or of humanity and use its submarines to sink every vessel that sought to approach either the ports of Great Britain and Ireland or the western coasts of Europe or any of the ports controlled by the enemies of Germany within the Mediterranean. That had seemed to be the object of the German submarine warfare earlier in the war, but since April of last year the Imperial Government had somewhat restrained the commanders of its undersea craft in conformity with its promise then given to us that passenger boats should not be sunk and that due warning would be given to all other vessels which its submarines might seek to destroy, when no resistance was offered or escape attempted, and care taken that their crews were given at least a fair chance to save their lives in their open boats. The precautions taken were meager and haphazard enough, as was proved in distress instance after instance in the progress of the

SOURCE: *Cong. Rec.*, 65th Cong., 1st sess, LV, 102.

cruel and unmanly business, but a certain degree of restraint was observed. The new policy has swept every restriction aside. Vessels of every kind, whatever their flag, their character, their cargo, their destination, their errand, have been ruthlessly sent to the bottom without warning and without thought of help or mercy for those on board, the vessels of friendly neutrals along with those of belligerents. Even hospital ships and ships carrying relief to the sorely bereaved and stricken people of Belgium, though the latter were provided with safe conduct through the proscribed areas by the German Government itself and were distinguished by unmistakable marks of identity, have been sunk with the same reckless lack of compassion or of principle. I was for a little while unable to believe that such things would in fact be done by any government that had hither to subscribed to the humane practices of civilized nations. International law had its origin in the attempt to set up some law which would be respected and observed upon the seas, where no nation had the right of dominion and where lay the free highways of the world. By painful stage after painful stage has that law been built up, with meager enough results, indeed, after all was accomplished that could be accomplished, but always with a clear view, at least, of what the heart and conscience of mankind demanded. This minimum of right the German Government has swept aside under the plea of retaliation and necessity and because it had no weapons which it could use at sea except these which it is impossible to employ as it is employing them without throwing to the winds all scruples of humanity or of respect for the understandings that were supposed to underlie the intercourse of the world. I am not now thinking of the loss of property involved, immense and serious as that is, but only of the wanton and wholesale destruction of the lives of non-combatants, men, women, and children, engaged in pursuits which have always, even in the darkest periods of modern history, been deemed innocent and legitimate. Property can

be paid for; the lives of peaceful and innocent people cannot be. The present German submarine warfare against commerce is a warfare against mankind.

It is a war against all nations. American ships have been sunk, American lives taken, in ways which it has stirred us very deeply to learn of, but the ships and people of other neutral and friendly nations have been sunk and overwhelmed in the waters in the same way. There has been no discrimination. The challenge is to all mankind. Each nation must decide for itself how it will meet it. The choice we make for ourselves must be made with a moderation of counsel and a temperateness of judgment befitting our character and our motives as a nation. We must put excited feelings away. Our motive will not be revenge or the victorious assertion of the physical might of the nation, but only the vindication of right, of human right, of which we are only a single champion.

When I addressed the Congress on the twenty-sixth of February last I thought that it would suffice to assert our neutral rights with arms, our right to use the seas against unlawful interference, our right to keep our people safe against unlawful violence. But armed neutrality, it now appears, is impracticable. Because submarines are in effect outlaws when used as the German submarines have been used against merchant shipping, it is impossible to defend ships against their attacks as the law of nations has assumed that merchantmen would defend themselves against privateers or cruisers, visible craft giving chase upon the open sea. It is common prudence in such circumstances, grim necessity indeed, to endeavor to destroy them before they have shown their own intention. They must be dealt with upon sight, if dealt with at all. The German Government denies the right of neutrals to use arms at all within the areas of the sea which it has proscribed, even in the defense of rights which no modern publicist has ever before questioned their right to defend. . . . There is one choice we cannot make, we are incapable of making: we will not choose the path of submission and suffer the most sacred rights of our Nation and our people to be ignored or violated. The wrongs against which we now array ourselves are no common wrongs; they cut to the very roots of human life. With a profound sense of the solemn and even tragical character of the step I am taking and of the grave responsibilities which it involves, but in unhesitating obedience to what I deem my constitutional duty, I advise that the Congress declare the recent course of the Imperial German Government to be in fact nothing less than war against the government and people of the United States; that it formally accept the status of belligerent which has thus been thrust upon it; and that it take immediate steps not only to put the country in a more thorough state of defense but also to exert all its power and employ all its resources to bring the Government of the German Empire to terms and end the war. What this will involve is clear. It will involve the utmost practicable cooperation in counsel and action with the governments now at war with Germany, and, as incident to that, the most liberal financial credits, in order that our resources may so far as possible be added to theirs. It will involve the organization and mobilization of all material resources of the country to supply the materials of war and serve the incidental needs of the Nation in the most abundant and yet the most economical and efficient way possible. . . .

While we do these things, these deeply momentous things, let us be very clear, and make very clear to all the world, what our motives and our objects are. My own thought has not been driven from its habitual and normal course by the unhappy events of the last two months, and I do not believe that the thought of the Nation has been altered or clouded by them. I have exactly the same things in mind now that I had in mind when I addressed the Senate on the twenty-second of January last; the same that I had in mind when I addressed the Congress on the third of February and on the twenty-sixth of February. Our object now,

as then, is to vindicate the principles of peace and justice in the life of the world as against selfish and autocratic power and to set up amongst the really free and self-governed peoples of the world such a concert of purpose and of action as will henceforth insure the observance of those principles. Neutrality is no longer feasible or desirable where the peace of the world is involved and the freedom of its peoples, and the menace to that peace and freedom lies in the existence of autocratic governments backed by organized force which is controlled wholly by their will, not by the will of their people. We have seen the last of neutrality in such circumstances. We are at the beginning of an age in which it will be insisted that the same standards of conduct and of responsibility for wrong done shall be observed among nations and their governments that are observed among the individual citizens of civilized states.

We have no quarrel with the German people. We have no feeling towards them but one of sympathy and friendship. It was not upon their impulse that their government acted in entering this war. It was not with their previous knowledge or approval. It was a war determined upon as wars used to be determined upon in the old, unhappy days when peoples were nowhere consulted by their rulers and wars were provoked and waged in the interest of dynasties or of little groups of ambitious men who were accustomed to use their fellow men as pawns and tools. Self-governed nations do not fill their neighbor states with spies or set the course of intrigue to bring about some critical posture of affairs which will give them an opportunity to strike and make conquest. Such designs can be successfully worked out only under cover and where no one has the right to ask questions. Cunningly contrived plans of deception or aggression, carried, it may be, from generation to generation, can be worked out and kept from the light only within the privacy of courts or behind the carefully guarded confidences of a narrow and privileged class. They are happily impossible where public opinion commands and insists upon full information concerning all the nation's affairs.

We are accepting this challenge of hostile purpose because we know that in such a government, following such methods, we can never have a friend; and that in the presence of its organized power, always lying in wait to accomplish we know not what purpose, there can be no assured security for the democratic governments of the world. We are now about to accept gauge of battle with this natural foe to liberty and shall, if necessary, spend the whole force of the Nation to check and nullify its pretensions and its power. . . .

Just because we fight without rancor and without selfish object, seeking nothing for ourselves but what we shall wish to share with all free peoples, we shall, I feel confident, conduct our operations as belligerents without passion and ourselves observe with proud punctilio the principles of right and of fair play we profess to be fighting for. . . .

It will be all the easier for us to conduct ourselves as belligerents in a high spirit of right and fairness because we act without animus, not in enmity towards a people or with the desire to bring any injury or disadvantage upon them, but only in armed opposition to an irresponsible government which has thrown aside all considerations of humanity and of right and is running amuck. We are, let me say again, the sincere friends of the German people, and shall desire nothing so much as the early reestablishment of intimate relations of mutual advantage between us—however hard it may be for them, for the time being, to believed that this is spoken from our hearts. We have borne with their present Government through all these bitter months because of that friendship—exercising a patience and forbearance which would otherwise have been impossible. We shall, happily, still have an opportunity to prove that friendship in our daily attitude and actions towards the millions of men and women of German birth and native sympathy who live amongst us and share our life, and we shall be proud to prove it towards all who are in fact loyal to their neighbors and to the Government in the hour of test. They are, most of them, as true and loyal Americans as if they had never known any other fealty or allegiance. They will be prompt to stand with us in rebuking and restraining the few who may be of different mind and purpose. If there should be disloyalty, it will be dealt with with a firm hand of stern repression; but, if it lifts its head at all, it will lift it only here and there and without countenance except from a lawless and malignant few.

It is a distressing and oppressive duty, Gentlemen of the Congress, which I have performed in thus addressing you. There are, it may be, many months of fiery trial and sacrifice ahead of us. It is a fearful thing to lead this great peaceful people into war, into the most terrible and disastrous of all wars, civilization itself seeming to be in the balance. But the right is more precious than peace, and we shall fight for the things which we have always carried nearest our hearts—for democracy, for the right of those who submit to authority to have a voice in their own governments, for the rights and liberties of small nations, for a universal dominion of right by such a concert of free peoples as shall bring peace and safety to all nations and make the world itself at last free. To such a task we can dedicate our lives and our fortunes, everything that we are and everything that we have, with the pride of those who know that the day has come when America is privileged to spend her blood and her might for the principles that gave her birth and the peace which she has treasured. God helping her, she can do no other.

2.7   Wilson's Fourteen Points, Delivered to a Joint Session of Congress, January 8, 1918

There is no better example of Wilsonian idealism than the Fourteen Points, Woodrow Wilson's comprehensive agenda for ending the Great War in Europe (*Document 2.7*). Wilson's broad proposal was a direct reflection of his own crusading spirit, his belief in the American ideal, and his vision for a new world order—one in which the United States would be a major player. Wilson outlined his plan for peace before a joint session of Congress on January 8, 1918, even before most American soldiers had arrived in Europe. The Fourteen Points included references to the distinctly American concepts of the Open Door, freedom of the seas, and self-determination for the peoples of Europe. It also called for open diplomacy, arms control, and a "general association of nations" that would become the League of Nations. Ten months later the German government would agree to a peace based on Wilson's Fourteen Points. Only the League of Nations, however, would survive the Paris peace conference.

....

DOCUMENT 2.7

WILSON'S FOURTEEN POINTS, DELIVERED TO A JOINT SESSION OF CONGRESS, JANUARY 8, 1918

Gentlemen of the Congress:
Once more, as repeated before, the spokesmen of the Central Powers have indicated their desire to discuss the objects of the war and the possible basis of a general peace. Parleys have been in progress at Brest-Litovsk between Russian representatives and representatives of the Central Powers to which the attention of all the belligerents has been invited for the purpose of ascertaining whether it may be possible to extend these parleys into a general conference with regard to terms of peace and settlement.*

*At Brest-Litovsk the Soviet Union surrendered to Germany in March 1918. That treaty did not become a general peace treaty. Lenin and the Bolsheviks took over in Russia in late 1917.

SOURCE: *Cong. Rec.*, 65th Cong. 2d sess., LVI, 680.

The Russian representatives presented not only a perfectly definite statement of the principles upon which they would be willing to conclude peace but also an equally definite program of the concrete application of those principles. The representatives of the Central Powers, on their part, presented an outline of settlement which, if much less definite, seemed susceptible of liberal interpretation until their specific program of practical terms was added. That program proposed no concessions at all either to the sovereignty of Russia or to the preferences of the populations with whose fortunes it dealt, but meant, in a word, that the Central Empires were to keep every foot of territory their armed forces had occupied—every province, every city, every point of vantage as a permanent addition to their territories and their power.

It is a reasonable conjecture that the general principles of settlement which they at first suggested originated with the more liberal statesmen of Germany and Austria, the men who have begun to feel the force of their own people's thought and purpose, while the concrete terms of actual settlement came from the military leaders who have no thought but to keep what they have got. The negotiations have been broken off. The Russian representatives were sincere and in earnest. They cannot entertain such proposals of conquest and domination.

The whole incident is full of significance. It is also full of perplexity. With whom are the Russian representatives dealing? For whom are the representatives of the Central Empires speaking? Are they speaking for the majorities of their respective parliaments or for the minority parties, that military and imperialistic minority which has so far dominated their whole policy and controlled the affairs of Turkey and of the Balkan states which have felt obliged to become their associates in this war?

The Russian representatives have insisted, very justly, very wisely, and in the true spirit of modern democracy, that the conferences they have been holding with the Teutonic and Turkish statesmen should be held within open, not closed, doors, and all the world [will be the] audience, as was desired. To whom have we been listening, then? To those who speak the spirit and intention of the resolutions of the German Reichstag of the 9th of July last, the spirit and intention of the Liberal leaders and parties of Germany, or to those who resist and defy that spirit and intension and insist upon conquest and subjugation? Or are we listening, in fact, to both, unreconciled and in open and hopeless contradiction? These are very serious and pregnant questions. Upon the answer to them depends the peace of the world.

But, whatever the results of the parleys at Brest-Litovsk, whatever the confusions of counsel and of purpose in the utterances of the spokesmen of the Central Empires, they have again attempted to acquaint the world with their objects in the war and have again challenged their adversaries to say what their objects are and what sort of settlement they would deem just and satisfactory. There is no

good reason why that challenge should not be responded to, and responded to with the utmost candor. . . . Not once, but again and again, we have laid our whole thought and purpose before the world, not in general terms only, but each time with sufficient definition to make it clear what sort of definite terms of settlement must necessarily spring out of them. Within the last week [British Prime Minister] Lloyd George has spoken with admirable candor and in admirable spirit for the people and Government of Great Britain.

There is no confusion of counsel among the adversaries of the Central Powers, no uncertainty of principle, no vagueness of detail. The only secrecy of counsel, the only lack of fearless frankness, the only failure to make definite statement of the objects of the war, lies with Germany and her allies. The issues of life and death hang upon these definitions. No statesman who has the least conception of his responsibility ought for a moment to permit himself to continue this tragical and appalling outpouring of blood and treasure unless he is sure beyond a peradventure that the objects of the vital sacrifice are part and parcel of the very life of Society and that the people for whom he speaks think them right and imperative as he does.

There is, moreover, a voice calling for these definitions of principle and of purpose which is, it seems to me, more thrilling and more compelling than any of the many moving voices with which the troubled air of the world is filled. It is the voice of the Russian people. They are prostrate and all but helpless, it would seem, before the grim power of Germany, which has hitherto known no relenting and no pity. Their power, apparently, is shattered. And yet their soul is not subservient. They will not yield either in principle or in action. Their conception of what is right, of what is humane and honorable for them to accept, has been stated with a frankness, a largeness of view, a generosity of spirit, and a universal human sympathy which must challenge the admiration of every friend of mankind; and they have refused to compound their ideals or desert others that they themselves may be safe.

They call to us to say what it is that we desire, in what, if in anything, our purpose and our spirit differ from theirs; and I believe that the people of the United States would wish me to respond, with utter simplicity and frankness. Whether their present leaders believe it or not, it is our heartfelt desire and hope that some way may be opened whereby we may be privileged to assist the people of Russia to attain their utmost hope of liberty and ordered peace.

It will be our wish and purpose that the processes of peace, when they are begun, shall be absolutely open and that they shall involve and permit henceforth no secret understandings of any kind. The day of conquest and aggrandizement is gone by; so is also the day of secret covenants entered into in the interest of particular governments and likely at some unlooked-for moment to upset the peace of the world. It is this happy fact, now clear to the view of every public man whose thoughts do not still linger in an age that is dead and gone, which makes it possible for every nation whose purposes are consistent with justice and the peace of the world to avow now or at any other time the objects it has in view.

We entered this war because violations of right had occurred which touched us to the quick and made the life of our own people impossible unless they were corrected and the world secured once and for all against their recurrence. What we demand in this war, therefore, is nothing peculiar to ourselves. It is that the world be made fit and safe to live in; and particularly that it be made safe for every peace-loving nation which, like our own, wishes to live its own life, determine its own institutions, be assured of justice and fair dealing by the other peoples of the world as against force and selfish aggression. All the peoples of the world are in effect partners in this interest, and for our own part we see very clearly that unless justice be done to others that it will not be done to us. The programme of the world's peace, therefore, is our programme; and that

programme, the only possible programme, as we see it, is this:

I.   Open covenants of peace, openly arrived at, after which there shall be no private international understandings of any kind but diplomacy shall proceed always frankly and in the public view.

II. Absolute freedom of navigation upon the seas, outside territorial waters, alike in peace and in war, except as the seas may be closed in whole or in part by international action for the enforcement of international covenants.

III. The removal, so far as possible, of all economic barriers and the establishment of an equality of trade conditions among all the nations consenting to the peace and associating themselves for its maintenance.

IV. Adequate guarantees given and taken that national armaments will be reduced to the lowest point consistent with domestic safety.

V.   A free, open-minded, and absolutely impartial adjustment of all colonial claims, based upon a strict observance of the principle that in determining all such questions of sovereignty the interests of the populations concerned must have equal weight with the equitable claims of the government whose title is to be determined.

VI. The evacuation of all Russian territory and such a settlement of all questions affecting Russia as will secure the best and freest cooperation of the other nations of the world in obtaining for her an unhampered and unembarrassed opportunity for the independent determination of her own political development and national policy and assure her of a sincere welcome into the society of free nations under institutions of her own choosing; and, more than a welcome, assistance also of every kind that she may need and may herself desire. The treatment accorded Russia by her sister nations in the months to come will be the acid test of their good will, of their comprehension of her needs as distinguished from their own interests, and of their intelligent and unselfish sympathy.

VII. Belgium, the whole world will agree, must be evacuated and restored, without any attempts to limit the sovereignty which she enjoys in common with all other free nations. No other single act will serve as this will serve to restore confidence among the nations in the laws which they have themselves set and determined for the government of their relations with one another. Without this healing act the whole structure and validity of international law is forever impaired.

VIII. All French territory should be freed and the invaded portions restored, and the wrong done to France by Prussia in 1871 in the matter of Alsace-Lorraine, which has unsettled the peace of the world for nearly fifty years, should be righted, in order that peace may once more be made secure in the interests of all.

IX. A readjustment of the frontiers of Italy should be effected along clearly recognizable lines of nationality.

X. The peoples of Austria-Hungary, whose place among the nations we wish to see safeguarded and assured, should be accorded the freest opportunity of autonomous development.

XI. Rumania, Serbia, and Montenegro should be evacuated; occupied territories restored; Serbia accorded free and secure access to the sea; and the relations of the several Balkan states to one another determined by friendly counsel along historically established lines of allegiance and nationality; and international guarantees of the political and economic independence and territorial integrity of the several Balkan states should be entered into.

XII. The Turkish portions of the present Ottoman Empire should be assured a secure sovereignty, but the other nationalities which are now under Turkish rule should be assured an undoubted security of life and an absolutely unmolested opportunity of autonomous development, and the Dardanelles should be permanently opened as a free passage to the ships and commerce of all nations under international guarantees.

XIII. An independent Polish state should be erected which should include the territories inhabited by indisputably Polish populations, which should be assured a free and secure access to the sea, and whose political and economic independence and territorial integrity should be guaranteed by international covenant.

XIV. A general association of nations must be formed under specific covenants for the purpose of affording mutual guarantees of political independence and territorial integrity to great and small states alike.

In regard to these essential rectifications of wrong and assertions of right we feel ourselves to be intimate partners of all the governments and peoples associated together against the Imperialists. We cannot be separated in interest or divided in purpose. We stand together until the end.

For such arrangements and covenants we are willing to fight and to continue to fight until they are achieved; but only because we wish the right to prevail and desire a just and stable peace such as can be secured only by removing the chief provocations to war, which this program does remove.

We have no jealousy of German greatness, and there is nothing in this program that impairs it. We grudge her no achievement or distinction of learning or of pacific enterprise such as have made her record very bright and very enviable. We do not wish to injure her or to block in any way her legitimate influence or power. We do not wish to fight her either with arms or with hostile arrangements of trade if she is willing to associate herself with us and the other peace-loving nations of the world in covenants of justice and law and fair dealing.

We lavish her only to accept a place of equality among the peoples of the world—the new world in which we now live—instead of a place of mastery.

Neither do we presume to suggest to her any alteration or modification of her institutions. But it is necessary, we must frankly say, and necessary as a preliminary to any intelligent dealings with her on our part, that we should know whom her spokesmen speak for when they speak to us, whether for the Reichstag majority or for the military party and the men whose creed is imperial domination.

We have spoken now, surely, in terms too concrete to admit of any further doubt or ques-

tion. An evident principle runs through the whole program I have outlined. It is the principle of justice to all peoples and nationalities, and their right to live on equal terms of liberty and safety with one another, whether they be strong or weak.

Unless this principle be made its foundation, no part of the structure of international justice can stand. The people of the United States could act upon no other principle; and to the vindication of this principle they are ready to devote their lives, their honor, and everything that they possess. The moral climax of this the culminating and final war for human liberty has come, and they are ready to put their own strength, their own highest purpose, their own integrity and devotion to the test.

2.8   President Woodrow Wilson's Statement to the Senate Foreign Relations Committee, August 19, 1919
2.9   Senator William E. Borah's Speech Before the Senate in Opposition to Ratification of the League of Nations, November 19, 1919

America's intervention in the war gave Wilson the place he wanted at the peace table in Paris, along with influence in establishing what he hoped would be a new world order of international cooperation with the United States as a major player. Never before had an American president served as the chief negotiator of a peace treaty; nor had a president been away from the nation for so long—for much of the period between December 1918 and June 1919, but Wilson's actions seemed intended to dramatize his desire to ensure his goal of a lasting peace. He returned to the United States to confront the task of winning Senate approval for the Versailles Treaty that he had helped negotiate. What followed was a debate, as one historian has written, that was "no less important than the great debate of 1787 to 1789 over the ratification of the Constitution." Wilson had proposed—as a signatory of the Versailles Treaty—that the United States participate in a system of collective security, the League of Nations. The League was included in the treaty, thus it would be up to the Senate to accept or reject America's entrance into the League, but to a larger degree the fate of the League and possibly the future of world peace actually rested on the response from the American people. The American people, however, were in no mood for world involvement. During the 1918 congressional election campaigns, Wilson had asked voters to support Democratic candidates in a show of support for his peace goals. They had not, voting in a Republican Congress that would make ratification of the Versailles Treaty difficult.

Wilson had worked hardest in Paris for the League, an organization that he believed would ultimately temper the harsh Allied peace terms and restrain imperialist ambitions in the future. He returned to Washington in February 1919 to open the new Congress, and was immediately besieged by a group of 37 senators who opposed various aspects of the League. Wilson agreed to make some changes and headed back to Paris to put the final touches on the treaty and the League.

At the heart of the League covenant was Article 10, which called for collective security. Here the League members agreed to "respect and preserve as against external aggression the territorial integrity and existing political independence of all Members of the League. In case of any such aggression or in case of any threat or danger of such aggression the Council shall advise upon the means by which this obligation shall be fulfilled." To many Americans, now moving toward postwar isolation, this unspecified obligation was difficult to accept. Would the United States be required to send troops to defend the collective security? Would the U.S. army be part of a world police force? U.S. involvement in the European war had, to many Americans, solved nothing; even the reasons for going to war in the first place were being questioned. Now should the United States become involved in an international organization that was essentially designed to keep the European peace? The national mood seemed to be away from international involvement.

Wilson argued that the League would rectify the wrongs of the treaty, while giving the United States a leadership position in world affairs. The treaty, including the Covenant of the League, was submitted to the Senate on July 10, 1919. But Henry Cabot Lodge, chairman of the Senate Foreign Relations Committee, had reservations. Lodge is often derided as an isolationist standing in the way of America's worldwide obligations, but in fact he simply believed in an American unilateral foreign policy, that the U.S. would be better off in world affairs acting alone. He also feared that Americans might not be willing to deliver the sacrifices the League demanded. He belonged to a group known as the "reservationists" who would agree to join the League, but with limited U.S. participation. Lodge packed the Foreign Relations Committee with critics and held hearings on the League in an attempt to tone down the American commitment, particularly as it related to Article 10. On August 19, Wilson went before the committee to make his arguments for the League. His statement follows as *Document 2.8*.

Wilson made little headway against Lodge and the Foreign Affairs Committee. The committee's minority report stated a willingness to support ratification of the treaty, but only after some 45 amendments were attached to it. Wilson responded by trying to convince the American people to pressure their representatives in Washington to ratify the treaty. His extended speaking trip to this end was exhausting. He collapsed in Pueblo, Colorado on September 25, 1919. A week later he suffered a severe stroke. Over the next months the treaty was defeated, at least in part because the ailing Wilson refused to compromise on any part of it. "Either we should enter the League fearlessly," he said, "accepting the responsibility and not fearing the role of leadership which we now enjoy, contributing our efforts toward establishing a just and permanent peace, or we should retire as gracefully as possible from the great concert of powers by which the world was saved." *Document 2.9* is a speech by William E. Borah of Idaho before the Senate on November 19, 1919. Borah was among a group opposing the League known as the "irreconcilables," those who opposed American entrance into the League on any terms. His speech was delivered two weeks after Wilson's stroke.

....

DOCUMENT 2.8

PRESIDENT WOODROW WILSON'S STATEMENT TO THE SENATE FOREIGN RELATIONS COMMITTEE, AUGUST 19, 1919

Nothing, I am led to believe, stands in the way of ratification of the treaty except certain doubts with regard to the meaning and implication of certain articles of the Covenant of the League of Nations; and I must frankly say that I am unable to understand why such doubts should be entertained. You will recall that when I had the pleasure of a conference with your committee and with the committee of the House of Representatives on Foreign Affairs at the White House in March last the questions now most frequently asked about the League of Nations were all canvassed with a view to their immediate clarification. The Covenant of the League was then in its first draft and subject to revision. It was pointed out that no express recognition was given to the Monroe Doctrine; that it was not expressly provided that the League should have no authority to act or to express a judgment on matters of domestic policy; that the right to withdraw from the League was not expressly recognized; and that the constitutional right of the Congress to determine all questions of peace and war was not sufficiently safeguarded. On my return to Paris all these matters were taken up again by the Commission on the

Humanity is the accuser, the U.S. Senate is the assassin, and the Treaty of Versailles is the victim in this commentary on the Senate's rejection of the treaty. Isolationists, who wanted to keep the United States out of European affairs, opposed the treaty because it included the Covenant for the League of Nations. *The Granger Collection, NY*

League of Nations and every suggestion of the United States was accepted. The views of the United States with regard to the questions I have mentioned had, in fact, already been accepted by the Commission and there was supposed to be nothing inconsistent with them in the draft of the Covenant first adopted—the draft which was the subject of our discussion in March—but no objection was made to saying explicitly in the text what all had supposed to be implicit in it. There was absolutely no doubt as to the meaning of any one of the resulting

SOURCE: *Senate Documents*. 66th Cong. 1st sess., XXXI, Doc. # 76.

provisions of the Covenant in the minds of those who participated in drafting them, and I respectfully submit that there is nothing vague or doubtful in their wording. The Monroe Doctrine is expressly mentioned as an understanding which is in no way to be impaired or interfered with by anything contained in the covenant, and the expression "regional understandings like the Monroe Doctrine" was used, not because any one of the conferees thought there was any comparable agreement anywhere else in existence or in contemplation, but only because it was thought best to avoid the appearance of dealing in such a document with the policy of a single nation. Absolutely nothing is concealed in the phrase.

With regard to domestic questions, Article 16 of the Covenant expressly provides that, if in case of any dispute arising between members of the League the matter involved is claimed by one of the parties "and is found by the council to arise out of a matter which by international law is solely within the domestic jurisdiction of that party, the council shall so report, and shall make no recommendations as to its settlement." The United States was by no means the only Government interested in the explicit adoption of this provision, and there is no doubt in the mind of any authoritative student of international law that such matters as immigration, tariffs, and naturalization are incontestably domestic questions with which no international body could deal without express authority to do so. No enumeration of domestic questions was undertaken because to undertake it, even by sample, would have involved the danger of seeming to exclude those not mentioned.

The right of any sovereign State to withdraw had been taken for granted, but no objection was made to making it explicit. Indeed, so soon as the views expressed at the White House conference were laid before the commission it was at once conceded that it was best not to leave the answer to so important a question to inference. No proposal was made to set up any tri-bunal to pass judgment upon the question whether a withdrawing Nation had in fact fulfilled "all its international obligations and all its obligations under the covenant." It was recognized that that question must be left to be resolved by the conscience of the Nation proposing to withdraw; and I must say that it did not seem to me worth while to propose that the article be made more explicit, because I knew that the United States would never itself propose to withdraw from the League if its conscience was not entirely clear as to the fulfillment of all its international obligations. It has never failed to fulfill them and never will. Article 10 is in no respect of doubtful meaning when read in the light of the covenant as a whole. The council of the League can only "advise upon" the means by which the obligations of that great article are to be given effect to. Unless the United States is a party to the policy or action in question, her own affirmative vote in the council is necessary before any advice can be given, for a unanimous vote of the council is required. If she is a party, the trouble is hers anyhow. And the unanimous vote of the council is only advice in any case. Each Government is free to reject it if it pleases. Nothing could have been made more clear to the conference than the right of our Congress under our Constitution to exercise its independent judgment in all matters of peace and war. No attempt was made to question or limit that right.

The United States will, indeed, undertake under Article 10 to "respect and preserve as against external aggression the territorial integrity and existing political independence of all members of the League," and that engagement constitutes a very grave and solemn moral obligation. But it is a moral, not a legal, obligation, and leaves our Congress absolutely free to put its own interpretation upon it in all cases that call for action. It is binding in conscience only, not in law.

Article 10 seems to me to constitute the very backbone of the whole covenant. Without it the League would be hardly more than an influential debating society. It has several times been suggested, in public debate and in private conference, that interpretations of the sense in which the United States accepts the engagements of the covenant should be embodied in the instrument of ratification. There can be no reasonable objection to such interpretations accompanying the act of ratification provided they do not form a part of the formal ratification itself. Most of the interpretations which have been suggested to me embody what seems to me the plain meaning of the instrument itself. But if such an interpretation should constitute a part of the formal resolution of ratification, long delays would be the inevitable consequence, inasmuch as all the many Governments concerned would have to accept, in effect, the language of the Senate as the language of the treaty before ratification would be complete. The assent of the German assembly at Weimar would have to be obtained, among the rest, and I must frankly say that I could only with the greatest reluctance approach that Assembly for permission to read the treaty as we understand it and as those who framed it quite certainly understood it. If the United States were to qualify the document in any way, moreover, I am confident from what I know of the many conferences and debates which accompanied the formulation of the treaty that our example would immediately be followed in many quarters, in some instances with very serious reservations, and that the meaning and operative force of the treaty would presently be clouded from one end of its clauses to the other. Pardon me, Mr. Chairman, if I have been entirely unreserved and plainspoken in speaking of the great matters we all have so much at heart. If excuse is needed, I trust that the critical situation of affairs may serve as my justification. The issues that manifestly hang upon the conclusions of the Senate with regard to peace and upon the time of its action are so grave and so clearly insusceptible of being thrust on one side or postponed that I have felt it necessary in the public interest to make this urgent plea, and to make it as simply and as unreservedly as possible.

DOCUMENT 2.9

SENATOR WILLIAM E. BORAH'S SPEECH BEFORE THE SENATE IN OPPOSITION TO RATIFICATION OF THE LEAGUE, NOVEMBER 19, 1919

When the league shall have been formed, we shall be a member of what is known as the council of the league. Our accredited representative will sit in judgment with the accredited representatives of the other members of the league to pass upon the concerns not only of our country but of all Europe and all Asia and the entire world. Our accredited representatives will be members of the assembly. They will sit there to represent the judgment of these 110,000,000 people—more than—just as we are accredited here to represent our constituencies. We can not send our representatives to sit in council with the representatives of the other great nations of the world with mental reservations as to what we shall do in case their judgment shall not be satisfactory to us. If we go to the council or to the assembly with any other purpose than that of complying in good faith and in absolute integrity with all upon which the council or the assembly may pass, we shall soon return to our country with our self-respect forfeited and the public opinion of the world condemnatory.

Why need you gentlemen across the aisle worry about a reservation here or there when we are sitting in the council and in the assembly and bound by every obligation in morals, which the President said was supreme above that of law, to comply with the judgment which are representative and the other representatives finally form? Shall we go there, Mr. President, to sit in judgment, and in case that judgment works for peace join with our allies, but in case it works for war withdraw our cooperation? How long would we stand as we now stand, a

SOURCE: *Cong. Rec.* 66th Cong. 1st sess., LVI, 8781.

The Treaty of Versailles marked the end of the Great War. Thirty-two Allied nations took part in drawing up the treaty, however the statesmen above, known in history as the Big Four, took charge of the primary negotiations. They are, left to right, Prime Minister David Lloyd George of Great Britain, Primier Vittorio Orlando of Italy, Primier Georges Clemenceau of France, and President Woodrow Wilson of the United States. The United States did not sign the treaty. *Courtesy National Archive Still Pictures*

great Republic commanding the respect and holding the leadership of the world, if we should adopt any such course . . . ?

We have said, Mr. President, that we would not send our troops abroad without the consent of Congress. Pass by now for a moment the legal proposition. If we create executive functions, the Executive will perform those functions without the authority of Congress. Pass that question by and go to the other question. Our members of the council are there. Article 11 is complete, and it authorizes the league, a member of which is our representative, to deal with matters of peace and war, and the league through its council and its assembly deals with the matter, and our accredited representative joins with the others in deciding upon a certain course, which involves a question of sending troops. What will the Congress of the United States do? What right will it have left, except the bare technical right to refuse, which as a moral proposition it will not dare to exercise? Have we not been told day by day for the last nine months that the Senate of the United States, a coordinate part of the treaty-making

power, should accept this league as it was written because the wise men sitting at Versailles had so written it, and has not every possible influence and every source of power in public opinion been organized and directed against the Senate to compel it to do that thing? How much stronger will be the moral compulsion upon the Congress of the United States when we ourselves have indorsed the proposition of sending our accredited representatives there to vote for us?

Ah, but you say that there must be unanimous consent, and that there is vast protection in unanimous consent. I do not wish to speak disparagingly; but has not every division and dismemberment of every nation which has suffered dismemberment taken place by unanimous consent for the last three hundred years? Did not Prussia and Austria and Russia by unanimous consent divide Poland? Did not the United States and Great Britain and Japan and Italy and France divide China and give Shantung to Japan? Was that not a unanimous decision? Close the doors upon the diplomats of Europe, let them sit in secret, give them the material to trade on, and there always will be unanimous consent. . . .

Mr. President, if you have enough territory, if you have enough material, if you have enough subject peoples to trade upon and divide, there will be no difficulty about unanimous consent.

Do our Democratic friends ever expect any man to sit as a member of the council or as a member of the assembly equal in intellectual power and in standing before the world with that of our representative at Versailles? Do you expect a man to sit in the council who will have made more pledges, and I shall assume made them in sincerity, for self-determination and for the rights of small peoples, than had been made by our accredited representative? And yet, what became of it? The unanimous consent was obtained nevertheless. But take another view of it. We are sending to the council one man. That one man represents 110,000,000 people. Here, sitting in the Senate, we have two from every State in the Union, and over in the other

House we have Representatives in accordance with population, and the responsibility is spread out in accordance with our obligations to our constituency. But now we are transferring to one man the stupendous power of representing the sentiment and convictions of 110,000,000 people in tremendous questions which may involve the peace or may involve the war of the world. . . .

What is the result of all this? We are in the midst of all the affairs of Europe. We have entangled ourselves with all European concerns. We have joined in alliance with all the European nations which have thus far joined the league, and all nations which may be admitted to the league. We are sitting there dabbling in their affairs and intermeddling in their concerns. In other words, Mr. President—and this comes to the question which is fundamental with me—we have forfeited and surrendered, once and for all, the great policy of "no entangling alliances" upon which the strength of this Republic has been founded for 150 years. My friends of reservations, tell me, where is the reservation in these articles which protects us against entangling alliances with Europe? Those who are differing over reservations, tell me, what one of them protects the doctrine laid down by the Father of this Country? That fundamental propositions surrendered, and we are a part of the European turmoils and conflicts from the time we enter this league. . . .

[British Prime Minister] Lloyd-George is reported to have said just a few days before the conference met at Versailles that Great Britain could give up much, and would be willing to sacrifice much, to have America withdraw from that policy. That was one of the great objects of the entire conference at Versailles, so far as the foreign representatives were concerned. [French President Georges] Clemenceau and Lloyd-George and others like them were willing to make any reasonable sacrifice which would draw America away from her isolation and into the internal affairs and concerns of Europe. This league of nations, with or without reservations, whatever else it does or does not

do, does surrender and sacrifice that policy; and once having surrendered and become a part of the European concerns, where, my friends, are you going to stop?

You have put in here a reservation upon the Monroe Doctrine. I think that, in so far as language could protect the Monroe Doctrine, it has been protected. But as a practical proposition, as a working proposition, tell me candidly, as men familiar with the history of your country and of other countries, do you think that you can intermeddle in European affairs and never permit Europe to intervene in our affairs . . . ?

Mr President, there is another and even a more commanding reason why I shall record my vote against this treaty. It imperils what I conceive to be the underlying, the very first principles of this Republic. It is in conflict with the right of our people to govern themselves free from all restraint, legal or moral, of foreign powers. . . .

Sir, since the debate opened months ago those of us who have stood against this proposition have been taunted many times with being little Americans. Leave us the word American, keep that in your presumptuous impeachment, and no taunt can disturb us, no gibe discompose our purposes. Call us little Americans if you will, but leave us the consolation and the pride which the term American, however modified, still imparts. . . . We have sought nothing save the tranquility of our own people and the honor and independence of our own Republic. No foreign flattery, no possible world glory and power have disturbed our poise or come between us and our devotion to the traditions which have made us a people or the policies which have made us a Nation, unselfish and commanding. If we have erred we have erred out of too much love for those things which from childhood you and we together have been taught to revere—yes, to defend even at the cost of limb and life. If we have erred it is because we have placed too high an estimate upon the wisdom of Washington and Jefferson, too exalted an opinion upon the patriotism of the sainted Lincoln. . . .

Senators, even in an hour so big with expectancy we should not close our eyes to the fact that democracy is something more, vastly more, than a mere form of government by which society is restrained into free and orderly life. It is a moral entity, a spiritual force, as well. And these are things which live only and alone in the atmosphere of liberty. The foundation upon which democracy rests is faith in the moral instincts of the people. Its ballot boxes, the franchise, its law, and constitutions are but the outward manifestations of the deeper and more essential thing—a continuing trust in the moral purposes of the average man and woman. When this is lost or forfeited your outward forms, however democratic in terms, are a mockery. Force may find expression through institutions democratic in structure equal with the simple and more direct processes of a single supreme ruler. These distinguishing virtues of a real republic you can not co-mingle with the discordant and destructive forces of the Old World and still preserve them. You can not yoke a government whose first law is that of force and hope to preserve the former. These things are in eternal war, and one must ultimately destroy the other. You may still keep for a time the outward form, you may still delude yourself, as others have done in the past, with appearances and symbols, but when you shall have committed this Republic to a scheme of world control based upon force, upon the combined military force of the four great nations of the world, you will have soon destroyed the atmosphere of freedom, of confidence in the self-governing capacity of the masses, in which alone a democracy may thrive. We may become one of the four dictators of the world, but we shall no longer be master of our own spirit. And what shall it profit us as a Nation if we shall go forth to the domination of the earth and share with others the glory of world control and lose that fine sense of confidence in the people, the soul of democracy?

Look upon the scene as it is now presented. Behold the task we are to assume, and then contemplate the method by which we are to deal with this task. Is the method such as to address itself to a Government "conceived in liberty and dedicated to the proposition that all men are created equal"? When this league, this combination, is formed four equal powers representing the dominant people will rule one-half of the inhabitants of the globe as subject peoples—rule by force, and we shall be a party to the rule of force. There is no other way by which you can keep people in subjection. You must either give them independence, recognize their rights as nations to live their own life and to set up their own form of government, or you must deny them these things by force. That is the scheme, the method proposed by the league. It proposes no other. We will in time become inured to its inhuman precepts and its soulless methods, strange as this doctrine now seems to a free people. If we stay with our contract we will come in time to declare with our associates that force—force, the creed of the Prussian military oligarchy—is after all the true foundation upon which must rest all stable government. Korea, despoiled and bleeding at every pore; India, sweltering in ignorance and burdened with inhuman taxes after more than one hundred years of dominant rule; Egypt, trapped and robbed of her birthright; Ireland, with 700 years of sacrifice for independence—this is the task, this is the atmosphere, and this is the creed in and under which we are to keep alive our belief in the moral purposes and self-governing capacity of the people, a belief without which the Republic must disintegrate and die. The maxim of liberty will soon give way to the rule of blood and iron. We have been pleading here for our Constitution. Conform this league, it has been said, to the technical terms of our charter, and all will be well. But I declare to you that we must go further and conform to those sentiments and passions for justice and freedom which are essential to the existence of democracy. . . .

Sir, we are told that this treaty means peace. Even so, I would not pay the price. Would you purchase peace at the cost of any part of our independence? We could have had peace in

1776—the price was high, but we could have had it. James Otis, Sam Adams, Hancock, and Warren were surrounded by those who urged peace and British rule. All through that long and trying struggle, particularly when the clouds of adversity lowered upon the cause, there was a cry of peace—let us have peace. We could have had peace in 1860; Lincoln was counseled by men of great influence and accredited wisdom to let our brothers—and, thank Heaven, they are brothers—depart in peace. But the tender, loving Lincoln, bending under the fearful weight of impending civil war, an apostle of peace, refused to pay the price, and a reunited country will praise his name forevermore—bless it because he refused peace at the price of national honor and national integrity. Peace upon any other basis than national independence, peace purchased at the cost of any part of our national integrity, is fit only for slaves, and even when purchased at such a price it is a delusion, for it can not last.

But your treaty does not mean peace—far, very far, from it. If we are to judge the future by the past it means war. Is there any guaranty of peace other than the guaranty which comes of the control of the war-making power by the people? Yet what great rule of democracy does the treaty leave unassailed? The people in whose keeping alone you can safely lodge the power of peace or war nowhere, at no time and in no place, have any voice in this scheme for world peace. Autocracy which has bathed the world in blood for centuries reigns supreme. Democracy is everywhere excluded. This, you say, means peace. . . .

Can you hope for peace when love of country is disregarded in your scheme, when the spirit of nationality is rejected, even scoffed at? Yet what law of that moving and mysterious force does your treaty not deny? With a ruthlessness unparalleled your treaty in a dozen instances runs counter to the divine law of nationality. Peoples who speak the same language, kneel at the same ancestral tombs, moved by the same traditions, animated by a common hope, are torn asunder, broken in pieces, divided, and parceled out to antagonistic nations. And this you call justice. This, you cry, means peace. Peoples who have dreamed of independence, struggled and been patient, sacrificed and been hopeful, peoples who were told that through this peace conference they should realize the aspirations of centuries, have again had their hopes dashed to earth. One of the most striking and commanding figures in this war, soldier and statesman, turned away from the peace table at Versailles declaring to the world, "The promise of the new life, the victory of the great humane ideals for which the peoples have shed their blood and their treasure without stint, the fulfillment of their aspirations toward a new international order and a fairer and better world, are not written into the treaty." No; your treaty means injustice. It means slavery. It means war. And to all this you ask this Republic to become a party. You ask it to abandon the creed under which it has grown to power and accept the creed of autocracy, the creed of repression and force.

CHAPTER 3

The Interwar Period and Preparing for War, 1920–1939

3.1 Five-Power Treaty, February 6, 1922

3.2 President Herbert Hoover's Disarmament Proposal, Delivered to the League of Nations, June 22, 1932

3.3 Letter from Joseph C. Grew, Ambassador to Japan, to Secretary of State Cordell Hull, May 11, 1933

3.4 The Consul General at Berlin (George Messersmith) to the Undersecretary of State, June 26, 1933

3.5 H. C. Engelbrecht and F. C. Hanighen, *Merchants of Death*, 1934

3.6 The Hirota Government's National Foreign Policies (Reported to Emperor Hirohito, August 15, 1936)

3.7 President Franklin Roosevelt's Address Before the Pan-American Conference for the Maintenance of Peace, Buenos Aires, Argentina, December 1, 1936

3.8 Neutrality Act of 1937, May 1, 1937

3.9 *The London Times* Reports Prime Minister Neville Chamberlain's Return from Munich, September 30, 1938

1922–1939 Timeline

Date	Year	Event
February 6, 1922	1922	Five-Power Treaty
August 27, 1928	1923	Kellogg-Briand Pact outlaws war
March 1929	1924	Herbert Hoover becomes president
October 1929	1925	U.S. stock market crash
June 22, 1932	1926	Hoover's disarmament proposal
January 30, 1933	1927	Hitler become Chancellor of Germany
March 1933	1928	Franklin Roosevelt becomes president
May 11, 1933	1929	Letter, Grew to Hull
June 26, 1933	1930	Letter, Messersmith to Undersecretary of State
August 15, 1936	1931	Foreign policy report to Emperor Hirohito
December 1, 1936	1932	FDR's Pan-American Conference speech
May 1, 1937	1933	Neutrality Act of 1937
July 1937	1934	Japan and China go to war
September 30, 1938	1935	Munich Accords
September 28, 1939	1936	Germany invades Poland beginning war in Europe

3.1   **Five-Power Treaty, February 6, 1922**
3.2   **President Herbert Hoover's Disarmament Proposal, Delivered to the League of Nations, June 22, 1932**

The Great War had left a bitter taste in the mouths of the American people. It had become a persuasive argument in the U.S. that the war had been a wholly European affair caused by a series of alliances (of the type that George Washington had warned the new nation against in his farewell speech) and that the U.S. had been dragged, as a truly unwilling participant, into that tangled mess in 1917. To avoid a similar fate in the future, most Americans believed that the United States in the postwar must engage its foreign policy alone—be free to make independent decisions in foreign affairs in order to preserve the national interests of security and prosperity. Through the 1920s and 1930s, however, it became clear that this policy of unilateral action had its limits and obvious failings. Consequently, the United States did not withdraw from world affairs in the two decades after World War I. It attempted to use nonmilitary means (chiefly legal, diplomatic, and economic) to influence world events, and to bring an end to war. Among the most prominent themes of American foreign policy in the interwar period was global disarmament.

The industrialized world held several disarmament conferences throughout the 1920s, including the Washington Naval Conference in November 1921. This conference, called by President Warren G. Harding, was designed to stop a naval arms race in the Pacific, and to neutralize a potential trouble spot in the Far East by safeguarding the integrity of a weak China. The conference convened in Washington in November 1921 and produced several treaties including what was considered the conference's greatest success, the Five-Power Treaty signed by the United States, Britain, France, Italy, and Japan on February 6, 1922 (*Document 3.1*). Another result of the Washington Arms Conference was the Four-Power Treaty. It was signed in December 1921 and took affect on August 19, 1923. The objective here again was to avoid war in the Pacific, with an obvious eye toward the growing conflict between the United States and Japan for control of the region. Other such international conferences included the Geneva Conference in 1927, the London Naval Conference of 1930, and another conference in Geneva in 1935–1936. America's involvement in these conferences demonstrates its international, but independent, diplomatic course in the era.

In 1932 the League of Nations proposed a World Disarmament Conference at Geneva. President Herbert Hoover hoped to be in the vanguard of world disarmament, and he submitted a proposal to the conference (*Document 3.2*). It was a noble pledge that reflected the American attitude toward the gathering war clouds: Stop the military build-up and there will be no war. But Hoover's proposal fell mostly on deaf ears. Europe and Japan had already begun rearming in anticipation of war. Their move toward rearmament promoted the growth of American isolationism.

DOCUMENT 3.1

FIVE-POWER TREATY, FEBRUARY 6, 1922

The United States of America, the British Empire, France, Italy, and Japan;

Desiring to contribute to the maintenance of the general peace, and to reduce the burdens of competition in armament;

Have resolved, with a view to accomplishing these purposes, to conclude a treaty to limit their respective naval armament. . . .

CHAPTER I

Article I. The Contracting Powers agree to limit their respective naval armament as provided in the present treaty.

Article II. The Contracting Powers may retain respectively . . . all other capital ships,(*) built or building, of the United States, the British Empire and Japan. . . .

Article III. Subject to the provisions of Article II, the Contracting Powers shall abandon their respective capital ship building programs, and no new capital ships shall be constructed or acquired by any of the Contracting Powers except replacement tonnage which may be constructed or acquired as specified. . . .

Article IV. The total capital ship replacement tonnage of the Contracting Powers shall not exceed in standard displacement, for the United States 525,000 tons . . . ; for the British Empire 525,000 tons . . . ; for France 175,000 tons. . . . ; for Italy 175,000 tons . . . ; for Japan 315,000 tons. . . .

Article V. No capital ships exceeding 35,000 tons . . . standard displacement shall be acquired by, or constructed by, for, or within the jurisdiction of, any of the Contracting Powers.

*ships of the largest class, including aircraft carriers.

SOURCE: *Foreign Relations of the United States, 1938,* I, 247–53.

Article VI. No capital ship of any of the Contracting Powers shall carry a gun with a caliber in excess of 16 inches (405 millimeters).

Article VII. The total tonnage for aircraft carriers of each of the Contracting Powers shall not exceed in standard displacement, for the United States 135,000 tons . . . ; for the British Empire 135,000 tons . . . ; for France 60,000 tons . . . ; for Italy 60,000 tons . . . ; for Japan 81,000 tons. . . .

Article IX. No aircraft carrier exceeding 27,000 tons . . . standard displacement shall be acquired by, or constructed by, for, or within the jurisdiction of, any of the Contracting Powers. . . .

Article XI. No vessel of war exceeding 10,000 tons . . . standard displacement, other than capital ship or aircraft carrier, shall be acquired by, or constructed by, for, or within the jurisdiction of, any of the Contracting Powers. . . .

Article XII. No vessels of war of any of the Contracting Powers, hereafter laid down, other than a capital ship, shall carry a gun with a caliber in excess of 8 inches (203 millimeters). . . .

Article XIV. No preparations shall be made in merchant ships in time of peace for the installation of warlike armaments for the purpose of converting such ships into vessels of war. . . .

Article XIX. The United States, the British Empire and Japan agree that the *status quo* at the time of the signing of the present Treaty, with regard to fortifications and naval bases, shall be maintained in their respective territories and possessions specified hereunder:

1. The insular possessions which the United States now holds or may hereafter acquire in the Pacific Ocean, except those adjacent to the coast of the United States, Alaska and the Panama Canal Zone, not including the Aleutian Islands, and the Hawaiian Islands;

2. Hong Kong and the insular possessions which the British Empire now holds or may acquire in the Pacific Ocean, east of

the meridian of 110 degrees east longitude, except those adjacent to the coast of Canada, and the Commonwealth of Australia and its Territories, and New Zealand;

3. Following the insular territories and the possessions of Japan in the Pacific Ocean, to wit: the Kurile Islands, the Bonin Islands, Amani-Oshima, the Loochoo Islands, Formosa and the Pescadores, and any insular territories or possessions in the Pacific Ocean which Japan may hereafter acquire.

The maintenance of the status quo under the foregoing provisions implies that no new fortifications or naval bases shall be established in the territories and possessions specified; that no measures shall be taken to increase the existing naval facilities for the repair and maintenance of naval forces, and that no increase shall be made in the coast defenses of the territories and possessions above specified. This restriction, however, does not preclude such repair and replacement of worn-out weapons and equipment as is customary in naval and military establishments in time of peace. . . .

CHAPTER II

Part 2

The following rules shall be observed for the scrapping of vessels of war which are to be disposed of in accordance with Articles II and III.

I.   A vessel to be scrapped must be placed in such condition that it cannot be put to combatant use.

II. This result must be finally affected in any one of the following ways:
   a. Permanent sinking of the vessel;
   b. Breaking the vessel up . . . ;
   c. Converting the vessel to target use exclusively. . . .

Part 3

Capital ships and aircraft carriers twenty years after the date of their completion may . . . be replaced by new construction. . . .

CHAPTER III

Article XXIII. The present Treaty shall remain in force until December 31st, 1936, and in case none of the Contracting Powers shall have given notice two years before that date of its intention to terminate the Treaty, it shall continue in force until the expiration of the two years from the date on which notice of termination shall be given by one of the Contracting Powers. . . .

DOCUMENT 3.2

PRESIDENT HERBERT HOOVER'S DISARMAMENT PROPOSAL, DELIVERED TO THE LEAGUE OF NATIONS, JUNE 22, 1932

The time has come when we should cut through the brush and adopt some broad and definite method of reducing the overwhelming burden of armament which now lies upon the toilers of the world. . . .

I propose that the arms of the world should be reduced by nearly one-third.

LAND FORCES

In order to reduce the offensive character of all land forces as distinguished from their defensive character, I propose the adoption of the presentation already made at the Geneva Conference for the abolition of all tanks, all chemical warfare and all large mobile guns. This would not prevent the establishment or increase of fixed fortifications of any character

SOURCE: *Public Papers of the Presidents: Herbert Hoover, 1932–1933*, 267–70.

for the defense of frontiers and seacoasts. It would give an increased relative strength to such defense as compared with attack.

I propose, further, that there should be a reduction of one-third in strength of all land armies over and above the so-called police component.

The land armaments of many nations are considered to have two functions. One is the maintenance of internal order in connection with the regular police forces of the country. The strength required for this purpose has been called the "police component." The other function is defense against foreign attack. The additional strength required for this purpose has been called the "defense component." While it is not suggested that these different components should be separated, it is necessary to consider this contention as to functions in proposing a practical plan of reduction in land forces. Under the Treaty of Versailles and the other peace treaties, the armies of Germany, Austria, Hungary and Bulgaria were reduced to a size deemed appropriate for the maintenance of internal order, Germany being assigned one hundred thousand troops for a population of approximately sixty-five million people. I propose that we should accept for all nations a basic police component of soldiers proportionate to the average which was thus allowed Germany and these other States. This formula with necessary corrections for Powers having colonial possessions should be sufficient to provide for the maintenance of internal order by the nations of the world. Having analyzed these two components in this fashion, I propose, as stated above, that there should be a reduction of one-third in the strength of all land armies over and above the police component.

AIR FORCES

All bombing-planes to be abolished. This will do away with the military possession of types of planes capable of attacks upon civil populations and should be coupled with the total prohibition of all bombardment from the air.

NAVAL FORCES

I propose that the treaty number and tonnage of battleships shall be reduced by one-third; that the treaty tonnage of aircraft-carriers, cruisers and destroyers shall be reduced by one-fourth; that the treaty tonnage of submarines shall be reduced by one-third and that no nation shall retain a submarine tonnage greater than 35,000 tons.

The relative strength of naval arms in battleships and aircraft-carriers as between the five leading naval Powers was fixed by the Treaty of Washington [the Five Power Treaty].

The relative strength in cruisers, destroyers and submarines was fixed as between the United States, Great Britain and Japan by the Treaty of London. For the purpose of this proposal it is suggested that the French and Italian strength in cruisers and destroyers be calculated as though they had joined in the Treaty of London on a basis approximating the so-called accord of March 1, 1931.

There are various technical considerations connected with these naval reductions which will be presented by the delegation at Geneva.

The effect of this plan would be to bring an enormous savings in cost of new construction and replacement of naval vessels. It would also save large amounts in the operating expense to all nations of land, sea and air forces. It would greatly reduce offensive strength compared to defensive strength in all nations.

These proposals are simple and direct. They call upon all nations to contribute something. The contribution here proposed will be relative and mutual. I know of nothing that would give more hope for humanity today than the acceptance of such a program with such minor changes as might be necessary. It is folly for the world to go on breaking its back over military expenditures, and the United States is willing to take its share of responsibility by making definite proposals that will relieve the world.

3.3 Letter from Joseph C. Grew, Ambassador to Japan, to Secretary of State Cordell Hull, May 11, 1933

3.4 The Consul General at Berlin (George Messersmith) to the Undersecretary of State, June 26, 1933

By 1931 the worldwide depression had spread to Japan and was quickly destroying that nation's fragile economy. With few natural resources and foreign trade quickly drying up, the Japanese economy was in trouble. When it became clear that the Tokyo government was incapable of dealing with these problems, the Japanese people began looking for solutions among the ultra-rightist nationalists. They, in turn, found their leadership among the military.

One answer to Japan's economic problems seemed to be in Manchuria, China's mineral rich northeastern province. In the fall of 1931, Japan seized Manchuria. In January 1932, Secretary of State Henry Stimson issued a stern warning that the United States would not recognize Japan's occupation. Two months later, Japan set up Manchukuo, a supposedly independent state in what was once Manchuria. When the League of Nations objected, Japan withdrew from the League. In May 1932 the Japanese prime minister was assassinated and Admiral Viscount Saito Makoto formed a new government under the direction of the emperor, Hirohito. From that point, Japan's government became increasingly representative of the growing power of the military and the ultra-rightist nationalists. It is in this atmosphere that Joseph Grew, Ambassador to Japan, sent a letter to Secretary of State Cordell Hull in Washington expressing his concern over the turn of events in Japan (*Document 3.3*).

At nearly the same moment Germany was going through many of the same types of changes as Japan. American aid to postwar Europe had kept most European economies reasonably strong through much of the 1920s. But the Great Depression, which struck the American economy after 1929, forced the U.S. to cut that aid and curtail trade. The depression quickly spread to Europe, causing a disastrous economic depression in Germany that fostered the growth of radicalism from both the left and the right. In the 1932 Reichstag elections, Adolf Hitler's Nazi party pulled over 40 percent of the vote, making it the most powerful political party in Germany. In January of the next year, an aging and senile Paul von Hindenburg, president of the Republic, called on Hitler to fill the office of Chancellor and form a new government. These incidents provoked the U.S. Consul General to Germany, George Messersmith, to send a letter (*Document 3.4*) to the state department in Washington. Not unlike Ambassador Grew in Japan, Messersmith saw something sinister and threatening in these events unfolding in Germany. Written only months apart, these two letters reflect the changes taking place in Asia and Europe—changes that would, nearly ten years later, pull the United States into the wars against Germany and Japan.

DOCUMENT 3.3

LETTER FROM JOSEPH C. GREW, AMBASSADOR TO JAPAN, TO SECRETARY OF STATE CORDELL HULL, MAY 11, 1933

My dear Mr. Secretary:

For your information I am enclosing a copy of a special report from the Military Attaché of the Embassy, describing the Japanese Army's methods of increasing its strength by means of voluntary contributions from the people and indicating, in the closing paragraphs, the tremendous military power which Japan is developing. This report gives an admirable picture of one phase of Japan's fighting strength, but I would like to describe to you, briefly the whole picture as I see it; that is, the strength of the Japanese nation as a whole and particularly the strength of the combined Japanese fighting machine. Japan is so often spoken of as a small, over-crowded nation cooped up within the confines of a few small islands, without natural resources, and largely dependent upon foreign sources for its food stuffs, that people in other countries sometimes fail to appreciate the facts and to realize the actual and potential power of these people.

The Japanese Empire is not a small country, as compared with the countries of Europe, at least. The Empire itself, without "Manchukuo," has an area considerably greater than that of France or Germany and much more than that of either Spain or Italy. Including the area of "Manchukuo," which to all practical purposes is under Japanese control, the total area of Japan and its dependencies is greater than that of France, Germany, Spain, Switzerland, Belgium, Netherlands and Demark combined. The population of the Japanese Empire proper is 90 millions; with that of "Manchu-

kuo" it is around 120 millions, or nearly the same as that of the United States. And these people (or that part of them which is of the Japanese race) are intelligent, industrious, energetic, extremely nationalistic, war-loving, aggressive and, it must be admitted, somewhat unscrupulous. So Japan cannot be considered as a small or a weak country. Nor is it living on the verge of starvation, keeping the wolf from the door by super-human exertions. Japan can and does raise enough foodstuffs (even without "Manchukuo") to feed the population quite comfortably, and in years of large harvests is embarrassed by the surplus of foodstuffs. However, if the population continues to increase at its present rate, the food problem will become real and pressing within the next generation. Moreover, the nation has developed its industries in recent years until it is able to supply itself with all the necessities of life, and can build all the ships, and make all the airplanes, tanks, guns, ammunition, chemicals, etc. , needed to wage a severe war, if it is not too protracted. Furthermore, it has large reserves of war material, such as petroleum, nitrates, etc., not produced within the country.

So much for the country and its people and industries. Turning to the armed forces of the country, it is my opinion that Japan probably has the most complete, well-balanced, coordinated and therefore powerful fighting machine in the world today. I do not refer to the army only, but to the combination of sea, land and air forces, backed up as they are by enormous reserves of trained men, by industrial units coordinated with the fighting machine and by large reserves of supplies. The different units of Japan's machine may be exceeded in size by equivalent units of other nations, but taken as a whole[,] the machine, I believe, is equal, if not superior, to that of any other nation. Thus, France has a large navy, but a much smaller army. The United States is weaker than Japan on land and about equal on the sea, but it is probably potentially superior in the air. Of course, it would take a group of naval, military,

SOURCE: Department of State, *Peace and War: United States Foreign Policy, 1931–1941* (Washington, USGPO, 1943), 191–92.

aviation and industrial experts to calculate accurately the relative strength of the fighting machines of the world, but I think that if such could be done, the strength of Japan's combined machine would give a shock to many people. The machine probably could not stand a protracted, severe war, as industrial supplies would become exhausted, but for a quick, hard push I do not believe that the machine has its equal in the world.

Relative to the strength which could conceivably be brought against it, I consider the Japanese fighting machine immeasurably stronger than any other. Thus, France's army is not large if all the forces which could be brought against it in Europe are considered, nor is Great Britain's navy large when compared with the combined naval forces of the European powers. But Japan has no potential enemy in Asia capable of defeating her fighting machine as a whole, not even Soviet Russia it is believed, while American and European countries are too far from Japan to offer any serious menace. Japan's relative strength, therefore, is much greater than that of any other Power.

However, although we are faced with this tremendously powerful fighting machine across the Pacific, I think that our anxiety can be lessened by the fact that this machine does not seem to be designed for aggressive action outside of the Far East. The Japanese fighting machine, unless I am very much mistaken, is designed for the purpose of keeping Western nations from interfering as Japan carries out its ambitions in Asia, whatever they may be. It is true that the Japanese fighting forces consider the United States as their potential enemy, and sometimes direct their maneuvers against a potential American attack by sea or air, but that is because they think that the United States is standing in the path of the nation's natural expansion and is more apt to interfere with Japan's ambitions than are the European nations.

Whether directed at us or not, however, I believe that it would be well for us to keep this tremendous Japanese fighting machine in mind when discussing disarmament.

More than the size of the nation or the strength of its fighting machine, however, the thing that makes the Japanese nation actually so powerful and potentially so menacing, is the national morale and *esprit de corps*—a spirit which perhaps has not been equaled since the days when the Mongol hordes followed Genghis Khan in his conquest of Asia. The force of a nation bound together with great moral determination, fired with national ambition, and peopled by a race with unbounded capacity for courageous self-sacrifice is not easy to overestimate.

Respectfully yours,
Joseph Grew

DOCUMENT 3.4

THE CONSUL GENERAL AT BERLIN (GEORGE MESSERSMITH) TO THE UNDERSECRETARY OF STATE, JUNE 26, 1933

I think the [State] Department must be exceedingly careful in its dealings with Germany as long as the present Government is in power as it has no spokesman who can really be depended upon, and those who hold the highest positions are capable of actions which really outlaw them from ordinary intercourse.

I think we must recognize that while the Germany to-day wants peace, it is by no means a peaceful country or one looking forward to a long period of peace. The present German Government and its adherents desire peace ardently for the present because they need peace to carry through the changes in Germany which they want to bring about. What they want to do, however, definitely is to make Ger-

SOURCE: U.S. Department of State, *Peace and War: United States Foreign Policy, 1931–1941* (Washington: USGPO, 1942), 191–92.

many the most capable instrument of war that there has ever existed. The Minister of Education, speaking yesterday, said that a Spartan spirit must be developed among the German youth. Wherever one goes in Germany one sees people drilling, from children of five and six on, up to those well into middle age. A psychology is being developed in Germany. If this government remains in power for another year and carries on in the same measure in this direction, it will go far towards making Germany a danger to world peace for years to come.

This is a very disjointed and incoherent letter. I am dictating it under pressure as I wish to catch the courier pouch. What I do want to say really is that for the present this country is headed in directions which can only carry ruin to it and will create a situation here dangerous to world peace. With few exceptions, the men who are running this Government are of a mentality that you and I cannot understand. Some of them are psychopathic cases and

would ordinarily be receiving treatment somewhere. Others are exalted and in a frame of mind that knows no reason. The majority are woefully ignorant and unprepared for the tasks which they have to carry through every day. Those men in the party and in responsible positions who are really worth-while, and there are quite a number of these, are powerless because they have to follow the orders of superiors who are suffering from the abnormal psychology prevailing in the country. It is impossible for us to talk about tariffs or monetary policy or any of these matters with a Germany whose leaders do not think in any sense along the lines that we do. While their representatives are talking at London and seem to be just like everybody else, the most fantastic experiments on financial or economic lines are being definitely considered in their home country. . . .

Very Sincerely yours,
George S. Messersmith

3.5   H. C. Engelbrecht and F. C. Hanighen, *Merchants of Death*, 1934

By the 1930s disillusionment with the last war, combined with the growing clouds of what appeared to be a coming war, served to foster a strong peace movement in the U.S. For many Americans the nation had been dragged into the European war in 1917 for no other reason than to settle the petty scores of the European nations. As German nationalism and militarism began to rise again, and it appeared that another European war was just beyond the horizon, Americans began to look at the reasons for the nation's involvement in the Great War and to try and avoid similar situations in the future.

It was a common belief that the United States had entered the war, at least in part, to protect the private investments of American bankers, financiers, and industrialists who had loaned millions of dollars to the Allies. When it appeared that England and the Allies might not win, the argument went, the investors feared for their money and pushed the Wilson administration to enter the war against Germany to protect their investments. This argument certainly had a logical ring. Millions of private dollars had been sent to the Allies, and just as it appeared that they might lose the war, the

United States entered. But those who believed in this "devil theory," as it was often called, never produced the cause-and-effect evidence that America's actions were at the behest of the Wall Street investors.

Post-war disillusionment produced a similar argument that the heads of the world's armaments industry had somehow caused the war in order to increase their profits. Again, the evidence was lacking. But it was clear that the world armaments industry had profited mightily from the war; and as Europe (and possibly the world), moved again toward war, many in the American peace movement tried to expose what were called "the merchants of death," the world arms makers who needed war to make a profit, even survive. One result was the Nye Commission, an arms inquiry sponsored in the Senate by Gerald P. Nye, a North Dakota Republican. The Nye Commission failed to prove that the munitions makers had any effect on the cause of the war, or that they had in any way been instrumental in America's intervention in 1917. But as the Nye Commission deliberated through much of 1934 several popular books and articles appeared that made strong arguments against the arms industry. The most important of these was *Merchants of Death* by Helmuth C. Engelbrecht and Frank Hanighen. Well written and full of evidence and backed by footnotes, *Merchants of Death* certainly had more impact on the American psyche than the findings of the Nye Commission. It made bestseller lists and was a Book-of-the-Month Club selection. *Document 3.5* is the first chapter of *Merchants of Death*.

....

DOCUMENT 3.5

H. C. ENGELBRECHT AND F. C. HANIGHEN, *MERCHANTS OF DEATH,* 1934

In 1930, as a result of the endeavors of disarmament advocates, a treaty was signed between the United States, Great Britain and Japan. While it fell far short of disarming these powers, it did agree on a joint policy of naval limitation and so prevented for a time a costly naval building competition between these countries. President Hoover submitted the treaty to the Senate for ratification. At this point an organization called the Navy League entered the picture. It raised strenuous objections to the treaty on the ground that it "jeopardized American security." The League failed to convince the Senate, however, and the treaty was ratified.

Presumably the Navy League was a collection of individuals who distrusted international efforts to disarm and who believed that a large navy would insure the safety of the United States and of it citizens. Some might assail these conservatives for clinging to reactionary ideas, but their point of view was a recognized patriotic policy upheld by many who had no connection to the League. But what was the Navy League and who were its backers?

Representative Claude H. Tavvener made a speech in Congress in 1916 which revealed the results of his investigations into the nature and character of the League. He cited the League's official journal to show that eighteen men and one corporation were listed as "founders." The corporation was the Midvale Steel Company from which the government had bought more than $20,000,000 worth of armor plate, to say nothing of other materials. Among the individual founders were Charles M. Schwab, president of Bethlehem Steel Corporation, which makes armor plate and other war material; J. P. Morgan, of the United States Steel Corpora-

SOURCE: H. C. Engelbrecht and F. C. Hanighen, *Merchants of Death* (Dodd, Meade, 1934), 1–11.

tion, which would profit heavily from large naval orders; Colonel R. M. Thompson, of the International Nickel Company, which dealt in nickel, that metal so necessary in making shells; and B. F. Tracy, former Secretary of the Navy, who became attorney for the Carnegie Steel Company. More than half of the founders of the energetic League were gentlemen whose business would benefit by large naval appropriations. It is evident from this that American arms makers have employed the Navy League to prevent naval disarmament.

In Europe their colleagues are even more active. Hitler has now become the symbol of the return of Germany militarism. Even before he managed to obtain supreme power there was speculation as to his financial backers. Obviously they included German industrialists fearful of socialism, communism, and the labor unions, nationalists smarting under the "insults" of the Versailles treaty, and a host of other discontented folk. But on the list of these contributors supplying funds to the Hitler movement were names of two capitalists—Von Arthaber and Von Duschnitz—directors of Skoda, the great armament firm of Germany's neighbor and enemy, Czechoslovakia.

Interlocking directorates are a familiar phenomenon in the United States. The real controller of industries is frequently found in the most unexpected places. In Europe the same system prevails. And so it appears that Messrs. Von Arthaber and Von Duschnitz represent a firm which is controlled by still another firm. The head of this holding company is neither German nor Czech. He is a French citizen, M. Eugene Schneider, president of the Schneider-Creusot Company which for a century has dominated the French arms industry and which through its subsidiaries now controls most of the important arms factories in central Europe. Some of Hitler's financial support, then, was derived from a company owed by a leading French industrialist and arms maker.

Arms merchants also own newspapers and mold public opinion. M. Schneider is more than just president of Creusot. He is the mov-

ing spirit of another great combine, the Comite des Forges. This French steel trust through one of its officers has controlling shares in the Paris newspaper *Le Temps*, the counterpart of *The New York Times*, and the *Journal des Debats*, which corresponds to the *New York Herald Tribune*. These two powerful papers constantly warn their readers of the "danger of disarmament" and of the menace of Germany. Thus M. Schneider is in a position to pull two strings, one linked to Hitler and German militarism, the other tied to the French press and French militarism.

Arms merchants have long carried on a profitable business arming the potential enemies of their own country. In England today in Bedford Park there is a cannon captured by the British from the Germans during the World War. It bears a British trademark, for it was sold to Germany by a British firm before the war. English companies also sold mines to the Turks by which British men-of-war were sunk in the Dardanelles during the war. The examples of this international trade in arms before the war are legion, as will be shown.

Nor are they lacking today. Recently the trial of the British engineers in Soviet Russia brought up the name of Vickers, the engineering firm which employed the accused. But Vickers has other lines than building dams for Bolsheviks. It is the largest armament trust in Great Britain. For years relations between the Soviets and Great Britain were such that the Soviets were convinced that Britain would lead the attack of the "capitalist powers" on Russia. Yet in 1930 Vickers sold 60 of its latest and most powerful tanks to the Soviets.

Today Russia is less of a problem to England than is Germany. The rise of Hitler has reawakened much of the pre-war British suspicion of Germany. Germany was forbidden by the Treaty of Versailles to have a military air force. Yet in 1933, at a time when relations between the two countries were strained, the Germans placed an order with an English aircraft manufacturer for 60 of the most efficient fighting planes on the market, and the order would have been filled had not the British Air Ministry intervened and refused to permit the British manufacturer to supply the planes.

Arms makers engineer "war scares." They excite governments and peoples to fear their neighbors and rivals, so that they may sell more armaments. This is an old practice worked often in Europe before the World War and still in use. Bribery is frequently closely associated with war scares. Both are well illustrated in the Seletzki scandal in Rumania. Bruno Seletzke was the Skoda agent in Rumania. In March, 1933, the Rumanian authorities discovered that this Czech firm had evaded taxes to the extent of 65 million lei. In searching Seletzki's files, secret military documents were found which pointed to espionage. The files were sealed and Seletzki's affairs were to undergo a thorough "airing."

A few days later the seals were found broken and many documents were missing. Seletzki was now held for trial and his files were carefully examined. The findings at that time pointed to widespread corruption of important government and army officials. Sums amounting to more than a billion lei had been distributed among the "right" officials, hundreds of thousands had been given to "charity" or spent on "entertainment," because the persons receiving these sums "will be used by us some day." The war scare of 1930 was revealed as a device to secure Rumanian armament orders, for Russia at that time was represented as ready to invade Bessarabia, and Rumania was pictured as helpless against this threat; all the hysteria vanished over night when Skoda was given large armament orders by the Rumanian government. General Popescu who was involved shot himself in his study and other officials were exceedingly nervous about the revelations which might yet come. It was never revealed who Seletzki's friends in the Rumanian government had been.

All these incidents took place in times of peace. Presumably arms merchants become strictly patriotic once their countries start warlike operations. Not at all! During the World

War at one time there were two trials going on in France. In one, Bolo Pasha was facing charges of trying to corrupt French newspapers in the interest of the Central Powers. He was convicted and executed. In the other, a group of French industrialists were tried for selling war material to Germany through Switzerland. Although the facts were proved, these industrialists were released because they had also supplied the French armies. This is but one of the number of sensational instances of trading with the enemy during the war.

Dealers in arms are scrupulously careful in keeping their accounts collected. Previous to the World War, Krupp had invented a special fuse for hand grenades. The English company, Vickers, appropriated this invention during the war and many Germans were killed by British grenades equipped with this fuse. When the war was over, Krupp sued Vickers for violation of patent rights, demanding the payment of one shilling per fuse. The total claimed by Krupp was 123,000,000 shillings. The case was settled out of court and Krupp received payment in stock of one of Vickers's subsidiaries in Spain.

Reading such accounts many people are shocked. They picture a group of unscrupulous villains who are using every device to profit from human suffering and death. They conjure up a picture of a well-organized, ruthless conspiracy to block world peace and to promote war. Theirs is an ethical reaction easily understood. For the business of placing all our vaunted science and engineering in the service of Mars and marketing armaments by the most unrestricted methods of modern salesmanship is indeed a thoroughly anti-social occupation.

But the arms merchant does not see himself as a villain. According to his lights he is simply a business man who sells his wares under prevailing business practices. The uses to which his products are put and the results of his traffic are apparently no concern of his, no more than they are, for instance, of an automobile salesman. Thus there are many naive statements of arms makers which show their complete indifference about anything related to their industry save its financial success. One British arms manufacturer, for instance, compared his enterprise to that of a house-furnishing company which went so far as to encourage matrimony to stimulate more purchases of house furnishings. The arms maker felt that he, too, was justified in promoting his own particular brand of business.

Neither of these two points of view—the average man's accusation and the arms maker's defense—is an adequate statement of the issues involved. One may be horrified by the activities of an industry which thrives on the greatest of human curses; still it is well to acknowledge that the arms industry did not create the war system. On the contrary, the war system created the arms industry. And our civilization which, however, reluctantly, recognizes war as the final arbiter in international disputes, is also responsible for the existence of the arms maker.

Who—to be specific—has the power to declare war? All constitutions in the world (except Spain) vest the war-making power in the government or in the representatives of the people. They further grant the power to conscript man-power to carry on such conflicts. Why is there no ethical revolt against these constitutions? Governments also harbor and foster forces like nationalism and chauvinism, economic rivalry and exploiting capitalism, territorial imperialism and militarism. Which is the most potent for war, these elements or the arms industry? The arms industry is undeniably a menace to peace, but it is an industry to which our present civilization clings and for which it is responsible.

It is an evidence of the superficiality of many peace advocates that they should denounce the arms industry and accept the present state of civilization which fosters it. Governments today spend approximately four and a half billion dollars every year to maintain their war machines. This colossal sum is voted every year by representatives of the people. There are, of course, some protests against these enormous military outlays and a handful of individuals carry their protest so far as to refuse to render

military service and to pay taxes. But by and large it is believed that "natural security" demands these huge appropriations. The root of the trouble, therefore, goes far deeper than the arms industry. It lies in the prevailing temper of peoples toward nationalism, militarism, and war, in the civilization which forms this temper and prevents any drastic and radical change. Only when this underlying basis of the war system is altered, will war and its concomitant, the arms industry, pass out of existence.

While critics of the arms makers are thus frequently lacking in a thorough understanding of the problems involved, the apologists of the arms makers, who defend the purely commercial and nonpolitical nature of the traffic in arms, are far from profound. The fact is that the armament maker is the right-hand man of all war and navy departments, and, as such, he is a supremely important political figure. His sales to his home government are political acts, as much as, perhaps even more so, than the transactions of a tax collector. His international traffic is an act of international politics and is so recognized in solemn international treaties. The reason this aspect has never been emphasized is that most nations are extremely anxious to continue the free and uninterrupted commerce in armaments, because they do not and cannot manufacture the arms they deem necessary for their national safety. From this the curious paradox arises that an embargo on arms is everywhere considered an act of international politics, while the international sales of arms, even in war time, is merely business.

This is the complex situation which breeds such a singular intellectual confession. The world at present apparently wants both the war system and peace; it believes that "national safety" lies in preparedness, and it denounces the arms industry. This is not merely confused thinking, but a striking reflection of the contradictory forces at work in our social and political life. Thus it happens that so-called friends of peace frequently uphold the institution of armies and navies to preserve "national security," support "defensive wars," and advocate military training in colleges. On the other hand, arms makers sometimes make dramatic gestures for peace. Nobel, the Dynamite King, established the worlds most famous peace prize; Andrew Carnegie endowed a peace foundation and wrote pamphlets on the danger of armaments; Charles Schwab declared that he would gladly scrap all his armor plants if it would bring peace to the world; and Du Pont recently informed its stockholders that it was gratified that the world was rebelling against war.

Out of this background of conflicting forces the arms maker has risen and grown powerful, until today he is one of the most dangerous factors in world affairs—a hindrance to peace, a promoter of war. He has reached this position not through any deliberate plotting or planning of his own, but simply as a result of the historic forces of the nineteenth century. Granting the nineteenth century with its amazing development of science and invention, its industrial and commercial evolution, its concentration of economic wealth, its close international ties, its spread and intensification of nationalism, its international political conflicts, the modern armament maker with all his evils was inevitable. If the arms industry is a cancer on the body of modern civilization, it is not an extraneous growth; it is the result of the unhealthy condition of the body itself.

3.6 The Hirota Government's National Foreign Policies (Reported to Emperor Hirohito, August 15, 1936)

By the mid-1930s the Japanese had come to see themselves as the dominant force (both political and economic) for the future in East Asia. They called this expansion of influence the Greater East Asia Co-prosperity Sphere. The primary threat to this Japanese expansion was the Western powers, specifically the old European colonial powers, plus the Soviet Union and the United States. All of these nations continued to maintain interests in Asia, and all, the Japanese believed, would have to be removed in some way before Japan could dominate East Asia, and its power and economy would be secure for the future. In August 1936 the government of Prime Minister Hirota Koki (in office only since March) reported to the emperor its strategy for expansion of the Japanese empire into the regions of Asia that it did not already occupy. That report is excerpted in *Document 3.6*. Washington's objections to this expansion would be instrumental in drawing the United States into the war in the Pacific in December 1941.

DOCUMENT 3.6

THE HIROTA GOVERNMENT'S NATIONAL FOREIGN POLICIES (REPORTED TO EMPEROR HIROHITO, AUGUST 15, 1936)

The aims of our state administration are to stabilize the government at home, and to promote better diplomatic and trade relations abroad. It is in line with the fundamental principles of the Empire that we should seek to become in name and in fact a stabilizing power for assuring peace in East Asia, thereby ultimately contributing to the peace and welfare of humanity. The fundamental national policy for Japan dictated by the prevailing domestic and international situation, is the securing of a firm diplomatic and defensive position on the East Asiatic Continent and the extension of national influence as far as the South Seas. The following is the outline of the basic program for the realization of these aims:

a. It is the embodiment of the spirit of the Japanese way of life to attempt to achieve unity in East Asia based on a "live-and-let-live" principle. This may be accomplished by destroying the Great Powers' East Asiatic policy of aggression. This should be the principle aim of our foreign policy.

b. National defense will be brought to a level necessary for Japan to secure her position as the stabilizing power in East Asia. This will be accomplished through preservation of her peace and safeguarding her development.

c. Our basic policies for the continent include the elimination of the menace of the Soviet Union by assisting in the sound development of Manchukuo and strengthening the Japan-Manchukuo defense set-up, preparing against Great Britain and the United States economic development by bringing about close cooperation of Manchukuo, Japan and China. In carrying out these policies, care must be exercised to avoid aggravating friendly relations with other nations.

d. In our national and economic expansion to the South Seas, especially to the outer South Seas area, our influence will be extended gradually and by peaceful means, with the utmost care being exercised to avoid provoking other nations. This development, together with the healthy growth of Manchukuo, will contribute to the repletion of our national strength.

All our domestic and international policies will be adjusted and unified along lines of the basic national policies mentioned above. New administrative policies and actions in conformity with the current situation will be affected, and the following measures will be taken for this purpose:

a. National defense and armament.

1. The repletion of Army forces will aim at a strength to resist the forces the Soviet Union can employ in the Far East at the outbreak of hostilities.

2. Naval rearmament will be brought to a level sufficient to secure command of the Western Pacific against the United States Navy.

b. Foreign policy will be revamped with a view to achieving our fundamental national policy.

The Army and Navy, while avoiding all direct action, will do everything possible to facilitate the working of the diplomatic machinery. . . .

Foreign policy will be based on the accomplishment of our national policy. In order to bring all actions into line with national policy, close liaison will be maintained with all civil and military authorities dispatched abroad. Moreover, positive guidance will be given to the people and complete control will be affected over diplomacy. For the protection and promotion of our just and proper national

SOURCE: Military History Section Headquarters, Army Forces Far East, Distributed by the Office of the Chief of Military History Department of the Army, *Political Strategy Prior to the Outbreak of War,* (December 31, 1952), Japanese Monograph No. 144, Part 1, Appendix 1.

rights and interests, a self-effacing attitude is to be avoided and a positive one taken. At the same time, efforts will be made to allay the Great Powers' suspicion and apprehension toward the Empire. . . .

In recent years, the Soviet Union has strengthened sharply its national defense and international position. It has reinforced its forces in the Far East to an unwarranted degree, exerting increasing military and revolutionary pressure against this region. Moreover, the Soviet Union is planning the communization of all areas of this region, seeking to force the Empire into still more disadvantageous positions. This is a direct menace to the national security of the Empire and a serious obstacle to the execution of current East Asian policy. Therefore, emphasis will be laid for the present on the frustration of Soviet aggressive designs in the Far East. . . .

The improvement of friendly relations between our country and the United States might greatly contribute to offsetting British and Soviet influences. However, in view of the fact that the United States is engaged in rearming and views the development of our China policy with great concern in the light of her traditional Far Eastern policy, there is danger that she may assist China, making that country dependent on the West. Moreover, it is feared that this would eventually create a situation exceedingly unfavorable to the execution of our policy against the Soviet Union. Therefore, we must seek the United States' understanding of our just attitude through respect for her commercial interests in China. At the same time, we should endeavor to improve friendly relations based on economic interdependence, thereby causing the United States to refrain from interfering with our Far Eastern policy.

Since the development of the political situation in Europe has an important bearing on East Asia, efforts must be exerted to turn it to our advantage, particularly to hold the Soviet Union in check.

Great Britain and Japan have many areas of conflicting interests. In view of the fact that Great Britain, among the Western powers, has the greatest stake in the Far East and since the attitude of other European countries depends largely upon that of Great Britain, it is especially important for us to take the initiative at this time to improve relations with Great Britain. In this way Great Britain may side with us in our relations with the Soviet Union and act as a counterbalance against the Soviets, thereby lessening the obstacles lying in the way of our overseas expansion. Since the adjustment of Anglo-Japanese relations in China will have far-reaching results, we must endeavor to take appropriate measures for breaking the deadlock over China and for making an over-all adjustment to Anglo-Japanese relations. This is to be accomplished through efforts to get Great Britain to recognize and respect Japan's special and vital interests, especially in China, and also through respecting Great Britain's rights and interests there. We must, nevertheless, guard against Great Britain, lest she adopt a policy of applying pressure against Japan in concert with other powers, particularly the United States, the Soviet Union and China.

Germany, in here relations with the Soviet Union, is in much the same position as Japan. In view of the special relationship between France and the Soviet Union, it is deemed advantageous for Germany to act in concert with Japan in matters of national defense and anti-Communist policy. Therefore, our friendly relations with Germany are to be improved and measures are to be taken to realize Japanese-German collaboration as occasion demands. Moreover, this relationship is to be expanded to include such countries as Poland, with a view to checking the Soviet Union. In addition, efforts are to be made to enlighten Moslem nations and European and Asian countries neighboring the Soviet Union, with attention paid to the improvement of friendly relations with those nations.

Occupying an important position in our global trade relations and being an area indispensable for the industrial and national defense of the Empire, as well as a natural field for our racial development, the Southern Region must be studied as an area for our expansion. But our advance in that area must be conduced peacefully and gradually, with the utmost efforts to prevent provocation of other countries and to allay their misgivings against the Empire.

As for the Philippines, we look forward to her complete independence and, if called upon, be ready to guarantee her neutrality. For our expansion into the Netherlands East Indies, it is extremely important that we allay the misgivings of the people toward us and convert them to a pro-Japanese nation. Appropriate measures, therefore, will be taken for this purpose. If need be [,] a non-aggression pact with Holland will be concluded. Thailand and other

underdeveloped nations should be given proper guidance and assistance on the basis of our principle of co-existence and co-prosperity.

Overseas trade is not only indispensable for the maintenance and betterment of the economic life of our nation but also contributes to the improvement of our finances and the state of our international obligations. It is particularly important, under the current domestic and international situation, that foreign trade be expanded to the utmost. Thus, we must develop our economic power by rationalizing our foreign trade and at the same time acquiring important natural resources through proper adjustment of our interests to those of other powers.

3.7   President Franklin Roosevelt's Address Before the Pan-American Conference for the Maintenance of Peace, Buenos Aires, Argentina, December 1, 1936

Through at least the first two decades of the century the United States had intervened in Latin American affairs fairly freely. These interventions, mostly military in nature, caused a great deal of distrust and resentment of the United States. By the beginning of the 1920s Washington began to see the necessity of winning back the trust of the Latin American nations and maintaining friendly neighbors in the hemisphere. In 1921 the Harding administration paid the $25 million to Colombia that it had demanded for canal rights in Panama in 1903. U.S. forces left the Dominican Republic in 1924 after some eight years of occupation. A year later Marines left Nicaragua, but that nation remained embroiled in civil war and the troops were sent back in.

In 1928, at the sixth Pan-American Conference in Havana, Charles Evans Hughes, at the head of the American delegation sent by President Coolidge, announced troop withdrawals from both Nicaragua and Haiti. This was widely perceived as the beginning of the end of U.S. involvement in Latin American affairs. President Hoover began those troop withdrawals; they were completed under President Roosevelt.

At the Pan-American conference in Montevideo, Uruguay in December 1933, all the nations of the Western Hemisphere signed a pact giving their pledge to the "Good Neighbor Policy," a plan of mutual trust and U.S. aid outlined by Roosevelt. For the Latin American nations, the key to the Good Neighbor Policy was that "No state has the right to intervene in the international or external affairs of another." Although U.S. presidents since Roosevelt have continued to meddle in Latin American affairs, the

Good Neighbor Policy became the foundation of U.S.–Latin American relations for the remainder of the century, and led to the establishment of the Organization of American States in 1948.

In December 1936, Roosevelt addressed the seventh Pan-American conference in Buenos Aries (*Document 3.7*). The primary accomplishment of the 1936 conference was that the nations of Latin America agreed to maintain peace in their region. Bolivia and Paraguay had fought a costly war between 1932 and 1935. Roosevelt, however, focused his speech on the problems that a European war might have on the Western Hemisphere. The title of his speech: "Can We, the Republics of the New World, Help the Old World to Avert the Catastrophe Which Impends?"

DOCUMENT 3.7

PRESIDENT FRANKLIN ROOSEVELT'S ADDRESS BEFORE THE PAN-AMERICAN CONFERENCE FOR THE MAINTENANCE OF PEACE, BUENOS AIRES, ARGENTINA, DECEMBER 1, 1936

On the happy occasion of the convening of this Conference I address you thus, because members of a family need no introduction or formalities when, in pursuance of excellent custom, they meet together for their common good. . . .

Three years ago the American family met in nearby Montevideo, the great capital of the Republic of Uruguay. They were dark days. A shattering depression, unparalleled in its intensity, held us, with the rest of the world, in its grip. And in our own Hemisphere a tragic war was raging between two of our sister Republics.

Yet, at that conference there was born not only hope for our common future but a greater measure of mutual trust between the American democracies than had ever existed before. In this Western Hemisphere the night of fear has been dispelled. Many of the intolerable burdens of economic depression have been lightened and, due in no small part to our common ef-

SOURCE: Edgar Nixon, ed., *Franklin D. Roosevelt and Foreign Affairs*, Vol. III, Sept. 1935–Jan. 1937 (1969), 516–21.

forts, every Nation of this Hemisphere is today at peace with its neighbors.

This is no conference to form alliances, to divide the spoils of war, to partition countries, to deal with human beings as though they were pawns in a game of chance. Our purpose, under happy auspices, is to assure the continuance of the blessings of peace.

Three years ago, recognizing that a crisis was being thrust upon the New World, with splendid unanimity our twenty-one Republics set an example to the whole world by proclaiming a new spirit, a new day, in the affairs of this Hemisphere.

While the succeeding period has justified in full measure all that was said and done at Montevideo, it has unfortunately emphasized the seriousness of threats to peace among other Nations. Events elsewhere have served only to strengthen our horror of war and all that war means. The men, women, and children of the Americas know that warfare in this day and age means more than the mere clash of armies: they see the destruction of cities and of farms; they foresee that children and grandchildren, if they survive, will stagger for long years not only under the burden of poverty but also amid the threat of broken society and the destruction of constitutional government. I am profoundly convinced that the plain people everywhere in the civilized world today wish to live in peace one with another. And still leaders and Governments resort to war. Truly, if the genius of mankind that has invented the weapons of death cannot discover the means of preserving peace, civilization as we know it lives in an evil day.

But we cannot now, especially in view of our common purpose, accept any defeatist attitude. We have learned by hard experience that peace is not to be had for the mere asking; that peace, like other great privileges, can be obtained only by hard and painstaking effort. We are here to dedicate ourselves and our countries to that work.

You who assemble today carry with you in your deliberations the hopes of millions of human beings in other less fortunate lands. Beyond the ocean we see continents rent asunder by old hatreds and new fanaticisms. We hear the demand that injustice and inequality be corrected by resorting to the sword and not by resorting to reason and peaceful justice. We hear the cry that new markets can be achieved only through conquest. We read that the sanctity of treaties between Nations is disregarded.

We know, too, that vast armaments are rising on every side and that the work of creating them employs men and women by the millions. It is natural, however, for us to conclude that such employment is false employment; that it builds no permanent structures and creates no consumers' goods for the maintenance of a lasting prosperity. We know that Nations guilty of these follies inevitably face the day when either their weapons of destruction must be used against their neighbors or when an unsound economy, like a house of cards, will fall apart.

In either case, even though the Americas become involved in no war, we must suffer too. The madness of a great war in other parts of the world would affect us and threaten our good in a hundred ways. And the economic collapse of any Nation or Nations must of necessity harm our own prosperity.

Can we, the Republics of the New World, help the Old World to avert the catastrophe which impends? Yes; I am confident that we can.

First, it is our duty by every honorable means to prevent any future war among ourselves. This can best be done through the strengthening of the processes of constitutional democratic government; by making these processes conform to the modern need for unity and efficiency and, at the same time, preserving the individual liberties of our citizens. By so doing, the people of our Nations, unlike the people of many Nations who live under other forms of governments can and will insist on their intention to live in peace. Thus will democratic government be justified throughout the world.

In this determination to live at peace among ourselves we in the Americas make it at the same time clear that we stand shoulder to shoulder in our final determination that others who, driven by war madness or land hunger, might seek to commit acts of aggression against us will find a Hemisphere wholly prepared to consult together for our mutual safety and our mutual good. I repeat what I said in speaking before the Congress and the Supreme Court of Brazil: "Each one of us has learned the glories of independence. Let each one of us learn the glories of interdependence."

Secondly, and in addition to the perfecting of the mechanisms of peace, we can strive even more strongly than in the past to prevent the creation of those conditions which give rise to war. Lack of social or political justice within the borders of any Nation is always cause for concern. Through democratic processes we can strive to achieve for the Americas the highest possible standard of living conditions for all our people. Men and women blessed with political freedom, willing to work and able to find work, rich enough to maintain their families and to educate their children, contented with their lot in life and on terms of friendship with their neighbors, will defend themselves to the utmost, but will never consent to take up arms for a war of conquest.

Interwoven with these problems is the further self-evident fact that the welfare and prosperity of each of our Nations depend in large part on the benefits derived from commerce among ourselves and with other Nations, for our present civilization rests on the basis of an international exchange of commodities. Every

Nation of the world has felt the evil effects of recent efforts to erect trade barriers of every known kind. Every individual citizen has suffered from them. It is no accident that the Nations which have carried this process farthest are those which proclaim most loudly that they require war as an instrument of their policy. It is no accident that attempts to be self-sufficient have led to falling standards for their people and to ever-increasing loss of the democratic ideals in a mad race to pile armament on armament. It is no accident that, because of these suicidal policies and the suffering attending them, many of their people have come to believe with despair that the price of war seems less than the price of peace. This state of affairs we must refuse to accept with every instinct of defense, with every exhortation of enthusiastic hope, with every use of mind and skill.

I cannot refrain here from reiterating my gratification that in this, as in so many other achievements, the American Republics have given a salutary example to the world. The resolution adopted at the Inter-American Conference at Montevideo endorsing the principles of liberal trade policies has shown forth like a beacon in the storm of economic madness which has been sweeping over the entire world during these later years. Truly, if the principles there embodied find still wider application in your deliberations, it will be a notable contribution to the cause of peace. For my own part I have done all in my power to sustain the consistent efforts of my Secretary of State in negotiating agreements for reciprocal trade, and even though the individual results may seem small, the total of them is significant. These policies in recent weeks have received the approval of the people of the United States, and they have, I am sure, the sympathy of the other Nations here assembled.

There are many other causes for war— among them, long-festering feuds, unsettled frontiers, territorial rivalries. But these sources of danger which still exist in the Americas, I am thankful to say, are not only few in number but already on the way to peaceful adjudication.

While the settlement of such controversies may necessarily involve adjustments at home or in our relations with our neighbors which may appear to involve material sacrifice, let no man or woman forget that there is no profit in war. Sacrifices in the cause of peace are infinitesimal compared with the holocaust of war.

Peace comes from the spirit and must be grounded in faith. In seeking peace, perhaps we can best begin by proudly affirming the faith of the Americas: the faith in freedom and its fulfillment, which has proved a mighty fortress beyond reach of successful attack in half the world.

That faith arises from a common hope and a common design given us by our fathers in differing form but with a single aim: freedom and security of the individual, which has become the foundation of our peace.

If, then, by making war in our midst impossible, and if within ourselves and among ourselves we can give greater freedom and fulfillment to the individual lives of our citizens, the democratic form of representative government will have justified the high hopes of the liberating fathers. Democracy is still the hope of the world. If we in our generation can continue its successful application in the Americas, it will spread and supersede other methods by which men are governed and which seem to most of us to run counter to our ideals of human liberty and human progress.

Three centuries of history sowed the seeds which grew into our Nations; the fourth century saw those Nations become equal and free and brought us to a common system of constitutional government; the fifth century is giving to us a common meeting ground of mutual help and understanding. Our Hemisphere has at last come of age. We are here assembled to show its unity to the world. We took from our ancestors a great dream. We here offer it back as a great unified reality.

Finally, in expressing our faith of the Western World, let us affirm:

That we maintain and defend the democratic form of constitutional representative government.

That through such government we can more greatly provide a wider distribution of culture, of education, of thought, and of free expression.

That through it we can obtain a greater security of life for our citizens and a more equal opportunity for them to prosper.

That through it we can best foster commerce and the exchange of art and science between Nations.

That through it we can avoid the rivalry of armaments, avert hatreds, and encourage goodwill and true justice.

That through it we offer hope for peace and a more abundant life to the peoples of the whole world.

But this faith of the Western World will not be complete if we fail to affirm our faith in God. In the whole history of mankind, far back into the dim past before man knew how to record thoughts or events, the human race has been distinguished from other forms of life by the existence, the fact, of religion. Periodic attempts to deny God have always come and will always come to naught.

In the constitution and in the practice of our Nations is the right of freedom of religion. But this ideal, these words, presuppose a belief and a trust in God.

The faith of the Americas, therefore, lies in the spirit. The systems, the sisterhood, of the Americas is impregnable so long as her Nations maintain that spirit.

In that faith and spirit we will have peace over the Western World. In that faith and spirit we will all watch and guard our Hemisphere. In that faith and spirit may we also, with God's help, offer hope to our brethren overseas.

3.8 Neutrality Act of 1937, May 1, 1937

By the mid-1930s, when it became clear that war in Europe was on the horizon, the United States began to devise ways of staying out of the impending conflict. Many Americans believed that the nation had been drawn into World War I, at least in part because it had not remained strictly neutral. Through the 1930s the United States, in a series of difficultly-worded neutrality acts, declared its neutrality over and over in an almost desperate attempt to avoid war. The first Neutrality Act, passed in August 1935, seemed aimed at avoiding the types of crises that had dragged the United States into World War I. Passed just as Italy invaded Ethiopia, the Neutrality Act of 1935 prohibited Americans from sending arms to belligerent nations. It also forbade U.S. ships from dealing in the arms trade and warned American passengers that they traveled in war zones at their own risk. The 1936 Neutrality Act, passed just as FDR was preparing to run for a second term and as Francisco Franco was poised to overthrow the Spanish Republic, effectively tightened the first act by prohibiting loans to belligerent nations.

In the Neutrality Act of 1937 (*Document 3.8*), Congress hoped to strengthen even further the preceding neutrality acts, but at the suggestion of financier Bernard Baruch the 1937 act contained a clause that quietly changed the face of American neutrality: "Cash and Carry." This new crinkle allowed warring nations to purchase various materiel from the United States provided they paid up immediately and carried the goods away in their own ships. This, of course, allowed the

United States to profit from the neutral trade while minimizing the risk of becoming involved in a major war. Cash and Carry, however, had an inherent weakness: It did not differentiate between aggressor nations and victims, and there was no certainty that only America's friends would benefit from the program. When Japan invaded China in the summer of 1937, Roosevelt refused to invoke the 1937 Act because Japan, with its large navy and ability to transport goods across the Pacific, might have benefited greatly from the program. China, on the other hand, had no ability either to pay for or transport goods, thus it would have suffered further from Japan's aggressions.

The war in Europe began on September 1, 1939 when Hitler invaded Poland, and Britain and France responded by declaring war. Americans split over how to react. Interventionists wanted to aid America's old allies, France and Britain. On the other hand, isolationists such as Senator William Borah resisted any steps that might draw the nation into another war. Borah and his followers particularly feared that significant aid to the European democracies might ultimately commit the United States to intervention against its will to protect its investments—as in 1917.

President Franklin Roosevelt, however, had come to the conclusion that neutrality was no longer useful in a world that was increasingly divided and quickly moving toward global war. Insisting that his motives were to keep the United States out of war, Roosevelt asked Congress to repeal the neutrality acts. The attempt failed and FDR was forced to accept another statement of neutrality, the Neutrality Act of 1939. Initiated by congressional isolationists in the face of the growing world conflict, this act reiterated much of what was in the earlier acts, in addition to the cash and carry clause.

....

NEUTRALITY ACT OF 1937, MAY 1, 1937

Section 1. Whenever the President shall find that a state of civil strife exists in a foreign state and that such civil strife is of a magnitude or is being conducted under such conditions that the export of arms, ammunition, or implements of war from the United States to such foreign state would threaten or endanger the peace of the United States, the President shall proclaim such fact, and it shall thereafter be unlawful to export . . . arms, ammunition, or implements of war from any place in the United States to such foreign state. . . .

SOURCE: *U.S. Statutes at Large*, XLIX, pt. 1, 1153.

Section 2. Whenever the President shall have issued a proclamation under the authority of section 1 of this Act . . . it shall thereafter be unlawful . . . to export or transport . . . from the United States to any belligerent state wherein civil strife exists . . . any articles or materials whatever until all rights, title, and interests therein shall have been transferred to some foreign government, agency, institution association, partnership, corporation, or national. The ship of such articles or materials shall be required to file with the collector of the port from which they are to be exported a declaration under oath that there exists in citizens of the United States no right, title, or interest in such articles or materials. . . . Any such declaration so filed shall be a conclusive estoppel against any claim of any citizen of the United States of right, interest, or title in such articles or materials. Insurance written by underwriters on any articles or materials the export of which is prohibited by this Act, or on articles or materials carried by an American vessel in violation of subsection (a) of this sections, shall not be deemed an American interest therein, and no insurance policy issued on such articles or materials and no loss incurred thereunder or by the owner of the vessel carrying the same shall be made a basis of any claim put forward by the Government of the United States. . . .

Section 9. Whenever the President shall have issued a proclamation under the authority of section 1 of this Act it shall thereafter be unlawful for any citizen of the United States to travel on any vessel of the state or states named in such proclamation, except in accordance with such rules and regulations as the President shall prescribe. . . .

Section 10. Whenever the President shall issue a proclamation under the authority of section 1, it shall thereafter be unlawful, until such proclamation is revoked, for any American vessel engaged in commerce with any belligerent state, or any state wherein civil strife exists, named in such proclamation, to be armed or to carry any armament, arms, ammunition, or implements of war, except small arms and ammunition therefore which the President may deem necessary . . . for the preservation of discipline aboard the vessel.

3.9 *The London Times* Reports Prime Minister Neville Chamberlain's Return from Munich, September 30, 1938

One primary principle of American foreign policy is that an aggressor cannot be appeased, that to do so only invites a greater war. That lesson was learned at Munich in 1938, when British Prime Minister Neville Chamberlain agreed to allow Hitler to occupy the Sudetenland in Czechoslovakia in exchange for a promise to bring an end to his aggressions. Chamberlain's attempt at appeasing Hitler failed.

This event has had a great impact on U.S. foreign policy. President Harry Truman, in his memoirs, referred specifically to the appeasement of Hitler as the lesson he evoked in deciding to invade Korea in 1950; and President George Bush, just prior to intervening in the Persian Gulf in 1991, said as events escalated, "no more Munichs." Indeed, Chamberlain's actions at Munich are seen by most Americans as cowardly, causing a greater, more destructive war against a much more powerful Germany just a year later. There are those, however, who still view Chamberlain's actions as a personal sacrifice for the purpose of delaying the outbreak of war and buying Britain precious time to rearm. Certainly, Britain was not prepared for a land war against Germany in the fall of 1938.

Czechoslovakia, however, was prepared. It had a larger land force than Germany in 1938, and it was better mechanized. The Czechs had even allied with France, then the most powerful land force in Europe, and the Soviet Union. Both nations had promised to come to the aid of Czechoslovakia if it were attacked by Germany.

The situation in central Europe became extremely tense when Hitler, in March, 1938, annexed Austria and then began making demands on Czechoslovakia to surrender control of the Sudetenland, a mostly German-speaking region in western and northern Czechoslovakia. War seemed imminent—a war that might include Soviet troops marching across Eastern Europe on its way to defend the Czechs. Chamberlain responded as peacemaker by making several trips to Germany to meet with Hitler. Hitler, however, continued to demand the Sudetenland, and in September, in Munich, Chamberlain and Hitler signed the Munich Accords that surrendered the Sudetenland to Germany. The decisions were made without consulting the Prague government and with the agreement of the French.

The Czech Crisis, as it was called, was defused, and war was averted. Hitler, it was assumed, would be satisfied. The Munich agreement was considered a triumph in the West. Roosevelt, in fact, sent a two-word telegram to Chamberlain: "Good man." And there was an added bonus: A now-stronger Germany in Central Europe would serve as a restraint against Soviet expansion into Eastern Europe. Chamberlain returned to London in triumph. On the evening of September 30, he delivered a short speech at Heston Airport in London and then drove to his residence at 10 Downing Street where he made his "peace for our time" statement that won cheers for the moment but defined appeasement as folly for the future. Document 3.9 recounts both speeches. A London Times editorial on the events entitled "A New Dawn," follows Chamberlain's speeches.

Chamberlain's triumph turned to tragedy when Hitler, almost immediately, demanded the remainder of Czechoslovakia, now seriously weakened by its loss of the Sudetenland and abandonment by its allies. In March 1939 Hitler swallowed Czechoslovakia—again unopposed. The following month Italy absorbed Albania. Britain and France, surprised at the turn of events, announced immediately that they would go to war to protect Poland.

....

DOCUMENT 3.9

THE LONDON TIMES REPORTS PRIME MINISTER NEVILLE CHAMBERLAIN'S RETURN FROM MUNICH, SEPTEMBER 30, 1938

THE NATION THANKED

Then, amid continuous cheers, the Prime Minister stepped towards a microphone and spoke a message to the nation. He said:—

> There are only two things I want to say. First of all, I received an immense number of letters during all these anxious days—and so has my wife—

letters of support and approval and gratitude, and I cannot tell you what an encouragement that has been to me. I want to thank the British people for what they have done. Next I want to say that the settlement of the Czechoslovak problem which has now been achieved is, in my view, only a prelude to a larger settlement in which all Europe may find peace.

This morning I had another talk with the German Chancellor, Herr Hitler, and here is a paper which bears his name upon it as well as mine. Some of you perhaps have already heard what it contains, but I would just like to read it to you.

Mr. Chamberlain then read the joint declaration, and there was a further burst of cheering. There were more cheers as policemen made a way for him to his car, and the drive to London began to the singing of "For he's a jolly good fellow." As Mr. Chamberlain drove

SOURCE: *London Times* October 1, 1938.

past the cheering Eton boys to the airport exit his car was surrounded by crowds who could not be held back by the police, and amid the enthusiasm many people tried to open the doors of the car to shake him by the hand.

Mounted police eventually made a way, and the Prime Minister drove slowly through the pressing and cheering crowds—among whom were hundreds of children waving tiny flags—towards London and the still greater welcome that was the acknowledgment of a victory gained for peace. . . .

DOWNING STREET SPEECH

Now the cries were "Speech, speech," and Mr. Chamberlain held up his hand for silence. It took several minutes for the great crowd to settle down into something like quietude, and then the Prime Minister's voice came down to them. "My good friends," he said, "this is the second time in our history that there has come back from Germany to Downing Street peace with honour."

At this the cheering broke out unrestrainedly, and it was some time before the Prime Minister could continue. "I believe," he went on, "it is peace for our time. We thank you from the bottom of our hearts."

The response was immediate. "We thank you," came back from the crowd below. "God bless you." Mr. Chamberlain paused for a moment and then said: "And now I recommend you to go home and sleep quietly in your beds." The significance of the phrase was not lost on his hearers. But before they went they sang "For he's a jolly good fellow" and then, with a deep fervor, the National Anthem.

All along the route from Heston to Buckingham Palace and from the Palace to Downing Street scenes of enthusiasm had been repeated and cheers from windows were joined in those from the crowds filling the streets.

Even after 10 o'clock, bouquet after bouquet was handed in at 10 Downing Street, to be added to the earlier tributes, and until late in the evening happy crowds demonstrated in Whitehall and the West End of London, traffic often being brought almost to a standstill, and it was nearly midnight before the last of the crowds had departed from outside Buckingham Palace.

A NEW DAWN

[A *London Times* Editorial]

No conqueror returning from a victory on the battlefield has come home adorned with nobler laurels than Mr. Chamberlain from Munich yesterday; and King and people alike have shown by the manner of their reception their sense of his achievement. The terms of settlement in the Czech-German dispute, reached in the small hours of the morning and published in the later issues of *The Times* of yesterday, had been seen to deliver the world from a menace of extreme horror while doing rough-and-ready justice between the conflicting claims. Yet even this great service to humanity was already beginning to appear as the lesser half of the Prime Minister's work in Munich. He himself announced it as the prelude to a larger settlement. He had not only relegated an agonizing episode to the past; he had found for the nations a new hope for the future. The joint declaration made by Herr Hitler and Mr. Chamberlain proclaims that "the desire" of the two peoples never to go to war with "one another again" shall henceforth govern the whole of their relationships. There have been times when such a manifesto could be dismissed as a pious platitude, likely to be forgotten long before an occasion could arise for it to be practically tested. The present, it is fair to think, is not such a time. The two statesmen plainly recognize in their declaration that there are still sources of differences between Great Britain and Germany, which for the sake of the peace of Europe must be settled at an early date; it is in direct relation to these that they pledge themselves to the methods of peaceful consultation, and so demonstrate that they expect to be taken at the full value of their word. By inserting a specific reference to the Anglo-German Naval Agreement, as well as to the negotiations

We, the German Führer and Chancellor and the
British Prime Minister, have had a further
meeting today and are agreed in recognising that
the question of Anglo-German relations is of the
first importance for the two countries and for
Europe.

We regard the agreement signed last night
and the Anglo-German Naval Agreement as symbolic
of the desire of our two peoples never to go to
war with one another again.

We are resolved that the method of
consultation shall be the method adopted to deal
with any other questions that may concern our two
countries, and we are determined to continue our
efforts to remove possible sources of difference
and thus to contribute to assure the peace of
Europe.

[signatures: Adolf Hitler and Neville Chamberlain]

September 30, 1938.

German Chancellor Adolf Hitler and British Prime Minister Neville Chamberlain signed this note on September 30, 1938. The note is based on the Munich Accords and certifies a peaceful relationship between Great Britain and Germany. To gain the peace, Chamberlain relinquished to Hitler the Sudetenland, a portion of Czechoslovakia. The lesson for the world was that aggressors cannot be appeased. The note was published in the *London Times* on October 1. *THE TIMES Oct. 1, 1938, p. 14/Remember When*

so happily concluded at Munich, the Fuhrer reminds us of an earnest of his good intentions, which the British people, in the new atmosphere, will readily acknowledge.

Civilization had been so near to the brink of collapse that any peaceful issue from the dispute of the last months would have been an overwhelming relief. . . . That [the terms of the accord] should be bitterly resented in Czechoslovakia must add to the profound sympathy which has always been felt in England with one of the smaller and, as it seemed to many, the more promising countries emerging from the [Versailles Treaty]. Yet the loss of the Sudaten territories had long been unavoidable, nor was it desirable that it should be avoided. . . . At any rate—the Prague Government, the only dissentient, having been induced to acquiesce in succession—the issue narrowed down to finding the means for an orderly execution of an agreed plan. That on such an issue the whole world should be plunged into war was the monstrous prospect that had to be contemplated until less than three days ago. It would inevitably have been realized if Herr Hitler had insisted on a spectacular "conquest" of the Sudetenland by German troops. The Czechs would certainly have resisted in arms, nor would any Power have had the right to attempt to dissuade them. France would have been drawn in by direct obligation to Czechoslovakia; Great Britain and the Soviet Union would have been certain to come to the help of France; and so the widening conflict would have involved all those peoples throughout the world who had watched with ever-increasing revulsion the development of brutal methods of national aggrandizement, and through that the time had come to make a stand against them.

These methods have been publicly renounced by their principal exponents, to whom the peace-loving peoples should be ready to give full credit for their professions. But, at the moment when the current racing towards the precipice seemed irresistible, it was the leadership of the British Prime Minister that showed how immense were the forces ranged on the side of reason against violence. The gathering

urgency of persuasion was reinforced by unmistakable proofs of resolution for defense. France mobilized her army and manned her impregnable lines. Preparation in England, though slower in starting, as is the national habit, became at the crucial moment universal and formidable. The Fleet was mobilized; the anti-aircraft forces were brought into readiness; and civilians, taking post for emergency under voluntary as well as official schemes, showed plainly that the nation would not flinch. The Dominions were prompt to affirm their unanimity with the Mother Country. These things were not a threat, nor is it to be supposed that the German Chancellor would yield to threats; but there is no doubt that the evidence that Mr. Chamberlain offered concessions from strength and not from weakness won him a respect that might not otherwise have been accorded. Meanwhile other authoritative voices were uplifted for peace; the President of the United States spoke out for humanity, the Italian Duce, responding to the Prime Minister's leadership, acknowledged that peace is a supreme interest to dictators as to other national rulers. Herr Hitler deferred, as no man need be ashamed of doing, to the protest of the whole world against war. . . .

By the terms thus concluded the most dangerous threat of war in Europe is at last removed, and by the joint declaration we are given the hope that others will be peacefully eliminated. That . . . achievement, by common consent, we owe first and foremost to the Prime Minister. Had the Government of the United Kingdom been in less resolute hands it is as certain as it can be that war, incalculable in its range, would have broken out against the wishes of every people concerned. . . .

CHAPTER **4**

U.S. Foreign Policy and World War II

4.1 President Franklin Roosevelt's Fireside Chat on the Dangers of Nazi Domination of Europe, December 29, 1940

4.2 Charles Lindbergh, "We Cannot Win This War for England," May 1941

4.3 The Atlantic Charter, August 14, 1941

4.4 FDR Responds to the *Greer* Incident, September 11, 1941

4.5 Memorandum Handed by the Japanese Ambassador (Nomura) to the Secretary of State at 2:20 P.M., December 7, 1941

4.6 FDR's War Message to Congress, December 8, 1941

4.7 The Yalta Conference Accords, February 1945

4.8 Henry Stimson Explains Why the Bomb Was Necessary

4.9 Was the Bomb Necessary?

1940–1945 Timeline

Date	Year	Event
December 29, 1940	1940	FDR's Fireside Chat on Nazism
May 1941		Charles Lindburgh, "We Cannot Win This War for England"
August 14, 1941		Atlantic Charter signed
September 11, 1941	1941	FDR responds to the *Greer* incident
December 7, 1941		Japanese memorandum to Hull
December 8, 1941		FDR's war message to Congress
June 4, 1942	1942	Battle of Midway
February 1943		German defeat at Stalingrad
May 1943		German defeat in North Africa
June 6, 1944		Allies land at Normandy
October 20, 1944	1943	MacArthur retakes Philippines
February 1945		Yalta Conference
April 1945		FDR dies. Harry Truman becomes president
May 8, 1945	1944	V-E Day
August 6, 1945		Hiroshima
August 9, 1945		Nagasaki
August 14, 1945	1945	V-J Day

4.1   **President Franklin Roosevelt's Fireside Chat on the Dangers of Nazi Domination of Europe, December 29, 1940**

4.2   **Charles Lindbergh, "We Cannot Win This War for England," May 1941**

4.3   **The Atlantic Charter, August 14, 1941**

The United States proclaimed its strict neutrality immediately after the war began in Europe. But as Hitler occupied or neutralized most of the European continent, only the old American ally Great Britain stood in the way of Germany's domination of nearly all of Western Europe. Many Americans abandoned the isolationist sentiment of the two post-World War I decades and began arguing that the United States should assist Britain. But the isolationist impulse persisted.

In December 1940, President Roosevelt, in one of his most important fireside chats, spoke directly to the isolationists (*Document 4.1*). He warned of the dangers of isolationism, and what might become of the Western world if Britain were overcome by "the Nazi masters of Germany." The tone of the speech is a clear call for war preparation, to stop Germany, and to be the arsenal for democracy. The speech was delivered by the president as a radio address on December 29, and then delivered before Congress several days later.

In October 1940, just days before the presidential election, FDR told a crowd in Boston, "I shall say it again and again. Your boys are not going to be sent into any foreign wars." However, in January, just after his third inaugural, Roosevelt proposed a bill that would bring a final end to American neutrality. In March, 1941, following a long debate, Congress passed the Lend Lease Act, giving the president the power he wanted to aid Britain. The lend-lease aspect of the bill was designed to eliminate the problem of postwar debt. The isolationists had argued that floating loans to Britain (or any other belligerent nation) would cause a replay of the massive war debt problems that followed World War I. By "lending" the materiel to Britain, Congress seemed to be saying, there would be no postwar debt problem.

Roosevelt's talk of preparedness and Congress' willingness to abandon neutrality brought out the full force of the isolationists. Led by such prominent figures in American history as Herbert Hoover and Charles Lindbergh, the isolationists would have their say. They were joined by other prominent figures, including senators George Norris and William Borah, and historians Carl Becker and Charles Beard. Several domestic reformers in the Roosevelt administration also embraced isolationism, or simply non-intervention. They feared that the resources needed to fight the European war might undercut the successes of the New Deal.

The most ardent isolationist organization in the United States was the America First Committee. Organized in 1940 with the expressed purpose of keeping the nation out of the European war, America First could claim Charles Lindbergh as a spokesman. Possibly the most popular figure in the nation at the time, Lindbergh was a national hero and symbol, and his convictions carried tremendous weight with the American people. *Document 4.2* is Lindburgh's address to the New York America First Committee, delivered one month after the passage of the Lend-Lease Act.

In August 1941 Roosevelt and British Prime Minister Winston Churchill met in secret for a four-day conference aboard the British battleship *Prince of Wales* off the Coast of Newfoundland. The result was the Atlantic Charter (*Document 4.3*), a joint statement of shared goals for the war against Germany. The United States was four months from officially entering the war, but here Roosevelt committed the United States to the British war effort.

The Charter, in its eight points, was filled with Wilsonian rhetoric, calling for collective security, self-determination, freedom of the seas, and liberal trade practices. Roosevelt even suggested a new League of Nations, a proposal that Churchill rejected, to be brought up again when Nazi Germany was defeated. Churchill, an ardent imperialist, insisted that the charter protect the British colonial system. To that end, a short phrase was added: "with due respect for [Britain's] existing obligations."

Following the meeting, the United States conducted a secret and undeclared war against German shipping in the North Atlantic. Churchill returned to tell his cabinet that the American president agreed to "wage war" against Germany, "but not declare it" and to do "everything" to "force an 'incident.'"

DOCUMENT 4.1

PRESIDENT FRANKLIN ROOSEVELT'S FIRESIDE CHAT ON THE DANGERS OF NAZI DOMINATION OF EUROPE, DECEMBER 29, 1940

My Friends:

This is not a fireside chat on war. It is a talk on national security; because the nub of the whole purpose of your President is to keep you now, and your children later, and your grandchildren much later, out of a last-ditch war for the preservation of American independence and all the things that American independence means to you and to me and to ours.

Never before since Jamestown and Plymouth Rock has our American civilization been in such danger as now.

For, on September 27, 1940, by an agreement signed in Berlin, three powerful nations, two in Europe and one in Asia, joined themselves together in the threat that if the United States of America interfered with or blocked the expansion program of these three nations—a program aimed at world control—they would unite in ultimate action against the United States.

The Nazi masters of Germany have made it clear that they intend not only to dominate all life and thought in their own country, but also to enslave the whole of Europe, and then to use the resources of Europe to dominate the rest of the world. . . .

Some of our people like to believe that wars in Europe and Asia are of no concern to us. But it is a matter of most vital concern to us that European and Asiatic war-makers should not gain control of the oceans which lead to this hemisphere.

One hundred and seventeen years ago the Monroe Doctrine was conceived by our Government as a measure of defense in the face of a threat against this hemisphere by an alliance in Continental Europe. Thereafter, we stood on

SOURCE: Samuel I. Rosenman, ed., *The Public Papers and Addresses of Franklin D. Roosevelt*, IX, *Aid to the Democracies* (1941), 633–44.

guard in the Atlantic, with the British as neighbors. There was no treaty. There was no "unwritten agreement."

And yet, there was the feeling, proven correct by history, that we as neighbors could settle any disputes in peaceful fashion. The fact is that during the whole of this time the Western Hemisphere has remained free from aggression from Europe or from Asia.

Does anyone seriously believe that we need to fear attack anywhere in the Americas while a free Britain remains our most powerful naval neighbor in the Atlantic? Does anyone seriously believe, on the other hand, that we could rest easy if the Axis powers were our neighbors there?

If Great Britain goes down, the Axis powers will control the continents of Europe, Asia, Africa, Australasia, and the high seas—and they will be in a position to bring enormous military and naval resources against this hemisphere. It is no exaggeration to say that all of us, in all the Americas, would be living at the point of a gun—a gun loaded with explosive bullets, economic as well as military.

We should enter upon a new and terrible era in which the whole world, our hemisphere included, would be run by threats of brute force. To survive in such a world, we would have to convert ourselves permanently into a militaristic power on the basis of war economy.

Frankly and definitely there is danger ahead—danger against which we must prepare. But we well know that we cannot escape danger, or the fear of danger, by crawling into bed and pulling the covers over our heads.

Some nations of Europe were bound by solemn non-intervention pacts with Germany. Other nations were assured by Germany that they need never fear invasion. Non-intervention pact or not, the fact remains that they were attacked, overrun and thrown into the modern form of slavery at an hour's notice, or even without any notice at all. As an exiled leader of one of these nations said to me the other day, "The notice was a minus quality. It was given

to my Government two hours after German troops had poured into my country in a hundred places."

The fate of these nations tells us what it means to live at the point of a Nazi gun.

The Nazis have justified such actions by various pious frauds. One of these frauds is the claim that they are occupying a nation for the purpose of "restoring order." Another is that they are occupying or controlling a nation on the excuse that they are "protecting it" against the aggression of somebody else.

There are those who say that the Axis powers would never have any desire to attack the Western Hemisphere. That is the same dangerous form of wishful thinking which has destroyed the powers of resistance of so many conquered peoples. The plain facts are that the Nazis have proclaimed, time and again, that all other races are their inferiors and therefore subject to their orders. And most important of all, the vast resources and wealth of this American Hemisphere constitute the most tempting loot in all the round world.

Let us no longer blind ourselves to the undeniable fact that the evil forces which have crushed and undermined and corrupted so many others are already within our own gates. Your Government knows much about them and every day is ferreting them out. . . .

There are also American citizens, many of them in high places, who, unwittingly in most cases, are aiding and abetting the work of these agents. I do not charge the American citizens with being foreign agents. But I do charge them with doing exactly the kind of work that the dictators want done in the United States.

These people not only believe that we can save our own skins by shutting our eyes to the fate of other nations. Some of them go much further than that. They say that we can and should become the friends and even the partners of the Axis powers. Some of them even suggest that we should imitate the methods of the dictatorships. Americans never can and never will do that.

The experience of the past two years has proven beyond doubt that no nation can appease the Nazis. Not many can tame a tiger into a kitten by stroking it. There can be no appeasement with ruthlessness. There can be no reasoning with an incendiary bomb. We know now that a nation can have peace with the Nazis only at the price of total surrender.

Even the people of Italy have been forced to become accomplices of the Nazis; but at this moment they do not know how soon they will be embraced to death by their allies.

The American appeasers ignore the warning to be found in the fate of Austria, Czechoslovakia, Poland, Norway, Belgium, the Netherlands, Denmark, and France. They tell you that the Axis powers are going to win anyway, that all this bloodshed in the world could be saved; that the United States might just as well throw its influence into the scale of a dictated peace, and get the most out of it that we can.

They call it a "negotiated peace." Nonsense! Is it a negotiated peace if a gang of outlaws surrounds your community and on threat of extermination makes you pay tribute to save your own skins?

Such a dictated peace would be no peace at all. It would be only another armistice, leading to the most gigantic armament race and the most devastating trade wars in all history. And in these contests the Americas would offer the only real resistance to the Axis powers.

With all their vaunted efficiency, with all their parade of pious purpose in this war, there are still in their background the concentration camp and the servants of God in chains.

The history of recent years proves that shootings and chains and concentration camps are not simply the transient tools but the very altars of modern dictatorship. They may talk of a "new order" in the world, but what they have in mind is only a revival of the oldest and the worst tyranny. In that there is no liberty, no religion, no hope. The proposed "new order" is the very opposite of a United States of Europe or a United States of Asia. It is not a Government based upon the consent of the governed.

It is not a union of the ordinary, self-respecting men and women to protect themselves and their freedom and their dignity from oppression. It is an unholy alliance of power and pelf to dominate and enslave the human race.

The British people and their allies today are conducting an active war against this unholy alliance. Our own future security is greatly dependent on the outcome of that fight. Our ability to "keep out of war" is going to be affected by that outcome. Thinking in terms of today and tomorrow, I make the direct statement to the American people that there is far less chance of the United States getting into war if we do all we can now to support the nations defending themselves against attack by the Axis than if we acquiesce in their defeat, submit tamely to an Axis victory, and wait our turn to be the object of attack in another war later on.

If we are to be completely honest with ourselves, we must admit that there is risk in any course we may take. But I deeply believe that the great majority of our people agree that the course that I advocate involves the least risk now and the greatest hope for world peace in the future.

The people of Europe who are defending themselves do not ask us to do their fighting. They ask us for the implements of war, the planes, the tanks, the guns, the freighters which will enable them to fight for their liberty and for our security. Emphatically we must get these weapons to them in sufficient volume and quickly enough so that we and our children will be saved the agony and suffering of war which others have had to endure.

Let not the defeatists tell us that it is too late. It will never be earlier. Tomorrow will be later than today.

Certain facts are self-evident.

In a military sense Great Britain and the British Empire are today the spearhead of resistance to world conquest. They are putting up a fight which will live forever in the story of human gallantry.

There is no demand for sending an American Expeditionary Force outside our own borders. There is no intention by any member of your Government to send such a force. You can, therefore, nail any talk about sending armies to Europe as deliberate untruth.

Our national policy is not directed toward war. Its sole purpose is to keep war away from our country and our people.

Democracy's fight against world conquest is being greatly aided, and must be more greatly aided, by the rearmament of the United States and by sending every ounce and every ton of munitions and supplies that we can possibly spare to help the defenders who are in the front lines. It is no more unneutral for us to do that than it is for Sweden, Russia and other nations near Germany to send steel and ore and oil and other war materials into Germany every day in the week.

We are planning our own defense with the utmost urgency; and in its vast scale we must integrate the war needs of Britain and the other free nations which are resisting aggression.

This is not a matter of sentiment or of controversial personal opinion. It is a matter of realistic, practical military policy, based on the advice of our military experts who are in close touch with existing warfare. These military and naval experts and the members of the Congress and the Administration have a single-minded purpose—the defense of the United States.

This nation is making a great effort to produce everything that is necessary in this emergency—and with all possible speed. This great effort requires great sacrifice. . . .

We must be the great arsenal of democracy. For us this is an emergency as serious as war itself. We must apply ourselves to our task with the same resolution, the same sense of urgency, the same spirit of patriotism and sacrifice as we would show were we at war.

We have furnished the British great material support and we will furnish far more in the future.

There will be no "bottlenecks" in our determination to aid Great Britain. No dictator, no combination of dictators, will weaken that determination by threats of how they will construe that determination.

The British have received invaluable military support from the heroic Greek army, and from the forces of all the governments in exile. Their strength is growing. It is the strength of men and women who value their freedom more highly than they value their lives.

I believe that the Axis powers are not going to win this war. I base that belief on the latest and best information.

We have no excuse for defeatism. We have every good reason for hope—hope for peace, hope for the defense of our civilization and for the building of a better civilization in the future.

I have the profound conviction that the American people are now determined to put forth a mightier effort than they have ever yet made to increase our production of all the implements of defense, to meet the threat to our democratic faith.

As President of the United States I call for that national effort. I call for it in the name of this nation which we love and honor and which we are privileged and proud to serve. I call upon our people with absolute confidence that our common cause will greatly succeed.

DOCUMENT 4.2

CHARLES LINDBERGH, "WE CANNOT WIN THIS WAR FOR ENGLAND," MAY 1941

I know I will be severely criticized by the interventionists in America when I say we should not enter a war unless we have a reasonable chance of winning. That, they will claim, is far too materialistic a standpoint. . . . But I do not believe that our American ideals, and our way of life, will gain through an unsuccessful war. And I know that the United States is not prepared to wage war in Europe successfully at this time. . . .

I have said before, and I will say again, that I believe it will be a tragedy to the entire world if the British Empire collapses. That is one of the

SOURCE: *Vital Speeches of the Day* (May 1941), 424–26.

main reasons why I opposed this war before it was declared, and why I have constantly advocated a negotiated peace. I did not feel that England and France had a reasonable chance of winning. France has now been defeated; and . . . it is now obvious that England is losing the war. I believe this is realized even by the British Government. But they have one last desperate plan remaining. They hope that they may be able to persuade us to send another American Expeditionary Force to Europe and to share with England militarily, as well as financially, the fiasco of this war.

I do not blame England for this hope, or for asking for our assistance. . . . But we in this country have a right to think of the welfare of America first, just as the people in England thought first of their own country when they encouraged the smaller nations of Europe to fight against hopeless odds. When England asks us to enter this war, she is considering her own future, and that of her empire. In making our reply, I believe we should consider the future of the United States and that of the Western Hemisphere.

It is not only our right, but it is our obligation as American citizens to look at this war objectively and to weigh our chances for success if we should enter it. I have attempted to do this, especially from the standpoint of aviation; and I have been forced to the conclusion that we cannot win this war for England, regardless of how much assistance we send. . . .

There is a policy open to this nation that will lead to success—a policy that leaves us free to allow our own way of life, and to develop our own civilization. It is not a new and untried idea. It was advocated by Washington. It was incorporated in the Monroe Doctrine. Under its guidance, the United States has become the greatest nation in the world.

It is based on the belief that the security of a nation lies in the strength and character of its own people. It recommends the maintenance of armed forces sufficient to defend this hemisphere from attack by any combination of foreign powers. It demands faith in an independent American destiny. This is the policy of the American First Committee today. It is a policy not of isolation, but of independence; not of defeat, but of courage. It is a policy that led this nation to success during the most trying years of our history, and it is a policy that will lead us to success again. We have weakened ourselves for many months, and still worse, we have divided our own people by this dabbling in Europe's wars. While we should have been concentrating on American defense we have been forced to argue over foreign quarrels. We must turn our eyes and our faith back to our own country before it is too late. . . .

The United States is better situated from a military standpoint than any other nation in the world. Even in our present condition of unpreparedness no foreign power is in a position to invade us today. If we concentrate on our own defenses and build the strength that this nation should maintain, no foreign army will ever attempt to land on American shores.

War is not inevitable for this country. Such a claim is defeatism in the true sense. No one can make us fight abroad unless we ourselves are willing to do so. No one will attempt to fight us here if we arm ourselves as a great nation should be armed. Over a hundred million people in this nation are opposed to entering the war. If the principles of democracy mean anything at all, that is reason enough for us to stay out. If we are forced into a war against the wishes of an overwhelming majority of our people, we will have proved democracy such a failure at home that there will be little use fighting for it abroad.

The time has come when those of us who believe in an independent American destiny must band together and organize for strength. . . .

These people—the majority of hardworking American citizens, are with us. They are the true strength of our country. And they are beginning to realize as you and I, that there are times when we must sacrifice our normal interests in life in order to insure the safety and the welfare of our nation. . . .

If you believe in an independent destiny for America, if you believe that this country should not enter the war in Europe, we ask you to join the America First Committee in its stand. We ask you to share our faith in the ability of this nation to defend itself, to develop its own civilization, and to contribute to the progress of mankind in a more constructive and intelligent way than has yet been found by the warring nations of Europe. We need your support, and we need it now. The time to act is here. I thank you.

DOCUMENT 4.3

THE ATLANTIC CHARTER, AUGUST 14, 1941

The President of the United States of America and the Prime Minister, Mr. Churchill, representing His Majesty's Government in the United Kingdom, being met together, deem it right to make known certain common principles in the national policies of their respective countries on which they base their hopes for a better future for the world.

First, their countries seek no aggrandizement, territorial or other;

Second, they desire to see no territorial changes that do not accord with the freely expressed wishes of the peoples concerned;

Third, they respect the right of all peoples to choose the form of government under which they will live; and they wish to see sovereign rights and self-government restored to those who have been forcibly deprived of them;

SOURCE: Samuel I. Rosenman, ed., *The Public Papers and Addresses of Franklin D. Roosevelt*, X, *Call to Battle Stations* (1950), 31.

Fourth, they will endeavor, with due respect for their existing obligations, to further the enjoyment by all states, great or small, victor or vanquished, of access, on equal terms, to trade and to the raw materials of the world which are needed for their economic prosperity;

Fifth, they desire to bring about the fullest collaboration between all nations in the economic field with the object of securing, for all, improved labor standards, economic advancement and social security;

Sixth, after the final destruction of the Nazi tyranny, they hope to see established a peace which will afford to all nations the means of dwelling in safety within their own boundaries, and which will afford assurance that all the men in all the lands may live out their lives in freedom from fear and want;

Seventh, such a peace should enable all men to traverse the high seas and oceans without hindrance;

Eighth, they believe that all of the nations of the world, for realistic as well as spiritual reasons must come to the abandonment of the use of force. Since no future peace can be maintained if land, sea or air armaments continue to be employed by nations which threaten, or may threaten, aggression outside of their frontiers, they believe, pending the establishment of a wider and permanent system of general security, that the disarmament of such nations is essential. They will likewise aid and encourage all other practicable measures which will lighten for peace-loving peoples the crushing burden of armaments.

FRANKLIN D. ROOSEVELT
WINSTON S. CHURCHILL

4.4 **FDR Responds to the *Greer* Incident, September 11, 1941**

Well before the American people realized it, the U.S. Navy was at war with Germany in the Atlantic. Even before the Atlantic Charter was signed in Newfoundland in August 1941, the navy was engaged in escorting convoys through the western Atlantic as far as Iceland, where they could be picked up by the Royal Navy. At the same time, U.S. destroyers often shadowed German U-boats until British ships could be called in for the kill. As the U.S. Navy became more and more involved in operations in the Atlantic it seemed certain that some sort of military event was inevitable. It seems probable that Roosevelt may have sought an incident to induce America's entrance into the war.

On September 4, the *USS Greer* began shadowing a German U-boat in the North Atlantic. After a British plane dropped depth charges on the U-boat, the Germans fired a torpedo at the *Greer*. The shot missed. The *Greer* responded with depth charges. They also missed.

With a few omissions and adjustments in the story to make his case more credible, Roosevelt responded with a message to the nation on September 11 (*Document 4.4*). Often called his "Shoot on Sight Speech," Roosevelt made it clear that the U.S. Navy was about to become more active in the Atlantic. Generally, the American public supported FDR's tough line. In mid-October, a German torpedo hit the *USS. Kearney* while it was on escort duty near Iceland. The *Kearney* survived the attack. Then on October 31 the *Ruben James* was sunk west of Iceland. Congress responded by amending the neutrality acts to allow merchant ships operating in the North Atlantic to carry arms. The U.S. was taking short steps toward war with Germany.

....

DOCUMENT 4.4

FDR RESPONDS TO THE *GREER* INCIDENT, SEPTEMBER 11, 1941

My fellow Americans:
    The Navy Department of the United States has reported to me that on the morning of September 4 the United States destroyer *Greer*, proceeding in full daylight toward Iceland, had reached a point southeast of Greenland. She was carrying American mail to Iceland. She was flying the American flag. Her identity as an American ship was unmistakable.

SOURCE: *New York Times*, October 31, 1948.

She was then and there attacked by a submarine. Germany admits that it was a German submarine. The submarine deliberately fired a torpedo at the *Greer*, followed later by another torpedo attack. In spite of what Hitler's propaganda bureau has invented, and in spite of what any American obstructionist organization may prefer to believe, I tell you the blunt fact that the German submarine fired first upon this American destroyer without warning, and with deliberate design to sink her.

Our destroyer, at the time, was in waters which the Government of the United States had declared to be waters of self-defense-surrounding outposts of American protection in the Atlantic. . . .

This was piracy—legally and morally. It was not the first nor the last act of piracy which the Nazi government has committed against the American flag in this war. Attack has followed attack. . . .

In the face of all this, we Americans are keeping our feet on the ground. Our type of democratic civilization has outgrown the thought of feeling compelled to fight some other nation by reason of any single piratical attack on one of our ships. We are not becoming hysterical or losing our sense of proportion. Therefore, what I am thinking and saying does not relate to any isolated episode.

Instead, we Americans are taking a long-range point of view in regard to certain fundamentals and to a series of events on land and on sea which must be considered as a whole— as a part of a world pattern. It would be unworthy of a great nation to exaggerate an isolated incident, or to become inflamed by some one act of violence. But it would be inexcusable folly to minimize such incidents in the face of evidence which makes it clear that the incident is not isolated, but part of a general plan.

The important truth is that these acts of international lawlessness are a manifestation of a design which has been made clear to the American people for a long time. It is the Nazi design to abolish the freedom of the seas, and to acquire absolute control and domination of the seas for themselves.

For with control of the seas in their own hands, the way can become clear for their next step—domination of the United States and the Western Hemisphere by force. Under Nazi control of the seas, no merchant ship of the United States or of any other American republic would be free to carry on any peaceful commerce, except by the condescending grace of this foreign and tyrannical power. The Atlantic Ocean which has been, and which should always be, a free and friendly highway for us would then become a deadly menace to the commerce of the United States, to the coasts of the United States, and to the inland cities of the United States. . . .

To be ultimately successful in world mastery Hitler knows that he must get control of the seas. He must first destroy the bridge of ships which we are building across the Atlantic, over which we shall continue to roll the implements of war to help destroy him and all his works in the end. He must wipe out our patrol on sea and in the air. He must silence the British Navy.

It must be explained again and again to people who like to think of the United States Navy as an invincible protection that this can be true only if the British Navy survives. That is simple arithmetic. For if the world outside the Americas falls under Axis domination, the shipbuilding facilities which the Axis Powers would then possess in all of Europe, in the British Isles, and in the Far East would be much greater than all the shipbuilding facilities and potentialities of all the Americas—not only greater but two or three times greater. Even if the United States threw all its resources into such a situation, seeking to double and even redouble the size of our Navy, the Axis Powers, in control of the rest of the world, would have the manpower and the physical resources to out-build us several times over.

It is time for all Americans of all the Americas to stop being deluded by the romantic notion that the Americas can go on living happily and peacefully in a Nazi-dominated world. . . .

It is now clear that Hitler has begun his campaign to control the seas by ruthless force and by wiping out every vestige of international law and humanity. His intention has been made clear. The American people can have no further illusions about it. No tender whisperings of appeasers that Hitler is not interested in the Western Hemisphere, no soporific lullabies that a wide ocean protects us from him can long have any effect on the hard-headed, farsighted, and realistic American people. . . .

This attack on the *Greer* was no localized military operation in the North Atlantic. This was no mere episode in a struggle between two nations. This was one determined step toward creating a permanent world system based on force, terror, and murder.

And I am sure that even now the Nazis are waiting to see whether the United States will by silence give them the green light to go ahead on this path of destruction.

The Nazi danger to our western world has long ceased to be a mere possibility. The danger is here now—not only from a military enemy, but from an enemy of all law, all liberty, all morality, all religion.

There has now come a time when you and I must see the cold, inexorable necessity of saying to these inhuman, unrestrained seekers of world conquest and permanent world domination by the sword, "You seek to throw our children and our children's children into your form of terrorism and slavery. You have now attacked our own safety. You shall go no further."

Normal practices of diplomacy—note writing—are of no possible use in dealing with international outlaws who sink our ships and kill our citizens. One peaceful nation after another has met disaster because each refused to look the Nazi danger squarely in the eye until it actually had them by the throat. The United States will not make that fatal mistake. . . .

We have sought no shooting war with Hitler. We do not seek it now. But, neither do we want peace so much that we are willing to pay for it by permitting him to attack our naval and merchant ships while they are on legitimate business.

I assume that the German leaders are not deeply concerned by what we Americans say or publish about them. We cannot bring about the downfall of Naziism by the use of long-range invectives. But when you see a rattlesnake poised to strike you do not wait until he has struck before you crush him.

These Nazi submarines and raiders are the rattlesnakes of the Atlantic. They are a menace to the free pathways of the high seas. They are a challenge to our sovereignty. They hammer at our most precious rights when they attack ships of the American flag—symbols of our independence, our freedom, our very life. . . .

Do not let us split hairs. Let us not ask ourselves whether the Americas should begin to defend themselves after the fifth attack, or the tenth attack, or the twentieth attack. The time for active defense is now.

Do not let us split hairs. Let us not say, "We will only defend ourselves if the torpedo succeeds in getting home, or if the crew and the passengers are drowned." This is the time for prevention of attack. . . .

In the waters which we deem necessary for our defense American naval vessels and American planes will no longer wait until Axis submarines lurking under the water, or Axis raiders on the surface of the sea, strike their deadly blow-first.

Upon our naval and air patrol—now operating in large numbers over a vast expanse of the Atlantic Ocean—falls the duty of maintaining the American policy of freedom of the seas—now. That means very simply and clearly, that our patrolling vessels and planes will protect all merchant ships—not only American ships but ships of any flag—engaged in commerce in our defensive waters. They will protect them from submarines; they will protect them from surface raiders. . . .

My obligation as President is historic; it is clear. It is inescapable.

It is no act of war on our part when we decide to protect the seas which are vital to American defense. The aggression is not ours. Ours is solely defense.

But let this warning be clear. From now on, if German or Italian vessels of war enter the waters, the protection of which is necessary for American defense, they do so at their own peril.

The orders which I have given as Commander in Chief to the United States Army and Navy are to carry out that policy—at once.

The sole responsibility rests upon Germany. There will be no shooting unless Germany continues to seek it.

That is my obvious duty in this crisis. That is the clear right of this sovereign Nation. That is the only step possible, if we would keep tight the wall of defense which we are pledged to maintain around this Western Hemisphere. . . .

The American people have faced other grave crises in their history—with American courage and American resolution. They will do no less today. They know the actualities of the attacks upon us. They know the necessities of a bold defense against these attacks. They know that the times call for clear heads and fearless hearts.

And with that inner strength that comes to a free people conscious of their duty and of the righteousness of what they do, they will—with Divine help and guidance—stand their ground against this latest assault upon their democracy, their sovereignty, and their freedom.

4.5 Memorandum Handed by the Japanese Ambassador (Nomura) to the Secretary of State at 2:20 P.M., December 7, 1941

4.6 FDR's Roosevelt's War Message to Congress, December 8, 1941.

In February 1941 Japan sent a negotiator to the United States, Admiral Kichisaburo Nomura. But Japan's continued encroachments in East Asia made negotiations between Nomura and Secretary of State Cordell Hull nearly impossible. These talks, Hull later wrote, seemed "to come to a certain point and then start going around and around in the same circle." In July, when Japan invaded Indochina, the United States and Britain responded by freezing Japanese assets and insisting that Japan end its war in Asia. From that the Japanese government concluded that war with the United States was inevitable.

On December 7, Nomura delivered a note to Hull explaining Japan's position on the unfolding events in the Pacific. The note (*Document 4.5*) was intended as a declaration of war. Nomura had been instructed by his foreign office in Tokyo to burn his codebooks and deliver the message at 1:00 P.M. Washington time, 7:00 A.M. in Hawaii. Because typists in Nomura's office had difficulty decoding the message from Tokyo, Normura did not deliver the message to Hull until 2:20. The attack on Pearl Harbor had already begun. Hull had, in fact, seen the message as a result of U.S. decoding, but because he did not perceive it as a formal declaration he did nothing about it. After he read the note in Nomura's presence, Hull told Nomura, "In all my fifty years of service I have never seen a document that was more crowded with infamous falsehoods and distortions . . . on a scale so huge that I never imagined until today that any Government on this planet was capable of uttering them."

The Japanese attack on Pearl Harbor in Hawaii on that morning was intended to deliver a crippling blow that might even damage the American will to fight a war in the Pacific. On the same day Japan struck American installations in the Philippines along with several British colonial outposts in Southeast Asia. The attack was devastating. It quieted the isolationists in Congress, and it dragged the United States into the second major world war of the twentieth century. *Document 4.6* is President Roosevelt's impassioned war message to Congress, delivered the day after the attack.

DOCUMENT 4.5

MEMORANDUM HANDED BY THE JAPANESE AMBASSADOR (NOMURA) TO THE SECRETARY OF STATE AT 2:20 P.M., December 7, 1941

The Government of Japan, prompted by a genuine desire to come to an amicable understanding with the Government of the United States in order that the two countries by their joint efforts may secure the peace of the Pacific Area and thereby contribute toward the realization of world peace, has continued negotiations with the utmost sincerity since April last with the Government of the United States regarding the adjustment and advancement of Japanese-American relations and the stabilization of the Pacific Area.

The Japanese Government has the honor to state frankly its views concerning the claims the American Government has persistently maintained as well as the measures the United States and Great Britain have taken toward Japan during these eight months.

It is the immutable policy of the Japanese Government to insure the stability of East Asia and to promote world peace and thereby to enable all nations to find each its proper place in the world.

Ever since the China Affair broke out owing to the failure on the part of China to comprehend Japan's true intentions, the Japanese Government has striven for the restoration of peace and it has consistently exerted its best efforts to prevent the extension of war-like disturbances. It was also to that end that in September last year Japan concluded the Tripartite Pact with Germany and Italy.

However, both the United States and Great Britain have resorted to every possible measure to assist the Chungking regime so as to obstruct the establishment of a general peace be-

tween Japan and China, interfering with Japan's constructive endeavours toward the stabilization of East Asia. Exerting pressure on the Netherlands East Indies, or menacing French Indo-China, they have attempted to frustrate Japan's aspiration to the ideal of common prosperity in cooperation with these regions. Furthermore, when Japan in accordance with its protocol with France took measures of joint defence of French Indo-China, both American and British Governments, willfully misinterpreting it as a threat to their own possessions, and inducing the Netherlands Government to follow suit, they enforced the assets freezing order, thus severing economic relations with Japan. While manifesting thus an obviously hostile attitude, these countries have strengthened their military preparations perfecting an encirclement of Japan, and have brought about a situation which endangers the very existence of the Empire.

Nevertheless, to facilitate a speedy settlement, the Premier of Japan proposed, in August last, to meet the President of the United States for a discussion of important problems between the two countries covering the entire Pacific area. However, the American Government, while accepting in principle the Japanese proposal, insisted that the meeting should take place after an agreement of view had been reached on fundamental and essential questions.

Subsequently, on September 25th the Japanese Government submitted a proposal based on the formula proposed by the American Government, taking fully into consideration past American claims and also incorporating Japanese views. Repeated discussions proved of no avail in producing readily an agreement of view. The present cabinet, therefore, submitted a revised proposal, moderating still further the Japanese claims regarding the principal points of difficulty in the negotiation and endeavoured strenuously to reach a settlement. But the American Government, adhering steadfastly to its original assertions, failed to display in the slightest degree a spirit of conciliation. The negotiation made no progress.

SOURCE: U.S. Department of State, *Peace and War: United States Foreign Policy, 1931–1941* (Washington: US-GPO, 1943), 830–37.

Therefore, the Japanese Government, with a view to doing its utmost for averting a crisis in Japanese-American relations, submitted on November 20th still another proposal in order to arrive at an equitable solution of the more essential and urgent questions which, simplifying its previous proposal, stipulated the following points:

1. The Governments of Japan and the United States undertake not to dispatch armed forces into any of the regions, excepting French Indo-China, in the Southeastern Asia and the Southern Pacific area.
2. Both Governments shall cooperate with the view to securing the acquisition in the Netherlands East Indies of those goods and commodities of which the two countries are in need.
3. Both Governments mutually undertake to restore commercial relations to those prevailing prior to freezing of assets. The Government of the United States shall supply Japan the required quantity of oil.
4. The Government of the United States undertakes not to resort to measures and actions prejudicial to the endeavours for the restoration of general peace between Japan and China.
5. The Japanese Government undertakes to withdraw troops now stationed in French Indo-China upon either the restoration of peace between Japan and China or the establishment of an equitable peace in the Pacific Area; and it is prepared to remove the Japanese troops in the southern part of French Indo-China to the northern part upon the conclusion of the present agreement.

As regards China, the Japanese Government, while expressing its readiness to accept the offer of the President of the United States to act as "introducer" of peace between Japan and China as was previously suggested, asked for an undertaking on the part of the United States to do nothing prejudicial to the restoration of Sino-Japanese peace when the two parties have commenced direct negotiations.

The American Government not only rejected the above-mentioned new proposal, but made known its intention to continue its aid to Chiang Kai-shek; and in spite of its suggestion mentioned above, withdrew the offer of the President to act as so-called "introducer" of peace between Japan and China, pleading that time was not yet ripe for it. Finally on November 26th, in an attitude to impose upon the Japanese Government those principles it has persistently maintained, the American Government made a proposal totally ignoring Japanese claims, which is a source of profound regret to the Japanese government.

From the beginning of the present negotiation the Japanese Government has always maintained an attitude of fairness and moderation, and did its best to reach a settlement, for which it made all possible concessions often in spite of great difficulties. As for the China question which constituted an important subject of the negotiation, the Japanese Government showed a most conciliatory attitude. As for the principle of non-discrimination in international commerce, advocated by the American Government, the Japanese Government expressed its desire to see the said principle applied throughout the world, and declared that along with the actual practice of this principle in the world, the Japanese Government would endeavour to apply the same in the Pacific Area including China, and made it clear that Japan had no intention of excluding from China economic activities of third powers pursued on an equitable basis. Furthermore, as regards the question of withdrawing troops from French Indo-China, the Japanese Government even volunteered, as mentioned above, to carry out an immediate evacuation of troops from Southern French Indo-China as a measure of easing the situation.

It is presumed that the spirit of conciliation exhibited to the utmost degree by the Japanese Government in all these matters is fully appreciated by the American Government.

On the other hand, the American Government, always holding fast to theories in disregard of realities, and refusing to yield an inch on its impractical principles, caused undue delay in the negotiation. It is difficult to understand this attitude of the American Government and the Japanese Government desires to call the attention of the American Government especially to the following points:

1. The American Government advocates in the name of world peace those principles favorable to it and urges upon the Japanese Government the acceptance thereof. The peace of the world may be brought about only by discovering a mutually acceptable formula through recognition of the reality of the situation and mutual appreciation of one another's position. An attitude such as ignores realities and imposes one's selfish views upon others will scarcely serve the purpose of facilitating the consummation of negotiations.

    Of the various principles put forward by the American Government as a basis of the Japanese-American Agreement, there are some which the Japanese Government is ready to accept in principle, but in view of the world's actual conditions, it seems only a utopian ideal on the part of the American Government to attempt to force their immediate adoption.

    Again, the proposal to conclude a multilateral non-aggression pact between Japan, United States, Great Britain, China, the Soviet Union, the Netherlands and Thailand, which is patterned after the old concept of collective security, is far removed from the realities of East Asia.

2. The American proposal contained a stipulation which states: "Both Governments will agree that no agreement, which either has concluded with any third power or powers, shall be interpreted by it in such a way as to conflict with the fundamental purpose of this agreement, the establishment and preservation of peace throughout the Pacific area." It is presumed that the above provision has been proposed with a view to restrain Japan from fulfilling its obligations under the Tripartite Pact when the United States participates in the War in Europe, and, as such, it cannot be accepted by the Japanese Government.

    The American Government, obsessed with its own views and opinions, may be said to be scheming for the extension of the war. While it seeks, on the one hand, to secure its rear by stabilizing the Pacific Area, it is engaged, on the other hand, in aiding Great Britain and preparing to attack, in the name of self-defense, Germany and Italy, two Powers that are striving to establish a new order in Europe. Such a policy is totally at variance with the many principles upon which the American Government proposes to found the stability of the Pacific Area through peaceful means.

3. Whereas the American Government, under the principles it rigidly upholds, objects to settle international issues through military pressure, it is exercising in conjunction with Great Britain and other nations pressure by economic power. Recourse to such pressure as a means of dealing with international relations should be condemned as it is at times more inhumane than military pressure.

4. It is impossible not to reach the conclusion that the American Government desires to maintain and strengthen, in coalition with Great Britain and other Powers, its dominant position it has hitherto occupied not only in China but in other areas of East Asia. It is a fact of history that the countries of East Asia for the past hundred years or more have been compelled to observe the status quo under the Anglo-American policy of imperialistic exploitation and to sacrifice themselves to the prosperity of the two nations. The Japanese Government cannot tolerate the perpetuation of such a situation since it

directly runs counter to Japan's fundamental policy to enable all nations to enjoy each its proper place in the world.

The stipulation proposed by the American Government relative to French Indo-China is a good exemplification of the above-mentioned American policy: Thus the six countries,—Japan, the United States, Great Britain, the Netherlands, China and Thailand,—excepting France, should undertake among themselves to respect the territorial integrity and sovereignty of French Indo-China and equality of treatment in trade and commerce would be tantamount to placing that territory under the joint guarantee of the Governments of those six countries. Apart from the fact that such a proposal totally ignores the position of France, it is unacceptable to the Japanese Government in that such an arrangement cannot but be considered as an extension to French Indo-China of a system similar to the Nine Power Treaty structure which is the chief factor responsible for the present predicament of East Asia.

5. All the items demanded of Japan by the American Government regarding China such as wholesale evacuation of troops or unconditional application of the principle of non-discrimination in international commerce ignored the actual conditions of China, and are calculated to destroy Japan's position as the stabilizing factor of East Asia. The attitude of the American Government in demanding Japan not to support militarily, politically or economically any regime other than the regime at Chungking, disregarding thereby the existence of the Nanking Government, shatters the very basis of the present negotiation. This demand of the American Government falling, as it does, in line with its above-mentioned refusal to cease from aiding the Chungking regime, demonstrates clearly the intention of the American Government to ob-

struct the restoration of normal relations between Japan and China and the return of peace to East Asia.

In brief, the American proposal contains certain acceptable items such as those concerning commerce, including the conclusion of a trade agreement, mutual removal of the freezing restrictions, and stabilization of yen and dollar exchange, or the abolition of extra-territorial rights in China. On the other hand, however, the proposal in question ignores Japan's sacrifices in the four years of the China Affair, menaces the Empire's existence itself and disparages its honour and prestige. Therefore, viewed in its entirety, the Japanese Government regrets that it cannot accept the proposal as a basis of negotiation.

The Japanese Government, in its desire for an early conclusion of the negotiation, proposed simultaneously with the conclusion of the Japanese-American negotiation, agreements to be signed with Great Britain and other interested countries. The proposal was accepted by the American Government. However, since the American Government has made the proposal of November 26th as a result of frequent consultation with Great Britain, Australia, the Netherlands and Chungking, and presumably by catering to the wishes of the Chungking regime in the questions of China, it must be concluded that all these countries are at one with the United States in ignoring Japan's position.

Obviously it is the intention of the American Government to conspire with Great Britain and other countries to obstruct Japan's efforts toward the establishment of peace through the creation of a new order in East Asia, and especially to preserve Anglo-American rights and interests by keeping Japan and China at war. This intention has been revealed clearly during the course of the present negotiation. Thus, the earnest hope of the Japanese Government to adjust Japanese-American relations and to preserve and promote the peace of the Pacific through cooperation with the American Government has finally been lost.

The Japanese Government regrets to have to notify hereby the American Government that in view of the attitude of the American Government it cannot but consider that it is impossible to reach an agreement through further negotiations.

[WASHINGTON,] December 7, 1941.

DOCUMENT 4.6

FDR'S WAR MESSAGE TO CONGRESS, DECEMBER 8, 1941

Yesterday, December 7, 1941—a date which will live in infamy—the United States of America was suddenly and deliberately attacked by naval and air forces of the empire of Japan.

The United States was at peace with that nation and, at the solicitation of Japan, was still in conversation with its government and its Emperor looking toward the maintenance of peace in the Pacific.

Indeed, one hour after Japanese air squadrons had commenced bombing Oahu the Japanese Ambassador to the United States and his colleague delivered to our Secretary of State a formal reply to a recent American message. While this reply stated that it seemed useless to continue the existing diplomatic negotiations, it contained no threat or hint of war or armed attack.

It will be recorded that the distance of Hawaii from Japan makes it obvious that the attack was deliberately planned many days or even weeks ago. During the intervening time the Japanese Government has deliberately sought to deceive the United States by false statements and expressions of hope for continued peace.

The attack yesterday on the Hawaiian Islands has caused severe damage to American naval and military forces. Very many American lives have been lost. In addition American ships have been reported torpedoed on the high seas between San Francisco and Honolulu.

Yesterday the Japanese Government also launched an attack against Malaya.

Last night Japanese forces attacked Hong Kong.

Last night Japanese forces attacked Guam.

Last night Japanese forces attacked the Philippine Islands.

Last night the Japanese attacked Wake Island.

This morning the Japanese attacked Midway Island.

Japan has, therefore, undertaken a surprise offensive extending throughout the Pacific area. The facts of yesterday speak for themselves. The people of the United States have already formed their opinions and well understand the implications to the very life and safety of our nation.

As Commander in Chief of the Army and Navy, I have directed that all measures be taken for our defense.

Always will we remember the character of the onslaught against us.

No matter how long it may take us to overcome this premeditated invasion, the American people in their righteous might will win through to absolute victory.

I believe I interpret the will of the Congress and of the people when I assert that we will not only defend ourselves to the uttermost but will make very certain that this form of treachery shall never endanger us again.

Hostilities exist. There is no blinking at the fact that our people, our territory and our interests are in grave danger.

With confidence in our armed forces—with the unbounded determination of our people—we will gain the inevitable triumph—so help us God.

I ask that the Congress declare that since the unprovoked and dastardly attack by Japan on Sunday, December 7, a state of war has existed between the United States and the Japanese Empire.

SOURCE: *Cong. Rec.,* 77th Cong. 1st sess., LXXXVII (pt. 9), p. 9519.

4.7 The Yalta Conference Accords, February 1945

There was probably no more disillusioning aspect of World War II than the failures at Yalta. The American people fought to free those who were under the oppressive thumb of fascist totalitarianism only to see large parts of Europe and Asia dominated by Soviet totalitarianism. In the years after the war, as the Cold War hardened, many Americans traced the postwar problems to Yalta, where, it seemed, Roosevelt had given away Eastern Europe and parts of Asia to the Soviets. It was not true, but Yalta has remained a sour note in the otherwise spectacular victory that was World War II.

The Yalta Accords were divided into nine sections: (1) the establishment of a world organization (that would later become the United Nations), (2) the "Declaration on Liberated Europe," (3) the dismemberment of postwar Germany, (4) reparations payments, (5) the trial of war criminals, and the future of specific regions of the world, including (6) Poland, (7) Iran, (8) Yugoslavia, and (9) Japan. Clearly, the purpose of the Accords was to restructure the postwar world. Included here in *Document 4.7* is the "Declaration on Liberated Europe," followed by the portions of the Accords dealing with postwar Poland and Japan.

The "Declaration on Liberated Europe" is an ambiguous and vaguely worded document calling for the formation of governments in Eastern Europe that would be "broadly representative of all democratic elements in the population and pledged to the earliest possible establishment through free elections of governments responsive to the will of the people." It was designed by Roosevelt mostly to convince Congress of the democratic nature of the Accords, and also for U.S. public consumption. Ultimately, it held no weight, and it bound Soviet Premier Josef Stalin to nothing.

Throughout the Yalta Conference, Roosevelt and Churchill argued for a democratic government in Poland. Stalin agreed, but he also made it clear that he would have a friendly government in Poland as a buffer between the Soviet Union and the West. When Churchill reminded Stalin that Britain had gone to war in 1939 to protect Poland's sovereignty, Stalin replied flatly: "The Prime Minister has said that for Great Britain the question of Poland is a question of honor. For Russia it is not only a question of honor but of security. . . . During the last thirty years our German enemy has passed through this corridor twice."

But with Poland in the hands of Soviet troops, Churchill and Roosevelt were in no position to argue effectively. The result was a compromise over the issue that was included in the Yalta Accords. There would be a "reorganized" Polish government made up of Lublin Poles (placed in power by the Soviets) and the London Poles (pro-Western Poles in exile). Stalin agreed in the Accords to allow "the inclusion of democratic leaders from Poland itself and from Poles abroad," and then to allow "free and unfettered elections." When the president returned to Washington his chief of staff, William Leahy, commented that the Russians could stretch the Yalta agreement on Poland "all the way from Yalta to Washington without technically breaking it." "I know, Bill," Roosevelt responded, "but it's the best I can do for Poland at this time."

The Yalta agreements pertaining to Japan were more easily resolved. FDR hoped to obtain Stalin's aid in defeating Japan, something the Soviet leader was willing to do in exchange for concessions in the Far East. Roosevelt considered this a bargain. Stalin would receive what imperial Russia had lost at the beginning of the century in the Russo-Japanese War: the Kurile Islands and southern Sakhalin Island. In addition, the Soviets would receive joint control, with the Chinese, of Manchuria's railways, and control of Port Arthur and Dairen (Lushun). The Yalta Accords also reflect Roosevelt's insistence that Stalin recognize Jiang Jieshi (Chiang Kai-shek) and the Nationalist Chinese as the only legitimate government in China. This was important to FDR's greater plan for East Asia because it denied Soviet support to Mao Zedong and the Chinese Communists. The Nationalists and the Communists had been locked in a bloody civil war since the late 1920s and it seemed certain that once the war against Japan ended the Chinese Civil War would resume. Roosevelt feared that a hot war in Asia between Communist and non-Communist forces might damage U.S.-Soviet relations—or worse, draw the United States and the U.S.S.R. into a third world war. He hoped that by pushing Stalin to support the Nationalist Chinese instead of the Communists, the Communists would be forced to join a coalition government with the Nationalists and a resumption of the Chinese Civil War would be averted. Ultimately, the plan failed because Jiang refused to join a coalition, while Mao and the Communists had developed enough strength (partly through clandestine Soviet aid) to defeat the Nationalists.

Roosevelt returned to the United States following Yalta and told Congress that the Big Three had agreed on all issues, especially on the question of democratic elections in Eastern Europe. The agreement, he said, would "bring order and security after the chaos of war, and . . . give some assurance of lasting peace among the nations of the world. . . ." *Time* magazine hailed the event: "By any standard, the Crimea Conference was a great achievement." Walter Lippmann chimed in: "There has been no more impressive international conference in our time." It seemed a triumph, which added to the nation's disillusionment when the Yalta accords broke down almost immediately. The agreements at Yalta had in no way bound Stalin to remove his troops from Eastern Europe, or to hold free elections there. Just two weeks after Yalta the Soviets placed a puppet government in Rumania and the failure of the conference became clear. Roosevelt wrote Stalin of his "astonishment," "anxiety," and "bitter resentment" over the situation, and he admonished the Soviet premier for not allowing elections in Poland. To Churchill, Roosevelt wrote of his growing distrust of Stalin and of his intentions to increase the pressure on the Soviets: "Our armies will in a very few days be in a position that will permit us to become 'tougher' than has heretofore appeared advantageous to the war effort." Just as the Soviet stranglehold on Eastern Europe grew tighter in mid-April, FDR died, taking with him the hope that goodwill would somehow shape a secure postwar world order.

DOCUMENT 4.7

THE YALTA CONFERENCE ACCORDS, FEBRUARY 1945

DECLARATION ON LIBERATED EUROPE

The following declaration has been approved:

The Premier of the Union of Soviet Socialist Republics, the Prime Minister of the United Kingdom and the President of the United States of America have consulted with each other in the common interests of the peoples of their countries and those of liberated Europe. They jointly declare their mutual agreement to concert during the temporary period of instability in liberated Europe the policies of their three Governments in assisting the peoples liberated from the domination of Nazi Germany and the peoples of the former Axis satellite states of Europe to solve by democratic means their pressing political and economic problems.

The establishment of order in Europe and the rebuilding of national economic life must be achieved by processes which will enable the liberated peoples to destroy the last vestiges of Nazism and fascism and to create democratic institutions of their own choice. This is a principle of the Atlantic Charter—the right of all peoples to choose the form of government under which they will live—the restoration of sovereign rights and self-government to those peoples who have been forcibly deprived of them by the aggressor nations.

To foster the conditions in which the liberated peoples may exercise these rights, the three Governments will jointly assist the people of any European liberated state or former Axis satellite state in Europe where, in their judgment conditions require, (a) to establish condi-

SOURCE: *Papers Relating to the Foreign Relations of the United States, 1945, The Conferences of Malta and Yalta* (1955), 975–84.

tions of internal peace; (b) to carry out emergency measures for the relief of distressed peoples; (c) to form interim governmental authorities broadly representative of all democratic elements in the population and pledged to the earliest possible establishment through free elections of Governments responsive to the will of the people; and (d) to facilitate where necessary the holding of such elections. . . .

When, in the opinion of the three Governments, conditions in any European liberated state or former Axis satellite state in Europe make such action necessary, they will immediately consult together on the measures necessary to discharge the joint responsibilities set forth in this declaration.

By this declaration we reaffirm our faith in the principles of the Atlantic Charter, our pledge in the Declaration by the United Nations and our determination to build in cooperation with other peace-loving nations world order, under law, dedicated to peace, security, freedom and general well-being of all mankind. . . .

POLAND

The following declaration on Poland was agreed to by the conference:

A new situation has been created in Poland as a result of her complete liberation by the Red Army. This calls for the establishment of a Polish Provisional Government which can be more broadly based than was possible before the recent liberation of the western part of Poland. The Provisional Government which is now functioning in Poland should therefore be reorganized on a broader democratic basis with the inclusion of democratic leaders from Poland itself and from Poles abroad. This new Government should then be called the Polish Provisional Government of National Unity.

M. Molotov, Mr. Harriman and Sir A. Clark Kerr are authorized as a commission to consult in the first instance in Moscow with members of the present Provisional Government and with other Polish democratic leaders from within Poland and from abroad, with a view to the reorganization of the present Government along the above lines. This Polish Provisional Government of National Unity shall be pledged to the holding of free and unfettered elections as soon as possible on the basis of universal suffrage and secret ballot. In these elections all democratic and anti-Nazi parties shall have the right to take part and to put forward candidates.

When the Polish Provisional Government of National Unity has been properly formed in conformity with the above, the Government of the U.S.S.R., which now maintains diplomatic relations with the present Provisional Government of Poland, and the Government of the United Kingdom and the Government of the United States of America will establish diplomatic relations with the new Polish Provisional Government of National Unity, and will exchange Ambassadors by whose reports the respective Governments will be kept informed about the situation in Poland. . . .

AGREEMENT REGARDING JAPAN

The leaders of the three great powers—the Soviet Union, the United States of America and Great Britain—have agreed that in two or three months after Germany has surrendered and the war in Europe has terminated, the Soviet Union shall enter into the war against Japan on the side of the Allies on condition that:

1. The *status quo* in Outer Mongolia (the Mongolian People's Republic) shall be preserved;
2. The former rights of Russia violated by the treacherous attack of Japan in 1904 shall be restored, viz:
    a. The southern part of Sakhalin as well as the island adjacent to it shall be returned to the Soviet Union.
    b. The commercial port of Dairen shall be internationalized, the preeminent interests of the Soviet Union in this port being safeguarded, and the lease of Port Arthur as a naval base of the U.S.S.R. restored.
    c. The Chinese-Eastern Railroad and the South Manchurian Railroad, which provide an outlet to Dairen, shall be jointly operated by the establishment of a joint Soviet-Chinese company, it being understood that the preeminent interests of the Soviet Union shall be safeguarded and that China shall retain full sovereignty in Manchuria;
3. The Kurile Islands shall be handed over to the Soviet Union. It is understood that the agreement concerning Outer Mongolia and the ports and railroads referred to above will require concurrence of Generalissimo Chaing Kai-shek. The President will take measures in order to obtain this concurrence on advice from Marshal Stalin.

The heads of the three great powers have agreed that these claims of the Soviet Union shall be unquestionably fulfilled after Japan has been defeated.

For its part, the Soviet Union expresses its readiness to conclude with the National Government of China a pact of friendship and alliance between the U.S.S.R. and China in order to render assistance to China with its armed forces for the purpose of liberating China from the Japanese yoke.

JOSEPH V. STALIN
FRANKLIN D. ROOSEVELT
WINSTON S. CHURCHILL
February 11, 1945

4.8   Henry Stimson Explains Why the Bomb Was Necessary

4.9   Was the Bomb Necessary?

On April 12, 1945, an anxious Harry S. Truman took the oath of office of President of the United States. Roosevelt had died earlier that day in Warm Springs, Georgia, and he had taken with him the knowledge of much of the nation's foreign policy. FDR had, for the most part, served as his own secretary of state, establishing policy, dealing with world leaders on a one-to-one basis, making decisions alone. As vice president, Truman had not been advised on any of the behind-the-scenes intricacies of the nation's foreign policies; by his own admission, he knew only what he read in the papers.

On the day he took office, Truman met with his cabinet. When the meeting adjourned, Secretary of State Stimson remained in the Cabinet Room to inform the new president that a new weapon was under development. That, Truman recalled, was all Stimson would say. Only in that way did Harry Truman learn of the Manhattan Project.

The Manhattan Project had its origins in late 1939 when several refugee scientists from Europe, including Albert Einstein and Leo Szilard, notified Roosevelt that the Germans might be capable of developing an atomic bomb. Based on that information, Roosevelt established the Manhattan Project under the direction of J. Robert Oppenheimer. The project had cost some $2 billion. It required the construction of thirty-seven installations in nineteen states and Canada, and employed over 120,000 people. When Truman took office the project was less than four months from success.

By then the war in Europe would be over. But Japan had not surrendered, and General George Marshall had told Truman that an invasion of the Japanese home islands might cost the lives of as many as 500,000 American soldiers. For over five decades, historians and military figures have debated the accuracy of Marshall's estimate, but Truman (who revered Marshall and even mentioned the half-million figure in his memoirs) made decisions based on that number.

The bomb was successfully tested near Alamogordo, New Mexico on July 16 while Truman was attending the Potsdam Conference outside Berlin with Churchill and Stalin. On August 6 the president was on his way home aboard the *U.S.S Augusta* when he was informed that the bomb had been dropped on Hiroshima. Between those two dates Truman was faced with the decision of whether or not to use the bomb, and how to use it.

Throughout his life, Truman took total responsibility for the decision to drop the bomb, but because he came to events so abruptly and with no knowledge of past decisions relating to the production of the bomb or plans for its use, he naturally relied heavily on advice from men like Stimson. When the bomb became a viable weapon following the test in New Mexico, it was Stimson who advised Truman to use the bomb immediately. *Document 4.8* is Stimson's reasoning for giving that advice to the president.

The passages here are from an article Stimson wrote for *Harper's* magazine in February 1947. Clearly, Stimson saw himself split between the horrible choices of not using the bomb and allowing more men to die in battle, or using it to end the war by causing the deaths of many thousands of Japanese civilians. The title is "The Decision to Use the Atomic Bomb." Stimson's *Harper's* article was later incorporated into a book written by Stimson and McGeorge Bundy. Stimson's reasoning has become, more or less, the accepted view of the Truman administration's decision to drop the bomb.

But not everyone agreed. *Document 4.9* is a portion of a book, *Great Mistakes of the War*, by Hanson W. Baldwin, a writer on military affairs. The book was published in 1950. Baldwin argues that the bomb was unnecessary, that it had no discernable impact on Japan's decision to surrender.

....

DOCUMENT 4.8

HENRY STIMSON EXPLAINS WHY THE BOMB WAS NECESSARY

The principal political, social, and military objective of the United States in the summer of 1945 was the prompt and complete surrender of Japan. Only the complete destruction of her military power could open the way to lasting peace.

Japan, in July 1945, had been seriously weakened by our increasingly violent attacks. It is known to us that she had gone so far as to make tentative proposals to the Soviet Government, hoping to use the Russians as mediators in a negotiated peace. These vague proposals contemplated the retention of Japan of important conquered areas and were therefore not considered seriously. There was as yet no indication of any weakening in the Japanese determination to fight rather than accept unconditional surrender. If she should persist in her fight to the end, she had still a great military force.

In the middle of July, 1945, the intelligence section of the War Department General Staff estimated Japanese military strength as follows: in the home islands, slightly under 2,000,000; in Korea, Manchuria, China proper, and Formosa, slightly over 2,000,000; in French Indo-China, Thailand, and Burma, over 200,000; in the East Indies area, including the Philippines,

over 500,000; in the by-passed Pacific islands, over 100,000. The total strength of the Japanese Army was estimated at about 5,000,000 men. These estimates later proved to be in very close agreement with official Japanese figures.

The Japanese Army was in much better condition than the Japanese Navy and Air Force. The Navy had practically ceased to exist except as a harrying force against an invasion fleet. The Air Force had been reduced mainly to reliance upon Kamikaze, or suicide, attacks. These latter, however, had already inflicted serious damage on our seagoing forces, and their possible effectiveness in a last ditch fight was a matter of real concern to our naval leaders.

As we understood it in July, there was a very strong possibility that the Japanese Government might determine upon resistance to the end, in all the areas of the Far East under its control. In such an event the Allies would be faced with the enormous task of destroying an armed force of five million men and five thousand suicide aircraft, belonging to a race which had already amply demonstrated its ability to fight literally to the death.

The strategic plans of our armed forces for the defeat of Japan, as they stood in July, had been prepared without reliance upon the atomic bomb, which had not yet been tested in New Mexico. We were planning an intensified sea and air blockade, and greatly intensified strategic air bombing through the summer and early fall, to be followed on November 1 by an invasion of the southern island of Kyushu. This would be followed in turn by an invasion of the main island of Honshu in the spring of 1946. The total U.S. military and naval force involved

SOURCE: Henry L. Stimson and McGeorge Bundy, *On Active Service in Peace and War* (New York: Harper and Row, 1947), 617–21, 624–27, 630–33.

The Yalta Conference, in February 1945, was planned to make decisions about the end of the war in both Europe and Asia. Those decisions were made. However, Yalta also set the stage for the postwar world. Many Americans still count the Yalta Conference as the origination point of the Cold War. Seated left to right are the Big Three: British Prime Minister Winston Churchill, United States President Franklin Roosevelt, and Soviet Primer Josef Stalin. *Courtesy National Archive Still Pictures #111-SC260486*

in this grand design was of the order of 5,000,000 men; if all those indirectly concerned are included, it was larger still.

We estimated that if we should be forced to carry this plan to its conclusion, the major fighting would not end until the latter part of 1946, at the earliest. I was informed that such operations might be expected to cost over a million casualties, to American forces alone. Additional large losses might be expected among our allies and, of course, if our campaign were successful and if we could judge by previous experience, enemy casualties would be much larger than our own.

It was already clear in July that even before the invasion we would be able to inflict enormously severe damage on the Japanese homeland by combined application of "conventional" sea and air power. The critical question was whether this kind of action would induce surrender. It therefore became necessary to consider very carefully the probable state of mind of the enemy, and to assess with accuracy the line of conduct which might end his will to resist.

With these considerations in mind, I wrote a memorandum for the President [Truman], on July 2, which I believe fairly represents the thinking of the American Government as it finally took shape in action. This memorandum was prepared after discussion and general agreement with Joseph C. Grew, acting Secretary of State, and Secretary of the Navy [James] Forrestal, and when I discussed it with the President, he expressed his general approval. . . .

Memorandum for the President

July 2, 1945

PROPOSED PROGRAM FOR JAPAN

1. The plans of operation up to and including the first landing have been authorized and the preparations for the operation are now actually going on. . . .
2. There is reason to believe that the operation for the occupation of Japan following the landing may be a very long, costly, and arduous struggle on our part. The terrain, much of which I have visited several times, has left the impression on my memory of being one which would be susceptible to a last ditch defense such as has been made on Iwo Jima and Okinawa and which of course is very much larger than either of those two areas. According to my recollection it will be much more unfavorable with regard to tank maneuvering than either the Philippines or Germany.
3. If we once land on one of the main islands and begin a forceful occupation of Japan, we shall probably have cast the die of last ditch resistance. The Japanese are highly patriotic and certainly susceptible to calls for fanatical resistance to repel an invasion. Once started in actual invasion, we shall in my opinion have to go through with an even more bitter fight than in Germany. We shall incur the losses incident to such a war and we shall have to leave the Japanese islands even more thoroughly destroyed than was the case with Germany. . . .
4. The question then comes: Is there any alternative to such a forceful occupation of Japan which will secure for us the equivalent of an unconditional surrender of her forces and a

permanent destruction of her power again to strike an aggressive blow at the "peace in the Pacific?" I am inclined to think that there is enough such chance to make it well worth while our giving them a warning of what is to come and definite opportunity to capitulate. As suggested above, it should be tried before the actual forceful occupation of the homeland islands is begun. . . . . I believe Japan *is* susceptible to reason in such a crisis to a much greater extent than is indicated by our current press and other current comment. . . . [T]he warning must be tendered before the actual invasion has occurred and while the impending destruction, though clear beyond peradventure, has not yet reduced her to fanatical despair. If Russia is part of the threat, the Russian attack, if actual, must not have progressed too far. Our own bombing should be confined to military objectives as far as possible.

Henry L. Stimson
Secretary of War

It is important to emphasize the double character of the suggested warning. It was designed to promise destruction if Japan resisted, and I hope, if she surrendered.

It will be noted that the atomic bomb is not mentioned in this memorandum. On grounds of secrecy the bomb was never mentioned except when absolutely necessary, and furthermore, it had not been tested. It was of course well forward in our minds, as the memorandum was written and discussed, that the bomb would be the best possible sanction if our warning were rejected. . . .

There was much discussion in Washington about the timing of the warning to Japan. The controlling factor in the end was the date already set for the Potsdam meeting of the Big Three.* It was President Truman's decision that

---

*The Potsdam meeting outside Berlin was held in mid-to-late July. The "Big Three" in attendance were Truman, Stalin, and Churchill. Churchill was defeated in a national election and replaced in mid-meeting by Clement Atlee.

such a warning should be solemnly issued by the U.S. and U.K. from this meeting, with the concurrence of the head of the Chinese Government, so that it would be plain that *all* of Japan's principal enemies were in entire unity. This was done, in the Potsdam ultimatum of July 26. . . .

On July 28 the Premier of Japan, [Kantaro] Suzuki, rejected the Potsdam ultimatum by announcing that it was "unworthy of public notice." In the face of this rejection we could only proceed to demonstrate that the ultimatum had meant exactly what it said when it stated that if the Japanese continued the war, "the full application of our military power, backed by our resolve, will mean the inevitable and complete destruction of the Japanese armed forces and just as inevitably the utter devastation of the Japanese homeland."

For such a purpose the atomic bomb was an eminently suitable weapon. The New Mexico test occurred while we were at Potsdam, on July 16. It was immediately clear that the power of the bomb measured up to our highest estimates. We had developed a weapon of such a revolutionary character that its use against the enemy might well be expected to produce exactly the kind of shock on the Japanese ruling oligarchy which we desired, strengthening the position of those who wished peace, and weakening that of the military party.

Because of the importance of the atomic mission against Japan, the detailed plans were brought to me by the military staff for approval. With President Truman's warm support I struck off the list of suggested targets the city of Kyoto. Although it was a target of considerable military importance, it had been the ancient capital of Japan and was a shrine of Japanese art and culture. We determined that it should be spared. I approved four other targets including the cities of Hiroshima and Nagasaki.

Hiroshima was bombed on August 6, and Nagasaki on August 9. These two cities were active working parts of the Japanese war effort, One was an army center; the other was naval and industrial. Hiroshima was the headquar-

ters of the Japanese Army defending southern Japan and was a major military storage and assembly point. Nagasaki was a major seaport and it contained several large industrial plants of great wartime importance. We believed that our attacks had struck cities which must certainly be important to the Japanese military leaders, both Army and Navy, and we waited for a result. We waited one day.

Many accounts have been written about the Japanese surrender. After a prolonged Japanese Cabinet session in which the deadlock was broken by the Emperor himself, the offer to surrender was made on August 10. It was based on the Potsdam terms, with a reservation concerning the sovereignty of the Emperor.

While the Allied reply made no promises other than those already given, it implicitly recognized the Emperor's position by prescribing that his power must be subject to the orders of the Allied supreme commander. These terms were accepted on August 14 by the Japanese, and the instrument of surrender was formally signed on September 2, in Tokyo Bay. Our great objective was thus achieved, and all the evidence I have seen indicates that the controlling factor in the final Japanese decision to accept our terms of surrender was the atomic bomb.

The two atomic bombs which we had dropped were the only ones we had ready, and our rate of production at the time was very small. Had the war continued until the projected invasions on November 1, additional fire raids of B-29's would have been more destructive of life and property than the very limited number of atomic raids which we could have executed in the same period. But the atomic bomb was more than a weapon of terrible destruction; it was a psychological weapon. In March, 1945, our Air Forces had launched the first great incendiary raid on the Tokyo area. In this raid more damage was done and more casualties were inflicted than was the case at Hiroshima. Hundreds of bombers took part and hundreds of tons of incendiaries were dropped. Similar successive raids burned out a great part of the urban area of Japan, but the Japanese fought on. On August 6 one B-29 dropped a single atomic bomb on Hiroshima. Three days later a second bomb was dropped on Nagasaki and the war was over. So far as the Japanese could know, our ability to execute atomic attacks, if necessary by many planes at a time, was unlimited. . . .

The bomb thus served exactly the purpose we intended. . . .

In order to end the war in the shortest possible time and to avoid the enormous losses of life which other wise confronted us, I felt that we must use the Emperor as our instrument to command and compel his people to cease fighting and subject themselves to our authority through him, and that to accomplish this we must give him and his controlling advisers a compelling reason to accede to our demands. This reason furthermore must be of such a nature that his people could understand his decision. The bomb seemed to me to furnish a unique instrument for that purpose.

My chief purpose was to end the war in victory with the least possible cost in the lives of the men in the armies which I had helped raise. In the light of the alternatives which, on a fair estimate, were open to us I believe that no man, in our position and subject to our responsibilities, holding in his hands a weapon of such possibilities for accomplishing this purpose and saving those lives, could have failed to use it and afterwards looked his countrymen in the face.

As I read over what I have written, I am aware that much of it, in this year of peace, may have a harsh and unfeeling sound. It would perhaps be possible to say the same things and say them more gently. But I do not think it would be wise. As I look back over the five years of my service as Secretary of War, I see too many stern and heart-rending decisions to be willing to pretend that war is anything else than what it is. The face of war is the face of death; death is an inevitable part of every order that a wartime leader gives. The decision to use the atomic bomb was a decision that brought death to over a hundred thousand

Japanese. No explanation can change that fact and I do not wish to gloss over it. But this deliberate premeditated destruction was our least abhorrent choice. The destruction of Hiroshima and Nagasaki put an end to the Japanese war. It stopped the fire raids, and the strangling blockade; it ended the ghastly specter of a clash of great land armies.

In this last great action of the Second World War we were given final proof that war is death. War in the twentieth century has grown steadily more barbarous, more destructive, more debased in all its aspects. Now, with the release of atomic energy, man's ability to destroy himself is very nearly complete. The bombs dropped on Hiroshima and Nagasaki ended the war. They also made it wholly clear that we must never have another war. This is the lesson men and leaders everywhere must learn, and I believe that when they learn it they will find a way to lasting peace. There is no other choice.

DOCUMENT 4.9

WAS THE BOMB NECESSARY?

The utilization of the atomic bomb against a prostrate and defeated Japan in the closing days of the war exemplifies . . . the narrow, astigmatic concentration of our planners upon one goal, and one goal alone: victory. . . .

To accept the Stimson thesis that the atomic bomb should have been used as it was used, it is necessary first to accept the contention that the atomic bomb achieved or hastened victory, and second, and more important, that it helped to consolidate the peace or to further the political aims for which war was fought.

History can accept neither contention.

Let us examine the first. The atomic bomb was dropped in August. Long before that month started our forces were securely based in Okinawa, the Marianas and Iwo Jima; Germany had been defeated; our fleet had been

SOURCE: Hanson W. Bladwin, *The Great Mistakes of the War* (Harper, 1949), 88–92, 95, 102, 104–107.

cruising off the Japanese coast with impunity bombarding the shoreline; our submarines were operating in the Sea of Japan; even inter-island ferries had been attacked and sunk. . . . Food was short; mines and submarines and surface vessels and planes clamped an iron blockade around the main islands; raw materials were scarce. . . . The enemy, in a military sense, was in a hopeless strategic position by the time the Potsdam demand for unconditional surrender was made on July 26. . . .

Not only was the Potsdam ultimatum merely a restatement of the politically impossible—unconditional surrender—but it could hardly be construed as a direct warning of the atomic bomb and was not taken as such by anyone who did not know the bomb had been created. A technical demonstration of the bomb's power may well have been unfeasible, but certainly a far more definite warning could have been given; and it was hard to believe that a target objective in Japan with but sparse population could not have been found. The truth is we did not try; we gave no specific warning. . . .

[In] fact, our only warning to a Japan already militarily defeated, and in a hopeless situation, was the Potsdam demand for unconditional surrender issued on July 26, when we knew Japanese surrender attempts had started. Yet when the Japanese surrender was negotiated about two weeks later, after the bomb was dropped, our unconditional surrender demand was made conditional and we agreed, as Simson had originally proposed we should do, to continuation of the Emperor upon his imperial throne.

We were, therefore, twice guilty. We dropped the bomb at a time when Japan already was negotiating for an end of the war but before those negotiations could come to fruition. We demanded unconditional surrender, then dropped the bomb and accepted conditional surrender, a sequence which indicates pretty clearly that the Japanese would have surrendered, even if the bomb had not been dropped, had the Potsdam Declaration included our promise to permit the Emperor to remain on his imperial throne. . . .

It is therefore clear today—and was clear to many even as early as the spring of 1945—that the military defeat of Japan was certain; the atomic bomb was not needed.

But if the bomb did not procure victory, did it hasten it?

In April, 1945, as the United States was establishing a foothold on Okinawa, the Russians in effect denounced their neutrality agreement with Japan, and from then until July 12, the new cabinet was moving rapidly toward surrender attempts.

On July 12, fourteen days before we issued the Potsdam Proclamation, these attempts reached a clearly defined point. Prince [Fumimaro] Konoye was received by the Emperor on that day and ordered to Moscow as a peace plenipotentiary to "secure peace at any price." On July 13 Moscow was notified officially by the Japanese foreign office that the "Emperor was desirous of peace."

It was hoped that Moscow would inform the United States and Britain at the Potsdam conference of Japan's desire to discuss peace. But instead of an answer from the "Big Three," Ambassador [Naotake] Sato in Moscow was told by [Soviet Foreign Minister V.M.] Molotov on August 8 of Russia's entry into the war against Japan, effective immediately.

However, since early May—well before the disappointing denouement to the most definite peace attempts the Japanese had yet made—the six-man Supreme War Direction Council in Japan had been discussing peace. On June 20, the Emperor told the Council that it "was necessary to have a plan to close the war at once as well as a plan to defend the home islands."

The Council was deadlocked three to three, and Premier [Kantaro] Suzuki, to break the deadlock, had decided to summon a Gozen-kaigi* at which the Emperor himself could make the decision for peace or further war. Suzuki knew his Emperor's mind; [Emperor] Hirohito had been convinced for some weeks

*a meeting of elder statesmen, summoned in times of crisis

that peace was the only answer to Japan's ordeal.

The first atomic bomb was dropped on Hiroshima on August 6; Russia entered the war on August 8; and a second atomic bomb was dropped on Nagasaki on August 9. The dropping of the first bomb, and the Russian entry into the war, gave Suzuki additional arguments for again putting the issue before the Supreme War Direction Council, and, on August 9, he won their approval for the Gozenkaigi. But neither the people of Japan nor their leaders were as impressed with the atomic bomb as were we. The public did not know until after the war what had happened to Hiroshima; and even so, they had endured fire raids against Tokyo which had caused more casualties than the atomic bomb and had devastated a greater area than destroyed at Hiroshima. The Supreme War Direction Council was initially told that a fragment of the Hiroshima bomb indicated that it was made in Germany, that it appeared to be a conventional explosive of great power, and that there was only one bomb available. When the Gozenkaigi actually was held on August 14, five days after the second bomb was dropped, War Minister Anami and the chiefs of the Army and Navy General Staff—three members of the war Council who had been adamant for continuation of the war—were still in favor of continuing it; those who had wanted peace still wanted it. In other words, the bomb changed no opinions; the Emperor himself, who had already favored peace, broke the deadlock. . . .

For whether or not the atomic bomb hastened victory, it is quite clear it has not won the peace. . . .

In estimating the effect of the use of the bomb upon the peace, we must remember, first, that we used the bomb for one purpose, and one only: not to secure a more equable peace, but to hasten victory. By using the bomb we

have become identified, rightfully or wrongly, as inheritors of the mantle of Genghis Khan and all those of past history who have justified the use of utter ruthlessness in war.

It may well be argued, of course, that war—least of all modern war—knows no humanity, no rules, and no limitations, and that death by the atomic bomb is no worse than death by fire bombs or high explosives or gas or flame throwers. . . .

Yet surely those methods—particularly the extension of unrestricted warfare to enemy civilians—defeated any peace aims we might have had, and had little appreciable effect in hastening military victory. For in any totalitarian state, the leaders rather than the people must be convinced of defeat, and the indiscriminate use of mass or area weapons, like biological agents and the atomic bomb, strike at the people, not the rulers. We cannot succeed, therefore, by such methods, in drawing that fine line between ruler and ruled that ought to be drawn in every war; we cannot hasten military victory by slaughtering the led; such methods only serve to bind the led closer to their leaders. . . .

The American public is tending to accept the nefarious doctrine that the ends justify the means, the doctrine of exigency. What we have done to ourselves—and Hiroshima and Nagasaki were heavy blows to a weakening moral structure. . . .

We have embarked upon Total War with a vengeance; we have done our best to make it far more total. If we do not soon reverse this trend, if we do not cast about for means to limit and control war, if we do not abandon the doctrine of expediency, of unconditional surrender, of total victory, we shall someday ourselves become the victims of our own theories and practices.

CHAPTER 5

Origins of the Cold War, 1945–1952

5.1 President Harry S. Truman's Statement on the Fundamentals of American Foreign Policy, October 27, 1945

5.2 Henry Wallace's Madison Square Garden Speech, September 12, 1946

5.3 The Novikov Letter, September 1946

5.4 The Truman Doctrine, March 12, 1947

5.5 Secretary of State George Marshall's Report to the Senate Committee on Foreign Affairs, January 8, 1948

5.6 "X" and Containment. George Kennan, "The Sources of Soviet Conduct"

5.7 Walter Lippmann Responds to "Mr. X"

5.8 Declaration of the Founding of the Cominform, September 1947

5.9 National Security Council Paper #68, April 1950

5.10 Truman's Decision to Enter the War in Korea, June 1950

1945–1951 Timeline

October 27, 1945	1945	President Truman's statement on foreign policy
September 12, 1946		Henry Wallace's Madison Square Garden speech
September 1946	1946	Novikov Letter
March 12, 1947		Truman Doctrine
July 1947		George Kennan, "Sources of Soviet Conduct"
September 1947	1947	Founding of the Cominform
December 1947		Walter Lippmann responds to Kennan
January 8, 1948	1948	General George Marshall on foreign affairs
July 1948		Berlin Airlift begins
November 1948	1949	Truman elected to a full term
October 1, 1949		Mao Zedong declares the Peoples Republic of China
April 1950		NSC #68
June 25, 1950	1950	North Korea invades South Korea
June 30, 1950		Truman's decision to enter the war in Korea
April 11, 1951	1951	Truman relieves MacArthur

5.1 President Harry S. Truman's Statement on the Fundamentals of American Foreign Policy, October 27, 1945

5.2 Henry Wallace's Madison Square Garden Speech, September 12, 1946

World War II brought considerable devastation to Western Europe. Britain, France, Belgium, Germany, and Italy all lay in rubble, but most importantly their economic bases were destroyed by the war. It was the conventional wisdom at the time that a weak economic base was fertile ground for the spread of extremism. If anyone questioned that, there was the example of the rise of fascism in Europe out of the devastation and economic calamity following World War I. Now, following World War II, communism was the great fear; and many believed that the weak economies of Western Europe might invite the spread of what America's first ambassador to the Soviet Union, William Bullitt, called the "red amoeba." Italy, and even France, seemed to be moving toward a home-grown style of communism. It quickly became clear that if the United States did not aid in a European economic recovery, two problems would likely occur: Western Europe would become vulnerable to Soviet incursions; and the U.S. economy would falter for lack of strong overseas trading partners. In fact, it was a common fear that without European trade the American economy would return to the 1930s depression.

The first selection (*Document 5.1*) is Truman's Statement on the Fundamentals of American Foreign Policy, delivered in New York on October 27, 1945. It was Truman's first important statement on foreign policy in the weeks following the Potsdam Conference, the dropping of the bomb, and the end of the war in the Pacific. Many of his remarks were clearly aimed at the Soviet Union. The shadow of Woodrow Wilson should be apparent in many of Truman's statements.

Not all Americans believed that the end of the war meant a confrontation with the Soviets. Many Americans, particularly those on the political left, believed that the United States should do all in its power to maintain a peaceful coexistence with the Soviet Union based on common international interests. The chief spokesman of this opinion was Henry Agard Wallace. Wallace had served as Franklin Roosevelt's vice president in his third term, but was forced off the ticket by Democratic moderates at the 1944 Democratic convention in favor of Truman. Wallace went on to serve as Secretary of Commerce in Roosevelt's fourth-term cabinet, and then continued in that position under Truman. Many New Dealers and liberal-labor types believed that Wallace would be an ideal candidate to lead the Democrats in 1948.

In September 1946 Wallace spoke on U.S. foreign policy before a rally of supporters at Madison Square Garden. At a moment when the administration was moving rapidly toward an anti-Soviet stance, Wallace spoke out against British imperialism and called for a "friendly" policy toward the Soviet Union. Just prior to the speech, Truman told reporters that he had read the speech and approved of its content. The next day he released a statement claiming that he only approved Wallace's right to make such statements. Almost immediately, Truman's secretary of state, James Byrnes (who was strongly anti-Soviet), insisted that the president make a foreign policy choice. Truman asked for Wallace's resignation and chose Byrnes' hard-line stance and the anti-Soviet path. *Document 5.2* is Wallace's speech.

As the cold war hardened, Wallace's arguments for peace and coexistence with the Soviets increasingly lost credibility. He ran as a third party candidate on the Progressive party ticket in 1948, but the Democrats, fearing a bolt of the left, successfully branded Wallace a communist sympathizer during the campaign. He received only about a million votes.

DOCUMENT 5.1

PRESIDENT HARRY S. TRUMAN'S STATEMENT ON THE FUNDAMENTALS OF AMERICAN FOREIGN POLICY, OCTOBER 27, 1945

The foreign policy of the United States is based firmly on fundamental principles of righteousness and justice. In carrying out those principles we shall firmly adhere to what we believe to be right; and we shall not give our approval to any compromises with evil.

But we know that we cannot attain perfection in this world overnight. We shall not let our search for perfection obstruct our steady progress toward international cooperation. We must be prepared to fulfill our responsibilities as best we can, within the framework of our fundamental principles, even though we have to operate in an imperfect world.

Let me restate the fundamentals of the foreign policy of the United States:

1. We seek no territorial expansion or selfish advantage. We have no plans for aggression against any other state, large or small. We have no objective which need clash with the peaceful aims of any other nation.
2. We believe in the eventual return of sovereign rights and self-government to all peoples who have been deprived of them by force.
3. We shall approve no territorial changes in any friendly part of the world unless they accord with the freely expressed wishes of the people concerned.
4. We believed that all peoples who are prepared for self-government should be permitted to choose their own form of government by their own freely expressed choice, without interference from any foreign source. That is true in Europe, in Asia, in Africa, as well as in the Western Hemisphere.
5. By the combined and cooperative action of our war Allies, we shall help the defeated enemy states establish peaceful democratic governments of their own free choice. And we shall try to attain a world in which Nazism, Fascism, and military aggression cannot exist.
6. We shall refuse to recognize any government imposed upon any nation by the force of any foreign power. In some cases it may be impossible to prevent forceful imposition of such a government. But the United States will not recognize any such government.
7. We believe that all nations should have the freedom of the seas and equal rights to the navigation of boundary rivers and waterways and of rivers and waterways which pass through more than one country.
8. We believe that all states which are accepted in the society of nations should have access on equal terms to the trade and the raw materials of the world.
9. We believe that the sovereign states of the Western Hemisphere, without interference from outside the Western Hemisphere, must work together as good neighbors in the solution of their common problems.

SOURCE: Harry S. Truman, *Memoirs: Vol. 1, 1945, Year of Decisions* (1955), 589–90.

10. We believe that full economic collaboration between all nations, great and small, is essential to the improvement of living conditions all over the world, and to the establishment of freedom from fear and freedom from want.

11. We shall continue to strive to promote freedom of expression and freedom of religion throughout the peace-loving areas of the world.

12. We are convinced that the preservation of peace between nations requires a United Nations Organization composed of all the peace-loving nations of the world who are willing jointly to use force if necessary to insure peace.

That is the foreign policy which guides the United States now. That is the foreign policy with which it confidently faces the future.

DOCUMENT 5.2

HENRY WALLACE'S MADISON SQUARE GARDEN SPEECH, SEPTEMBER 12, 1946

. . . Tonight I want to talk about peace—and how to get peace. Never have the common people of all lands so longed for peace. Yet, never in a time of comparative peace have they feared war so much.

Up till now peace has been negative and unexciting. War has been positive and exciting. Far too often, hatred and fear, intolerance and deceit have had the upper hand over love and confidence, trust and joy. Far too often, the law of nations has been the law of the jungle; and the constructive spiritual forces of the Lord have bowed to the destructive forces of Satan.

During the past year of so, the significance of peace has been increased immeasurably by the atom bomb, guided missiles, and airplanes which soon will travel as fast as sound. Make no mistake about it—another war would hurt

the United States many times as much as the last war. We cannot rest in the assurance that we invented the atom bomb—and therefore that this agent of destruction will work best for us. He who trusts in the atom bomb will sooner or later perish by the atom bomb—or something worse.

I say this as one who steadfastly backed preparedness throughout the thirties. We have no use for namby-pamby pacifism. But we must realize that modern inventions have now made peace the most exciting thing in the world—and we should be willing to pay a just price for peace. If modern war can cost us four hundred billion dollars, we should be willing and happy to pay much more for peace. But certainly, the cost of peace is to be measured not in dollars but in the hearts and minds of men.

The price of peace—for us and for every nation in the world—is the price of giving up prejudice, hatred, fear, and ignorance.

Let's get down to cases here at home.

First, we have prejudice, hatred, fear and ignorance of certain races. The recent mass lynching in Georgia was not merely the most unwarranted, brutal act of mob violence in the United States in recent years; it was also an illustration of the kind of prejudice that makes war inevitable.

Hatred breeds hatred. The doctrine of racial superiority produces a desire to get even on the part of its victims. If we are to work for peace in the rest of the world, we here in the United States must eliminate racism from our unions, our business organizations, our educational institutions, and our employment practices. Merit alone must be the measure of the man.

Second, in payment for peace, we must give up prejudice, hatred, fear, and ignorance in the economic world. This means working earnestly, day after day, for a larger volume of world trade. It means helping undeveloped areas of the world to industrialize themselves with the help of American technical assistance and loans.

SOURCE: John Morton Blum, ed., *The Price of Vision: The Diary of Henry A. Wallace* (Boston: Houghton Mifflin, 1973), 663–68.

We should welcome the opportunity to help along the most rapid possible industrialization in Latin America, China, India, and the Near East. For as the productivity of these peoples increases, our exports will increase.

We all remember the time, not so long ago, when the high tariff protectionists blindly opposed any aid to the industrialization of Canada. But look at our exports to Canada today. On a per capita basis our Canadian exports are seven times greater than our exports to Mexico.

I supported the British loan of almost four billion dollars because I knew that without this aid in the rehabilitation of its economy, the British government would have been forced to adopt totalitarian trade methods and economic warfare of a sort which would have closed the markets of much of the world to American exports.

For the welfare of the American people and the world it is even more important to invest four billion dollars in the industrialization of undeveloped areas in the so-called backward nations, thereby promoting the long-term stability that comes from an ever-increasing standard of living. This would not only be good politics and good morals. It would be good business.

The United States is the world's greatest creditor nation. And low tariffs by creditor nations are a part of the price of peace. For when a great creditor demands payment, and at the same time, adopts policies which make it impossible for the debtors to pay in goods—the first result is the intensification of depression over large areas of the world; and the final result is the triumph of demagogues who speak only the language of violence and hate.

Individual Republicans may hold enlightened views—but the Republican Party as a whole is irrevocably committed to tariff and trade policies which can only mean worldwide depression, ruthless economic warfare, and eventual war. And if the Republicans were in power in the United States today, intelligent people all over the world would fear that once more we would be headed straight for boom, busts, and worldwide chaos.

I noticed in the papers recently that Governor Dewey* doesn't like my prophecies. I said weeks before the last [1944] election—and said it repeatedly—that Franklin Roosevelt would carry thirty-six states and have a popular majority of three million. Of course, Mr. Dewey didn't like that one. I say now—as I have said repeatedly—that Republican foreign economic policies carried into action would mean disaster for the nation and the world. Mr. Dewey won't like that one either.

The Republican Party is the party of economic nationalism and political isolationism—and as such is anachronistic as the dodo and as certain to disappear. The danger is that before it disappears it may enjoy a brief period of power during which it can do irreparable damage to the United States and the cause of world peace.

Governor Dewey has expressed himself as favoring an alliance of mutual defense with Great Britain as the key to our foreign policy. This may sound attractive because we both speak the same language and many of our customs and traditions have the same historical background. Moreover, to the military men, the British Isles are our advanced air base against Europe.

Certainly we like the British people as individuals. But to make Britain the key to our foreign policy would be, in my opinion, the height of folly. We must not let the reactionary leadership of the Republican Party force us into that position. We must not let British balance-of-power manipulations determine whether and when the United States gets into war.

Make no mistake about it—the British imperialistic policy in the Near East alone, combined with the Russian retaliation, would lead the United States straight to war unless we have a clearly defined and realistic policy of our own.

Neither of these two great powers wants war now, but the danger is that whatever their

---

*Thomas Dewey was governor of New York. He ran against FDR in 1940 and lost, winning only ten states. In 1948, Dewey would lose to Truman.

intentions may be, their current policies may eventually lead to war. To prevent war and insure our survival in a stable world, it is essential that we look abroad through our own American eyes and not through the eyes of either the British Foreign Office or a pro-British or anti-Russian press.

In this connection, I want one thing clearly understood. I am neither anti-British nor pro-British—neither anti Russian nor pro-Russian. And just two days ago, when President Truman read these words, he said that they represented the policy of his administration.

I plead for an America vigorously dedicated to peace—just as I plead for opportunities for the next generation throughout the world to enjoy the abundance which now, more than ever before, is the birthright of man.

To achieve lasting peace, we must study in detail just how the Russian character was formed—by invasions of Tartars, Mongols, Germans, Poles, Swedes, and French; by the czarist rule based on ignorance, fear, and force; by the intervention of the British, French, and Americans in Russian affairs from 1919 to 1921; by the geography of the huge Russian land mass situated strategically between Europe and Asia; and by the vitality derived from the rich Russian soil and the strenuous Russian climate. Add to all this the tremendous emotional power which Marxism and Leninism gives to the Russian leaders—and then we can realize that we are reckoning with a force which cannot be handled successfully by a "Get tough with Russia" policy. "Getting tough" never bought anything real and lasting—whether for schoolyard bullies or businessmen or world powers. The tougher we get, the tougher the Russians will get.

Throughout the world there are numerous reactionary elements which had hoped for Axis victory—and now profess great friendship for the United States. Yet, these enemies of yesterday and false friends of today continually try to provoke war between the United States and Russia. They have no real love of the United States. They only long for the day when the United States and Russia will destroy each other.

We must not let our Russian policy be guided or influenced by those inside or outside the United States who want war with Russia. This does not mean appeasement.

We most earnestly want peace with Russia—but we want to be met halfway. We want cooperation. And I believe that we can get cooperation once Russia understands that our primary objective is neither saving the British Empire nor purchasing oil in the Near East with the lives of American soldiers. We cannot allow national oil rivalries to force us into war. All of the nations producing oil, whether inside or outside of their own boundaries, must fulfill the provisions of the United Nations Charter and encourage the development of world petroleum reserves so as to make the maximum amount of oil available to all nations of the world on an equitable peaceful basis—and not on the basis of fighting the next war

For her part, Russia can retain our respect by cooperating with the United Nations in a spirit of open-minded and flexible give-and-take.

The real peace treaty we now need is between the United States and Russia. On our part, we should recognize that we have no more business in the *political* affairs of eastern Europe than Russia has in the *political* affairs of Latin America, western Europe, and the United States. We may not like what Russia does in eastern Europe. Her type of land reform, industrial expropriation, and suppression of basic liberties offends the great majority of the people of the United States.

But whether we like it or not the Russians will try to socialize their sphere of influence just as we try to democratize our sphere of influence. This applies also to Germany and Japan. We are striving to democratize Japan and our area of control in Germany, while Russia strives to socialize eastern Germany

As for Germany, we all must recognize that an equitable settlement, based on a unified Germany nation, is absolutely essential to any lasting European settlement. This means that Russia must be assured that never again can German industry be converted into military might to be used against her—and Britain. Western Europe and the United States must be certain that Russia's German policy will not become a tool of Russian design against western Europe.

The Russians have no more business in stirring up native communists to political activity in western Europe, Latin America, and the United States than we have interfering in the politics of eastern Europe and Russia. We know what Russia is up to in eastern Europe, for example, and Russia knows what we are up to. We cannot permit the door to be closed against our trade in eastern Europe any more than we can in China. But at the same time we have to realize that the Balkans are closer to Russia than to us—and that Russia cannot permit either England or the United States to dominate the politics of that area.

China is a special case and although she holds the longest frontier in the world with Russia, the interests of world peace demand that China remain free from any sphere of influence, either politically or economically. We insist that the door to trade and economic development opportunities be left wide open in China as in all the world. However, the open door to trade and opportunities for economic development in China are meaningless unless there is a unified and peaceful China—built on the cooperation of the various groups in that country and based on a hands-off policy of the outside powers.

We are still arming to the hilt. Our excessive expenses for military purposes are the chief cause of our unbalanced budget. If taxes are to be lightened we must have the basis of a real peace with Russia—a peace that cannot be broke by extremist propagandists.

Russian ideas of social-economic justice are going to govern nearly a third of the world. Our ideas of free-enterprise democracy will govern much of the rest. The two ideas will endeavor to prove which can deliver the most satisfaction to the common man in their respective areas of political dominance. But by mutual agreement, this competition should be put on a friendly basis. Let the results of the two systems speak for themselves.

Meanwhile, we should close our ears to those among us who would have us believe that Russian communism and our free enterprise system cannot live, one with another, in a profitable and productive peace.

Under friendly peaceful competition the Russian world and the American world can gradually become more alike. The Russians will be forced to grant more and more of the personal freedoms; and we shall become more and more absorbed with the problems of social-economic justice.

Russia must be convinced that we are not planning for war against her and we must be certain that Russia is not carrying on territorial expansion or world domination through native communists faithfully following every twist and turn in the Moscow party line. But in this competition, we must insist on an open door for trade throughout the world. There will always be an ideological conflict—but that is no reason why diplomats cannot work out a basis for both systems to live safely in the world side by side.

Once the fears of Russia and the United States Senate have been allayed by practical regional political reservations, I am sure that concern over the veto power would be greatly diminished. Then the United Nations would have a really great power in those areas which are truly international and not regional. In the worldwide, as distinguished from the regional field, the armed might of the United Nations should be so great as to make opposition useless. Only the United Nations should have atomic bombs and its military establishment should give special emphasis to air power. It should have control of the strategically located air bases in which the United States and Britain have encircled the world. And not only should individual nations be prohibited from manufacturing atomic bombs, guided missiles, and military aircraft for bombing purposes, but no nation should be allowed to spend on its military establishment more than 15 percent of its budget.

Practically and immediately, we must recognize that we are not yet ready for World Federation. Realistically, the most we can hope for now is a safe reduction in military expense and a long period of peace based on mutual trust between the Big Three.

During this period, every effort should be made to develop as rapidly as possible a body of international law based on moral principles and not on the Machiavellian principles of deceit, force, and distrust—which, if continued, will lead the modern world to rapid disintegration.

In brief, as I see it today, the World Order is bankrupt—and the United States, Russia, and England are the receivers. These are the hard facts of power politics on which we have to build a functioning, powerful United Nations and a body of international law. And as we build, we must develop fully the doctrine of the rights of small peoples as contained in the United Nations Charter. This law should ideally apply as much to Indonesians and Greeks as to the Bulgarians and Poles—but practically, the application may be delayed until both British and Russians discover the futility of their methods.

In the full development of the rights of small nations, the British and Russians can learn a lesson from the Good Neighbor policy of Franklin Roosevelt. For under Roosevelt, we in the Western Hemisphere built a workable system of regional internationalism that fully protected the sovereign rights of every nation—a system of multi-lateral action that immeasurably strengthened the whole of world order.

In the United States an informed public opinion will be all-powerful. Our people are peace-minded. But they often express themselves too late—for events today move much faster than public opinion. The people here, as everywhere in the world, must be convinced that another war is not inevitable. And through mass meetings such as this, and through persistent pamphleteering, the people can be organized for peace—even though a large segment of our press is propagandizing our people for war in the hope of scaring Russia. And we who look on this war-with-Russia talk as criminal foolishness must carry our message direct to the people—even though we may be called communists because we dare to speak out.

I believe that peace—the kind of peace I have outlined tonight—is the basic issue, both in the congressional campaign this fall and right on through the presidential election in 1948. How we meet this issue will determine whether we live not in "one world" or "two worlds"—but whether we live at all.

5.3 The Novikov Letter, September 1946

Almost immediately after the war both the United States and the Soviets began to distrust each other—as they had, in fact, distrusted each other before and even during the war. Both sides searched for some insight into the other's intent, and many of those answers came, at first, from diplomats. In early 1946 George Kennan, an advisor at the American embassy in Moscow, wrote his Long Telegram to the State Department in Washington appraising Soviet conduct and intentions. Much of what Kennan wrote in that telegram was reiterated in an article in *Foreign Affairs* a year later.

In September 1946 the Soviet ambassador to Washington, Nicolai Novikov, compiled a letter detailing what he believed was the U.S. objectives in the postwar world, and how the Soviet Union should deal with what he saw as a hostile power intent on using its power to extract concessions from the Soviet Union (*Document 5.3*). As the Soviet ambassador to the U.S., Novikov carried great weight in Moscow and his opinions on U.S. intentions surely influenced Soviet policy toward the U.S. in those early years of the Cold War.

One important aspect of the Novikov letter is the marked distinction he sees between the foreign policies of the Roosevelt and Truman administrations. He also seems to see a major demarcation in U.S. foreign policy with the firing of Secretary of Commerce Henry Wallace (which occurred in the same month that Novikov wrote the letter) and the appointment of James Byrnes as Secretary of State.

In 1989 Novikov published his memoirs. His opinion of the U.S. and U.S. intentions following the war had changed very little in the intervening 43 years.

....

DOCUMENT 5.3

THE NOVIKOV LETTER, SEPTEMBER 1946

The foreign policy of the United States, which reflects the imperialist tendencies of American monopolistic capital, is characterized in the postwar period by a striving for world supremacy. This is the real meaning of the many statements by President Truman and other representatives of American ruling circles; that the United States has the right to lead the world. All the forces of American diplomacy—the army, the air force, the navy, industry, and science— are enlisted in the service of this foreign policy. For this purpose broad plans for expansion have been developed and are being implemented through diplomacy and the establishment of a system of naval and air bases stretching far beyond the boundaries of the United States, through the arms race, and through the creation of ever-newer types of weapons.

The foreign policy of the United States is conducted now in a situation that differs greatly from the one that existed in the prewar period. This situation does not fully conform to the calculations of those reactionary circles which hoped that during the Second World War they would succeed in avoiding, at least for a long time, the main battles in Europe and Asia. They calculated that the United States of America, if it was unsuccessful in completely avoiding direct participation in the war, would enter it only at the last minute, when it could easily affect the outcome of the war, completely insuring its interests.

In this regard, it was thought that the main competitors of the United States would be crushed or greatly weakened in the war, and the United States by virtue of this circumstance would assume the role of the most powerful factor in resolving the fundamental questions of the postwar world. These calculations were also based on the assumption, which was very widespread in the United States in the initial stages of the war, that the Soviet Union, which had been subjected to the attack of German Fascism in June 1941, would also be exhausted or even completely destroyed as a result of the war.

Reality did not bear out the calculations of the American imperialists. The two main aggressive powers, fascist Germany and militarist Japan, which were at the same time the main competitors of the United States in both the economic and foreign policy fields, were thoroughly defeated. The third great power, Great Britain, which had taken heavy blows during the war, now faces enormous economic and political difficulties. The political foundations of the British Empire were appreciably shaken, and crises arose, for example, in India, Palestine, and Egypt.

Europe has come out of the war with a completely dislocated economy, and the economic devastation that occurred in the course of the war cannot be overcome in a short time. All of the countries of Europe and Asia are experiencing a colossal need for consumer goods, industrial and transportation equipment, etc. Such a situation provides American monopolistic capital with prospects for enormous shipments of goods and the importation of capital into these countries—a circumstance that would permit it to infiltrate their national economies. Such a development would mean a serious strengthening of the economic position of the United States in the whole world and would be a stage on the road to world domination by the United States.

On the other hand, we have seen a failure of calculations on the part of U.S. circles which assumed that the Soviet Union would be destroyed in the war or would come out of it so weakened that it would be forced to go begging to the United States for economic assistance. Had that happened, they would have been able to dictate conditions permitting the United States to carry out its expansion in Europe and Asia without hindrance from the U.S.S.R.

In actuality, despite all of the economic difficulties of the postwar period connected with the enormous losses inflicted by the war and the German fascist occupation, the Soviet Union continues to remain economically independent of the outside world and is rebuilding its national economy with its own forces.

At the same time the USSR's international position is currently stronger than it was in the prewar period. Thanks to the historical victories of Soviet weapons, the Soviet armed forces are located on the territory of Germany and other formerly hostile countries, thus guaranteeing that these countries will not be used again for an attack on the USSR. In formerly hostile countries, such as Bulgaria, Finland, Hungary, and Romania, democratic reconstruction has established regimes that have undertaken to strengthen and maintain friendly relations with the Soviet Union. In the Slavic countries that were liberated by the Red Army or with its assistance—Poland, Czechoslovakia, and Yugoslavia—democratic regimes have also been established that maintain relations with the Soviet Union on the basis of agreements on friendship and mutual assistance.

The enormous relative weight of the USSR in international affairs in general and in the European countries in particular, the independence of its foreign policy, and the economic and political assistance that it provides to neighboring countries, both allies and former enemies, has led to the growth of the political influence of the Soviet Union in these countries and to the further strengthening of democratic tendencies in them. Such a situation in Eastern and Southeastern Europe cannot help but be regarded by the American imperialists as an obstacle in the path of the expansionist policy of the United States.

The foreign policy of the United States is not determined at present by the circles in the Democratic Party that (as was the case during Roosevelt's lifetime) strive to strengthen the cooperation of the three great powers that constituted the basis of the anti-Hitler coalition during the war. The ascendance to power of President Truman, a politically unstable person but with certain conservative tendencies, and the subsequent appointment of [James] Byrnes as Secretary of State meant a strengthening of the influence of U.S. foreign policy of the most reactionary circles of the Democratic party. The constantly increasing reactionary nature of the foreign policy course of the United States, which consequently approached the policy advocated by the Republican party, laid the groundwork for close cooperation in this field between the far right wing of the Democratic party and the Republican party. This cooperation of the two parties, which took shape in both houses of Congress in the form of an unofficial bloc of reactionary Southern Democrats and the old guard of the Republicans headed by [senators Arthur] Vandenberg and [Robert] Taft, was especially clearly manifested in the essentially identical foreign policy statements issued by figures of both parties. In Congress and at international conferences, where as a rule leading Republicans are represented in the delegations of the United States, the Republicans actively support the foreign policy of the government. This is the source of what is called, even in official statements, "bipartisan" foreign policy.

At the same time, there has been a decline in the influence on foreign policy of those who follow Roosevelt's course for cooperation among peace-loving countries. Such persons in the government, in Congress, and in the leadership of the Democratic party are being pushed farther and farther into the background. The contradictions in the field of foreign policy and existing between the followers of [Henry] Wallace and [Claude] Pepper, on the one hand, and the adherents of the reactionary "bipartisan" policy, on the other, were manifested with great clarity recently in the speech by Wallace that led to his resignation from the post as Secretary of Commerce. Wallace's resignation means the victory of the reactionary course that Byrnes is conducting in cooperation with Vandenberg and Taft.

Obvious indications of the U.S. effort to establish world dominance are also to be found in the increase in military potential in peacetime and in the establishment of a large number of naval and air bases both in the United States and beyond its borders.

In the summer of 1946, for the first time in the history of the country, Congress passed a law on the establishment of a peacetime army, not on a volunteer basis but on the basis of universal military service. The size of the army, which is supposed to amount to about one million persons as of July 1, 1947, was also increased significantly. The size of the navy at the conclusion of the war decreased quite insignificantly in comparison with wartime. At the present time, the American navy occupies first place in the world, leaving England's navy far behind, to say nothing of those of other countries. . . .

One of the stages in the achievement of dominance over the world by the United States is its understanding with England concerning the partial division of the world on the basis of mutual concessions. The basic lines of the secret agreement between the United States and England regarding the division of the world consist, as shown by facts, in their agreement on the inclusion of Japan and China in the sphere of influence of the United States in the Far East, while the United States, for its part, has agreed not to hinder England either in resolving the Indian problem or in strengthening its influence in Siam and Indonesia. In connection with this division, the United States at the present time is in control of China and Japan without any interference from England.

The American policy in China is striving for the complete economic and political submission of China to the control of American monopolistic capital. Following this policy, the American government does not shrink even from interference in the internal affairs of China. At the present time in China, there are more than 50,000 American soldiers. In a number of cases, American Marines participated directly in military operations against [Mao Zedong's] people's liberation forces. . . .

China is gradually being transformed into a bridgehead for the American armed forces. American air bases are located all over its territory. The main ones are found in Peking, Tsingtao, Tientsin, Nanking, Shanghai, Chendu, Chungking, and Kunming. The main American naval base in China is located in Tsingtao. The headquarters of the 7th Fleet is also there. In addition more than 30,000 U.S. Marines are concentrated in Tsingtao and its environs. The measures carried out in northern China by the American army show that it intends to stay there for a long time.

In Japan, despite the presence there of only a small contingent of American troops, control is in the hands of the Americans. Although English capital has substantial interests in the Japanese economy, English foreign policy toward Japan is conducted in such a way as not to hinder the Americans from carrying out their penetration of the Japanese national economy and subordinating it to their influence. In the Far Eastern Commission in Washington and in the Allied Council in Tokyo, the English representatives as a rule make common cause with U.S. representatives conducting this policy. . . .

In recent years American capital has penetrated very intensively into the economy of the Near Eastern countries, in particular into the oil industry. At present there are American oil concessions in all of the Near Eastern countries that have oil deposits (Iraq, Bahrain, Kuwait, Egypt, and Saudi Arabia). American capital, which made its first appearance in the oil industry of the Near East, only in 1927, now controls 42 percent of all proven reserves in the Near East, excluding Iran. Of the total proven reserves of 26.8 billion barrels, over 11 billion barrels are owned by U.S. concessions. Striving to ensure further development of their concessions in different countries (which are often very large—Saudi Arabia, for example), the American oil companies plan to build a trans-Arabian pipeline to transport oil from the

American concession in Saudi Arabia and in other countries on the southeastern shore of the Mediterranean Sea to ports in Palestine and Egypt. . . .

The "hard-line" policy with regard to the USSR announced by Byrnes after the rapprochement of the reactionary Democrats with the Republicans is at present the main obstacle on the road to cooperation of the Great Powers. It consists mainly of the fact that in the postwar period the United States no longer follows a policy of strengthening cooperation among the Big Three . . . but rather has striven to undermine the unity of these countries. The objective has been to impose the will of other countries on the Soviet Union. . . .

The present policy of the American government with regard to the USSR is also directed at limiting or dislodging the influence of the Soviet Union from neighboring countries. In implementing this policy in former enemy or Allied countries adjacent to the USSR, the United States attempts, at various international conferences or directly in these countries themselves, to support reactionary forces with the purpose of creating obstacles to the process of democratization of these countries. In so doing, it also attempts to secure positions for the penetration of American capital into their economies.

5.4   The Truman Doctrine, March 12, 1947
5.5   Secretary of State George Marshall's Report to the Senate Committee on Foreign Affairs, January 8, 1948

*D*ocument 5.4 is the Truman Doctrine, one of the very pillars of America's postwar foreign policy. In early 1947 it became clear that the British had neither the will nor the resources to counter communist aggressions in Greece. At the same time (and in the same region of the world) the Soviets were pressuring Turkey for control of the Dardanelles, the Soviet Union's only access to the Mediterranean. Truman responded by asking Congress for $400 million in aid to Greece and Turkey—along with a pledge to aid "free peoples," he said, against "subjugation by armed minorities or by outside pressures." Some contemporary observers argued that this was unnecessarily alarmist language in an apparent effort to persuade the American people to accept his proposal and to push Congress to appropriate the aid. Others, however, believed that Truman was warning the nation of impending Soviet aggressions. In his memoirs, Truman wrote: "This was, I believed, the turning point in America's foreign policy, which now declared that wherever aggression, direct or indirect, threaten the peace, the security of the United States was involved." Thus the United States committed aid to any nation fighting communist aggression.

On June 5, 1947 Secretary of State George Marshall, speaking at Harvard University, announced a plan to reconstruct the economies of Europe. Known first as the European Recovery Plan, Marshall's proposal was later named after its initiator, the Marshall Plan.

The Truman Doctrine and the Marshall Plan went hand in hand. The first was directed at the military and political confrontation of the Soviet Union; the second was the economic side of that same philosophy. Even Truman called the Marshall Plan the "second half of the same walnut."

Document 5.5 is Marshall's testimony before the Senate Foreign Relations Committee on January 8, 1948. Congress had already approved $880,000 in interim economic relief for Europe, and Marshall argued that the United States should proceed with a long-range economic plan for the European nations. The Soviet Union, by this time, had already rejected the Marshall Plan for those areas it controlled in Eastern Europe, and had established the Molotov Plan designed to do for Eastern Europe what the United States intended to do in the west. Also by this time communists had staged a coup in Hungary. It would be just a month before they would do the same in Czechoslovakia.

....

DOCUMENT 5.4

THE TRUMAN DOCTRINE, MARCH 12, 1947

The gravity of the situation which confronts the world today necessitates my appearance before a joint session of the Congress.

The foreign policy and the national security of this country are involved.

One aspect of the present situation, which I present to you at this time for your consideration and decision, concerns Greece and Turkey.

The United States has received from the Greek Government an urgent appeal for finan-

cial and economic assistance. Preliminary reports from the American Economic Mission now in Greece and reports from the American Ambassador in Greece corroborate the statement of the Greek Government that assistance is imperative if Greece is to survive as a free nation.

I do not believe that the American people and the Congress wish to turn a deaf ear to the appeal of the Greek Government.

Greece is not a rich country. Lack of sufficient natural resources has always forced the Greek people to work hard to make both ends meet. Since 1940, this industrious, peace loving country has suffered invasion, four years of cruel enemy occupation, and bitter internal strife.

When forces of liberation entered Greece they found that the retreating Germans had destroyed virtually all the railways, roads, port

SOURCE: *Public Papers of the Presidents: Harry S. Truman, 1947*, 176–80.

facilities, communications, and merchant marine. More than a thousand villages had been burned. Eighty-five percent of the children were tubercular. Livestock, poultry, and draft animals had almost disappeared. Inflation had wiped out practically all savings.

As a result of these tragic conditions, a militant minority, exploiting human want and misery, was able to create political chaos which, until now, has made economic recovery impossible.

Greece is today without funds to finance the importation of those goods which are essential to bare subsistence. Under these circumstances the people of Greece cannot make progress in solving their problems of reconstruction. Greece is in desperate need of financial and economic assistance to enable it to resume purchases of food, clothing, fuel and seeds. These are indispensable for the subsistence of its people and are obtainable only from abroad. Greece must have help to import the goods necessary to restore internal order and security so essential for economic and political recovery.

The Greek Government has also asked for the assistance of experienced American administrators, economists and technicians to insure that the financial and other aid given to Greece shall be used effectively in creating a stable and self-sustaining economy and in improving its public administration.

The very existence of the Greek state is today threatened by the terrorist activities of several thousand armed men, led by Communists, who defy the government's authority at a number of points, particularly along the northern boundaries. A Commission appointed by the United Nations Security Council is at present investigating disturbed conditions in northern Greece and alleged border violations along the frontier between Greece on the one hand and Albania, Bulgaria, and Yugoslavia on the other.

Meanwhile, the Greek Government is unable to cope with the situation. The Greek army is small and poorly equipped. It needs supplies and equipment if it is to restore authority to the government throughout Greek territory.

Greece must have assistance if it is to become a self-supporting and self-respecting democracy.

The United States must supply this assistance. We have already extended to Greece certain types of relief and economic aid but these are inadequate.

There is no other country to which democratic Greece can turn. No other nation is willing and able to provide the necessary support for a democratic Greek Government.

The British Government, which has been helping Greece, can give no further financial or economic aid after March 31. Great Britain finds itself under the necessity of reducing or liquidating its commitments in several parts of the world, including Greece.

We have considered how the United Nations must assist in this crisis. But the situation is an urgent one requiring immediate action, and the United Nations and its related organizations are not in a position to extend help of the kind that is required.

It is important to note that the Greek Government has asked for our aid in utilizing effectively the financial and other assistance we may give to Greece, and in improving its public administration. It is of the utmost importance that we supervise the use of any funds made available to Greece, in such a manner that each dollar spent will count toward making Greece self-supporting, and will help to build an economy in which a healthy democracy can flourish.

No government is perfect. One of the chief virtues of a democracy, however, is that its defects are always visible and under democratic processes can be pointed out and corrected. The government of Greece is not perfect. Nevertheless it represents 85 percent of the members of the Greek Parliament who were chosen in an election last year. Foreign observers, including 692 Americans, considered this election to be a fair expression of the views of the Greek people.

The Greek Government has been operating in an atmosphere of chaos and extremism. It has made mistakes. The extension of aid by this country does not mean that the United

States condones everything that the Greek Government has done or will do. We have condemned in the past, and we condemn now, extremist measures of the right or the left. We have in the past advised tolerance, and we advise tolerance now.

Greece's neighbor, Turkey, also deserves our attention.

The future of Turkey as an independent and economically sound state is clearly no less important to the freedom-loving peoples of the world than the future of Greece. The circumstances in which Turkey finds itself today are considerably different from those of Greece. Turkey has been spared the disasters that have beset Greece. And during the war, the United States and Great Britain furnished Turkey with material aid.

Nevertheless, Turkey now needs our support.

Since the war Turkey has sought additional financial assistance from Great Britain and the United States for the purpose of effecting that modernization necessary for the maintenance of its national integrity.

That integrity is essential to the preservation of order in the Middle East.

The British Government has informed us that, owing to its own difficulties, it can no longer extend financial or economic aid to Turkey.

As in the case of Greece, if Turkey is to have the assistance it needs, the United States must supply it. We are the only country able to provide that help. I am fully aware of the broad implications involved if the United States extends assistance to Greece and Turkey, and I shall discuss these implications with you at this time.

One of the primary objectives of the foreign policy of the United States is the creation of conditions in which we and other nations will be able to work out a way of life free from coercion. This was a fundamental issue in the war with Germany and Japan. Our victory was won over countries which sought to impose their will, and their way of life, upon other nations.

To ensure the peaceful development of nations, free from coercion, the United States has taken a leading part in establishing the United Nations. The United Nations is designed to make possible lasting freedom and independence for all its members. We shall not realize our objectives, however, unless we are willing to help free peoples to maintain their free institutions and their national integrity against aggressive movements that seek to impose upon them totalitarian regimes. This is no more than a frank recognition that totalitarian regimes imposed upon free peoples, by direct or indirect aggression, undermine the foundations of international peace and hence the security of the United States.

The peoples of a number of countries of the world have recently had totalitarian regimes forced upon them against their will. The Government of the United States has made frequent protests against coercion and intimidation, in violation of the Yalta agreement, in Poland, Rumania, and Bulgaria. I must also state that in a number of other countries there have been similar developments.

At the present moment in world history nearly every nation must choose between alternative ways of life. The choice is too often not a free one. One way of life is based upon the will of the majority, and is distinguished by free institutions, representative government, free elections, guarantees of individual liberty, freedom of speech and religion, and freedom from political oppression. The second way of life is based upon the will of a minority forcibly imposed upon the majority. It relies upon terror and oppression, a controlled press and radio, fixed elections, and the suppression of personal freedoms.

I believed that it must be the policy of the United States to support free peoples who are resisting attempted subjugation by armed minorities or by outside pressures.

I believe that we must assist free peoples to work out their own destinies in their own way. I believe that our help should be primarily through economic and financial aid which is essential to economic stability and orderly political processes.

The world is not static, and the *status quo* is not sacred. But we cannot allow changes in the *status quo* in violation of the Charter of the United Nations by such methods as coercion, or by such subterfuges as political infiltration. In helping free and independent nations to maintain their freedom, the United States will be giving effect to the principles of the Charter of the United Nations.

It is necessary only to glance at a map to realize that the survival and integrity of the Greek nation are of grave importance in a much wider situation. If Greece should fall under the control of an armed minority, the effect upon its neighbor, Turkey, would be immediate and serious. Confusion and disorder might well spread throughout the entire Middle East.

Moreover, the disappearance of Greece as an independent state would have a profound effect upon those countries in Europe whose peoples are struggling against great difficulties to maintain their freedoms and their independence while they repair the damages of war.

It would be an unspeakable tragedy if these countries, which have struggled so long against overwhelming odds, should lose that victory for which they sacrificed so much. Collapse of free institutions and loss of independence would be disastrous not only for them but for the world. Discouragement and possibly failure would quickly be the lot of neighboring peoples striving to maintain their freedom and independence.

Should we fail to aid Greece and Turkey in this fateful hour, the effect will be far reaching to the West as well as to the East.

We must take immediate and resolute action.

I therefore ask the Congress to provide authority for assistance to Greece and Turkey in the amount of $400,000,000 for the period ending June 30, 1948. In requesting these funds, I have taken into consideration the maximum amount of relief assistance which would be furnished to Greece out of the $350,000,000 which I recently requested that the Congress authorize for the prevention of starvation and suffering in countries devastated by the war.

In addition to funds, I ask the Congress to authorize the detail of American civilian and military personnel to Greece and Turkey, at the request of those countries, to assist in the tasks of reconstruction, and for the purpose of supervising the use of such financial and material assistance as may be furnished. I recommend that authority also be provided for the instruction and training of selected Greek and Turkish personnel. . . .

This is a serious course upon which we embark.

I would not recommend it except that the alternative is much more serious.

The United States contributed $341 billion toward winning World War II. This is an investment in world freedom and world peace.

The assistance that I am recommending for Greece and Turkey amounts to little more than 1/10th of 1 percent of this investment. It is only common sense that we should safeguard this investment and make sure that it is not in vain.

The seeds of totalitarian regimes are nurtured by misery and want. They spread and grow in the evil soil of poverty and strife. They reach their full growth when the hope of a people for a better life has died.

We must keep that hope alive.

The free peoples of the world look to us for support in maintaining their freedoms. If we falter in our leadership, we may endanger the peace of the world—and we shall surely endanger the welfare of this nation.

Great responsibilities have been placed upon us by the swift movement of events. I am confident that the Congress will face these responsibilities squarely.

DOCUMENT 5.5

SECRETARY OF STATE GEORGE MARSHALL'S REPORT TO THE SENATE COMMITTEE ON FOREIGN AFFAIRS, JANUARY 8, 1948

On December 19 [1947] the President placed before you the recommendations of the executive branch of the Government for a

---

SOURCE: *Hearings Before the Committee on Foreign Relations*, U.S. Senate, 80th Cong. 2d Sess, 1948, pt. 1, 1–10.

program of United States assistance to European economic recovery.

This program will cost our country billions of dollars. It will impose a burden on the American taxpayer. It will require sacrifices today in order that we may enjoy security and peace tomorrow. Should the Congress approve the program for European recovery, as I urgently recommend, we Americans will have made a historic decision of our peacetime history.

A nation in which the voice of its people directs the conduct of its affairs cannot embark on an undertaking of such magnitude and significance for light or purely sentimental reasons. Decisions of this importance are dictated by the highest considerations of national interest. There are none higher, I am sure, than the establishment of enduring peace and the maintenance of true freedom for the individual. In the deliberations of the coming weeks I ask that the European recovery program be judged in these terms and on this basis.

As Secretary of State and as the initial representative of the executive branch of the Government in the presentation of the program to your community, I will first outline my convictions as to the extent and manner in which American interests are involved in European recovery.

Without the reestablishment of economic health and vigor in the free countries of Europe, without the restoration of their social and political strength necessarily associated with economic recuperation, the prospect for the American people, and for free people everywhere, to find peace with justice and well-being and security for themselves and their children will be gravely prejudiced.

So long as hunger, poverty, desperation, and resulting chaos threaten the great concentrations of people in western Europe—some 270,000,000—there will steadily develop social unease and political confusion on every side. Left to their own resources there will be, I believe, no escape from economic distress so intense, social discontents so violent, political confusion so widespread, and hopes of the future so shattered that the historic base of

western civilization, of which we are by belief and inheritance an integral part, will take on a new form in the image of the tyranny that we fought to destroy in Germany. The vacuum which the war created in western Europe will be filled by the forces of which wars are made. Our national security will be seriously threatened. We shall in effect live in an armed camp, relegated and controlled. Be if we furnish effective aid to support the now visible reviving hope of Europe, the prospect should speedily change. The foundation of political vitality is economic recovery. Durable peace requires the restoration of western European vitality.

We have engaged in a great war. We poured out our resources to win that war. We fought it to make real peace possible. Though the war has ended the peace has not commenced. We must not fail to complete that which we commenced. The peoples of western Europe have demonstrated their will to achieve a genuine recovery by entering into a great cooperative effort. Within the limits of their resources they formally undertake to establish the basis for the peace which we all seek, but they cannot succeed without American assistance. Dollars will not save the world, but the world today cannot be saved without dollars. . . .

I will confine my remarks to the three basic questions involved: First, "Why does Europe need help?" Second, "How much help is needed?" And third, "How should help be given?"

The "why": Europe is still emerging from the devastation and dislocation of the most destructive war in history. Within its own resources Europe cannot achieve within a reasonable time economic stability. The war more or less destroyed the mechanism whereby Europe supported itself in the past and the initial rebuilding of that mechanism requires outside assistance under existing circumstances.

The western European participating countries, with a present population of almost twice our own, constitute an interdependent area containing some of the most highly industrialized nations of the world. Production has become more and more specialized, and depends in large part on the processing of raw materials, largely imported from abroad, into finished goods and the furnishing of services to other areas. These goods and services have been sold throughout the world and the proceeds therefrom paid for the necessary imports.

The war smashed the vast and delicate mechanism by which European countries made their living. It was the war which destroyed coal mines and deprived the workshop of sufficient mechanical energy. It was the war which destroyed steel mills and thus cut down the workshop's material for fabrication. It was the war which destroyed transportation lines and equipment and thus made the ability to move goods and people inadequate. It was the war which destroyed livestock herds, made fertilizers unobtainable and thus reduced soil fertility. It was the war which destroyed merchant fleets and thus cut off accustomed income from carrying the world's goods. It was the war which destroyed or caused the loss of so much of foreign investments and the income which it has produced. It was the war which bled inventories and working capital out of existence. It was the war which shattered business relationships and markets and the sources of raw material. The war disrupted the flow of vital raw materials from southeast Asia, thereby breaking the pattern of multilateral trade which formerly provided, directly or indirectly, large dollar earnings for western Europe. In the postwar period artificial and forcible reorientation to the Soviet Union of eastern European trade had deprived western Europe of sources of foodstuffs and raw material from that area. Here and there the present European situation has been aggravated by unsound or destructive policies pursued in one or another country, but the basic dislocations find their source directly in the war.

The inability of the European workshop to get food and raw materials required to produce the exports necessary to get the purchasing power for food and raw materials is the worst of the many vicious circles that beset the European peoples. Not withstanding the fact that industrial output, except in western Germany, has almost regained its prewar volume, under the changed conditions this is not nearly enough. The loss of European investments abroad, the destruction of merchant fleets, and the disappearance of other sources of income, together with increases in populations to be sustained, make necessary an increase in production far above prewar levels, even sufficient for a living standard considerably below prewar standards.

This is the essence of the economic problems of Europe. This problem would exist even though it were not complicated by the ideological struggle in Europe between those who want to live as freemen and those small groups who aspire to dominate by the method of police states. The solution would be much easier, of course, if all the nations of Europe were cooperating. But they are not. Far from cooperating, the Soviet Union and the Communist parties have proclaimed their determined opposition to a plan for European economic recovery. Economic distress is to be employed to further political ends.

There are many who accept the picture that I have just drawn but who raise a further question: "Why must the United States carry so great a load in helping Europe?" The answer is simple. The United States is the only country in the world today which has the economic power and productivity to furnish the needed assistance.

I wish now to turn to the other questions which we must answer. These are "how much" aid is required and "how" should that aid be given[?]

Three principles should determine the amount and timing of our aid. It must be adequate. It must be prompt, it must be effectively applied.

The objective of the European recovery program submitted for your consideration is to achieve lasting economic recovery for western Europe; recovery in the sense that after our aid has terminated, the European countries will be able to maintain themselves by their own efforts on a sound economic basis.

Our assistance, if we determine to embark on this program to aid western Europe, must be adequate to do the job. The initial increment of our aid should be fully sufficient to get the program under way on a broad, sound basis and not in a piecemeal manner. An inadequate program would involve a wastage of our resources with an ineffective result. Either undertake to meet the requirements of the problem or don't undertake it at all.

I think it must be plain to all that the circumstances which have given birth to this program call for promptness in decision and vigor in putting the project into operation. The sooner this program can get under way the greater its chances of success. Careful consideration and early action are not incompatible.

The interim-aid law which the Congress enacted last December was designated as a stop-gap measure to cover the period until April first of this year. In the meantime it would be possible to consider the long-term recovery measure which we are now discussing. Unless the program can be placed in operation on or soon after April 1, there will undoubtedly be a serious deterioration in some of the basic conditions upon which the whole project is predicted.

It is proposed that the Congress now authorize the program for its full four and one-quarter year duration, although appropriations are being requested only for the first fifteen months. Annual decisions on appropriations will afford full opportunity for review and control. But a general authorization now for the longer term will provide a necessary foundation for the continuing effort and cooperation of the European countries.

The amounts, form, and conditions of the recommended program of American aid to European recovery have been presented in President Truman's message to the Congress on December 9, 1947. They were further explained in the proposed draft legislation and background material furnished to this committee at that time by the Department of State. Taking as the basis genuine European cooperation—the maximum of self-help and mutual help on the part of the participating European countries—the program aims to provide these countries until the end of June, 1952, with those portions of their essential imports from the Western Hemisphere which they themselves cannot pay for. These essential imports include not only the food, fuel, and other supplies but also equipment and materials to enable them to increase their productive capacity. They must produce and export considerably more goods than they did in prewar times if they are to become self-supporting even at a lower standard of living. . . .

In each succeeding year of the program, increased production and increased trade from Europe is expected to reduce the amount of assistance needed, until after mid-1952, when it is calculated that the participating countries will have recovered ability to support themselves.

The recommended program of $6.8 billion for the first fifteen months reflects a searching and comprehensive investigation by the executive branch of European needs and of availabilities in the United States and other supplying countries. . . .

The total estimated cost of the program is now put at somewhere between 15.1 to 17.8 billion [dollars]. But this will depend on developments each year, the progress made, and unforeseeable variations in the weather as it affects crops. The over-all cost is not capable of precise determination so far in advance.

In developing the program of American assistance, no question has been more closely examined than the ability of the United States to provide assistance in the magnitudes proposed. Both in terms of physical resources and in terms of financial capacity our ability to support such a program seems clear. Representatives of the executive branch more closely familiar than I with the domestic economy will provide further testimony on this issue. But I should like to remind you of the conclusions of the three special committees which explored this matter in detail during the summer and fall.

The proposed program does involve some sacrifice on the part of the American people, but it should be kept in mind that the burden of the program diminishes rapidly after the first fifteen months. Considerations of the cost must be related to the momentous objective, on the one hand, and to the probable price of the alternatives. The $6.8 billion proposed for the first fifteen months is less than a single month's charge of the war. A world of continuing uneasy half-peace will create demands for constantly mounting expenditures for defense. This program should be viewed as an investment in peace. In those terms, the cost is low. . . .

We will be working with a group of nations each with a long and proud history. The peoples of these countries are highly skilled, able, and energetic and justly proud of their cultures. They have ancient traditions of self-reliance and are eager to take the lead in working out their own salvation.

We have stated in many ways that American aid will not be used to interfere with the sovereign rights of these nations and their own responsibility to work out their won salvation. I cannot emphasize too much my profound conviction that the aid we furnish must not be tied to conditions which would, in effect, destroy the whole moral justification for our cooperative assistance toward European partnership.

We are dealing with democratic governments. One of the major justifications of asking the American people to make the sacrifice necessary under this program is the vital stake that the United States has in helping to preserve democracy in Europe. As democratic governments they are responsive, like our own, to the peoples of their countries—and we would not have it otherwise. We cannot expect any democratic government to take upon itself obligations or accept conditions which run counter to the basic national sentiment of its people. This program calls for free cooperation among nations mutually respecting one another's sincerity of purpose in the common endeavor—a cooperation which we hope will long outlive the period of American assistance. . . .

The fulfillment of the mutual pledges of these nations would have profound effects in altering for the better the future economic condition of the European Continent. The Paris Conference itself was one major step, and the participating nations have not waited on American action before taking further steps, many of which required a high order of practical courage. They have moved forward toward a practical working arrangement for the multilateral clearing of trade. France and Italy, whose financial affairs suffered greatly by war and occupation, are taking energetic measures to establish monetary stability—an essential prerequisite to economic recovery. British coal production is being increased more quickly than even the more hopeful forecasts, and there is prospect of the early resumption of exports to the Continent. The customs union among Belgium, the Netherlands, and Luxembourg is now in operation. Negotiations for a Franco-Italian customs union are proceeding. . . .

The operation of the program must be related to the foreign policy of the Nation. The importance of the recovery program in our foreign affairs needs no argument. To carry out this relationship effectively will require cooperation and teamwork, but I know of no other way by which the complexities of modern world affairs can be met. It should, I think, be constantly kept in mind that this great project, which would be difficult enough in a normal international political climate, must be carried to success against the avowed determination of the Soviet Union and the Communist Party to oppose and sabotage it at every turn. . . .

What are the prospects of success of such a program for the economic recovery of a continent? It would be absurd to deny the existence of obstacles and risks. Weather and the extent of world crops are unpredictable. The possible extent of political sabotage and the effectiveness with which its true intentions are unmasked and thus made susceptible to control cannot be fully foreseen. All we can say is this program does provide the means for success and if we maintain the will for success I believe that success will be achieved.

To be quite clear, this unprecedented endeavor of the New World to help the Old is neither sure nor easy. It is a calculated risk. But there can be no doubts as to the alternatives. The way of life that we have known is literally in balance.

Our country is now faced with a momentous decision. If we decided that the United States is unable or unwilling effectively to assist in the reconstruction of western Europe, we must accept the consequences of its collapse into the dictatorship of police states. . . .

I think it is of the greatest importance in considering this program that the people, as well as the Congress, thoroughly understand the critical situation. We have heard the comment several times that we won a victory, but we still have not won a peace. It goes much further than that. In some portions of the world there is more fighting now than there was during the war. You are aware of that. There is political instability. There are efforts to almost change the face of Europe, contrary to the interests of mankind in advancing civilization, certainly as we understand and desire it. The whole situation is critical in the extreme.

We happen to be, very fortunately for ourselves, the strongest nation in the world today, certainly economically, and I think in most other respects. There will be requirements in this program for certain sacrifices. But I feel that when you measure those sacrifices against what we are fighting for you will get a very much better idea of the necessities of the case.

I would like to close by saying that this is a complex program. It is a difficult program. And you know, far better than I do, the political difficulties involved in this program. But there is no doubt whatever in my mind that if we decide to do this thing we can do it successfully, and there is no doubt in my mind that the whole world hangs in the balance, as to what it is to be, in connection with what we are endeavoring to put forward here.

5.6 "X" and Containment. George Kennan, "The Sources of Soviet Conduct"
5.7 Walter Lippmann Responds to "Mr. X"

In February 1946 George Kennan, a low-level counselor at the U.S. Embassy in Moscow and an expert on Soviet affairs, sent a 600-word telegram to the State Department outlining the character of the Soviet Union. He focused mostly on the historical antecedents of a totalitarian Soviet leadership with expansionist tendencies and driven to act by impulses of paranoia and ideology. In this "Long Telegram," Kennan hinted at the idea that the United States should adopt a foreign policy of containment, an aggressive strategy that would contain an expansionist Soviet Union within its borders. About 18 months later, Kennan, writing under the pseudonym "X," further spelled out this containment strategy in an article in *Foreign Affairs* (Document 5.6). The Long Telegram and the "X" article are usually identified as the source of the containment strategy that remained a primary tenet of U.S. foreign policy throughout the cold war. However, it might also be argued that the Truman administration was already implementing a containment policy against the Soviets in several regions of the world.

Kennan's chief critic was Walter Lippmann, a titan of twentieth century American journalism. In a series of newspaper articles that were collected into a book entitled *The Cold War*, Lippmann argued eloquently that Kennan's containment strategy was untenable, unrealistic, and too expensive. The portion of Lippmann's book aimed directly at Kennan's "X" article is excerpted in *Document 5.7*.

Kennan went on to head the State Department's Policy Planning Staff until 1950. In 1952 he served a short time as ambassador to the Soviet Union. In the Kennedy administration he was named ambassador to Yugoslavia after being passed over for a cabinet post because of his opposition to the nuclear arms race ("stop the madness," he proclaimed), and for his belief that the United States should recognize the Chinese government of Mao Zedong, a move that Kennedy believed was politically impossible.

Later in his life Kennan insisted that the disagreement with Lippmann was a "misunderstanding almost tragic in its dimensions." He did not, he said, intend that his strategy of containment be interpreted as military containment. However, during the late 1940s and early 1950s when the Kennan-Lippmann debate over containment was being waged, Kennan did not take the opportunity to disavow the military interpretation of his strategy.

....

DOCUMENT 5.6

"X" AND CONTAINMENT. GEORGE KENNAN, "THE SOURCES OF SOVIET CONDUCT"

The political personality of Soviet power as we know it today is the product of ideology and circumstances: ideology inherited by the present Soviet leaders from the movement in which they had their political origin, and circumstances of the power which they now have exercised for nearly three decades in Russia. There can be few tasks of psychological analysis more difficult than to try to trace the interaction of these two forces and the relative role of each in the determination of official Soviet conduct. Yet the attempt must be made if that conduct is to be understood and effectively countered.

It is difficult to summarize the set of ideological concepts with which the Soviet leaders came

into power. Marxian ideology, in its Russian-Communist projection, has always been in process of subtle evolution. The materials on which it bases itself are extensive and complex. But the outstanding features of Communist thought as it existed in 1916 may perhaps be summarized as follows: (a) that the central factor in the life of man, the fact which determines the character of public life and the "physiognomy of society," is the system by which material goods are produced and exchanged; (b) that the capitalist system of production is a nefarious one which inevitably leads to the exploitation of the working class by the capital-owning class and is incapable of developing adequately the economic resources of society or of distributing fairly the material goods produced by human labor; (c) that capitalism contains the seeds of its own destruction and must, in view of the inability of the capital-owning class to adjust itself to economic change, result eventually and inescapably in a revolutionary transfer of power to the working class; and (d) that imperialism, the final phase of capitalism, leads directly to war and revolution.

SOURCE: X, "The Sources of Soviet Conduct," *Foreign Affairs* XXV (July 1947), 566–82.

The rest may be outlined in Lenin's own words: "Unevenness of economic and political development is the inflexible law of capitalism. It is from this that the victory of Socialism may come originally in a few capitalist countries or even in a single capitalist country. The victorious proletariat of that country, having expropriated the capitalists and having organized Socialist production at home, would rise against the remaining capitalist world, drawing to itself in the process the oppressed classes of other countries." It must be noted that there is no assumption that capitalism would perish without proletarian revolution. A final push was needed from a revolutionary proletariat movement in order to tip over the tottering structure. . . .

Now the outstanding circumstance concerning the Soviet regime is that down to the present day this process of political consolidation has never been completed and the men in the Kremlin have continued to be predominately absorbed with the struggle to secure and make absolute power which they seized in November 1917. They have endeavoured to secure it primarily against forces at home, within Soviet society itself. But they have also endeavoured to secure it against the outside world. For ideology, as we have seen, taught them that the outside world was hostile and that it was their duty eventually to overthrow the political forces beyond their borders. . . . It is an undeniable privilege of every man to prove himself right in the thesis that the world is his enemy; for if he reiterates it frequently enough and makes it the background of his conduct he is bound eventually to be right. . . .

This began at an early date. In 1924 Stalin specifically defended the retention of the "organs of suppression," meaning, among others, the army and the secret police, on the ground that "as long as there is a capitalist encirclement there will be danger of intervention with all the consequences that flow from that danger." In accordance with that theory, and from that time on, all internal opposition forces in Russia have consistently been portrayed as agents of foreign forces of reaction antagonistic to Soviet power.

By the same token, tremendous emphasis has been placed on the original Communist thesis of basic antagonism between the capitalist and the Socialist worlds. It is clear, from many indications, that this emphasis is not found in reality. The real facts concerning it have been confused by the existence abroad of genuine resentment provoked by Soviet philosophy and tactics and occasionally by the existence if great centers of military power, notably the Nazi regime in Germany and the Japanese Government of the late 1930s, which did indeed have aggressive designs against the Soviet Union. But there is ample evidence that the stress laid in Moscow on the menace confronting the Soviet society from the world outside its borders is founded not in the realities of foreign antagonism but in the necessity of explaining away the maintenance of dictatorial authority at home.

Now the maintenance of this pattern of Soviet power, namely, the pursuit of unlimited authority domestically, accompanied by the cultivation of the semi-myth of implacable foreign hostility, has gone far to shape the actual machinery of Soviet power as we know it today. Internal organs of administration which did not serve this purpose withered on the vine. Organs which did serve this purpose became vastly swollen. The security of Soviet power came to rest on the iron discipline of the Party, on the severity and ubiquity of the secret police, and on the uncompromising economic monopolism of the state. The "organs of suppression," in which the Soviet leaders had sought security from rival forces, became in large measures the masters of those whom they were designed to serve. Today the major part of the structure of Soviet power is committed to the perfection of the dictatorship and to the maintenance of the concept of Russia as in a state of siege, with the enemy lowering beyond the walls. And the millions of human beings who form that part of the structure of power must defend at all costs this concept of Russia's position, for without it they are themselves superfluous.

As things stand today, the rulers can no longer dream of parting with these organs of suppression. The quest for absolute power, pursued now for nearly three decades with a ruthlessness unparalleled (in scope at least) in modern times, has again produced internally, as it did externally, its own reaction. The excesses of the police apparatus have fanned the potential opposition to the regime into something far greater and more dangerous than it could have been before those excesses began.

But least of all can the rulers dispense with the fiction by which the maintenance of dictatorial power has been defended. For this fiction has been canonized in Soviet philosophy by the excesses already committed in its name; and it is now anchored in the Soviet structure of thought by bonds far greater than those of mere ideology.

II

So much for the historical background. What does it spell in terms of the political personality of Soviet power as we know it today?

Of the original ideology, nothing has been officially junked. Belief is maintained in the basic badness of capitalism, in the inevitability of its destruction, in the obligation of the proletariat to assist in that destruction and to take power into its own hands. But stress has come to be laid primarily on those concepts which relate most specifically to the Soviet regime itself: to its position as the sole truly Socialist regime in a dark and misguided world, and to the relationships of power within it.

The first of these concepts is that of the innate antagonism between capitalism and Socialism. We have seen how deeply that concept has become imbedded in foundations of Soviet power. It has profound implications for Russia's conduct as a member of international society. It means that there can never be on Moscow's side any sincere assumption of a community of aims between the Soviet Union and powers which are regarded as capitalism. It must invariably be assumed in Moscow that the aims of the capitalist world are antagonistic to the Soviet regime and therefore to the interests of the peoples it controls. If the Soviet government occasionally sets its signature to documents which would indicate the contrary, this is to be regarded as a tactical maneuver permissible in dealing with the enemy (who is regarded without honor) and should be taken in the spirit of *caveat emptor*. Basically, the antagonism remains. It is postulated. And from it flow many of the phenomena which we would find disturbing in the Kremlin's conduct of foreign policy: the secretiveness, the lack of frankness, the duplicity, the wary suspiciousness, and the basic unfriendliness of purpose. These phenomena are there to stay, for the foreseeable future. There can be variations of degree and of emphasis. When there is something the Russians want from us, one or the other of these features of their policy may be thrust temporarily into the background; and when that happens there will always be Americans who will leap forward with gleeful announcements that "the Russians have changed," and some who will even try to take credit for having brought about such "changes." But we should not be misled by tactical maneuvers. These characteristics of Soviet policy, like the postulate from which they flow, are basic to the internal nature of Soviet power, and will be with us, whether in the foreground or in the background, until the internal nature of Soviet power is changed.

This means that we are going to continue for a long time to find the Russians difficult to deal with. It does not mean that they should be considered as embarked upon a do-or-die program to overthrow our society by a given date. The theory of the inevitability of the eventual fall of capitalism has the fortunate connotation that there is no hurry about it. The forces of progress can take their time in preparing the final *coup de grace*. Meanwhile, what is vital is that the "Socialist fatherland"—that oasis of power which has been already won for Socialism in the person of the Soviet Union—should be cherished and defended by all good Communists at home and abroad, its fortunes promoted, its enemies badgered and confounded.

The promotion of premature, "adventuristic" revolutionary projects abroad which might embarrass Soviet power in any way would be an inexcusable, even a counterrevolutionary act. The cause of Socialism is the support and promotion of Soviet power, as defined in Moscow.

This brings us to the second of the concepts important to the contemporary Soviet outlook. That is the infallibility of the Kremlin. The Soviet concept of power, which permits no focal points of organization outside the Party itself, requires that the Party leadership remain in theory the sole repository of truth. For if truth were to be found elsewhere, there would be justification for its expression in organized activity. But it is precisely what the Kremlin cannot and will not permit.

The leadership of the Communist Party is therefore always right, and has always been right ever since in 1929 Stalin formalized his personal power by announcing that decisions of the Politburo were being taken unanimously.

On the principle of infallibility there rests the iron discipline of the Communist Party. In fact, the two concepts are mutually self-supporting. Perfect discipline requires recognition of infallibility. Infallibility requires the observance of discipline. The two together go far to determine the behaviorism of the entire Soviet apparatus of power. But their effect cannot be understood unless a third factor be taken into account: namely, the fact that the leadership is at liberty to put forward for tactical purposes any particular thesis which it finds useful to the cause at any particular moment and to require the faithful and unquestioning acceptance of that thesis by the members of the movement as a whole. This means that truth is not a constant but is actually created, for all intents and purposes, by the Soviet leaders themselves. . . .

But we have seen that the Kremlin is under no ideological compulsion to accomplish its purposes in a hurry. Like the Church, it is dealing in ideological concepts which are of long-term validity, and it can afford to be patient. It has no right to risk the existing achievements of the revolution for the sake of vain baubles of the future. The very teachings of Lenin himself require great caution and flexibility in the pursuit of Communist purposes. Again, these precepts are fortified by the lessons of Russian history: of centuries of obscure battles between nomadic forces over stretches of vast unfortified plain. Here caution, circumspection, flexibility and deception are the valuable qualities; and their value finds natural appreciation in the Russian or the oriental mind. Thus the Kremlin has no compunction about retreating in the face of superior force. And being under the compulsion of no timetable, it does not get panicky under the necessity for such a retreat. Its political action is a fluid stream which moves constantly, wherever it is permitted to move, toward a given goal. Its main concern is to make sure that it has filled every nook and cranny available to it in the basin of world power. But if it finds unassailable barriers in its path, it accepts these philosophically and accommodates itself to them. The main thing is that there should always be pressure, unceasing constant pressure, toward the desired goal. There is no trace of any feeling in Soviet psychology that that goal must be reached at any time.

These considerations make Soviet diplomacy at once easier and more difficult to deal with than the diplomacy of individual aggressive leaders like Napoleon and Hitler. On the one hand it is more sensitive to contrary force, more ready to yield on individual sectors of the diplomatic front when that force is felt to be too strong, and thus more rational in the logic and rhetoric of power. On the other hand it cannot be easily defeated or discouraged by a single victory on the part of its opponents. And the patient persistence by which it is animated means that it can be effectively countered not by sporadic acts which represent the momentary whims of democratic opinion but only by intelligent long-range policies on the part of Russia's adversaries—policies no less steady in their purpose, and no less variegated and resourceful in their application, than those of the Soviet Union itself.

In these circumstances it is clear that the main element of any United States policy toward the Soviet Union must be that of a long-term, patient but firm and vigilant containment of Russia expansive tendencies. It is important to note, however, that such a policy has nothing to do with outward histrionics: with threats or blustering or superfluous gestures of outward "toughness." While the Kremlin is basically flexible in its reaction to political realities, it is by no means unamenable to considerations of prestige. Like almost any other government, it can be placed by tactless and threatening gestures in a position where it cannot afford to yield even though this might be dictated by its sense of realism. The Russian leaders are keen judges of human psychology, and as such they are highly conscious that loss of temper and of self-control is never a source of strength in political affairs. They are quick to exploit such evidences of weakness. For these reasons, it is a *sine qua non* of successful dealing with Russia that the foreign government in question should remain at all times cool and collected and that its demands on Russian policy should be put forward in such a manner as to leave the way open for a compliance not too detrimental to Russian prestige.

III

In the light of the above, it will be clearly seen that the Soviet pressure against the free institutions of the Western world is something that can be contained by adroit and vigilant application of counterforce at a series of constantly shifting geographical and political points, corresponding to the shifts and maneuvers of Soviet policy, but which cannot be charmed or talked out of existence. The Russians look forward to a duel of infinite duration, and they see that already they have scored great successes. It must be borne in mind that there was a time when the Communist Party represented far more of a minority in the sphere of Russian national life than Soviet power today represents in the world community.

But if ideology convinces the rulers of Russia that truth is on their side and that they can therefore afford to wait, those of us on whom that ideology has no claim are free to examine objectively the validity of that premise. The Soviet thesis not only implies complete lack of control by the West over its own economic destiny, it likewise assumes Russian unity, discipline and patience over an infinite period. Let us bring this apocalyptic vision down to earth, and suppose that the Western world finds the strength and resourcefulness to contain Soviet power over a period of ten to fifteen years. . . .

In addition to this, we have the fact that Soviet economic development, while it can list certain formidable achievements, has been precariously spotty and uneven. Russian Communists who speak of the "uneven development of capitalism" should blush at the contemplation of their own national economy. Here certain branches of economic life, such as the metallurgical and machine industries, have been pushed out of all proportion to other sectors of the economy. Here is a nation striving to become in a short period one of the great industrial nations of the world while it has no highway network worthy of the name and only a relatively primitive network of railways. Much has been done to increase efficiency of labor and to teach primitive peasants something about the operation of machines. But the maintenance is still a crying deficiency of all Soviet economy. Construction is hasty and poor in quality. Depreciation must be enormous. And in vast sectors of economic life it has not yet been possible to instill into labor anything like that general culture of production and technical self-respect which characterizes the skilled worker of the West.

It is difficult to see how these deficiencies can be corrected at an early date by a tired and dispirited population working largely under the shadow of fear and compulsion. And as long as they are not overcome, Russia will remain economically a vulnerable, and in a certain sense an impotent, nation, capable of exporting its enthusiasm and of radiating the strange charm of its political vitality but unable to back up those articles of export by the real evidences of material power and prosperity. . . .

Who can say whether, in these circumstances, the eventual rejuvenation of the higher spheres of authority (which can only be a matter of time) can take place smoothly and peacefully, or whether rivals in the quest for higher power will eventually reach down into these politically immature and inexperienced masses in order to find support for their respective claims. If this were to ever happen, strange consequences could flow for the Communist Party: for the membership at large has been exercised only in the practices of iron discipline and obedience and not in the arts of compromise and accommodation. And if disunity were ever to seize and paralyze the Party, the chaos and weakness of Russian society would be revealed in forms beyond description. For we have seen that Soviet power is only a crust concealing an amorphous mass of human beings among whom no independent organizational structure is tolerated. In Russia there is not even such a thing as local government. The present generation of Russians have never known spontaneity of collective action. If, consequently, anything were to ever to occur to disrupt the unity and efficacy of the Party as a political instrument, Soviet Russia might be changed overnight from one of the strongest to one of the weakest and most pitiable of national societies.

Thus the future of Soviet power may not be by any means more secure as Russian capacity for self-delusion would make it appear to the men in the Kremlin. That they can keep power themselves, they have demonstrated. That they can quietly and easily turn it over to others remains to be proved. Meanwhile, the hardships of their rule and the vicissitudes of international life have taken a heavy toll of the strength and hopes of the great people on whom their power rests. It is curious to note that the ideological power of Soviet authority is strongest today in areas beyond the frontiers of Russia, beyond the reach of its police power. This phenomenon brings to mind a comparison used by Thomas Mann in his great novel *Buddenbrooks*. Observing that human institutions often show the greatest outward brilliance at a moment when inner decay is in reality farthest advanced, he compared the Buddenbrook family, in the days of its greatest glamour, to one of those stars whose light shines most brightly on this world when in reality it has long ceased to exist. And who can say with assurance that the strong light still cast by the Kremlin on the dissatisfied peoples of the Western world is not the powerful afterglow of a constellation which is in actuality on the wane? This cannot be proved. And it cannot be disproved. But the possibility remains (and in the opinion of this writer it is a strong one) that Soviet power, like the capitalist world of its conception, bears within it the seeds of its own decay, and that the sprouting of these seeds is well advanced.

IV

It is clear that the United States cannot expect in the foreseeable future to enjoy political intimacy with the Soviet regime. It must continue to regard the Soviet Union as a rival, not a partner, in the political arena. It must continue to expect that Soviet politics will reflect no abstract love of peace and stability, no real faith in the possibility of a permanent happy coexistence of the Socialist and capitalist worlds, but rather a cautious, persistent pressure toward the disruption and weakening of all rival influence and rival power.

Balanced against this are the facts that Russia, as opposed to the Western world in general, is still by far the weaker party, that Soviet policy is highly flexible, and that Soviet society may well contain deficiencies which will eventually weaken its own total potential. This would of itself warrant the United States entering with reasonable confidence upon a policy of firm containment, designed to confront the Russians with unalterable counterforce at every point where they show signs of encroaching upon the interests of a peaceful and stable world.

But in actuality the possibilities for American policy are by no means limited to holding the line and hoping for the best. It is entirely possible for the United States to influence by its actions the internal developments, both within Russia and throughout the international Communist movement, by which Russian policy is largely determined. This is not only a question of the modest measure of informational activity which this government can conduct in the Soviet Union and elsewhere, although that too is important. It is rather a question of the degree to which the United States can create among the peoples of the world generally the impression of a country which knows what it wants, which is coping successfully with the problems of its internal life and with the responsibilities of a world power, and which has a spiritual vitality capable of holding its own among the major ideological currents of the time. To the extent that such an impression can be created and maintained, the aims of Russian Communism must appear sterile and quixotic, the hopes and enthusiasm of Moscow's supporters must wane, and added strain must be imposed on the Kremlin's foreign policies. For the palsied decrepitude of the capitalist world is the keystone of Communist philosophy. Even the failure of the United States to experience the early economic depression which the ravens of Red Square have been predicting with such complacent confidence since hostilities ceased would have such deep and important repercussions throughout the Communist world.

By the same token, exhibitions of indecision, disunity and internal disintegration within this country have an exhilarating effect on the whole Communist movement. At each evidence of these tendencies, a thrill of hope and excitement goes through the Communist world; a new jauntiness can be noted in the Moscow tread; new groups of foreign supporters climb onto what they can only view as the bandwagon of international politics; and Russian pressure increases all along the line in international affairs.

It would be an exaggeration to say that American behavior unassisted and alone could exercise a power of life and death over the Communist movement and bring about the early fall of Soviet power in Russia. But the United States has it in its power to increase enormously the strains under which Soviet policy must operate, to force upon the Kremlin a far greater degree of moderation and circumspection than it has had to observe in recent years, and in this way to promote tendencies which must eventually find their outlet in either the breakup or the gradual mellowing of Soviet power. For no mystical, messianic movement—particularly not that of the Kremlin—can face frustration indefinitely without eventually adjusting itself in one way or another to the logic of that state of affairs.

Thus the decision will fall in large measure on this country itself. The issue of Soviet-American relations is in essence a test of the overall worth of the United States as a nation among nations. To avoid destruction the United States need only measure up to its own best traditions and prove itself worthy of preservation as a great nation.

Surely, there was never a fairer test of national quality that this. In the light of these circumstances, the thoughtful observer of Russian-American relations will find no cause for complaint in the Kremlin's challenge to American society. He will rather experience a certain gratitude to a Providence which, by providing the American people with this implacable challenge, has made their entire security as a nation dependent on pulling themselves together and accepting the responsibilities of moral and political leadership that history plainly intended them to bear.

DOCUMENT 5.7

WALTER LIPPMANN RESPONDS TO "MR. X"

Mr. X's article is . . . not only an analytical interpretation of the sources of Soviet conduct. It is also a document of primary importance on the sources of American foreign policy—of at least that part of it which is known as the Truman Doctrine.

SOURCE: Walter Lippmann, *The Cold War: A Study in U.S. Foreign Policy* (New York, 1947), 9–20, 24–28, 52, 60–61, 62.

As such I am venturing to examine it critically in this essay. My criticism, I hasten to say at once, does not arise from any belief or hope that our conflict with the Soviet government is imaginary or that it can be avoided, or ignored or easily disposed of. I agree entirely with Mr. X that the Soviet pressure "cannot be charmed or talked out of existence." I agree entirely that the Soviet power will expand unless it is prevented from expanding because it is confronted with the power, primarily American power, that it must respect. But I believe and shall argue, that the strategical conception and plan which Mr. X recommends is fundamentally unsound, and that it cannot be made to work, and that the attempt to make it work will cause us to squander our substance and our prestige.

We must begin with the disturbing fact, which anyone who will reread the article can verify for himself, that Mr. X's conclusions depend upon the optimistic prediction that the "Soviet power . . . bears within itself the seeds of its own decay, and that the sprouting of these seeds is well advanced"; that if "anything were ever to occur to disrupt the unity and efficacy of the party as a political instrument, Soviet Russia might be changed overnight from one of the strongest to one of the weakest and most pitiable of national societies"; and "that Soviet society may well contain deficiencies which will eventually weaken its own total potential."

Of this optimistic prediction Mr. X himself says that it "cannot be proved. And it cannot be disproved." Nevertheless, he concludes that the United States should construct its policy on the assumption that the Soviet power is inherently weak and impermanent, and that this unproved assumption warrants our entering "with reasonable confidence upon a policy of firm containment, designed to confront the Russians with unalterable counterforce at every point where they show signs of encroaching upon the interests of a peaceful and a stable world."

I do not find much ground for reasonable confidence in a policy which can be successful only if the most optimistic prediction should prove to be true. Surely a sound policy must be addressed to the worst and hardest that may be judged to be probable, and not to the best and easiest that may be possible.

As a matter of fact, Mr. X himself betrays a marked lack of confidence in his own diagnosis. For no sooner had he finished describing the policy of firm containment with unalterable counterforce at every point where the Russians show signs of encroaching, when he felt he must defend his conclusions against the criticism, one might almost say the wisecrack, that this is a policy of "holding the line and hoping for the best." His defense is to say that while he is proposing a policy of holding the line and hoping for the best, "in actuality the possibilities for American policy are by no means limited to holding the line and hoping for the best." The additional possibilities are not, however, within the scope of the authority of the Department of State: "the aims of Russian Communism must appear sterile and quixotic, the hopes and enthusiasms of Moscow's supporters must wane, and added strain must be imposed on the Kremlin's foreign policies" if "the United States can create among the peoples of the world generally the impression of a country which knows what it wants, which is coping successfully with the problems of its internal life and with the responsibilities of a world power, and which has a spiritual vitality capable of holding its own among the major ideological currents of the time."

This surely is a case of bolstering up the wishful thinking of "hoping for the best"— namely, the collapse of the Soviet power—by an extra strong dose of wishful thinking about the United States. There must be something deeply defective in Mr. X's estimates and calculations. For on his own showing, the policy cannot be made to work unless there are miracles and we get all the breaks.

In Mr. X's estimates there are no reserves for a rainy day. There is no margin of safety for bad luck, bad management, error and the unforeseen. He asks us to assume that the Soviet power is already decaying. He exhorts us to believe that our own highest hopes for ourselves will soon have been realized. Yet the policy he recommends is designed to deal effectively with the Soviet Union "as a rival, not a partner, in the political arena." Do we dare to assume, as we enter the arena and get set to run the race, that the Soviet Union will break its leg while the United States grows a pair of wings to speed it on its way?

Mr. X concludes his article on Soviet conduct and American policy by saying that "the thoughtful observer of Russian-American relations will . . . experience a certain gratitude to a Providence which, by providing the American people with this implacable challenge, has made their entire security as a nation dependent upon their pulling themselves together and accepting the responsibilities of moral and political leadership that history plainly intended them to bear." Perhaps. It may be that Mr. X has read the mind of Providence and that he knows what history plainly intended. But it is asking a good deal that the American people should stake their "entire security as a nation" upon a theory which, as he himself says, cannot be proved and cannot be disproved.

Surely it is by no means proved that the way to lead mankind is to spend the next ten or fifteen years, as Mr. X proposes we should, in reacting to "a series of constantly shifting geographical and political points, corresponding to the shifts and manoeuvres of Soviet policy." For if history has indeed intended us to bear the responsibility of leadership, then it is not leadership to adapt ourselves to the shifts and manoeuvres of Soviet policy at a series of constantly shifting geographical and political points. For that would mean for ten or fifteen years Moscow, not Washington, would define the issues, would make the challenges, would select the ground where the conflict was to be waged, and would choose the weapons. And the best that Mr. X can say for his own proposal is that if for a long period of time we can prevent the Soviet power from winning, the Soviet power will eventually perish or "mellow" because it has been "frustrated."

This is a dismal conclusion. Mr. X has, I believe, become bogged down in it because as he thought more and more about the conduct of the Soviets, he remembered less and less about the conduct of the other nations of the world. For while it may be true that the Soviet power would perish of frustration, if it were contained for ten or fifteen years, this conclusion is only half baked until he has answered the crucial question which remains: can the western world operate a policy of containment? Mr. X not only does not answer this question. He begs it, saying that it will be very discouraging to the Soviets if the western world finds the strength and resourcefulness to contain the Soviet power over a period of ten or fifteen years.

Now the strength of the western world is great, and we may assume that its resourcefulness is considerable. Nevertheless, there are weighty reasons for thinking that the kind of strength we have and the kind of resourcefulness we are capable of showing are peculiarly unsuited to operating a policy of containment.

How, for example, under the Constitution of the United States, is Mr. X going to work out an arrangement by which the Department of State has the money and the military power always available in sufficient amounts to apply "counterforce" at constantly shifting points all over the world? Is he going to ask Congress for a blank check on the Treasury and for a blank authorization to use the armed forces? Not if the American constitutional system is to be maintained. Or is he going to ask for an appropriation and for authority each time the Russians "show signs of encroaching upon the interests of a peaceful and stable world"? If that is his plan for dealing with the manoeuvres of a dictatorship, he is going to arrive at the points of encroachment with too little and he is going to arrive too late. The Russians, if they intend to encroach, will have encroached while Congress is getting ready to hold hearings.

A policy of shifts and manoeuvres may be suited to the Soviet system of government, which, as Mr. X tells us, is animated by patient persistence. It is not suited to the American system of government.

It is even more unsuited to the American economy which is unregimented and uncontrolled, and therefore cannot be administered according to a plan. Yet a policy of containment cannot be operated unless the Department of State can plan and direct exports and imports. For the policy demands that American goods be delivered or withheld at "constantly shifting geographical and political points corresponding to the shifts and manoeuvres of Soviet policy."

Thus Mr. X and the planners of policy in the State Department, and not supply and demand in the world market, must determine continually what portion of the commodities produced here may be sold in the United States, what portion is to be set aside for export, and then sold, lent, or given to this foreign country rather than to that one. The Department of State must be able to allocate the products of American industry and agriculture, to ration the goods allocated for export among the nations which are to contain the Soviet Union and to discriminate among them, judging correctly and quickly how much each nation must be given, how much each nation can safely be squeezed, so that all shall be held in line to hold the line against the Russians.

If then the Kremlin's challenge to American society is to be met by the policy which Mr. X proposes, we are committed to a contest, for ten or fifteen years, with the Soviet system which is planned and directed from Moscow. Mr. X is surely mistaken, it seems to me, if he thinks that a free and undirected economy like our own can be used by the diplomatic planners to wage a diplomatic war against a planned economy at a series of constantly shifting geographical and political points. He is proposing to meet the Soviet challenge on the ground which is most favorable to the Soviets, and with the very instruments, procedures, and weapons in which they have a manifest superiority. . . .

There is . . . however, no rational ground for confidence that the United States could muster "unalterable counterforce" at all the individual sectors. The Eurasian continent is a big place, and the military power of the United States, though it is very great, has certain limi-

tations which must be borne in mind if it is to be used effectively. We live on an island continent. We are separated from the theaters of conflict by the great oceans. We have a relatively small population, of which the greater proportion must in time of war be employed in producing, transporting and servicing the complex weapons and engines which constitute our military power. The United States has, as compared with the Russians, no adequate reserve of infantry. Our navy commands the oceans and we possess the major offensive weapons of war. But on the ground in the interior of the Eurasian continent, as we are learning in the Greek mountains, there may be many "individual sectors" where only infantry can be used as the "counterforce."

These considerations must determine American strategy in war and, therefore, also in diplomacy, whenever the task of diplomacy is to deal with a conflict and a contest of power. The planner of American diplomatic policy must use the kind of power we do have, not the kind we do not have. He must use that kind of power where it can be used. He must avoid engagements in those "Individual sectors of the diplomatic front" where our opponents can use the weapons in which they have superiority. But the policy of firm containment as defined by Mr. X ignores these tactical considerations. It makes no distinction among sectors. It commits the United States to confront the Russians with counterforce "at every point" along the line, instead of at those points which we have selected because, there at those points, our kind of sea and air power can best be exerted.

American military power is peculiarly unsuited to a policy of containment which has to be enforced persistently and patiently for an indefinite period of time. If the Soviet Union were an island like Japan, such a policy could be enforced by American sea and air power. The United States could, without great difficulty, impose a blockade. But the Soviet Union has to be contained on land, and "holding the line" is therefore a form of trench warfare.

Yet the genius of American military power does not lie in holding positions indefinitely. That requires a massive patience by great hordes of docile people. American military power is distinguished by its mobility, its speed, its range and its offensive striking force. It is, therefore, not an efficient instrument for a diplomatic policy of containment. It can only be the instrument of a policy which has as its objective a decision and a settlement. It can and should be used to redress the balance of power which has been upset by the war. But it is not designed for, or adapted to, a strategy of containing, waiting, countering, blocking, with no more specific objective than the eventual "frustration" of the opponent.

The Americans would themselves probably be frustrated by Mr. X's policy long before the Russians were. . . .

There is still greater disadvantage in a policy which seeks to "contain" the Soviet Union by attempting to make "unassailable barriers" out of the surrounding border states. They are admittedly weak. Now a weak ally is not an asset. It is a liability. It requires the diversion of power, money, and prestige to support it and to maintain it. These weak states are vulnerable. Yet the effort to defend them brings us no nearer to a decision or to a settlement of the main conflict. Worst of all, the effort to develop such an unnatural alliance of backward states must alienate the natural allies of the United States. . . .

Now the policy of containment as described by Mr. X, is an attempt to organize an anti-Soviet alliance composed in the first instance of peoples that are either on the shadowy extremity of the Atlantic community, or are altogether outside it. The active proponents of the policy have been concerned immediately with the anti-Soviet parties and factions of eastern Europe, with the Greeks, the Turks, the Iranians, the Arabs and Afghans, and with the Chinese Nationalists.

Instead of concentrating their attention and their efforts upon our allies of the Atlantic community, the makers and shapers of the policy of containment have for more than a year been reaching out for new allies on the perimeter of the Soviet Union. This new coalition, as we can see only too clearly in Greece, in Iran, in the Arab states and in China, cannot in fact be made to coalesce. Instead of becoming an unassailable barrier against the Soviet power, this borderland is a seething stew of civil strife. . . . Though impoverished and weakened, the nations of the Atlantic community are incomparably stronger, richer, more united and politically more democratic and mature than any of the nations of the Russian perimeter.

If the Soviet Union is, nevertheless, able to paralyze and disorganise them, then surely it can much more readily paralyze and disorganise the nations of the perimeter. They have never, in fact, been organized and effective modern states. Yet we are asked to believe that we can organize the perimeter of Russia, though the Russians are so strong and so cunning that we cannot consolidate the Atlantic community.

By concentrating our efforts on a diplomatic war in the borderlands of the Soviet Union, we have neglected—because we do not have unlimited power, resources, influence, and diplomatic brain power—the vital interests of our natural allies in western Europe, notably in reconstructing their economic life and in promoting a German settlement on which they can agree.

The failure of our diplomatic campaign in the borderlands, on which we have staked so much, too much, has conjured up the specter of a Third World War. The threat of a Russian-American war, arising out of the conflict in the borderlands, is dissolving the natural alliance of the Atlantic community. For the British, the French, and all the other Europeans see that they are placed between the hammer and the anvil. They realize, even if we do not realize it, that the policy of containment in the hope that the Soviet power will collapse by frustration, cannot be enforced and cannot be administered successfully, and that it must fail. Either Russia will burst through the barriers which are supposed to contain her, and all of Europe will be at her mercy, or at some point and some time, the diplomatic war will become a full-scale shooting war. In either event Europe is lost. Either Europe falls under the domination of Russia, or Europe becomes the battlefield of a Russian-American war. . . .

[The Western Europeans] remember Mr. Chamberlain's efforts to contain Hitler by a guarantee to Poland. They remember Mr. Hull's effort to contain Japan in China. They know that a policy of containment does not contain, that measures of "counterforce" are doomed to be too late and too little, that a policy of holding the line and hoping for the best means the surrender of the strategic initiative, the dispersion of our forces without prospect of a decision and a settlement, and in the end a war which, once begun, it would be most difficult to conclude. . . .

In the introduction to this essay, I said that Mr. X's article on "The Sources of Soviet Conduct" was "a document of primary importance on the sources of American foreign policy" in that it disclosed to the world the estimates, the calculations, and the conclusions on which is based that part of American foreign policy which is known as the Truman Doctrine. Fortunately, it seems to me, the Truman Doctrine does not have a monopoly. Though it is a powerful contender for the control of our foreign policy, there are at least two serious competitors in the field. One we may call the Marshall line, and the other is the American commitment to support the United Nations.

The contest between the Truman Doctrine on the one hand, the Marshall line and the support of the U.N on the other is the central drama within the State Department, within the Administration, within the government as a whole. The outcome is still undecided. . . .

Having observed, I believe quite correctly, that we cannot expect "to enjoy political intimacy with the Soviet regime," and that we must "regard the Soviet Union as a rival, not a partner in the political arena," and that "there can be no appeal to common purposes," Mr. X has reached the conclusion that all we can do is to "contain" Russia until Russia changes, ceases to be our rival, and becomes our partner.

The conclusion is, it seems to me, quite unwarranted. The history of diplomacy is the history of relations among rival powers, which did not enjoy political intimacy, and did not respond to appeals to common purposes. Nevertheless, there have been settlements. Some of them did not last very long. Some of them did. For a diplomat to think that rival and unfriendly powers cannot be brought to a settlement is to forget what diplomacy is about. There would be little for diplomats to do if the world consisted of partners, enjoying political intimacy, and responding to common appeals.

The method by which diplomacy deals with a world where there are rival powers is to organize a balance of power which deprives the rivals, however lacking in intimacy and however unresponsive to common appeals, of a good prospect of successful aggression. That is what a diplomat means by the settlement of a conflict among rival powers. He does not mean that they will cease to be rivals. He does not mean that they will all be converted to thinking and wanting the same things. He means that, whatever they think, whatever they want, whatever their ideological purposes, the balance of power is such that they cannot afford to commit aggression. . . .

Until a settlement which results in withdrawal is reached, the Red Army at the centre of Europe will control eastern Europe and will threaten western Europe. In those circumstances American power must be available, not to "contain" the Russians at scattered points, but to hold the whole Russian military machine, in check, and to exert a mounting pressure in support of a diplomatic policy which has as its concrete objective a settlement that means withdrawal. . . .

We shall be addressing ourselves to an objective to which our own power is suited—be it in diplomacy or in war. We shall be seeking an end that all men can understand, and one which expresses faithfully our oldest and best tradition—to be the friend and champion of nations seeking independence and an end to the rule of alien powers.

5.8   Declaration of the Founding of the Cominform at the Conference of the Communist Parties of Yugoslavia, Bulgaria, Hungary, Poland, the U.S.S.R., France, Czechoslovakia and Italy, September 1947

In September 1947 the Soviet Union called a meeting at Wiliza in Poland to be attended by the communist party leadership of the various European nations for the purpose of forming an international communist organization to be known as the Cominform. In 1943 Stalin had closed down the old Comintern, an organization formed after the 1917 revolution to encourage and spread communism throughout the world. He apparently hoped that the act would reassure the U.S. and Britain that he was a respectable ally and that the Soviets had ended its quest to orchestrate international communist revolutions. The new postwar Cominform was designed to replace the old Comintern, and with many of the main objectives as the old organization. The establishment of the Cominform was, to many Americans, definitive evidence that the Soviets were expansionist—that their wartime moderation was simply a ruse to win U.S. support against Germany, a nation they would never have defeated without U.S. military assistance. It also showed that Stalin no longer believed he needed to court the friendship of the U.S. and Britain.

It is also apparent from the declaration below, and from the following keynote speech by Politburo member A.A. Zhadanov (*Document 5.8*), that the Cominform was to be an international communist front against U.S. postwar imperialism. The communist leadership at Wiliza also saw the Truman Doctrine and the Marshall Plan as the primary tools of that imperialism.

....

DOCUMENT 5.8

DECLARATION OF THE FOUNDING OF THE COMINFORM AT THE CONFERENCE OF THE COMMUNIST PARTIES OF YUGOSLAVIA, BULGARIA, HUNGARY, POLAND, THE U.S.S.R., FRANCE, CZECHOSLOVAKIA AND ITALY, SEPTEMBER 1947

Fundamental changes have taken place in the international situation as a result of the Second World War. These changes are characterized by a new disposition of the basic political forces operating in the world arena. . . . While the war was on, the Allied States in the war against Germany and Japan united to comprise one camp. However . . . there were differences in the Allied camp as regards the definition of both war aims and the tasks of the postwar peace settlement. The Soviet Union and other democratic countries in Europe [desired] the eradication and the prevention of the possibility of new aggression on the part of Germany, and the establishment of a lasting all-round cooperation among the nations of Europe. The United States of America and Britain . . . set themselves another aim in the war: to rid themselves of competitors in the market (Germany and Japan) and to establish their dominant position. This difference in the defi-

SOURCE: M. Carlyle, ed., "The Founding of the Cominform: Conference at Wiliza," in *Documents on International Affairs, 1947–1948* (1952), 122–37.

nition of war aims and the tasks of the postwar settlement grew more profound after the war. Two diametrically opposed political lines took shape. On one side the policy of the USSR and the democratic countries was directed at undermining imperialism and consolidating democracy. On the other side, the policy of the United States and Britain was directed at strengthening imperialism and stifling democracy. In as much as the USSR and the countries of the new democracy became obstacles to the realization of these imperialist plans . . . [of] world domination and the smashing of democratic movements, a crusade was proclaimed against the USSR and the countries of the new democracy, bolstered also by threats of a new war on the part of the most zealous imperialist politicians in the United States and Britain.

Thus two camps were formed—the imperialist and anti-democratic camp having as its basic claim the establishment of world domination of American imperialism and the smashing of democracy, and the anti-imperialist and democratic camp having as its basic aim the undermining of imperialism, the consolidation of democracy, and the eradication of the remnants of fascism. The struggle between these two diametrically opposed camps . . . is taking place in a situation marked by the further aggravation of the general crisis of capitalism, the weakening of the forces of capitalism, and the strengthening of the forces of Socialism and democracy.

Hence the imperialist camp and its leading force, the United States, are displaying particularly aggressive activity. This activity is being developed simultaneously along all lines of military strategic planning, economic expansion, and ideological aggression. The Truman-Marshall plan is only a constituent part, the European subsection of the general plan for the policy of global expansion pursued by the United States in all parts of the world. The plan for the economic and political enslavement of Europe by American imperialism is being supplemented in China, Indonesia, and the South American countries. Yesterday's aggressors—the capitalist powers of Germany and Japan—are being groomed by the United States for a new role, that of instruments of the imperialist policies of the United States in Europe and Asia.

The arsenal of tactical weapons used by the imperialists is highly diversified. It combines direct threats of violence, blackmail and extortion, every means of political and economic pressure, bribery and utilization of internal contradictions and strife in order to strengthen its own positions, and all this concealed behind a liberal-pacifist mask designed to deceive and trap the politically inexperienced. . . .

To frustrate the plan of imperialist aggression the efforts of all the democratic anti-imperialist forces of Europe are necessary. . . . This imposes a special task on the Communist Parties. They must take into their hands the banner of the national independence and sovereignty of their countries. If the Communist Parties stick firmly to their positions, if they do not let themselves be intimidated and blackmailed, if they courageously safeguard democracy and the sovereignty, liberty and independence of other countries, if in their struggle against attempts to take the lead of all . . . who are ready to fight for the honour and national independence, no plans for enslavement of the countries of Europe and Asia can be carried into effect.

This is now one of the principal tasks of the Communist Parties.

It is essential to bear in mind that there is a vast difference between the desire of the imperialists to unleash a new war and the possibility of organizing such a war. The nations of the world do not want war. The forces standing for peace are so large and so strong that if these forces are staunch and firm in defending the peace, if they display stamina and resolution, the plans of the aggressors will meet with utter failure. It should not be forgotten that the war cries raised by the imperialist agents is intended to frighten the nervous and unstable elements, and by blackmail to win concessions.

The principal danger for the working classes lies in under-estimating their own strength and over-estimating the strength of the imperialist camp. Just as the Munich policy untied the hands of Hitlerite aggression in the past, so yielding to the policies of United States . . . is bound to make it still more arrogant and aggressive. Therefore, the Communist Parties must take the lead in resisting the plans of imperialist expansion and aggression in all spheres—state, political, economic and ideological. They must close their ranks, unite their efforts on the basis of a common anti-imperialist and democratic platform and rally around themselves all the democratic and patriotic forces of the nation. . . .

SPEECH BY A. A. ZHADANOV, MEMBER OF THE POLITBURO

The aggressive and frankly expansionist course to which American imperialism has committed itself since the end of the World War II finds expression in both the foreign and home policy of the United States. The active support rendered to the reactionary, anti-democratic forces all over the world, the sabotage of the Potsdam decisions (which call for the democratic reconstruction and the demilitarization of Germany), the protection given to the Japanese reactionaries, the extensive war preparations and the accumulation of atomic bombs—all this goes hand-in-hand in an offensive against the elementary democratic rights of the working people in the United States itself.

Although the U.S. suffered comparatively little from the war, the vast majority of Americans do not want another war, with its accompanying sacrifices and limitations. This has induced monopoly capital and its servitors among the ruling circles in the United States to resort to extraordinary means in order to crush the opposition to the aggressive expansionist and to secure a free hand for the further prosecution of this dangerous policy.

But the crusade against Communism, proclaimed by America's ruling circle with the backing of the capitalist monopolies, leads as a logical consequence to the attacks on the fundamental rights and interests of the American working people, to the fascization of America's

political life, and to the dissemination of the most savage and misanthropic theories and expansionist strategies designed to stifle all possible resistance within the country [and to] poison the minds of the politically backward and unenlightened American masses with the viruses of chauvinism and militarism, and in stultifying the average American with the help of all the diverse means of anti-Soviet and anti-Communist propaganda, including the cinema, the radio, the church and the press. . . .

The realization of the strategic plans for future aggression is connected with the desire to utilize to the utmost the war production facilities of the United States, which grew to enormous proportions by the end of World War II. American imperialism is persistently pursuing a policy of militarizing the country. Expenditures on the U.S. army and navy exceed $11 billion per annum in 1947–48. Thirty-five percent of America's budget was appropriated for the armed forces, or eleven times more than in 1938–1939. . . .

Economic expansion is an important supplement to . . . America's strategic plan. American imperialism is endeavoring, like a userer, to take advantage of the post-war difficulties in Europe, in particular the shortage of raw materials, fuel and food in the Allied countries that suffered most from the war, to dictate to them extortionate terms for any assistance rendered. With an eye to the impeding economic crisis, the United States is in a hurry to find new monopoly spheres of capital investment and markets for its goods. American economic "assistance" pursues the broad aim of bringing Europe into the bondage of American capitalism. The more drastic the economic situation of a country is, the harsher are the terms that the American monopolies endeavor to dictate to it.

But economic control logically leads to political subjugation. Thus the United States connects the extension of monopoly markets for its goods to the acquisition of new bridgeheads for its fight against the new democratic forces of Europe. In "saving" a country from starvation and collapse, the American monopolies at the same time seek to rob it of all vestige of independence. American "assistance" automatically involves a change in the policy of the country to which it is rendered. Individuals come to power who are prepared, on direction form Washington, to carry out a program of domestic and foreign policy suitable to the United States.

Lastly, the aspiration to world supremacy and the anti-democratic policy of the United States involves an ideological struggle. The principle purpose of the ideological part of the American strategy is to deceive public opinion by wrongly accusing the Soviet Union and the new democracies of aggressive intentions, thus representing the Anglo-Saxon bloc in a defensive role and absolving it of responsibility. . . .

[The Soviet Union's] devoted and heroic struggle against imperialism has earned it the affection and respect of working people in all countries. The military and economic might of the Soviet state, the invincible strength of the moral and political unity of Soviet society have been demonstrated to the whole world. The reactionary circles in the United States and Great Britain are anxious to erase the deep impression made by the Socialist system on the working people of the world. The warmongers fully realize that long ideological preparation is necessary before they can get their soldiers to fight against the Soviet Union.

In their ideological struggle against the USSR, the American imperialists, who have no great insight into political questions, demonstrate their ignorance by emphasizing that the Soviet Union is undemocratic and totalitarian, while the United States and Great Britain and the whole capitalist world are democratic. On this platform of ideological struggle—on this defense of bourgeois pseudo-democracy and condemnation of Communism as totalitarian—are united all the enemies of the working class . . . against the USSR. . . . Political ignoramuses that they are, they cannot understand that capitalists and landlords, (antagonistic classes and hence a plurality of parties), have long ceased to exist in the USSR. They would like to have in the USSR the

bourgeois parties, which are so dear to their hearts . . . as agencies of imperialism. But to their bitter regret these parties of the exploiting bourgeoisie have been doomed by history to disappear from the scene. . . .

At this present juncture, the expansionist ambitions of the United States find concrete expression in the Truman Doctrine and the Marshall Plan. Although they differ in form of presentation, both are an expression of a single policy. They are an embodiment of the American design to enslave Europe. . . .

The Truman Doctrine, which provides for the rendering of American assistance to all reactionary regimes that actively oppose the democratic peoples, bears a frankly aggressive character. . . . The Marshall Plan is a more carefully veiled attempt to carry through the same expansionist policy. The vague and deliberately guarded formulations of the Marshall Plan amount in essence to a scheme to create a bloc of states bound by obligations to the United States, and to grant American credits to European countries as a recompense for their renunciation of economic, and then of political, independence. . . .

Washington . . . invited the Soviet Union to take part in a discussion of the Marshall proposals. This step was taken in order to mask the hostile nature of proposals with respect to the USSR. The calculation was that, since it was well known beforehand that the USSR would refuse American assistance on the terms proposed by Marshall, it might be possible to shift the responsibility to the Soviet Union for declining to assist in the economic restoration of Europe, and thus incite against the USSR the European countries that are in need of real assistance. . . . Whereas the Truman plan was designed to terrorize and intimidate these countries, the Marshall Plan was designed to . . . lure them into a trap and then shackle them in the fetters of dollar assistance. In that case, the Marshall Plan would facilitate one of the most important objectives of the general American program, namely to restore the power of imperialism in the countries of the new democracy and to compel them to renounce close economic and political cooperation with the Soviet Union. . . . It thus became evident that in accepting the . . . Marshall Plan, Britain, France and the other Western European states fell dupes to the American chicanery. . . . The exposure of the American plan for the economic enslavement of the European countries is an indisputable service rendered by the . . . USSR and the new democracies.

5.9 National Security Council Paper #68, April 1950

*D*ocument 5.9 is from National Security Council paper #68, known universally as NSC-68. The National Security Council had been established in 1947 to coordinate the military services and to advise the president on foreign policy. In 1949 Truman ordered an analysis from the secretaries of state and defense on the ability of the United States to deal with a potential Soviet military challenge. In April 1950 NSC-68 was submitted to Truman. Written by a small committee of state and defense department officials under the leadership of Paul Nitze of the Policy Planning Staff, NSC-68 was an attempt to systematize the foreign policy of containment and to find a way to make the policy work. NSC-68 explains the world in terms of good and evil, free and slave, with the Soviets trying to dominate the Eurasian landmass, if not the world. The advice to Truman was to rearm the nation, and to fight against all instances of communist expansion.

Truman at first discounted the rearmament recommendations in NSC-6 8 as too expensive, especially in light of pushes in the political arena to balance the budget and reduce taxes. But when North Korea invaded the South in June, just two months after NSC-68 was sent to his desk, Truman began to see the need to rearm, and by September NSC-68 had become established U.S. policy. In 1950, before the outbreak of the Korean war and before the implementation of NSC-68, the Defense Department budget was $17.7 billion. By the end of the Korean war, the defense budget had grown to over $52 billion. NSC-68, along with the Korean war that appeared to make its implementation necessary, committed a major portion of the American economy to fighting communism abroad.

....

DOCUMENT 5.9

NATIONAL SECURITY COUNCIL PAPER #68, APRIL 1950

Within the past thirty-five years the world has experienced two tremendously violent global wars. It has witnessed two revolutions— the Russian and the Chinese—of extreme scope and intensity. It has also seen the collapse of five empires—the Ottoman, the Austro-Hungarian, German, Italian, and Japanese— and the drastic decline of two major imperial systems, the British and the French. During the span of one generation, the international distribution of power has been fundamentally altered. For several centuries it had proved impossible for any one nation to gain such preponderant strength that a coalition of other

SOURCE: *Papers Relating to the Foreign Relations of the United States, 1950*, I, (1977), 237–92.

nations could not in time face it with greater strength. The international scene was marked by recurring periods of violence and war, but a system of sovereign and independent states was maintained, over which no state was able to achieve hegemony.

Two complex sets of factors have now basically altered this historical distribution of power. First, the defeat of Germany and Japan and the decline of the British and French Empires have interacted with the development of the United States and the Soviet Union in such a way that power has increasingly gravitated to these two centers. Second, the Soviet Union, unlike previous aspirants to hegemony, is animated by a new fanatic faith, antithetical to our own, and seeks to impose its absolute authority over the rest of the world. Conflict has, therefore, become endemic and is waged, on the part of the Soviet Union, by violent or non-violent methods in accordance with the dictates of expediency. With the development of increasingly terrifying weapons of mass destruction, every individual faces the ever-resent possibility of annihilation should the conflict enter the phase of total war.

On the one hand, the people of the world yearn for relief from the anxiety arising from the risk of atomic war. On the other hand, any substantial further extension of the area under the domination of the Kremlin would raise the possibility that no coalition adequate to confront the Kremlin with greater strength could be assembled. It is in this context that this Republic and its citizens in the ascendancy of their strength stand in their deepest peril. The issues that face us are momentous, involving the fulfillment or destruction not only of this Republic but of civilization itself. They are issues which will not await our deliberations. With conscience and resolution this Government and the people it represents must now make new and fateful decisions. . . .

The fundamental design of those who control the Soviet Union and the international communist movement is to retain and solidify their absolute power, first in the Soviet Union and second in the areas now under their control. In the minds of the Soviet leaders, however, achievement of this design requires the dynamic extension of their authority and the ultimate elimination of any effective opposition to their authority.

The design, therefore, calls for the complete subversion or forcible destruction of the machinery of government and structure of society in the countries of the non-Soviet world and their replacement by an apparatus and structure subservient to and controlled from the Kremlin. To that end Soviet efforts are now directed toward the domination of the Eurasian land mass. The United States, as the principal center of power in the non-Soviet world and the bulwark of opposition to Soviet expansion, is the principal enemy whose integrity and vitality must be subverted or destroyed by one means or another if the Kremlin is to achieve its fundamental design. . . .

The Kremlin's design for world domination begins at home. The first concern of a despotic oligarchy is that the local base of its power and authority be secure. The massive fact of the iron curtain isolating the Soviet peoples from the outside world, the repeated political purges within the U.S.S.R. and institutionalized crimes of the [secret police] are evidence that the Kremlin does not feel secure at home. . . . Similar evidence in the satellite states of Eastern Europe leads to the conclusion that this same policy, in less advanced phases, is being applied to the Kremlin's colonial areas.

Being a totalitarian dictatorship, the Kremlin's objectives in these policies is the total subjective submission of the peoples now under its control. The concentration camp is the prototype of the society which these policies are designed to achieve, a society in which the personality of the individual is so broken and perverted that he participates affirmatively in his own degradation.

The Kremlin's policy toward areas not under its control is the elimination of resistance to its will and the extension of its influence and control. It is driven to follow this policy because it cannot . . . tolerate the existence of free societies; to the Kremlin the most mild and inoffensive free society is an affront, a challenge and a subversive influence. Given the nature of the Kremlin, and the evidence at hand, it seems clear that the ends toward which this policy is directed are the same as those where its control has already been established.

The means employed by the Kremlin in pursuit of this policy are limited only by considerations of expediency. Doctrine is not a limiting factor; rather it dictates the employment of violence, subversion and deceit, and rejects moral considerations. In any event, the Kremlin's conviction of its own infallibility has made its devotion to theory so subjective that past or present pronouncements as to doctrine offer no reliable guide to future actions. The only apparent restraints on resort to war are, therefore, calculations of practicality.

With particular reference to the United States, the Kremlin's strategic and tactical policy is affected by its estimate that we are not only the greatest immediate obstacle which stands between it and world domination, we are also the only power which could release forces in the free and Soviet worlds which could destroy it. The Kremlin's policy toward us is consequently animated by a peculiarly virulent blend of hatred and fear. Its strategy has been one of attempting to undermine the complex of forces, in this country and in the rest of the free world, on which our power is based. In this it has both adhered to doctrine and followed the sound principle of seeking maximum results with minimum risks and commitments. The present application of this strategy is a new form of expression for traditional Russian caution. However, there is no justification in Soviet theory or practice for predicting that, should the Kremlin become convinced that it could cause our downfall by one conclusive blow, it would seek that solution. . . .

The Kremlin has no economic intentions unrelated to its overall policies. Economics in the Soviet world is not an end in itself. The Kremlin's policy, in so far as it has to do with economics, is to utilize economic processes to contribute to the overall strength, particularly the war-making capacity of the Soviet system. The material welfare of the totalitariat is severely subordinated to the interest of the system. . . .

The Soviet Union is developing the military capacity to support its design for world domination. The Soviet Union actually possesses armed forces far in excess of those necessary to defend its national territory. These armed forces are probably not yet considered by the Soviet Union to be sufficient to initiate a war which would involve the United States. This excessive strength, coupled now with an atomic capability, provides the Soviet Union with great coercive power for use in time of peace in furtherance of its objectives and serves as a deterrent to the victims of its aggression from taking any action in opposition to its tactics which would risk war.

Should a major war occur in 1950 the Soviet Union and its satellites are considered by the Joint Chiefs of Staff to be in a sufficiently advanced state of preparation immediately to undertake and carry out the following campaigns:

a. To overrun Western Europe, with the possible exception of the Iberian and Scandinavian Peninsulas; to drive toward the oil-bearing areas of the Near and Middle East; and to consolidate Communist gains in the Far East.

b. To launch air attacks against the British Isles and air and sea attacks against the lines of communications of the Western Powers in the Atlantic and Pacific.

c. To attack selected targets with atomic weapons, now including the likelihood of such attacks against targets in Alaska, Canada, and the United States. Alternately, this capability, coupled with other actions open to the Soviet Union might deny the United Kingdom as an effective base of operations for allied forces. It also should be possible for the Soviet Union to prevent any allied "Normandy" type amphibious operations intended to force a reentry into the continent of Europe.

After the Soviet Union completed its initial campaigns and consolidated its positions in the ·

Western European area, it could simultaneously conduct:

a. Full-scale air and limited sea operations against the British Isles;
b. Invasions of the Iberian and Scandinavian Peninsulas;
c. Further operations in the Near and Middle East, continued air operations against the North American continent, and air and sea operations against Atlantic and Pacific lines of communications; and
d. Diversionary attacks in other areas.

During the course of the offensive operations listed . . . above, the Soviet Union will have an air defense capability with respect to the vital areas of its own and its satellites' territories which can oppose but cannot prevent allied air operations against these areas.

It is not known whether the Soviet Union possesses war reserves and arsenal capabilities sufficient to supply its satellite armies or even its own forces throughout a long war. It might not be in the interest of the Soviet Union to equip fully its satellite armies, since the possibility of defections would exist. . . .

[A] strong United States military position, plus increases in the armaments of the nations of Western Europe, should strengthen the determination of the recipient nations to counter Soviet moves and in the event of war could be considered as likely to delay operations and increase the time required for the Soviet Union to overrun Western Europe. In all probability, although United States backing will stiffen their determination, the armaments increase under the present aid programs will not be of any major consequence prior to 1952. Unless the military strength of the Western European nations is increased on a much larger scale than under current programs and at an accelerated rate, it is more than likely that those nations will not be able to oppose even by 1960 the Soviet armed forces in war with any degree of effectiveness. Considering the Soviet Union military capability, the long-range allied military objective in Western Europe must envisage an increased military strength in that area sufficient possibly to deter the Soviet Union from a major war or, in any event, to delay materially the overrunning of Western Europe and, if feasible, to hold a bridgehead on the continent against Soviet Union offensives. . . .

Our overall policy at the present time may be described as one designed to foster a world environment in which the American system can survive and flourish. It therefore rejects the concept of isolation and affirms the necessity of our positive participation in the world community.

This broad intention embraces two subsidiary policies. One is a policy which we would probably pursue even if there were not a Soviet threat. It is a policy of attempting to develop a healthy international community. The other is the policy of "containing" the Soviet system. The two policies are closely interrelated and interact on one another. Nevertheless, the distinction between them is basically valid and contributes to a clearer understanding of what we are trying to do.

The policy of striving to develop a healthy international community is the long-term constructive effort which we are engaged in. It was this policy which gave rise to our vigorous sponsorship of the United Nations. . . . It, as much as containment, underlay our efforts to rehabilitate Western Europe. Most of our international economic activities can likewise be explained in terms of this policy.

In a world of polarized power, the policies designed to develop a healthy international community are more than ever necessary to our own strength.

As for the policy of "containment," it is one which seeks by all means short of war to (1) block further expansion of Soviet power, (2) expose the falsities of Soviet pretensions, (3) induce a retraction of the Kremlin's control and influence and (4) in general, so foster the seeds of destruction within the Soviet system that the Kremlin is brought at least to the point of modifying its behavior to conform to generally accepted international standards.

It was and continues to be cardinal in this policy that we possess superior overall power in ourselves or in dependable combination with other like-minded nations. One of the most important ingredients of power is military strength. In the concept of "containment" the maintenance of a strong military posture is deemed to be essential for two reasons: (1) as an ultimate guarantee of our national security and (2) as an indispensable backdrop to the conduct of the policy of "containment." Without superior aggregate military strength, in being and readily mobilizable, a policy of "containment"—which is in effect a policy of calculated and gradual coercion—is no more than a policy of bluff.

At the same time, it is essential to the successful conduct of a policy of "containment" that we always leave open the possibility of negotiation with the U.S.S.R. A diplomatic freeze—and we are in one now—tends to defeat the very purpose of "containment" because it raises tensions at the same time that it makes Soviet retractions and adjustments in the direction of moderated behavior more difficult. It also tends to inhibit our initiative and deprives us of opportunities for maintaining a moral ascendance in our struggle with the Soviet system.

In "containment" it is desirable to exert pressure in a fashion which will avoid so far as possible directly challenging Soviet prestige, to keep open the possibility for the U.S.S.R. to retreat before pressure with a minimum loss of face and to secure political advantage from the failure of the Kremlin to yield or take advantage of the openings we leave it.

We have failed to implement adequately these two fundamental aspects of "containment." In the face of obviously mounting Soviet military strength ours has declined relatively. Partly as a byproduct of this, but also for other reasons, we now find ourselves at a diplomatic impasse with the Soviet Union, with the Kremlin growing bolder, with both of us holding on grimly to what we have and with ourselves facing difficult decisions. . . .

The United States now possesses the greatest military potential of any single nation in the world. The military weaknesses of the United States vis-à-vis the Soviet Union, however, include its numerical inferiority in . . . total manpower. Coupled with the inferiority of forces . . . the United States also lacks tenable positions from which to employ its forces in event of war. . . .

It is true that the United States armed forces are now stronger than ever before in other times of apparent peace; it is also true that there exists a sharp disparity between our actual military strength and our commitments. The relationship of our strength to our present commitments, however, is not alone the governing factor. The world situation, as well as commitments, should govern; hence, our military strength more properly should be related to the world situation confronting us. When our military strength is related to the world situation and balanced against the likely exigencies of such a situation, it is clear that our military strength is becoming dangerously inadequate.

If war should begin in 1950, the United States and its allies will have the military capability of conducting defensive operations to provide a reasonable measure of protection to the Western Hemisphere, bases in the Western Pacific, and essential military lines of communication; and an inadequate measure of protection to vital military bases in the United Kingdom and in the Near and Middle East. We will have the capability of conducting powerful offensive air operations against vital elements of the Soviet war-making capacity.

The scale of the operations listed in the preceding paragraph is limited by the effective forces . . . of the United States and its allies vis-à-vis the Soviet Union. Consistent with the aggressive threat facing us and in consonance with the overall strategic plans, the United States must provide to its allies on a continuing basis as large amounts of military assistance as possible without serious detriment to the United States operational requirements.

If the potential military capabilities of the United States and its allies were rapidly and effectively developed, sufficient forces could be produced probably to deter war, or if the Soviet Union chooses war, to withstand the initial Soviet attacks, to stabilize supporting attacks, and to retaliate in turn with even greater impact on the Soviet capabilities. From the military point of view alone, however, this would require not only the generation of the necessary military forces but also the development and stockpiling of improved weapons of all types.

Under existing peacetime conditions, a period of from two to three years is required to produce a material increase in military power. Such increased power could be provided in a somewhat shorter period in a declared period of emergency or in wartime through a full-out national effort. . . .

On the basis of current programs, the United States has a large potential military capability but an actual capability which, though improving, is declining relative to the U.S.S.R., particularly in light of its probably [atomic] bomb capability and possible [hydrogen] bomb capability. The same holds true for the free world as a whole relative to the Soviet world as a whole. If war breaks out in 1950 or in the next few years, the United States and its allies, apart from a powerful atomic blow, will be compelled to conduct delaying actions, while building up their strength for a general offensive. A frank evaluation of the requirements, to defend the United States and its vital interests and to support a vigorous initiative in the cold war, on the one hand, and of present capabilities, on the other, indicates that there is a sharp and growing disparity between them. . . .

Continuation of peace trends . . . will lead progressively to the withdrawal of the United States from most of its present commitments in Europe and Asia and to our isolation in the Western Hemisphere and its approaches. This would result not from a conscious decision but from a failure to take the actions necessary to bring our capabilities into line with our commitments and thus to withdrawal under pressure. This pressure might come from our present Allies, who will tend to seek other "solutions" unless they have confidence in our

determination to accelerate our efforts to build a successfully functioning political and economic system in the free world.

There are some who advocate a deliberate decision to isolate ourselves. Superficially, this has some attractiveness as a course of action, for it appears to bring our commitments and capabilities into harmony by reducing the former and by concentrating our present, or perhaps even reduced, military expenditures on the defense of the United States.

This argument overlooks the relativity of capabilities. With the United States in an isolated position, we would have to face the probability without meeting armed resistance. It would thus acquire a potential far superior to our own, and would promptly proceed to develop this potential with the purpose of eliminating our power, which would, even in isolation, remain as a challenge to it and as an obstacle to the imposition of its kind of order in the world. . . .

Some Americans favor a deliberate decision to go to war against the Soviet Union in the near future. It goes without saying that the idea of "preventive" war—in the sense of a military attack not provoked by a military attack upon us or our allies—is generally unacceptable to Americans. Its supporters argue that since the Soviet Union is in fact at war with the free world now and that since the failure of the Soviet Union to use all-out military force is explainable on the grounds of expediency, we are at war and should conduct ourselves accordingly. Some further argue that the free world is probably unable, except under the crisis of war, to mobilize and direct its resources to the checking and rolling back of the Kremlin's drive for world dominion. This is a powerful argument in the light of history, but the considerations against war are so compelling that the free world must demonstrate that this argument is wrong. The case for war is premised on the assumption that the United States could launch and sustain an attack of sufficient impact to gain a decisive advantage for the free world in a long war and perhaps to win an early decision.

The ability of the United States to launch effective offensive operations is now limited to attack with atomic weapons. A powerful blow could be delivered upon the Soviet Union, but it is estimated that these operations alone would not force or induce the Kremlin to capitulate and that the Kremlin would still be able to use the forces under its control to dominate most or all of Eurasia. This would probably mean a long and difficult struggle during which the free institutions of Western Europe and many freedom-loving people would be destroyed and the regenerative capacity of Western Europe dealt a crippling blow.

Apart from this, however, a surprise attack upon the Soviet Union, despite the provocativeness of the recent Soviet behavior, would be repugnant to many Americans. Although the American people would probably rally in support of the war effort, the shock of responsibility for the surprise attack would be morally corrosive. . . .

A more rapid build-up of political, economic, and military strength and thereby of confidence in the free world than is now contemplated is the only course which is consistent with progress toward achieving our fundamental purpose. The frustration of the Kremlin design requires the free world to develop a successful functioning political and economic system and a vigorous political offensive against the Soviet Union. These, in turn, require an adequate military shield under which they can develop. It is necessary to have the military power to deter, if possible, Soviet expansion, and to defeat, if necessary, aggressive Soviet or Soviet-directed actions of a limited or total character. The potential strength of the free world is great; its ability to develop these military capabilities and its will to resist Soviet expansion will be determined by the wisdom and will with which it undertakes to meet its political and economic problems. . . .

CONCLUSIONS

A continuation of present trends would result in a serious decline in the strength of the free world relative to the Soviet Union and its satellites. This unfavorable trend arises from the inadequacy of current programs and plans rather than from any error in our objectives and aims. These trends lead in the direction of isolation, not by deliberate decision but by lack of the necessary basis for a vigorous initiative in the conflict with the Soviet Union.

Our position as the center of power in the free world places a heavy responsibility upon the United States for leadership. We must organize and enlist the energies and resources of the free world in a positive program for peace which will frustrate the Kremlin design for world domination by creating a situation in the free world to which the Kremlin will be compelled to adjust. Without such a cooperative effort, led by the United States, we will have to make gradual withdrawals under pressure until we discover one day that we have sacrificed positions of vital interest.

It is imperative that this trend be reversed by a much more rapid and concerted build-up of the actual strength of the free world, and by means of an affirmative program intended to wrest the initiative from the Soviet Union, confront it with convincing evidence of the determination and ability of the free world to frustrate the Kremlin to the new situation. Failing that, the unwillingness of the Kremlin to accept equitable terms or its bad faith in observing them would assist in consolidating popular opinion in the free world in support of the measures necessary to sustain the build-up.

In summary, we must, by means of a rapid and sustained build-up of the political, economic, and military strength of the free world, and by means of an affirmative program intended to wrest the initiative from the Soviet Union, confront it with convincing evidence of the determination and ability of the free world to frustrate the Kremlin design of a world dominated by its will. Such evidence is the only means short of war which eventually may force the Kremlin to abandon its present course of action and to negotiate acceptable agreements on issues of major importance.

The whole success of the proposed program hangs ultimately on recognition by this Government, the American people, and all free peoples, that the cold war is in fact a real war in which the survival of the free world is at stake. Essential prerequisites to success are consultations with Congressional leaders designed to make the program the object of non-partisan legislative support, and a presentation to the public of a full explanation of the facts and implications of the present international situation. The prosecution of the program will require of us all the ingenuity, sacrifice, and unity demanded by the vital importance of the issue and the tenacity to persevere until our national objectives have been attained.

5.10 Truman's Decision to Enter the War in Korea, June 1950

On June 25, 1950 the communist government of North Korea launched a full-scale attack against South Korea. The event seemed to confirm all the forecastings of an expansionist communist monolith. Two days later the United Nations Security Council (with the Soviets absent in protest over the UN's refusal to recognize the communist government in Beijing) called on the members of the United Nations "to furnish such assistance to the Republic of Korea as may be necessary to repel the armed attack." On that same day President Truman announced that the United States would comply with the resolution by sending in armed forces. What followed was the Korean War, a bloody stalemate on the Korean peninsula that was the first hot spot, and the last outpost, of the cold war.

Truman thrust America into Korea more for political than diplomatic reasons. Just nine months before, Mao Zedong had announced the establishment of the Peoples Republic in China in Beijing. Republicans in Congress reacted by denouncing Truman for having "lost China" to communism. The issue ballooned into a political disaster for the Democrats with the potential of seriously damaging Democratic party foreign policy initiatives—as well as crippling Democratic candidates in up-coming elections. Truman was not about to be shackled with "losing Korea" as well. He collected his own thoughts on his decision to enter the Korean conflict in his memoirs (*Document 5.10*). His reasoning explained here, however, is more historical than political. Following in that same document, as it follows in his memoirs, is Truman's speech explaining the situation in Korea. There were, however, other factors that persuaded Truman to get involved in the situation unfolding on the Korean peninsula. Earlier in 1950, Joseph McCarthy, an obscure Republican senator from Wisconsin, played on America's anti-communist fears when he announced to a women's group in Wheeling, West Virginia that he had a list of over two hundred communists serving in the state department. McCarthy's claims seemed credible because of the "loss of China" just five months before, and the uncovering of several communist spy cases in the United States. In addition, the Soviet Union, in September 1949, had surprised the world by exploding its first atomic bomb, effectively removing the American monopoly on nuclear weapons. By the summer of 1950 it appeared that communism had taken a significant step forward in the world. To Truman, and to many Americans, the North Korean invasion of the south was simply another attempt at communist expansion, and it had to be stopped.

Truman was from the generation of Americans who had witnessed the situations that led to war in Europe in the 1930s. It should not be surprising that he evoked the memory of those incidents in his decision to enter the war in Korea—that the communists cannot be appeased.

DOCUMENT 5.10

TRUMAN'S DECISION TO ENTER THE WAR IN KOREA, JUNE 1950

On Saturday, June 24, 1950, I was in Independence, Missouri, to spend the weekend with my family and to attend to some personal family business.

It was a little after ten in the evening and we were sitting in the library of our home on North Delaware Street when the telephone rang. It was the Secretary of State calling from his home in Maryland.

"Mr. President," said Dean Acheson, "I have very serious news. The North Koreans have invaded South Korea."

My first reaction was that I must get back to the capital and I told Acheson so. He explained, however, that details were not yet available and that he thought I need not rush back until he called me again with further information. In the meantime, he suggested to me that we should ask the United Nations Security Council to hold a meeting at once and declare that an act of aggression had been committed against the Republic of Korea. I told him I agreed. . . .

Acheson's next call came through around eleven-thirty Sunday morning, just as we were getting ready to sit down to an early Sunday dinner. Acheson reported that the U.N. Security Council had been called into emergency session. Additional reports had been received

from Korea, and there was no doubt that an all-out invasion was under way there. . . . I informed the Secretary of State that I was returning to Washington at once. . . .

The plane left the Kansas City Municipal Airport at two o'clock and it took just a little over three hours to make the trip to Washington. I had time to think aboard the plane. In my generation, this was not the first occasion when the strong had attacked the weak. I recalled some earlier instances: Manchuria, Ethiopia, Austria. I remembered how each time that the democracies failed to act it had encouraged the aggressors to keep going ahead. Communism was acting in Korea just as Hitler, Mussolini, and the Japanese had acted ten, fifteen and twenty years earlier. I felt certain that if South Korea was allowed to fall Communist leaders would be emboldened to override nations closer to our own shores. If the Communists were permitted to force their way into the Republic of Korea without opposition from the free world, no small nation would have the courage to resist threats and aggression by stronger Communist neighbors. If this was allowed to go unchallenged it would mean a third world war, just as similar incidents had brought on the second world war. It was also clear to me that the foundations and the principles of the United Nations were at stake unless this unprovoked attack on Korea could be stopped. . . .

Throughout Monday the situation in Korea deteriorated rapidly. [Far East Commander, General Douglas] MacArthur's latest message was alarming:

". . . Piecemeal entry into action vicinity Seoul by South Korean Third and Fifth Divisions has not succeeded in stopping the penetration recog-

SOURCE: Harry S. Truman, *Memoirs*, Vol. 2, *Years of Trial and Hope*, 1946–1952 (1956), 377–86.

nized as the enemy main effort for the past 2 days with intent to seize the capital city of Seoul. Tanks entering suburbs of Seoul. . . . South Korean units unable to resist determined Northern offensive. . . . and our estimate is that a complete collapse is imminent."

There was now no doubt! The Republic of Korea needed help at once if it was not to be overrun. More seriously, a Communist success in Korea would put Red troops and planes within easy striking distance of Japan, and Okinawa and Formosa would be open to attack from two sides.

I told my advisers that what was developing in Korea seemed to me like a repetition on a larger scale of what had happened in Berlin. The Reds were probing for weaknesses in our armor; we had to meet their thrust without getting embroiled in a world-wide war.

I directed the Secretary of Defense to call General MacArthur on the scrambler phone and to tell him in person what my instructions were. He was to use air and naval forces to support the Republic of Korea with air and naval elements of his command, but only south of the 38th parallel. He was also instructed to dispatch the Seventh Fleet to the Formosa Strait. The purpose of this move was to prevent attacks by the Communists on Formosa as well as forays by Chiang Kai-shek against the mainland, this last to avoid reprisal actions by the Reds that might enlarge the area of conflict. . . .

That same morning, Tuesday, I asked a group of congressional leaders to meet with me so that I might inform them on the events and decisions of the past few days. . . . This is the statement I gave out to the press at the conclusion of this meeting with the congressional leaders:

STATEMENT BY THE PRESIDENT, JUNE 27, 1950

In Korea the Government forces, which were armed to prevent border raids and to preserve internal security, were attacked by invading forces from North Korea. The Security Council of the United Nations called upon the invading troops to cease hostilities and to withdraw to the 38th parallel. This they have not done, but on the contrary have pressed the attack. The Security Council called upon all members of the United Nations to render every assistance to the United Nations in the execution of this resolution. In these circumstances I have ordered United States air and sea forces to give the Korean Government troops cover and support. The attack upon Korea makes it plain beyond all doubt that Communism has passed beyond the use of subversion to conquer independent nations and will now use armed invasion and war. It has defied the orders of the Security Council of the United Nations issued to preserve international peace and security. In these circumstances the occupation of Formosa by Communist forces would be a direct threat to the security of the Pacific area and to the United States forces performing their lawful and necessary functions in that area.

Accordingly I have ordered the Seventh Fleet to prevent any attack upon Formosa. As a corollary of this action I am calling upon the Chinese Government on Formosa to cease all air and sea operations against the mainland. The Seventh Fleet will see that this is done. The determination of the future status of Formosa must await the restoration of security in the Pacific, a peace settlement with Japan, or consideration by the United Nations.

I have also directed that United States Forces in the Philippines be strengthened and that military assistance to the Philippine Government be accelerated.

I have similarly directed acceleration in the furnishing of military assistance to the forces of France and the Associated States in Indochina and the dispatch of a military mission to provide close working relations with those forces.

I know that all members of the United Nations will consider carefully the consequences of this latest aggression in Korea in defiance of the Charter of the United Nations. A return to the rule of force in international affairs would have far reaching effects. The United States will continue to uphold the rule of law. . . .

CHAPTER 6

···

New Look: U.S. Foreign Policy in the Age of Eisenhower

6.1   Secretary of State John Foster Dulles, "The Threat of a Red Asia," March 29, 1954

6.2   Secretary of State John Foster Dulles' Strategy of Massive Retaliation, January 12, 1954

6.3   Hans Morgenthau's Response to Dulles

6.4   Secretary of State John Foster Dulles Explains Events in Guatemala, June 30, 1954

6.5   E. Howard Hunt Explains Events in Guatemala

6.6   President Dwight Eisenhower's Speech in the Aftermath of the Suez Crisis and the Soviet Invasion of Hungary, January 5, 1957

6.7   Sputnik and the Space Race, *Newsweek,* October 14, 1957

6.8   Speech by Dr. Fidel Castro at the UN General Assembly, September 26, 1960

6.9   U.S. Response to Castro's Speech, October 14, 1960

6.10 Eisenhower's Farewell Address, January 18, 1961

1953–1961 Timeline

January 1953	1953	Dwight Eisenhower becomes president
January 12, 1954	1954	Secretary Dulles on massive retaliation
March 29, 1954		Secretary Dulles on Indochina
March 29, 1954	1955	Hans Morgenthau responds to Dulles' massive retaliation speech
June 30, 1954	1956	Dulles on Guatemala
October 29, 1956		Israel invades the Gaza and Sinai Peninsula
January 5, 1957	1957	Eisenhower on the Suez Crisis
October 4, 1957	1958	Soviets launch Sputnik
January 1, 1959	1959	Fidel Castro seizes power in Cuba
September 26, 1960		Castro speaks at the UN
October 14, 1960	1960	U.S. response to Castro's speech
January 18, 1961	1961	Eisenhower's farewell address

6.1   **Secretary of State John Foster Dulles, "The Threat of a Red Asia,"**
March 29, 1954

6.2   **Secretary of State John Foster Dulles' Strategy of Massive Retaliation,**
January 12, 1954

6.3   **Hans Morgenthau's Response to Dulles**

Dwight Eisenhower's election in 1952 brought in a new foreign policy initiative that the administration called "New Look." The architect of New Look was John Foster Dulles, Eisenhower's secretary of state and primary foreign policy advisor from 1952 to 1959. Dulles was an ardent anti-communist, a true cold warrior who believed with a religious passion that communism was a moral evil that must be contained with force of arms and at all costs. He was a career diplomat and international lawyer, the grandson of one secretary of state and the nephew of another. His view of the world was black and white, good and evil, with little room for neutrals or non-aligned nations. It was a viewpoint that brought sustained public support for the Eisenhower administration's foreign policy.

The Republicans in 1952 had run on a platform of budget cutting, and the Eisenhower-Dulles New Look foreign policy reflected that campaign promise. It was designed to be aggressive and engaging, but also inexpensive. Rather than rely on expensive ground forces and conventional weapons that had seemed so inconclusive in Korea, Eisenhower and Dulles intended to employ an aggressive nuclear strategy. "We have adopted a new principle," Vice President Richard Nixon told the nation. "Rather than let the Communists nibble us to death all over the world in little wars, we will rely in [the] future on [our] massive mobile retaliatory powers." Massive retaliation, as it was called, was intended as a warning to Moscow that the United States might respond with nuclear weapons as a deterrent against Soviet-sponsored aggression. While reducing the emphasis on expensive conventional ground forces, the United States would expand its air force significantly. As the left arm of massive retaliation, it would deliver the bombs (nuclear or conventional) when the time came. New Look was inexpensive and decisive, and it allowed the president to keep military spending to roughly $40 billion per year, below what even many Democrats in Congress believed was necessary. To Charles Wilson, the secretary of defense, it was "more bang for the buck."

Another aspect of New Look was Dulles' strategy of "brinkmanship," a policy of taking greater risks in diplomacy than in the past, a policy of making the Soviets believe that the United States would go to war when, in fact, it would not. Brinkmanship fit in well with New Look because it was both aggressive and inexpensive. The term comes from an interview Dulles gave to *Life* magazine in early 1956, an interview he probably wished he had not given. "The ability to get to the verge without getting into the war is the necessary art. If you cannot master it, you inevitably get into the war. If you try to run away from it, if you are scared to go to the brink, you are lost."

New Look was also designed to keep American soldiers out of combat—out of wars that could not be won, like in Korea. In the case of an outbreak of conventional warfare, particularly in Asia, Eisenhower and Dulles wanted to rely on either friendly indigenous forces to fight the communists, or give materiel support to America's allies to fight in Washington's interest. This strategy also fit well into the New Look framework. It was inexpensive, it kept American soldiers out of war, which quelled anti-war sentiment at home, and it furthered America's interests abroad.

Another aspect of the Ike-Dulles foreign policy was what has been called "pactomania," something of an extreme notion of the containment strategy that called for surrounding the Soviet Union and China with nations friendly to the United States—all done through a series of pacts, unilateral declarations, and mutual defense treaties. In Europe, Eisenhower and Dulles accepted NATO as the instrument of defense there. In Southeast Asia, Dulles built the Southeast Asia Treaty Organization (SEATO); and in the Middle East it was the Baghdad Pact (a document that the U.S. supported but did not sign). By the time Eisenhower left office in 1961 the Soviet-China communist bloc was surrounded by nations that had, one way or another, declared their allegiance to the United States, although only NATO maintained any real force.

Lastly in the arsenal of New Look was the strategy of covert military operations, an aspect of the Eisenhower foreign policy that was not made public. The chief force here was the Central Intelligence Agency (CIA), a mostly secret organization formed by Truman in the National Security Act of 1947 to consolidate all the various intelligence services that had grown up in Washington and in the several services. During Eisenhower's administration the CIA grew enormously in size and importance as another means of furthering American interests abroad. CIA-initiated operations were seldom expensive and the results were often immediately effective. The head of the CIA in this period was Allen Dulles, the brother of John Foster Dulles.

Some aspects of New Look had their antecedents in past strategies—like containment. Others, like covert operations and proxy armies, would establish precedents for future policies and actions.

Document 6.1 is an important foreign policy speech delivered by Secretary of State Dulles to the Overseas Press Club of America. Here Dulles argues the domino theory—the idea that if the United States does not stop the spread of communism in Vietnam, the Soviet Union will take over all of Southeast Asia. It is a foreshadowing of the American involvement in Vietnam in the next decade. In *Document 6.2* Dulles criticizes the Truman administration for allowing the communists to dictate events, for reacting to the moves of the communist world rather than acting and forcing the communists to react. He also explains the finer points of massive retaliation. *Document 6.3* is Hans Morgenthau's direct response to Dulles' speech. Morgenthau was a professor of political science at the University of Chicago and a frequent critic of U.S. foreign policy.

DOCUMENT 6.1

SECRETARY OF STATE JOHN FOSTER DULLES, "THE THREAT OF A RED ASIA," MARCH 29, 1954

Indochina is important for many reasons. First—and always first—are the human val-

SOURCE: *State Department, Bulletin*, April 12, 1954, 539–54.

ues. About 30 million people are seeking for themselves the dignity of self-government. Until a few years ago, they formed merely a French dependency. Now, their three political units—Vietnam, Laos and Cambodia—are exercising a considerable measure of independent political authority within the French Union. Each of the three is now recognized by the United States and by more than thirty other nations. They signed the Japanese Peace Treaty with us. Their independence is not yet complete. But the French Government in July 1953 declared its intention to complete that independence, and negotiations to consummate that pledge are actively under way.

The United States is watching this development with close attention and great sympathy. We do not forget that we were a colony that won its freedom. We have sponsored in the Philippines a conspicuously successful development of political independence. We feel a sense of kinship with those everywhere who yearn for freedom.

The Communists are attempting to prevent the orderly development of independence and to confuse the issue before the world. The Communists have, in these matters, a regular line which Stalin laid down in 1924.

The scheme is to whip up the spirit of nationalism so that it becomes violent. That is done by professional agitators. Then the violence is enlarged by Communist military and technical leadership and the provision of military supplies. In these ways, international Communism gets a strangle hold on the people and it uses that power to "amalgamate" the people into the Soviet orbit. "Amalgamation" is Lenin's and Stalin's word to describe their process.

"Amalgamation" is now being attempted in Indochina under the ostensible leadership of Ho Chi Minh. He was indoctrinated in Moscow. He became an associate of the Russian Borodin, when the latter was organizing the Chinese Communist Party which was to bring China into the Soviet orbit. Then Ho transferred his activities to Indochina.

Those fighting under the banner of Ho Chi Minh have largely been trained and equipped in Communist China. They are supplied with artillery and ammunition through the Soviet-Chinese Communist bloc. Captured materiel shows that much of it was fabricated by the Skoda Munitions Works in Czechoslovakia and transported across Russia and Siberia and then sent through China into Vietnam. Military supplies for the Communist armies have been pouring into Vietnam at a steadily increasing rate.

Military and technical guidance is supplied by an estimated 2,000 Communist Chinese.

They function with the forces of Ho Chi Minh in key positions—in staff sections of the high command, at the division level and in specialized units such as signal, engineer, artillery and transportation.

In the present stage, the Communists in Indochina use nationalistic anti-French slogans to win local support. But if they achieved military or political success, it is certain that they would subject the people to a cruel Communist dictatorship taking its orders from Peiping and Moscow.

The tragedy would not stop there. If the Communist forces won uncontested control over Indochina or any substantial part thereof, they would surely resume the same pattern of aggression against other free peoples in the area.

The propagandists of Red China and Russia make it apparent that the purpose is to dominate all of Southeast Asia.

Southeast Asia is the so-called "rice bowl" which helps to feed the densely populated region that extends from India to Japan. It is rich in many raw materials, such as tin, oil, rubber, and iron ore. It offers industrial Japan potentially important markets and sources of raw materials.

The area has great strategic value. Southeast Asia is astride the most direct and best developed sea and air routes between the Pacific and South Asia. It has major naval and air bases. Communist control of Southeast Asia would carry a grave threat to the Philippines, Australia and New Zealand, with whom we have treaties of mutual assistance. The entire Western pacific area, including the so-called "offshore island chain," would be strategically endangered.

President Eisenhower appraised the situation when he said that the area is of "transcendent importance."

The United States has shown in many ways its sympathy for the gallant struggle being waged in Indochina by the French forces and those of the Associated States. Congress has enabled us to provide material aid to the established governments and their peoples. Also, our diplomacy has sought to deter Communist China from open aggression in that area.

Secretary of State John Foster Dulles (right) and Eisenhower share a light moment on the White House lawn with Winston Churchill. Seated to the right, and apparently out of the conversation, is British Prime Minister Anthony Eden. *National Park Service/Dwight D. Eisenhower Library*

President Eisenhower, in his address of April 16, 1953, explained that a Korean armistice would be a fraud if it merely released aggressive armies for attack elsewhere. I said in September 1953 that if Red China sent its own Army into Indochina, that would result in grave consequences which might not be confined to Indochina.

Recent statements have been designed to impress upon potential aggressors that aggression might lead to action at places and by means of free-world choosing, so that aggression would cost more than it could gain.

The Chinese Communists have, in fact, avoided the direct use of their own Red armies in open aggression against Indochina. They have, however, largely stepped up their support of the aggression in that area. Indeed, they promoted that aggression by all means short of open invasion.

Under all the circumstances it seems desirable to clarify further the United States position.

Under the conditions of today, the imposition on Southeast Asia of the political system of Communist Russia and its Chinese Communist ally, by whatever means, would be a grave threat to the whole free community. The United States feels that that possibility should not be passively accepted, but should be met by united action. This might involve serious risks. But these risks are far less than those that will face us a few years from now, if we dare not be resolute today.

The free nations want peace. However, peace is not had merely by wanting it. Peace has to be worked for and planned for. Sometimes it is necessary to take risks to win peace just as it is necessary in war to take risks to win victory. The chances for peace are usually better by letting a potential aggressor know in advance where his aggression could lead him.

DOCUMENT 6.2

SECRETARY OF STATE JOHN FOSTER DULLES' STRATEGY OF MASSIVE RETALIATION, JANUARY 12, 1954

It is now nearly a year since the Eisenhower Administration took office. During that year I have often spoken of various parts of our foreign policies. Tonight I should like to present an overall view of those policies which relate to our security.

First of all, let us recognize that many of the preceding foreign policies were good. Aid to Greece and Turkey had checked the Communist drive to the Mediterranean. The European Recovery Program [Marshall Plan] has helped the peoples of Western Europe to pull out of the post-war morass. The Western powers were steadfast in Berlin and overcame the blockade with their airlift. As a loyal member of the United Nations, we reacted with force to repel the Communist attack in Korea. When that effort exposed our military weakness, we rebuilt rapidly our military establishment. We also sought a quick buildup of armed strength in Western Europe.

These were the acts of a nation which saw the danger of Soviet Communism; which realized that its own safety was tied up with that of others; which was capable of responding boldly and promptly to emergencies. These are pre-

SOURCE: *Department of State Bulletin*, Vol XXX, 107–10.

cious values to be acclaimed. Also, we can pay tribute to Congressional bi-partisanship which puts the nation above politics.

But we need to recall that what we did was in the main emergency action, imposed on us by our enemies. Let me illustrate.

We did not send our army into Korea because we judged, in advance, that it was sound military strategy to commit our army to fight land battles in Asia. Our decision had been to pull out of Korea. It was Soviet-inspired action that pulled us back. We did not decide in advance that it was wise to grant billions annually as foreign economic aid. We adopted that policy in response to the Communist efforts to sabotage the free economies of Western Europe. We did not build up our military establishment at a rate which involved huge budget deficits, a depreciating currency and a feverish economy, because this seemed, in advance, a good policy.

Indeed, we decided otherwise until the Soviet military threat was clearly revealed.

We live in a world where emergencies are always possible, and our survival may depend upon our capacity to meet emergencies. Let us pray that we shall always have that capacity. But, having said that, it is necessary also to say that emergency measures—however good for the emergency—do not necessarily make good permanent policies. Emergency measures are costly; they are superficial; and they imply that the enemy has the initiative. They cannot be depended on to serve our long-time interests.

This "long time" factor is of critical importance. The Soviet Communists are planning for what they call "an entire historical era," and we should do the same. They seek, through many types of maneuvers, gradually to divide and weaken the free nations by overextending them in efforts which, as Lenin put it, are "beyond their strength, so that they come to practical bankruptcy." Then, said Lenin, "our victory is assured." Then, said Stalin, will be "the moment for the decisive blow."

In the face of this strategy, measures cannot be judged adequate merely because they ward off an immediate danger. It is essential to do this, but it is also essential to do so without exhausting ourselves.

When the Eisenhower administration applied this test, we felt that some transformations were needed. It is not sound military strategy permanently to commit U.S. land forces to Asia to a degree that leaves us no strategic reserves. It is not sound economics, or good foreign policy, to support permanently other countries; for in the long run, that creates as much ill will as good will. Also, it is not sound to become permanently committed to military expenditures so vast they lead to "practical bankruptcy."

Change was imperative to assure the stamina needed for permanent security. But it was equally imperative that change should be accompanied by an understanding of our true purposes. Sudden and spectacular change had to be avoided. Otherwise, there might have been a panic among our friends and miscalculated aggression by our enemies. We can, I believe, make a good report in these respects.

We need allies and collective security. Our purpose is to make these relations more effective, less costly. This can be done by placing more reliance on deterrent power and less dependence on local defensive power.

This is accepted practice so far as local communities are concerned. We keep locks on our doors, but we do not have an armed guard in every home. We rely principally on a community security system so well equipped to punish any who break in and steal that, in fact, would-be aggressors are generally deterred. That is the modern way of getting maximum protection at a bearable cost. What the Eisenhower administration seeks is a similar international security system. We want, for ourselves and the other free nations, a maximum deterrent at a bearable cost.

Local defense will always be important. But there is no local defense which alone will contain the mighty land power of the Communist world. Local defenses must be reinforced by the further deterrent of massive retaliatory power. A potential aggressor must

know that he cannot always prescribe battle conditions that suit him. Otherwise, for example, a potential aggressor, might be tempted to attack in confidence that resistance would be confined to manpower. He might be tempted to attack in places where his superiority was decisive.

The way to deter aggression is for the free community to be willing and able to respond vigorously at places and with means of its own choosing. So long as our basic policy concepts were unclear, our military leaders could not be selective in building our military power. If an enemy could pick his time and place and method of warfare—and if our policy was to remain the traditional one of meeting aggression by direct and local opposition—then we needed to be ready to fight in the Arctic and in the Tropics; in Asia, the Near East, and in Europe; by sea, by land, and by air; with old weapons and with new weapons. . . .

Before military planning could be changed, the President and his advisors, as represented by the National Security Council, had to make some basic policy decisions. This has been done. The basic decision was to depend primarily upon a great capacity to retaliate, instantly, by means and at places of our choosing. Now the Department of Defense and the Joint Chiefs of Staff can shape our military establishment to fit what is our policy, instead of having to try to be ready to meet the enemy's many choices. That permits a selection of a military means instead of a multiplication of means. As a result, it is now possible to get, and share, more basic security at less cost.

Let us now see how this concept has been applied to foreign policy, taking first the Far East.

In Korea, this administration effected a major transformation. The fighting has been stopped on honorable terms. That was possible because the aggressor, already thrown back to and behind his place of beginning, was faced with the possibility that the fighting might, to his own great peril, soon spread beyond the limits and methods which he had selected.

The cruel toll of American youth and the nonproductive expenditure of many billions have been stopped. Also our armed forces are no longer largely committed to the Asian mainland. We can begin to create a strategic reserve which greatly improves our defensive posture.

This change gives added authority to the warning of the members of the United Nations which fought in Korea that, if the Communists renew the aggression, the United Nations response would not necessarily be confined to Korea. I have said in relation to Indochina that, if there were open Red Chinese army aggression there, that would have "grave consequences which might not be confined to Indochina." . . .

We do not, of course, claim to have found some magic formula that insures against all forms of Communist successes. It is normal that at some times and at some places there may be setbacks to the cause of freedom. What we expect to insure is that any setbacks will have only temporary and local significance, because they will leave unimpaired those free world assets which in the long run will prevail.

If we can deter such aggression as would mean general war, and that is our confident resolve, then we can let time and fundamentals work for us. We do not need self-imposed policies which sap our strength.

The fundamental, on our side, is the richness—spiritual, intellectual and material—that freedom can produce and the irresistible attraction it then sets up. That is why we do not plan ourselves to shackle freedom to preserve freedom. We intend that our conduct and example shall continue, as in the past to show all men how good can be the fruits of freedom.

If we relay on freedom, then it follows that we must abstain from diplomatic moves which would seem to endorse captivity. That would, in effect, be a conspiracy against freedom. I can assure you that we shall never seek security for ourselves by such a "deal. . . ."

If we persist in the courses I outline we shall confront dictatorship with a task that is, in the long run, beyond its strength. For unless it changes, it must suppress the human

desires that freedom satisfies—as we shall be demonstrating

If the dictators persist in their present course then it is they who will be limited to superficial successes, while their foundation crumbles under the tread of their iron boots. . . .

We can be sure that there is going on, even within Russia, a silent test of strength between the powerful rulers and the multitudes of human beings. Each individual no doubt seems by himself to be helpless in this struggle. But their aspirations in the aggregate make up a mighty force. There are signs that the rulers are bending to some of the human desires of their people. There are promises of more food, more household goods, more economic freedom. That does not prove that the Soviet rulers have themselves been converted. It is rather that they may be dimly perceiving a basic fact, that is that there are limits to the power of any ruler indefinitely to suppress the human spirit.

In that God-given fact lies our greatest hope. It is a hope that can sustain us. For even if the path ahead be long and hard, it need not be a warlike path; and we can know that at the end may be found the blessedness of peace.

DOCUMENT 6.3

HANS MORGENTHAU'S RESPONSE TO DULLES

The "Instant Retaliation" speech of Secretary Dulles, delivered on January 12 was presented as a major redefinition of the United States policy for the decade to come. . . . Through the confusion of these conflicting statements certain clear lines of argument can be seen. Congress and our allies have asked who will decide on "instant retaliation" and have been assured that their

SOURCE: Hans Morgenthau, "The Dulles Doctrine: 'Instant Retaliation,' " *The New Republic*, March 29, 1954, 10–14.

"constant acquiescence" is necessary. Army and Navy spokesmen have stressed that conventional weapons are still needed and this also is conceded. Objections have been advanced to the rigidity of the Dulles formula and in turn the Secretary of State acknowledges that its application in any given situation will turn on the facts. For all these modifications and qualifications, however, the doctrine itself has not been questioned by those in power. The January 12 speech stands on its essentials, as the expression of a major step by the National Security Council. It outlines a fundamental change that has taken place in United States strategy, and that is affirmed day by day, in important decisions such as those to eliminate three active Army divisions, to reduce naval personnel by 100,000 men, to extend the use of atomic weapons, and at the same time to warn our opponents that, in the event of new aggression in Korea, our counteraction will not stop short at the nation's Northern frontier. . . .

Mr. Dulles makes essentially five points which serve as the keystones of the new policy.

First, "emergency action imposed on us by our enemies" and exemplified by the Korean War and the Marshall Plan, must be replaced by a long-term plan which provides "a maximum deterrent at a bearable cost."

Second, we shall—and this is "the basic decision" made by the President and the National Security Council—"depend primarily upon a great capacity to retaliate, instantly, by means and at places of our choosing."

Third, as a corollary to "placing more reliance on deterrent power," we shall depend less on "local defensive power."

Fourth, "broadly speaking, foreign budgetary aid is being limited to situations where it clearly contributes to military strength."

Fifth, "if we can deter such aggression as would mean general war . . . then we can let time and fundamentals work for us. . . . The fundamental, on our side, is the richness—spiritual, intellectual and material—that freedom can produce and the irresistible attraction it then sets up." Thus "we shall confront dicta-

torship with a task that is, in the long run, beyond its strength. . . ."

The new policy assumes that the threats to the U.S. will take the form of open military aggression to be prevented by the threat, or answered by the reality, of atomic retaliation. With this assumption the new policy reverts to the pattern of the 40's when the American monopoly of the atomic bomb or at least of a stockpile of atomic bombs sufficient to wage successful atomic war stabilized the line of demarcation of 1945 between East and West. The virtual certainty that any step taken by the Soviet Union beyond that line would lead to the outbreak of a third world war, fought only by the U.S. with atomic weapons, may have prevented such a step from being taken. It may seem trite, but in view of the somnambulistic quality of such official argumentation it is not superfluous, to point out that a policy of atomic retaliation is a sure deterrent only if the retaliatory power has a monopoly or at least a vast superiority in the retaliatory weapon. But what if the power to be retaliated against is in a position to retaliate against the retaliation or to make retaliation impossible by prevention?

The new policy is intended in the future to make local aggression, Korean-style, impossible; for no government in its senses will embark upon local aggression in the knowledge that its industrial and population centers will be reduced to rubble in retaliation. In other words, the policy of atomic retaliation, by the vary fact of its announcement, removes the need for its implementation. However, this is not the end of the story. It is easy to imagine situations where local aggression will not be deterred by the threat of atomic retaliation but will be regarded by the aggressor nation of such vital importance to itself that it must be undertaken in spite of the risk of an atomic war. One can imagine a situation arising in central Europe which will induce the Soviet Union to take military measures which come under the heading of local aggression. . . .

The new policy shifts the emphasis from the conventional weapons to the new instruments of atomic power. By doing so, it recognizes what, at least in theory, has not always been recognized before, namely, that the United States has not the resources to oppose more than one local aggression at a time by local means. The United States would not have been able to fight two Korean Wars at the same time. By recognizing these limits of American strength, the new policy also recognizes that there may be local aggressions to which we have no answer at all, e.g. Indo-China, or against which our only answer is the atomic bomb. The shift from the traditional weapons of local defense to atomic weapons, then, on the one hand, limits our ability to meet local aggression by local means, as we did in Korea, and, on the other, increases the temptation to use the atomic bomb against local aggression where under the old strategy we might have used traditional weapons. In other words, the new policy tends to limit our choices. Formerly we could have met local aggression by doing nothing, by resisting it locally, or by striking at its source with atomic bombs. The new policy contracts the sphere within which the second alternative can operate. Confronted with a choice between doing nothing at all or dropping an atomic bomb, the new policy increases the incentive for doing the later. In the words of William Graham Sumner, "For what we prepare for is what we shall get."

Yet the chances that any of these contingencies will actually come to pass may well be small. For the immediate threat to the security to the West arises not from local aggression, Soviet inspired or otherwise, nor from atomic war deliberately embarked upon by the Soviet Union, but from the revolutionary fire which is sweeping through much of Asia, Africa, Western Europe and Latin America. Atomic retaliation can only be an answer to open military aggression. It stands to reason that to drop atomic bombs on Moscow or Peking is no answer to the threat of Communist revolution in Italy or Indo-China. The critical problem of national and social revolutions, that Moscow did not create but which it exploits, Mr. Dulles fails to face. The generalities of freedom are offered, of course; it is the specifics of freedom that concern the nations whose futures are now in doubt. . . .

Perhaps, however, the key to the new policy is to be sought not in such considerations of high political and military policy, but in the fact that in a speech of about 3,500 words there are no less than fifteen references to the comparative cost of the alternative policies and to the cheapness of the new one. Perhaps the *London Times* is right in saying: "It is indeed hard to see where and how the great strategic change has taken place, though it is not hard to recognize the economic reason why it has become politically desirable to assume that it has done so."

If economic interpretation of the new policy is correct, and much in the recent statements of the President and of Mr. Dulles point to its correctness, it may again be trite, but it is not superfluous, to remind the money saver that a Korean War, even one fought in perpetuity, is cheaper in every respect than an atomic war.

6.4 Secretary of State John Foster Dulles Explains Events in Guatemala, June 30, 1954
6.5 E. Howard Hunt Explains Events in Guatemala

A long with massive retaliation and brinkmanship was the New Look policy of covert action. These secret, inexpensive CIA-directed activities were designed to further American interests abroad without risking much in the process.

One of the most famous CIA covert operations in the period was the 1953 overthrow of the supposedly communist-leaning government of Mohammad Mosaddeq in Iran. A year later Eisenhower and Dulles found communism in the poor Latin American nation of Guatemala. There, Colonel Jacobo Arbenz had been elected to office in 1951 and was conducting labor land reforms in an attempt to drag his country out of economic blight. In the last days of 1953 the ambassador to Guatemala spent an evening with Arbenz in Guatemala City and sent his report back to Washington. "I came away," he wrote, "definitely convinced that if [Arbenz] is not a Communist he will certainly do until one comes along, and that normal approaches will not work in Guatemala."

Latin America had received little attention from Washington in the years following World War II, but here it seemed that communism was gaining a foothold in America's own backyard. When Arbenz accepted support from Guatemalan communists and then threatened to nationalize the United Fruit Company, Dulles (who had served on the board of directors of United Fruit before becoming secretary of state) claimed before the Court of Arbitration at The Hague that Guatemala had fallen into the web of international communism. Dulles' nightmare seemed to come true when Arbenz received a shipment of military supplies from Czechoslovakia.

Eisenhower responded by authorizing a CIA-directed coup, and he told the Dulles brothers, "I'm prepared to take any steps that are necessary to see that it succeeds." After a few CIA-orchestrated bombing missions over Guatemala City, Arbenz fled. He was succeeded by an American-sponsored military dictator, Castillo Armas. Communism was thwarted in Guatemala, but the incident remained a sore point in U.S.-Latin American relations for years to come. On June 30, 1954, Dulles delivered a radio address (*Document 6.4*) to explain to the American people what had happened in Guatemala.

It was E. Howard Hunt and a few CIA operatives who carried out the revolution itself. Hunt's account of events is *Document 6.5*. In this interview, Hunt mentions General Walter Bedell Smith and Thomas Corcoran as important players in the decision to intervene in Guatemala. Smith had been Eisenhower's chief of staff during World War II, then ambassador to the Soviet Union from 1946 to 1949, head of the CIA before Dulles, and undersecretary of state during the Guatemalan revolution. Possibly most importantly, Smith was one of Ike's closest personal friends. Tommy Corcoran, known by some as "Tommy the Cork," had earned his Washington reputation as a legendary aide inside the Roosevelt administration. In the postwar years he ran a Washington law firm and served as a high-powered lobbyist—the consummate Washington insider during the Eisenhower years. Hunt was later involved in several CIA attempts to overthrow Cuba's Fidel Castro, including the failed Bay of Pigs invasion in 1961. After resigning from the CIA in 1970, Hunt became covert operations chief for the Nixon White House, where he directed the burglary of Democratic party headquarters at the Watergate office complex in 1972.

....

DOCUMENT 6.4

SECRETARY OF STATE JOHN FOSTER DULLES EXPLAINS EVENTS IN GUATEMALA, JUNE 30, 1954

Tonight I should like to talk to you about Guatemala. It is a scene of dramatic events. They expose the evil purpose of the Kremlin to destroy the inter-American system and they test the ability of the American states to maintain the peaceful integrity of this hemisphere.

For several years now international communism has been probing here and there for nesting places in the Americas. It finally chose Guatemala as a spot which it could turn into an official base from which to breed subversion which would extend to the other American republics.

The intrusion of Soviet despotism was, of course, a direct challenge to the Monroe Doctrine, the first and most fundamental of our foreign policies. . . .

In Guatemala, international communism had an initial success. It began ten years ago when a revolution occurred in Guatemala. The revolution was not without justification. But the Communists seized on it, not as an opportunity for real reforms, but as a chance to gain political power.

Communist agitators devoted themselves to infiltrating the public and private organizations of Guatemala. They sent recruits to Russia for revolutionary training and indoctrination in such institutions as the Lenin School in Moscow.

Operating under the guise of reformers they organized the workers and peasants under Communist leadership. And having gained control of what they call the mass organizations, they moved on to take over the official press and radio of the Guatemalan Government.

They dominated the social security organization and ran the agrarian reform program. Through the technique of the so-called popular front they dictated to the Congress and the President.

The judiciary made one valiant attempt to protect its integrity and independence. But the Communists, using their control of the legislative body, caused the Supreme Court to be dissolved when it refused to give approval to a Communist-contrived law. Arbenz, who until this week was President of Guatemala, was openly manipulated by the leaders of communism.

Guatemala is a small country, but its power of standing alone is not a measure of the threat. The master plan of international communism is to gain a solid political base in this hemisphere. A base that then can be used to extend Communist penetration to the other peoples of the American Governments.

It was not the power of the Arbenz Government that concerned us, but the power behind it.

If world communism captured any American state, however small, a new and perilous front is established which will increase the dangers of the entire free world and require even greater sacrifices from the American people.

The situation in Guatemala had become so dangerous that the American states could not ignore it. And so at Caracas last month when the American states held their tenth inter-American conference, they adopted a momentous declaration. They said that the domination or the control of the political institution of any

SOURCE: *New York Times*, July 1, 1954.

American state by international communism would constitute a threat to the sovereignty and political independence of the American states endangering the peace of America.

There was only one American state that voted against that resolution. That state was Guatemala.

This Caracas Declaration precipitated a dramatic and rapidly moving chain of events. From their European base the Communist leaders moved quickly to build up the military power of their agents in Guatemala. In May a large shipment of arms was moved from behind the Iron Curtain into Guatemala. The shipment was thought to be secreted by false manifest and false clearances. The ostensible destination of the shipment was changed three times while the shipment was en route.

At the same time, the agents of international communism in Guatemala intensified their efforts to penetrate and to subvert the neighboring Central American states.

They attempted political assassinations and political strikes. They used their consular agents for political warfare. Many Guatemalan people protested against their being used by Communist dictatorship to serve the Communist's lust for power.

What was the response? It was mass arrests; the suppression of constitutional guarantees; the killing of opposition leaders, and other brutal tactics such as are normally employed by communism to secure the consolidation of its power.

In the face of these events and in accordance with the spirit of the Caracas Declaration, the nations of this Hemisphere laid further plans to grapple with the danger. The Arbenz Government responded with efforts to disrupt the inter-American system. And because this Guatemalan regime enjoyed the full support of Soviet Russia, which is a permanent member of the Security Council of the United Nations, Guatemala tried to bring this matter before the Security Council. It did so without first referring the matter to the American regional organization, as is called for both by the Charter of

the United Nations and by the treaty which creates the American Organization.

The Foreign Minister of Guatemala openly connived in this matter with the Foreign Minister of the Soviet Union. The two were in open correspondence and ill-concealed privity. The Security Council at first voted overwhelmingly to refer this Guatemalan matter to the Organization of American States and the vote was ten to one, but the one negative vote was a Soviet veto. And then that encouraged the Guatemalan Government to go on and with Soviet backing it redoubled its efforts to try to supplant the American system by Security Council jurisdiction.

However, last Friday the United Nations Security Council decided not to take up the Guatemalan matter, but to leave it in the first instance to the American states themselves. That was a triumph for the system of balance between regional organization and world organization, a balance which the American states had fought for and won when the Charter was drawn up at San Francisco.

And then the American states moved promptly to deal with the situation. Their peace commission left yesterday for Guatemala. And earlier the American states had voted overwhelmingly to call a meeting of the Foreign Ministers of the American states to consider the penetration of international communism in Guatemala and the measures required to eliminate it. Never before has there been so clear a call uttered with such a sense of urgency and strong resolve.

Throughout this period that I have outlined the Guatemalan Governments and Communist agents throughout the world have persistently attempted to obscure the real issue, that of Communist imperialism, by claiming that the United States is only interested in protecting American business. We regret that there have been disputes between the Government of Guatemala and the United Fruit Company. We have urged repeatedly that these disputes should be submitted to settlement by an international tribunal or by international arbitration. That's the way to dispose of problems of this sort. . . .

The people of Guatemala have now been heard from. Despite the armaments piled up by the Arbenz Government, it had been unable to enlist the spiritual cooperation of the people. Led by Colonel Castillo Armas, patriots arose in Guatemala to challenge the Communist leadership and to change it. Thus, a situation is being cured by the Guatemalans themselves.

Last Sunday, President Arbenz of Guatemala resigned and sought asylum, and other Communists and fellow-travelers are following his example. Tonight, just as I speak, Colonel Castillo Armas is in conference in El Salvadore with Colonel Monzon, the head of the council which has taken over the power in Guatemala City. It was this power which the just wrath of the Guatemalan people wrested from President Arbenz who took flight.

Now the future lies at the disposal of the Guatemalan people themselves. It lies at the disposal of leaders loyal to Guatemala who had not treasonably become the agents of an alien despotism which sought to use Guatemala for its own evil ends. . . . Need for vigilance is not past. Communism is still a menace everywhere, but the people of the United States and the other American republics can tonight feel that at least one grave danger has been averted. Also an example has been set which promises increased security of the future. The ambitious and unscrupulous will be less prone to feel that communism is the wave of their future.

DOCUMENT 6.5

E. HOWARD HUNT EXPLAINS EVENTS IN GUATEMALA

I always felt that in forming a task force to overthrow the communist government of Arbenz, that we did the right thing, but perhaps for the wrong reason: that reason being, I

SOURCE: CNN Interview with Howard Hunt (for program "Cold War"), 1997.

wanted it to be purely for our national security and to bolster and revere the Monroe Doctrine; whereas, when I was finally called up from Mexico City to confer with [General Walter] Bedell Smith and some of the other high-ranking members of our national security apparatus, it turned out that the reason that they were having a change of heart [in favor of intervention] was because Thomas Corcoran, who was the rather famous lobbyist working for the United Fruit Company, had persuaded Eisenhower and some other high dignitaries to take this matter under very close advisement and get going, do something about it.

So I felt a little bit betrayed when I learned that, because I thought, "Hey, you know, I'm working for the United States of America, I'm not a hireling for United Fruit." But I went ahead with my assigned tasks in any case, and if United Fruit benefited from it, that was part of the set game, I suppose you could say. . . .

I was not part of the military planning for this operation; I was in charge of the political and the psychological warfare aspects. And the old slogan "You can't beat someone with no one" was very much at the front of my mind, and from various sources I was able to pull together a sort of a preferential panel, or group of three prominent Guatemalans who were outside Guatemala. We could only deal with those who were outside, because those who were inside were in tough shape thanks to Arbenz's secret police.

[The key figure was] Colonel Castillo Armas. . . . I had his bio and his photographs and so forth: he was in refuge in Honduras at that time. I realized that "This has got to be our guy." He was an extraordinary fellow himself; he looked pure Mayan: he had the bronzed skin of the Central American Mayan or Aztec, and the hooked nose; a little, short, squat guy; very, very, durable individual. He'd been imprisoned by Arbenz for a long time, and had tunneled out of the prison with his bare hands, made his escape that way, and got into Honduras, where our chief of station contacted him and made his location available. . . .

[So] we went with Castillo Armas, and he had of course adherents from the army who were in exile with him in Honduras. And so it was a relatively simple thing for him to draw more people to himself. Once he was assured of the United States backing—and I didn't make that assurance to him; another member of the team did—then he went all out and got this group together, and told us what we were going to need and what his suggestions were to make the operation work.

On the U.S.-directed 1954 Guatemalan coup: I suppose the example that I can best turn to, although I rather hate to, is [that] what we wanted to do was to have a terror campaign: to terrify Arbenz particularly, terrify his troops, much as the German Stuka bombers terrified the populations of Holland, Belgium and Poland at the onset of World War II and just rendered everybody paralyzed.

We had acquired some aircraft, and the Guatemalan propaganda team prepared leaflets, which were in several phases. You know: "Beware: the day is coming," and so forth. And then the next air drop would have a slightly different theme, but they were all focusing basically on the main situation, which was that Arbenz was a "baddie," that he was selling Guatemala to a foreign power, i.e. the Soviet Union, and that this should not be tolerated by the Guatemalan populace.

And when the D-day actually came, these P-47s made a couple of low-level, relatively harmless strafing runs over the city. We didn't want to kill civilians; they dropped a few smoke bombs and concussion bombs to frighten people so that they just stayed indoors. And actually, the Guatemalan army was confined to barracks. When Arbenz tried to get a message out over his own transmitter, he found that his words were not being heard because our [radio] station in Guatemala was telling all

of Guatemala, and indeed all of Latin America . . . that Arbenz had fled; Arbenz and his cabinet had fled and left the country naked, and that was greeted with a lot of enthusiasm by the locals. . . .

Did it surprise me that they did not fight? Very much. We all anticipated an armed struggle—not of great proportions or of long duration, but we did anticipate [resistance]. . . . I found it hard to believe that there had been no bloodshed, no armed confrontation. Castillo Armas only had about 140 people working for him, a ragtag group if there ever was one. But then we had done the same thing in another part of the world a few years earlier. People don't have to be in spiffy uniforms, just so long as they can form a military presence and impress the population. . . .

The great mistake that the United States made at the termination of the project was that, as in so many other instances, having achieved objective "A," we turned our backs on Guatemala and went about other things that were of higher priority at that time to that Administration or succeeding Administration, and left this army colonel, Castillo Armas, in charge of a country without [giving] him any backing: we didn't send in advisers, we didn't do anything particularly financially for him. I guess we figured that United Fruit would take care of him. Whether they did or not, I don't know. But by the time he was assassinated three years later, by a soldier and his bodyguard (who was an ardent listener to Radio Moscow), there was no fall-back position. . . . Three years were insufficient for an untutored army colonel of questionable educational background to establish a kind of a democracy in Guatemala that we hoped would flourish and grow. But the United States has always done that: we settle for immediate objectives and, unlike the Soviets, did not have our eye on the distant future.

6.6   President Dwight Eisenhower's Speech in the Aftermath of the Suez Crisis and the Soviet Invasion of Hungary, January 5, 1957

The key to the Eisenhower administration's Middle East foreign policy was Egypt, the strongest Arab power in the region. Egypt's leader, Gamal Abdul Nasser, was a freewheeling Arab nationalist who had refused to accept the anti-communist line. "The Soviet Union," he told Dulles, "is more than a thousand miles away and we've never had any trouble with them. They have never attacked us. They have never occupied our territory. They have never had a base here." Nasser also refused to join the American anti-communist crusade because of Washington's continued support of Israel. In an attempt to pull Egypt and the other Arab states into the American sphere, the Eisenhower administration agreed to soften its support for Israel, but Nasser was never satisfied.

American interests in the Middle East went well beyond diplomacy. In 1953 American oil companies produced nearly 70 percent of the region's oil, the fuel that ran the industrial economies of the West. Eisenhower considered it his duty to protect that resource, and certainly to keep it from falling into Soviet hands.

Nasser's obstinance forced Eisenhower and Dulles to change their focus from Egypt to what Dulles called the "northern tier" of Arab states, and in 1955 Dulles was instrumental in bringing Turkey and Iraq into a defensive alliance, which was soon broadened to include Britain, Iran and Pakistan. This Baghdad Pact was to link NATO in the west with SEATO (South East Asia Treaty Organization) in the east and complete Dulles' plan to encircle the Soviet-Chinese Asian monolith. It was also designed to isolate Nasser, and possibly to raise Iraq to a leadership role in the Arab world at the expense of Egypt.

Nasser denounced the Baghdad Pact as a device of the Western imperialists, a scheme to split the Arab world, and a pro-Israeli alliance. Almost immediately he orchestrated an alliance with Saudi Arabia and Syria and announced that if the United States refused aid he would search for it elsewhere—presumably from the Soviets. Dulles responded by applying economic sanctions against Egypt, and this included halting all aid for the construction of Egypt's Aswan High Dam on the Nile River, the cornerstone of the nation's economic development plans. Nasser continued to flirt with the Soviet Union, holding the threat above Dulles' head often. And just as often Dulles pronounced it a bluff.

On July 26, 1956 Nasser surprised the world by announcing that he would nationalize the Suez Canal and use its revenues to build Aswan. He also made good on his threats to accept economic aid from the Soviets—nearly $500 million, two and one half times the amount offered by the United States and Britain. Washington's anti-Nasser policy, it seemed, had not only allowed a Soviet break into the Middle East, it had jeopardized the flow of oil to the NATO nations. "Don't think we intend to stand impotent and let this one man get away with it," Eisenhower told a group of congressmen.

Through the summer and fall of 1956 France and England contemplated a military campaign to take back the Suez. Israel, fearing a much-enhanced Egyptian power on its southern border as a result of Soviet aid, agreed that it might be willing to join in an invasion of Egypt. Eisenhower held them all off, promising a peaceful settlement of the issue. But on October 29, without consulting Washington, the Israelis invaded the Sinai and rushed toward the canal. Two days later British and French planes began bombing Egypt, and on November 5 British and French paratroopers invaded. Eisenhower acted quickly to condemn the invasion. We will not accept "one code of international conduct for those who oppose us and another for our friends," he told the American people. He introduced a resolution in the UN condemning the invasion, and threatening sanctions against the invaders. Finally on election day, November 6, England and France stood down. Israel agreed to a cease-fire two days later.

The Suez crisis helped increase U.S. prestige among the Arab states, but it hurt the NATO alliance, enhanced Nasser's prestige, and added to Arab-Israeli tensions. The Eisenhower administration began looking for a new Middle East policy, a policy that would maintain American influence in the region, lessen Nasser's influence, and keep the Soviets contained. The result was the Eisenhower Doctrine, a plan to aid the nations of the Middle East against communist expansion in the area. In his speech requesting Congressional support, (*Document 6.6*) Eisenhower asked Congress to allow him to use the armed forces to protect the nations of the Middle East "requesting such aid" against "overt armed aggression from any nation controlled by International Communism."

It was mostly rhetoric. Egypt and Syria, the only two nations in the region that might possibly come under Soviet influence, were not likely to request U.S. aid. Both nations, and Jordan, rejected the Eisenhower Doctrine immediately, and Iraq showed little interest. Israel denounced it as an American plan to strengthen the Arab nations. Only Lebanon, Iran, and Saudi Arabia came around to supporting the doctrine. But to most of the Arab nations the Eisenhower Doctrine was little more than attempted influence-building in their region.

At almost the same moment that the crisis erupted in the Middle East, the Soviet Union sent tanks into Budapest and crushed an anti-Soviet uprising. An estimated 30,000 Hungarian civilians and 7,000 Soviet soldiers died in the two days of fighting in the first week of November. Ike addresses that situation as well in the following document.

....

DOCUMENT 6.6

PRESIDENT DWIGHT EISENHOWER'S SPEECH IN THE AFTERMATH OF THE SUEZ CRISIS AND THE SOVIET INVASION OF HUNGARY, JANUARY 5, 1957

The Middle East has abruptly reached a new and critical stage in its long and important history. In past decades many of the countries

SOURCE: *Public Papers of the Presidents: Dwight D. Eisenhower, 1957*, 6–16.

in that area were not fully self-governing. Other countries exercised considerable authority in the area and the security of the region was largely built around their power. But since the First World War there has been a steady evolution toward self-government and independence. This development the United States has welcomed and has encouraged. Our country supports without reservation the full sovereignty and independence of each and every nation in the Middle East.

The evolution to independence has in the main been a peaceful process. But the area has been often troubled. Persistent cross-currents of distrust and fear with raids back and forth across national boundaries have brought about a high degree of instability in much of the Mid East. Just recently there has been hostilities involving Western European nations that once exercised much influence in the area. Also the relatively large attack by Israel in October has intensified the basic differences between that nation and its Arab neighbors. All this instability has been heightened and, at times, manipulated by International Communism.

Russia's rulers have long sought to dominate the Middle East. That was true of the Czars and it is true of the Bolsheviks. The reasons are not hard to find. They do not affect Russia's security, for no one plans to use the Middle East as a base for aggression against Russia. Never for a moment has the United States entertained such a thought.

The Soviet Union has nothing whatsoever to fear from the United States in the Middle East, or anywhere else in the world, so long as its rulers do not themselves first resort to aggression.

That statement I make solemnly and emphatically. Neither does Russia's desire to dominate the Middle East spring from its own economic interest in the area. Russia does not appreciably use or depend upon the Suez Canal. In 1955 Soviet traffic through the Canal represented only about three fourths of 1 percent of the total. The Soviets have no need for, and could provide no market for, the petroleum resources which constitute the principal natural wealth of the area. Indeed, the Soviet Union is a substantial exporter of petroleum products.

The reason for Russia's interest in the Middle East is solely that of power politics. Considering her announced purpose of Communizing the world, it is easy to understand her hope of dominating the Middle East.

This region has always been the crossroads of the continents of the Eastern Hemisphere. The Suez Canal enables the nations of Asia and Europe to carry on the commerce that is essential if these countries are to maintain well-rounded and prosperous economies. The Middle East provides a gateway between Eurasia and Africa.

It contains about two thirds of the presently known oil deposits of the world and it normally supplies the petroleum needs of many nations of Europe, Asia and Africa. The nations of Europe are peculiarly dependent upon this supply, and this dependency relates to transportation as well as to production. This has been vividly demonstrated since the closing of the Suez Canal and some of the pipelines. Alternate ways of transportation and, indeed, alternate sources of power can, if necessary, be developed. But these cannot be considered as early prospects. These things stress the immense importance of the Middle East. If the nations of that area should lose their independence, if they were dominated by alien forces hostile to freedom, that would be both a tragedy for the area and for many other free nations whose economic life would be subject to near strangulation. Western Europe would be endangered just as though there had been no Marshall Plan, no North Atlantic Treaty Organization. The free nations of Asia and Africa, too, would be placed in serious jeopardy. And the countries of the Middle East would lose the markets upon which their economies depend. All this would have the most adverse, if not disastrous, effect upon our own nation's economic life and political prospects. . . .

International Communism, of course, seeks to mask its purposes of domination by expressions of good will and by superficially attractive offers of political, economic and military aid. But any free nation, which is the subject of Soviet enticement, ought, in elementary wisdom, to look behind the mask. . . .

Soviet control of the satellite nations of Eastern Europe has been forcibly maintained in spite of solemn promises of a contrary intent, made during World War II.

Stalin's death brought hope that this pattern would change. And we read the pledge of the Warsaw Treaty of 1955 that the Soviet Union would follow in satellite countries "the principles of mutual respect for their independence and the sovereignty and non-interference in domestic affairs." But we have just seen the subjugation of Hungary by naked armed force. In the aftermath of this Hungarian tragedy, world respect for and belief in Soviet promises have sunk to a new low. International Communism needs and seeks a recognizable success.

Thus we have these simple and indisputable facts:

1. The Middle East, which has always been coveted by Russia, would today be prized more than ever by International Communism.
2. The Soviet rulers continue to show that they do not scruple to use any means to gain their ends.
3. The free nations of the Mid East need, and for the most part want, added strength to assure their continued independence.

Our thoughts naturally turn to the United Nations as a protector of small nations. Its charter gives it primary responsibility for the maintenance of international peace and security. Our country has given the United Nations its full support in relation to the hostilities in Hungary and in Egypt. The United Nations was able to bring about a cease-fire and withdrawal of hostile forces from Egypt because it was dealing with governments and peoples who had a decent respect for the opinions of mankind as reflected in the United Nations General Assembly. But in the case of Hungary, the situation was different. The Soviet Union vetoed action by the Security Council to require the withdrawal of Soviet armed forces from Hungary. And it has shown callous indifference to the recommendations, even the censure, of the General Assembly. The United Nations can always be helpful, but it cannot be a wholly dependable protector of freedom when the ambitions of the Soviet Union are involved. . . .

There is general recognition in the Middle East, as elsewhere, that the United States does not seek either political or economic domination over any other people. Our desire is a world environment of freedom, not servitude. On the other hand many, if not all, of the nations of the Middle East are aware of the danger that stems from International Communism

and welcome closer cooperation with the United States to realize for themselves the United Nations goals of independence, economic well-being and spiritual growth.

If the Middle East is to continue its geographic role of uniting rather than separating East and West; if its vast economic resources are to serve the well-being of the peoples there, as well as that of others; and if its cultures and religions and their shrines are to be preserved for the uplifting of the spirits of the peoples, then the United States must make more evident its willingness to support the independence of the freedom-loving nations of the area. . . . It is nothing new for the President and Congress to join to recognize that the national integrity of other free nations is directly related to our own security.

We have joined to create and support the security system of the United Nations. We have reinforced the collective security system of the United Nations by a series of collective defense arrangements. Today we have security treaties with forty-two other nations which recognize that our peace and security are intertwined. We have joined to take decisive action in relation to Greece and Turkey and in relation to Taiwan.

Thus, the United States through the joint action of the President and the Congress, or, in the case of treaties, the Senate, has manifested in many endangered areas its purpose to support free and independent governments—and peace—against external menace, notably the menace of International Communism. Thereby we have helped to maintain peace and security during a period of great danger. It is now essential that the United States should manifest through joint action of the President and the Congress our determination to assist those nations of the Mid East area, which desire that assistance.

The action which I propose would have the following features. It would, first of all, authorize the United States to cooperate with and assist any nation or group of nations in the general area of the Middle East in the development of economic strength dedicated to the maintenance of national independence.

It would, in the second place, authorize the Executive to undertake in the same region programs of military assistance and cooperation with any nation or group of nations which desires such aid.

It would, in the third place, authorize such assistance and cooperation to include the employment of the armed forces of the United States to secure and protect the territorial integrity and political independence of such nations, requesting such aid, against overt armed aggression from any nation controlled by International Communism.

These measures would have to be consonant with the treaty obligations of the United States, including the Charter of the United Nations and with any action or recommendations of the United Nations. They would also, if armed attack occurs, be subject to the overriding authority of the United Nations Security Council in accordance with the Charter.

The present proposal would, in the fourth place, authorize the President to employ, for economic and defensive military purposes, sums available under the Mutual Security Act of 1954, as amended, without regard to existing limitations. . . .

This program will not solve all the problems of the Middle East. Neither does it represent the totality of our policies for the area. There are the problems of Palestine and the relations between Israel and the Arab States, and the future of the Arab refugees. There is the problem of the future status of the Suez Canal. These difficulties are aggravated by International Communism. . . . Experience shows that indirect aggression rarely if ever succeeds where there is reasonable security against direct aggression; where the government disposes of loyal security forces, and where economic conditions are such as not to make Communism seem an attractive alternative. The program I suggest deals with all three aspects of this matter and thus with the problem of indirect aggression.

It is my hope and belief that if our purpose be proclaimed . . . that very fact will serve to halt any contemplated aggression. We shall have heartened the patriots who are dedicated to the independence of their nations. They will not feel that they stand alone, under the menace of great power. And I should add that patriotism is, throughout this area, a powerful sentiment. It is true that fear sometimes perverts true patriotism into fanaticism and to the acceptance of dangerous enticements from without. But if that fear can be allayed, then the climate will be more favorable to the attainment of worthy national ambitions. . . .

In the situation now existing, the greatest risk, as is often the case, is that ambitious despots may miscalculate. If power-hungry Communists should either falsely or correctly estimate that the Middle East is inadequately defended, they might be tempted to use open measures of armed attack. If so, that would start a chain of circumstances which would almost surely involve the United States in military action. I am convinced that the best insurance against this dangerous contingency is to make clear now our readiness to cooperate fully and freely with our friends of the Middle East in ways consonant with the purposes and principles of the United Nations. I intend promptly to send a special mission to the Middle East to explain the cooperation we are prepared to give.

6.7 **Sputnik and the Space Race,** *Newsweek*, **October 14, 1957**

America received something of a technological wake-up call in the first week in October 1957 when the Soviet Union announced the successful launch of a satellite into space. The event quickly came to represent an American failure, a major defeat that had to be overturned or the U.S. could lose the cold war. To make matters worse, an Atlas rocket had, just a week before, exploded gloriously just off Cape Canaveral in Florida. Russia, it seemed, had moved ahead of the U.S. in missile development; now they had ICBM capability—the capability of hitting the U.S. with missiles carrying nuclear weapons. It was a frightening thought. It was also apparent that the Soviets might win over nations straddling the fence between the cold war superpowers and tip the balance of power away from the U.S. America, it seemed, had lost both its technological advantage and its confidence. Clare Boothe Luce called it "an intercontinental outer-space raspberry to a decade of American pretensions that the American way of life was a gilt-edged guarantee of our material superiority."

The satellite was officially known as *Iskustvennyi Sputnik Zemil,* which means "Artificial Fellow Traveler Around the Earth." Quickly, the American press picked up Sputnik and the word jumped into the American vernacular. *Newsweek's* analysis of the Sputnik launch is *Document 6.7.*

At the same moment that the Sputnik launch hit the press, events at Central High School in Little Rock, Arkansas began to unfold. In response to the Supreme Court's *Brown v. the Board of Education* decision of 1954, Little Rock attempted to desegregate its school system. The result was violence, one of the first such events ever televised. Many Americans had begun to see the relationship between racism in the U.S. and the cold war, that much of the Third World (as the non-aligned nations were being called) had dark skin and saw American racism as an affront, and that the Soviets had used American racism in their own propaganda. In America's efforts to convince the Third World that the future lies with the U.S. and its allies, the first week in October was a significant setback.

....

DOCUMENT 6.7

SPUTNIK AND THE SPACE RACE, *NEWSWEEK*, OCTOBER 14, 1957

In the endless story of mankind's struggle to conquer the elements, the first week of October, in the year 1957, would be a milestone. In that week, future historians would note, the launching of an artificial satellite into the outer fringes of the earth's atmosphere marked man's first practical step toward the conquest of outer space. Now the once-wild dream of contact with the moon, or even with other planets, had assumed at least the outlines of reality.

For the brotherhood of man, this tremendous scientific achievement should have been an occasion of universal pride and triumph, a time of rejoicing. But the grim, sad fact was

SOURCE: *Newsweek,* October 14, 1957.

something entirely different. Because this achievement had been reached, in a torn world, by the controlled scientists of a despotic state—a state which had already given the word "satellite" the implications of ruthless servitude. Could the crushers of Hungary be trusted with this new kind of satellite, whose implications no man could measure?

So it was that for the free world, for its scientists, politicians, defense strategists, and ordinary citizens, the momentous announcement delivered by Soviet Russia last week had produced a mood—at best—of chagrin; at worst, the news brought simple fear.

For the United States, in particular, the Russian achievement added up to momentary defeat—defeat in three fields: In pure science, in practical know-how, and in psychological cold war. And there was no escaping the specter, however remote, of defeat on a broader scale.

It was tempting, of course, to fall into a more comfortable way of thinking. . . . The satellite represented a scientific triumph, not—in itself—a military threat. Was it not simply a case of the Russians having beaten us fairly at our own game? Shouldn't we be good sports about it?

Such a wishful point of view was put by a rocket scientist at Princeton: "We're like a U.S. Olympic team that's just lost the 440-yard relay to the Russians. We really ought to congratulate them. . . . " Sentiments like these were all well and good—if only the Reds played the same role of jolly good sports.

There was one particularly disquieting aspect: The effect of the Russian victory on America's borderline friends abroad. A thoughtful Los Angeles businessman summed it up: "This tips the balance to the uncommitted countries who want to go home with the winner. And God help us—we get this right on top of Little Rock. . . . "

Whatever is inside the "Red Moon," its 184 pounds is the tipoff to Russian progress. It indicates that the Russian moon was shot aloft not by the intricate and slender research rocket on which the U.S. has put its money (more than $100 million), but one of the big ones—a revamped intercontinental ballistic missile which probably weighed fifteen times as much as the U.S. Vanguard [rocket].

What had the Russians achieved with their inconspicuous Sputnik speeding through the near void?

1. They [have] clearly beaten the U.S. satellite workers in the keen scientific competition to get a data-gathering moon into outer space.
2. They [have] quickly and adroitly impressed hundreds of millions of people of the world with their technological prowess devoted to "peaceful" exploitation of space with all the fantasies of trips to the moon and beyond.
3. Most importantly, they [have] presented dramatic evidence to underscore their claims [of] having . . . rocketry and electronic controls of ICBM caliber. . . . Russian propagandists did not need to spell out the fact that a couple of dozen such rockets, equipped with dirty H-bombs instead of radio transmitters and batteries, could with very few technical changes be made to spew their lethal fallout over most of the U.S. or Europe. . . .

Today, first prize in the big rocket race is held firmly by the Russians. To the man in the street, the U.S. big missile picture seems to show mainly rockets in flames, rockets falling in smoke, rockets sitting helplessly on launching pads. The Russians, although they undoubtedly have had unannounced failures, have made known a series of dazzling successes culminating in Sputnik. . . .

The Pentagon feels there is still time to break the U.S. logjam and catch up. While the U.S. ICBM has yet to fly, there are no doubts in the military that both the Atlas and the Titan will be successful, or that Thor, Jupiter, and Polaris, the intermediate range ballistic missile (1,500 miles), will similarly succeed. Moreover, in the face of the Red triumph, there is complete outward confidence that in battlefield rockets, air defense missiles, air-to-air missiles, and air-to-ground missiles, we are up to par.

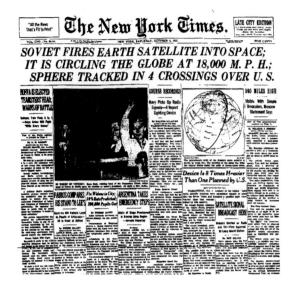

Sputnik I on its support stand before launching. The first news of *Sputnik* was not carried in Soviet newspapers until two days after the launch. *Sovfoto*

In fact, our whole approach to satellites has been somewhat different from Russia's. No U.S. scientist would say so openly—first, because they are full of open admiration for the Soviet scientists. But they keep stressing the fact [that] we are planning highly instrumental satellites, quite in contrast to the relatively simple, radio-signal-transmitting ball now rotating around the earth.

Nonetheless, whatever the confidence in Washington, it is inescapable that the Soviet satellite has been a stunning shock to the nation and is likely to bring heavy pressure on our military planners. The knowledge that a Soviet-made sphere is whirling over America many times a day will evoke a torrent of questions and there will have to be some solid answers.

Officials will parry as best they can, but behind the scenes they are surely going to work with greater dedication and speed to get the Atlas off on a good flight quickly. Economic and other restrictions on the missile programs will be lifted. Missilemen will now probably get what they want, even if their requests seem wasteful, or even if other parts of the defense program suffer.

The central fact that must be faced up to is this: As a scientific and engineering power, the Soviet Union has shown its mastery. The U.S. may have more cars and washing machines and toasters, but in terms of the stuff with which wars are won and ideologies imposed, the nation must now begin to view Russia as a power with a proven, frightening potential.

This is something our top scientists have known for some time, something the leaders of research and development have preached constantly within the military. They have urgently deplored the scarcity of youngsters going into science; they cry for the kind of economic sacrifice that it takes to win an epic struggle in space.

But the Administration and Congress have been confronted with persistent demands for economy. Both will listen to the missilemen now. The harsh fact is that whatever we're doing is not enough.

6.8 Speech by Fidel Castro at the UN General Assembly, September 26, 1960
6.9 U.S. Response to Castro's Speech, October 14, 1960

In 1959 a revolution in Cuba, and several events that followed, appeared to threaten U.S. security. In January 1960, Fidel Castro swept the dictatorial Fulgencio Batista out of power and established a government that, at first, appeared to be friendly to the U.S. But as Castro initiated a fairly strident policy that included land reform, confiscations of private property, and nationalization of industry he continually ran afoul of the Eisenhower administration. In May, Washington ended all economic aid to Cuba, and in July the president (on recommendation from Congress) ended the import of Cuban sugar. By mid-1960, Castro was being branded a communist by the U.S. government and in the American press. In response the United States became the object of Castro's increasingly virulent diatribes. Eventually Castro signed a trade agreement with Moscow.

In September 1960 Castro, accompanied by a large delegation, visited New York for the purpose of complaining of U.S. actions to the United Nations. On September 26, Castro spoke before the General Assembly for some four and one half hours, still a UN record but little more than a brief statement by Castro's long-winded standards. He explained his economic reforms in post-revolutionary Cuba, and chastised the United States for trying to subvert the will of an independent nation. His speech was interrupted many times by applause, and even cheering. Heavily edited here, it is *Document 6.8.*

Castro also took his complaints of U.S. encroachments to the UN National Security Council. Soviet Premier Nikita Khrushchev, infuriated by Castro's reports of U.S. attempts to undermine the Cuban government, warned the U.S. that "Soviet artillerymen can support Cuba with rocket fire" if the U.S. tried to invade. It was the first public pronouncement that the Soviet Union would defend Cuba.

The Cubans did not have a pleasant stay in New York. Their movements were restricted to Manhattan Island only, and they were constantly kept under surveillance. When a member of the Cuban delegation apparently chose to clean a chicken in his hotel room in Lower Manhattan the Cubans were evicted, finally taking refuge in what Castro called a "modest" hotel in Harlem—where he met with Nation Islam leader Malcolm X. Finally, Castro's airplane was confiscated by federal agents at LaGuardia Airport for nonpayment of debt. He flew back to Havana on a plane provided by the Soviets.

Because of Castro's harsh accusations toward the United States, the Eisenhower administration felt it needed to respond. *Document 6.9* is the U.S. response to Castro's speech, delivered on October 14 (less than a month before the election) to UN Secretary General Dag Hammerskjold. Then on January 3, 1961, just days before John Kennedy's inauguration, the Eisenhower administration broke diplomatic relations with the Castro regime. A CIA-initiated plan for an invasion of Cuba had already been in the works for some time.

DOCUMENT 6.8

SPEECH BY FIDEL CASTRO AT THE UN GENERAL ASSEMBLY, SEPTEMBER 26, 1960

Mr. President,
Fellow Delegates

Although it has been said of us that we speak at great length, you may rest assured that we shall endeavor to be brief and to put before you what we consider it our duty to say. We shall also speak slowly in order to co-operate with the interpreters.

Some people may think that we are very annoyed and upset by the treatment the Cuban delegation has received. This is not the case. We understand full well the reasons behind it. That is why we are not irritated. Nor should anybody worry that Cuba will not continue to the effort of achieving a worldwide understanding. That being so, we shall speak openly. . . .

Now, to the problem of Cuba. Perhaps some of you are well aware of the facts, perhaps others are not. It all depends on the sources of information, but, undoubtedly, the problem of Cuba, born within the last two years, is a new problem for the world. The world had not had many reasons to know that Cuba existed. For many, Cuba was something of an appendix of the United States. Even for many citizens of this country, Cuba was a colony of the United States. As far as the map is concerned, this was not the case: our country had a different color from that of the United States. But in reality Cuba was a colony of the United States.

How did our country become a colony of the United States? It was not because of its origins; the same men did not colonize the United States and Cuba. Cuba has a very different ethnic and cultural origin, and the difference has widened over the centuries. Cuba was the last country in America to free itself from Spanish

colonial rule, to cast off, with due respect to the representative of Spain, the Spanish colonial yoke; and because it was the last, it also had to fight more fiercely. . . .

The Cubans who fought for our independence, and at that very moment were giving their blood and their lives, believed in good faith in the joint resolution of the Congress of the United States of April 20, 1898, which declared that "Cuba is, and by right ought to be, free and independent." The people of the United States were sympathetic to the Cuban struggle for liberty. That joint declaration was a law adopted by the Congress of the United States through which war was declared on Spain. But that illusion was followed by a rude awakening. After two years of military occupation of our country, the unexpected happened: at the very moment that the people of Cuba, through their Constituent Assembly, were drafting the Constitution of the Republic, a new law was passed by the United States Congress, a law proposed by Senator Platt, bearing such unhappy memories for the Cubans. That law stated that the constitution of Cuba must have an appendix under which the United States would be granted the right to intervene in Cuba's political affairs and, furthermore, to lease certain parts of Cuba for naval bases or coal supply stations.

In other words, under a law passed by the legislative body of a foreign country, Cuban's Constitution had to contain an appendix with those provisions. Our legislators were clearly told that if they did not accept the amendment, the occupation forces would not be withdrawn. In other words, an agreement to grant another country the right to intervene and to lease naval bases was imposed by force upon my country by the legislative body of a foreign country. . . .

Then began the new colonization of our country, the acquisition of the best agricultural lands by United States firms, concessions of Cuban natural resources and mines, concessions of public utilities for exploitation purposes, commercial concessions of all types.

SOURCE: Document No. 4. Issued by the Embassy of Cuba, Colombo.

These concessions, when linked with the constitutional right—constitutional by force—of intervention in our country, turned it from a Spanish colony into an American colony.

Colonies do not speak. Colonies are not known until they have the opportunity to express themselves. That is why our colony and its problems were unknown to the rest of the world. In geography books reference was made to a flag and a coat of arms. There was an island with another color on the maps, but it was not an independent republic. Let us not deceive ourselves, since by doing so we only make ourselves ridiculous. Let no one be mistaken. There was no independent republic; there was only a colony where orders were given by the Ambassador of the United States. . . . Once again the Cuban people had to resort to fighting in order to achieve independence, and that independence was finally attained after seven bloody years of tyranny. Who forced this tyranny upon us? Those who in our country were nothing more than tools of the interests which dominated our country economically.

How can an unpopular regime, inimical to the interests of the people, stay in power unless it is by force? Will we have to explain to the representatives of our sister republics of Latin America what military tyrannies are? Will we have to outline to them how these tyrannies have kept themselves in power? Will we have to explain the history of several of those tyrannies which are already classical? Will we have to say what forces, what national and international interests support them?

The military group which tyrannized our country was supported by the most reactionary elements of the nation, and, above all, by the foreign interests that dominated the economy of our country. Everybody knows, and we understand that even the Government of the United States admits it, that that was the type of government favored by the monopolies. Why? Because by the use of force it was possible to check the demands of the people; by the use of force it was possible to suppress strikes

for improvement of living standards; by the use of force it was possible to crush all movements on the part of the peasants to own the land they worked; by the use of force it was possible to curb the greatest and most deeply felt aspirations of the nation.

That is why governments of force were favored by the ruling circles of the United States. That is why governments of force stayed in power for so long, and why there are governments of force still in power in America. Naturally, it all depends on whether it is possible to secure the support of the United States.

For instance, now they say they oppose one of these governments of force; the [Dominican Republic] Government of Trujillo. But they do not say they are against other governments of force—that of Nicaragua, or Paraguay, for example. The Nicaraguan one is no longer a government of force; it is a monarchy that is almost as constitutional as that of the United Kingdom, where the reins of power are handed down from father to son. The same would have occurred in my own country. It was the type of government of force—that of Fulgencio Batista—which suited the American monopolies in Cuba, but it was not, of course, the type of government which suited the Cuban people, and the Cuban people, at a great cost in lives and sacrifices, over threw the government.

What did the Revolution find when it came to power in Cuba? What marvels did the Revolution find when it came to power in Cuba? First of all the Revolution found that 600,000 able Cubans were unemployed—as many, proportionately, as were unemployed in the United States at the time of the great depression which shook this country and which almost created a catastrophe in the United States. That was our permanent unemployment. Three million out of a population of somewhat over 6,000,000 did not have electric lights and did not enjoy the advantages and comforts of electricity. Three and a half million out of a total of slightly more than 6,000,000 lived in huts, shacks and slums, without the slightest sanitary facilities. In the cities, rents took almost one third of family incomes. Electricity rates and rents were among the highest in the world.

Thirty-seven and one half percent of our population were illiterate; 70 per cent of the rural children had no teachers; 2 per cent of the population, that is, 100,000 persons out of a total of more than 6,000,000 suffered from tuberculosis. Ninety-five per cent of the children in rural areas were affected by parasites, and the infant mortality rate was therefore very high, just the opposite of the average life span.

On the other hand, 85 per cent of the small farmers were paying rents for the use of land to the tune of almost 30 per cent of their income, while one and one-half percent of the landowners controlled 46 per cent of the total area of the nation. Of course, the proportion of hospital beds to the number of inhabitants of the country was ridiculous, when compared with countries that only have halfway decent medical services.

Public utilities, electricity and telephone services all belonged to the United States monopolies. A major portion of the banking business, of the importing business and the oil refineries, the greater part of the sugar production, the best land in Cuba, and the most important industries in all fields belonged to American companies. The balance of payments in the last ten years, from 1950 to 1960, had been favorable to the United States with regard to Cuba to the extent of one thousand million dollars.

This is without taking into account the hundreds of millions of dollars that were extracted from the treasury of the country by the corrupt officials of the tyranny and were later deposited in United States or European Banks.

One thousand million dollars in ten years. This poor and underdeveloped Caribbean country, with 600,000 unemployed, was contributing greatly to the economic development of the most highly industrialized country in the world.

That was the situation we found, and it is probably not foreign to many of the countries represented in this Assembly, because, when all is said and done, what we have said about Cuba is like a diagnostic x-ray applicable to many of the countries represented here.

What alternative was there for the Revolutionary Government? To betray the people? Of course, as far as the President of the United States is concerned, we have betrayed our people, but it would certainly not have been considered so, if, instead of the Revolutionary Government being true to its people, it had been loyal to the big American monopolies that exploited the economy of our country. At least, let note be taken here of the wonders the Revolution found when it came to power. They were no more and no less than the usual wonders of imperialism, which are in themselves the wonders of the free world as far as we, the colonies, are concerned.

We surely cannot be blamed if there were 600,000 unemployed in Cuba and 37.5 per cent of the population were illiterate. We surely cannot be held responsible if 2 per cent of the population suffered from tuberculosis and 95 per cent were affected by parasites. Until that moment none of us had anything to do with the destiny of our country; until that moment, those who had something to do with the destiny of our country were the rulers who served the interests of the monopolies; until that moment, monopolies had been in control of our country. Did anyone hinder them? No one. Did anyone trouble them? No one. They were able to do their work, and there we found the result of their work. . . .

What has the Revolutionary Government done? What crime has the revolutionary Government committed to deserve the treatment we have received here, and the powerful enemies that events have shown us we have? . . .

And so the Revolutionary Government began to take the first steps. The first thing it did was to lower the rents paid by families by fifty per cent, a just measure, since, as I said earlier, there were families paying up to one third of their income. . . . Then another law was passed, a law canceling the concessions which had been granted by the tyranny of Batista to the Telephone Company, an American monopoly. Taking advantage of the fact our people were defenseless, they had obtained valuable concessions. The Revolutionary Government then cancelled these concessions and re-established normal prices for telephone services. Thus began the first conflict with the American monopolies.

The third measure was the reduction of electricity rates, which were the highest in the world. Then followed the second conflict with the American monopolies. We were beginning to appear communist; they were beginning to daub us in red because we had clashed head on with the interests of the United States monopolies.

Then followed the next law, an essential and inevitable law for our country, and a law which sooner or later will have to be adopted by all countries of the world, at least by those which have not yet adopted it: the Agrarian Reform Law. Of course, in theory everybody agrees with the Agrarian Reform Law. Nobody will deny the need for it unless he is a fool. No one can deny that agrarian reform is one of the essential conditions for the economic development of the country. In Cuba, even the big landowners agreed about the agrarian reform—only they wanted their own kind of reform, such as the one defended by many theoreticians; a reform which would not harm their interests, and above all, one which would not be put into effect as long as it could be avoided. This is something that is well known to the economic bodies of the United Nations, something nobody even cares to discuss any more. In my country it was absolutely necessary: more than 200,000 peasant families lived in the countryside without land on which to grow essential food crops.

Without an agrarian reform, our country would have been unable to take that step; we made an agrarian reform. Was it a radical agrarian reform? We think not. It was a reform adjusted to the needs of our development, and in keeping with our own possibilities of agricultural development. In other words, it was an agrarian reform which was to solve the problems of the landless peasants, the problem of supplying basic foodstuffs, the problem of rural unemployment, and which was to end, once and for all, the ghastly poverty which existed in the countryside of our native land.

And that is where the first major difficulty arose. In the neighboring Republic of Guatemala a similar case had occurred. And I honestly warn my colleagues of Latin America, Africa and Asia; whenever you set out to make a just agrarian reform, you must be ready to face a similar situation, especially if the best and largest tracts of land are owned by American monopolies, as was the case in Cuba. . . .

Then the problem of payment arose. Notes from the State Department rained on our Government. They never asked about our problems, not even out of sheer pity, or because of the great responsibility they had in creating such problems. They never asked us how many died of starvation in our country, or how many were suffering from tuberculosis, or how many were unemployed. No, they never asked about that. A sympathetic attitude towards our needs? Certainly not. All talks by the representatives of the Government of the United States centered upon the Telephone Company, the Electric Company, and the land owned by American Companies.

How could we solve the problem of payment? Of course, the first question that should have been asked was what we were going to pay with, rather than how. Can you gentlemen conceive of a poor underdeveloped country, with 600,000 unemployed and such a large number of illiterates and sick people, a country whose reserves have been exhausted, and which has contributed to the economy of a powerful country with one thousand million dollars in ten years—can you conceive of this country having the means to pay for the land affected by the Agrarian Reform Law, or the means to pay for it in the terms demanded?

What were the State Department aspirations regarding their affected interests? They wanted prompt, efficient and just payment. Do you understand that language? "Prompt, efficient, and just payment." That means, "pay now, in dollars, and whatever we ask for our land."

We were not 100 percent communist yet. We were just becoming slightly pink. We did not confiscate land; we simply proposed to pay for it in twenty years, and in the only way in which we could pay for it: in bonds, which would mature in twenty years at four and one-half per cent, or amortized yearly.

How could we pay for the land in dollars, and the amount they asked for it? It was absurd. Anyone can readily understand that, under those circumstances, we had to choose between making the agrarian reform, and not making it. If we choose not to make it, the dreadful economic situation of our country would last indefinitely. If we decided to make it, we exposed ourselves to the hatred of the Government of the powerful neighbor of the north.

We decided to go on with the agrarian reform. . . . But the truth is that in our country it was not only the land that was the property of the agrarian monopolies. The largest and most important mines were also owned by those monopolies. Cuba produces, for example, a great deal of nickel. All of the nickel was exploited by American interests . . . And so the Revolutionary Government passed a mining law which forced those monopolies to pay a 25 percent tax on the exportation of minerals. The attitude of the Revolutionary Government already had been too bold. It had clashed with the interests of the international electric trusts; it had clashed with the interests of the international telephone trusts; it had clashed with the interests of the mining trusts; it had clashed with the interests of the United Fruit Co; and it had in effect, clashed with the most powerful interests of the United States, which, as you know, are very closely linked with each other. And that was more than the Government of the United States—or rather, the representatives of the United States monopolies—could possibly tolerate. . . .

The attitude of the Cuban Revolution therefore had to be punished. Punitive actions of all sorts—even the destruction of those insolent people—had to follow the audacity of the Revolutionary Government.

On our honor, we swear that up to that moment we had not had the opportunity even to exchange letters with the distinguished Prime Minister of the Soviet Union, Nikita Khrushchev. That is to say that when, for the North American press and the international news agencies that supply information to the world, Cuba was already a Communist Government, a red peril ninety miles from the United States with a Government dominated by Communists, the Revolutionary Government had not even had the opportunity of establishing diplomatic and commercial relations with the Soviet Union. . . .

We wanted to sell our products and went in search of new markets. We signed a trade treaty with the Soviet Union, according to which we would sell one million tons of sugar and would purchase a certain amount of Soviet products or articles. Surely no one can say that this is an incorrect procedure. There may be some who would not do such a thing because it might displease certain interests. We really did not have to ask permission from the State Department in order to sign a trade treaty with the Soviet Union, because we considered ourselves, and we continue to consider ourselves and we will always consider ourselves, a truly independent and free country.

When the amount of sugar in stock began to diminish stimulating our economy, we received the hard blow: at the request of the executive power of the United States, Congress passed a law empowering the President or Executive power to reduce the import quotas for Cuban sugar to whatever limits might deem appropriate. The economic weapon was wielded against our Revolution. The justification for that attitude had already been prepared by publicity experts; the campaign had been on for a long time. You know perfectly well that in this country monopolies and publicity are one and the same thing. The economic weapon was wielded, our sugar quota was suddenly cut by about one million tons—sugar that had already been produced and prepared for the American market—in order to deprive our country of resources for its development, and thus reduce it to a state of impotence, with the natural political consequences. Such measures were expressly banned by Regional International Law.

Economic aggression, as all Latin American delegates here know, is expressly condemned by Regional International Law. However, the Government of the United States violated that law, wielded its economic weapon, and cut our sugar quota by about one million tons. They could do it. . . .

* * *

[T]he Government of the United States considers it has the right to promote and encourage subversion in our country. The Government of the United States is promoting the organization of subversive movements against the Revolutionary Government of Cuba, and we wish to denounce this fact in this General Assembly; we also wish to denounce specifically the fact that, for instance, a territory which belongs to Honduras, known as Islas Cisnes, the Swan Islands, has been seized [militarily] by the Government of the United States and that American marines are there, despite the fact that this territory belongs to Honduras. Thus, violating international law and despoiling a friendly people. [Also] the United States has established a powerful radio station on one of those Islands, in violation of international radio agreements, and has placed it at the disposal of the war criminals and subversive groups supported in this country; furthermore, military training is being conducted on that island, in order to promote subversion and the landing of armed forces in our country. . . .

I have here some declarations by Mr. Kennedy [then senator and presidential candidate] that would surprise anybody. On Cuba he says, "We must use all the power of the Organization of American States to prevent Castro from interfering in other Latin American countries, and we must use all that power to return freedom to Cuba." They are going to give freedom back to Cuba. "We must state our intention," he says, "of not allowing the Soviet Union to turn Cuba

into its Caribbean base . . . And we must make the Cuban people know that we sympathize with their legitimate economic aspirations. . . . " Why did they not feel sympathetic before? "That we know their love of freedom, and that we shall never be happy until democracy is restored in Cuba. . . . " What democracy? The democracy "made" by the imperialist monopolies of the Government of the United States?

"The forces in exile that are struggling for freedom," he says—note this very carefully so that you will understand why there are planes flying from American territory over Cuba. Pay close attention to what this gentleman has to say. "The forces that struggle for liberty in exile and in the mountains of Cuba should be supported and assisted, and in other countries of Latin America communism must be confined and not allowed to expand. . . . "

The problems which we have been describing in relation to Cuba can be applied just as well to all of Latin America. The control of Latin American economic resources by the monopolies, which, when they do not own the mines directly and are in charge of extraction, as the case with the copper of Chile, Peru, or Mexico, and with the oil of Venezuela—when this control is not exercised directly it is because they are the owners of the public utility companies, as is the case in Argentina, Brazil, Chile, Peru, Ecuador and Colombia, or the owners of telephone services, which is the case in Chile, Brazil, Peru, Venezuela, Paraguay and Bolivia, or they commercialize our products, as is the case with coffee in Brazil, Colombia, El Salvador, Costa Rica, and Guatemala, or with the cultivation, marketing and transportations of bananas by the United Fruit Co. in Guatemala, Costa Rica, and Honduras, or with the Cotton in Mexico and Brazil. In other words, the monopolies control the most important industries. Woe to those countries, the day they try to make an agrarian reform! They will be asked for immediate, efficient, and just payment. And if, in spite of everything they make an agrarian reform, the representative of the friendly country who comes to the United Nations will be confined to Manhattan; they will not rent hotel space to him; insult will be heaped upon him, and it is even possible that he may be physically mistreated by the police. . . .

The National General Assembly of the Cuban People proclaims before America, and proclaims here before the world, the right of the peasants to the land; the right of the workers to the fruits of their labor; the right of the children to education; the right of the sick to medical care and hospitalization; the right of young people to work; the right of students to free vocational training and scientific education; the right of Negroes, and Indians to full human dignity; the right of women to civil, social and political equality; the right of the elderly to security in their old age; the right of intellectuals, artists and scientists to fight through their works for a better world; the right of States to nationalize imperialist monopolies, thus rescuing their national wealth and resources; the right of nations to their full sovereignty; the right of peoples to convert their military fortresses into schools, and to arm their workers—because in this we too have to be arms-conscious, to arm our people in defense against imperialist attacks—their peasants, their students, their intellectuals, Negroes, Indians, women, young people, old people, all the oppressed and exploited, so that they themselves can defend their rights and their destinies.

Some people wanted to know what the policy of the Revolutionary Government of Cuba was. Very well, then, this is our policy.

DOCUMENT 6.9

U.S. RESPONSE TO CASTRO'S SPEECH, OCTOBER 14, 1960

On September 26, 1960, the Prime Minister of Cuba, Mr. Fidel Castro, addressed the General Assembly at considerable length

SOURCE: *New York Times*, October 15, 1960.

on the relations between the present Cuban regime and the United States. His speech contained many unfounded accusations, half-truths, malicious innuendos and distortions of history—all aimed against the historic friendship between Cuba and the United States, a friendship which he seems anxious to destroy.

The most important charges against the United States which Prime Minister Castro made in this address had already been considered and rejected in two meetings of the Organization of American States, consisting of twenty-one republics of the Western Hemisphere, before he made them in the General Assembly. The Foreign Ministers of the O.A.S. heard and rejected them at their meeting in San Jose, Costa Rica, in August. The delegates to the O.A.S. economic conference in Bogotá, Colombia, in September heard essentially the same charges from the representative of Cuba, and again rejected them. Now, in view of the repetition of these and other charges before the General Assembly, and out of respect for the opinions of the entire membership of the United Nations, the United States feels compelled once again to set the record straight. . . .

Prime Minister Castro has accused the United States of holding back Cuban development as a free nation. The facts are to the contrary. Cuba has not only consistently received higher prices from the United States for sugar than any other supplier but has also been a partner with the United States in a mutually preferential tariff with special low import duty rates. In per capita gross national product Cuba ranks third in Latin America. It is quite true that in the Republic of Cuba these developments were not matched, as the United States hoped they would be, by corresponding progress in eliminating corruption in public life, and achieving greater social justice and a more equitable distribution of the national income, in guaranteeing free elections, and insuring government of, by, and for the people—progress which only the Cuban people could make for themselves.

When Prime Minister Castro came to power in January, 1959, with promises to his people seemingly made in all sincerity, the United States hoped he would perfect their evolution by needed internal reforms. The United States tried to show its understanding and sympathy for his stated aims: honest and efficient government, the perfection of democratic processes, the economic development leading to higher living standards and to full employment. On June 11 and October 12, 1959, we expressed officially to the Cuban Government our full support for soundly conceived programs for rural development. We particularly endorsed its stated desire to do something for land reform. Not even the shock of the many executions in the first month following the establishment of the revolutionary government, nor the sharp attacks on the United States Government by high officials, could dampen the friendly feeling with which Prime Minister Castro was greeted when he came to the Untied States in April of 1959. There was a genuine reluctance to believe that Cuba, a country for which the people of the United States have long and special affection, could be embarked on an unfriendly course.

On January 26, 1960, President Eisenhower issued a major restatement of American policy toward Cuba, reaffirming the adherence of the United States Government to a policy of non-intervention in the domestic affairs of other countries, including Cuba, and explicitly recognizing the right of the Cuban Government and people in the exercise of their national sovereignty, "to undertake those social, economic and political reforms which, with due regard to their obligations under international law, they may think desirable," and expressing sympathy for the aspirations of the Cuban people.

Unfortunately, these policies of the United States were not reciprocated. The present Government of Cuba has deliberately and consciously sought to exacerbate relations with the United States. For openly announced political reasons Cuba's imports from the United States have been reduced to less than one-half of the level of two years ago. Property is not expropriated, but confiscated without payment, to serve political rather than social ends.

Growing intervention in Cuban affairs by the Soviet Union and Communist China is welcomed by the Government of Cuba. The present Cuban Government seeks to intervene in internal affairs of other American states and to undermine the inter-American system.

The present Cuban Government claims to speak for the Cuban people but denies them the right to choose their own spokesmen in free elections. It claims to believe in democracy, yet only the Communist party is permitted to function. It speaks of the rights of man, but Cuban jails are crowded with thousands of political prisoners.

It boasts of freedom of expression in Cuba, yet the editors of the great Cuban papers are all in exile, while every expression of opposition to the policies of the Government or to communism is suppressed as counter-revolutionary. It interferes with the free exercise of religion. It affirms the independence of the judiciary, but the right of a fair and impartial trial is denied those who differ with the government in power.

We regret that these things are true, but they are true. The people and Government of the United States, who are friends of the Republic of Cuba, still look to see her again become what her great son Marti declared he would have her be: "A democratic and cultured people zealously aware of her own rights and the rights of other."

6.10   Eisenhower's Farewell Address, January 18, 1961

World War II had brought together the forces of the United States military and the nation's industrial might. The cold war and then the Korean War pushed these two massive entities even closer. Military leaders wanted newer and better weaponry, while private industry was eager to produce the goods in exchange for lucrative government contracts. In the immediate postwar years, President Truman seemed to see this cooperative endeavor as an opportunity for sustained economic growth. But by the late 1950s, President Eisenhower had come to believe that the massive amounts being spent by this combination threatened the health of the nation's economy. This military-industrial complex, he warned, might also facilitate the rise of "misplaced power," or a scientific-technological elite. In his farewell address to the nation, (*Document 6.10*) Ike, not unlike George Washington, wished to leave public office by warning the American people against harmful trends that he believed could weaken the nation in the future. It was, he later said, "the most challenging message I could leave the people of this country."

····································

DOCUMENT 6.10

EISENHOWER'S FAREWELL ADDRESS, JANUARY 18, 1961

My fellow Americans, three days from now, after half a century in the service of our country, I shall lay down the responsibilities of office as, in traditional and solemn ceremony, the authority of the Presidency is vested in my successor.

This evening I come to you with a message of leavetaking and farewell, and to share a few final thoughts with you, my countrymen. . . .

We now stand ten years past the midpoint of a century that has witnessed four major wars among great nations. Three of these involved our country. Despite these holocausts, America is today the strongest, the most influential and most productive nation in the world. Understandably proud of this pre-eminence, we yet realize that America's leadership and prestige

depend, not merely upon our unmatched material progress, riches and military strength, but on how we use our power in the interests of world peace and human betterment.

Throughout America's adventure in free government our basic purposes have been to keep the peace; to foster progress in human achievement, and to enhance liberty, dignity, and integrity among people and among nations. To strive for less would be unworthy of a free and religious people. Any failure traceable to arrogance, or our lack of comprehension or readiness to sacrifice would inflict upon us grievous hurt both at home and abroad.

Progress toward these noble goals is persistently threatened by the conflict now engulfing the world. It commands our whole attention, absorbs our very beings. We face a hostile ideology—global in scope, atheistic in character, ruthless in purpose, and insidious in method. Unhappily, the danger it poses promises to be of indefinite duration. To meet it successfully, there is called for, not so much the emotional and transitory sacrifices of crisis, but

SOURCE: *Public Papers of the Presidents: Dwight D. Eisenhower, 1960–1961*, 1035–40.

rather those which enable us to carry forward steadily, surely, and without complaint the burdens of a prolonged and complex struggle—with liberty the stake. . . .

Crises there will continue to be. In meeting them, whether foreign or domestic, great or small, there is a recurring temptation to feel that some spectacular and costly action could become the miraculous solution to all current difficulties. A huge increase in newer elements of our defense; development of unrealistic programs to cure every ill in agriculture; a dramatic expansion in basic and applied research—these and many other possibilities, each possibly promising in itself, may be suggested as the only way to the road we wish to travel.

But each proposal must be weighed in the light of a broader consideration: The need to maintain balance in and among national programs—balance between the private and the public economy, balance between cost and hoped-for advantage—balance-between the clearly necessary and the comfortably desirable; balance between our essential requirements as a nation and the duties imposed by the Nation upon the individual; balance between actions of the moment and the national welfare of the future. Good judgment seeks balance and progress; lack of it eventually finds imbalance and frustration.

The record of many decades stands as proof that our people and their Government have in the main, understood these truths and have responded to them well, in the face of stress and threat. But threats, new in kind or degree, constantly arise. I mention two only.

A vital element in keeping the peace is our military establishment. Our arms must be mighty, ready for instant actions, so that no potential aggressor may be tempted to risk his own destruction.

Our military organization today bears little relation to that known by any of my predecessors in peacetime, or indeed by the fighting men of World War II or Korea. Until the latest of our world conflicts, the United States had no armaments industry. American makers of plowshares could, with time and as required, make

swords as well. But now we can no longer risk emergency improvision of national defense; we have been compelled to create a permanent armaments industry of vast proportions.

Added to this, three and one half million men and women are directly engaged in the defense establishment. We annually spend on military security more than the net income of all U.S. corporations.

This conjunction of an immense military establishment and a large arms industry is new in the American experience. The total influence—economic, political, even spiritual—is felt in every city, every statehouse, every office of the Federal Government.

We recognize the imperative need for this development. Yet we must not fail to comprehend its grave implications. Our toil, resources, and livelihood are all involved; so is the very structure of our society.

In the councils of government, we must guard against the acquisition of unwarranted influence, whether sought or unsought, by the military-industrial complex. The potential for the disastrous rise of misplaced power exists and will persist.

We must never let the weight of this combination endanger our liberties or democratic processes. We should take nothing for granted. Only an alert and knowledgeable citizenry can compel the proper meshing of the huge industrial and military machinery of defense with our peaceful methods and goals, so that security and liberty may prosper together.

Akin to, and largely responsible for the sweeping changes in our industrial-military posture, has been the technological revolution during recent decades. In this revolution, research has become central; it also becomes more formalized, complex, and costly. A steadily increasing share is conducted for, by, or at the direction of, the Federal Government.

Today, the solitary inventor, tinkering in his shop, has been overshadowed by task forces of scientists in laboratories and testing fields. In the same fashion, the free university, historically the fountainhead of free ideas and scientific discovery, has experienced a revolution in the conduct of research.

Partly because of the huge costs involved, a Government contract becomes virtually a substitute for intellectual curiosity. For every old blackboard there are now hundreds of new electronic computers.

The prospect of domination of the Nation's scholars by Federal employment, project allocations, and the power of money is ever present—and is gravely to be regarded.

Yet, in holding scientific research and discovery in respect, as we should, we must also be alert to the equal and opposite danger that public policy could itself become the captive of a scientific-technological elite.

It is the task of statesmanship to mold, to balance, and to integrate these and other forces, new, and old, within the principles of our democratic system—ever aiming toward the supreme goals of our free society.

Another factor in maintaining balance involves the element of time. As we peer into society's future, we—you and I, and our Government—must avoid the impulse to live only for today, plundering, for our own ease the convenience, the previous resources of tomorrow.

We cannot mortgage the material assets of our grandchildren without risking the loss also of their political and spiritual heritage. We want democracy to survive for all generations to come, to become the insolvent phantom of tomorrow. . . .

Disarmament with mutual honor and confidence is a continuing imperative. Together we must learn how to compose differences, not with arms, but with intellect and decent purpose. Because this need is so sharp and apparent I confess that I lay down my official responsibilities in this field with a definite sense of disappointment. As one who has witnessed the horror and lingering sadness of war—as one who knows that another war could utterly destroy this civilization which has been so slowly and painfully built over thousands of years—I wish I could say tonight that a lasting peace is in sight.

Happily, I can say that war has been avoided. Steady progress toward our ultimate goal has been made. But, so much remains to be done. As a private citizen, I shall never cease to do what little I can to help the world advance along that road.

CHAPTER 7

Kennedy, Johnson, and an American Tragedy, 1961–1968

7.1   Dean Rusk Recalls the Bay of Pigs Incident, April 17, 1961

7.2   E. Howard Hunt Recalls the Bay of Pigs Invasion

7.3   President John Kennedy Addresses the Nation on the Cuban Missile Crisis, October 22, 1962

7.4   President John Kennedy, *Ich bin ein Berliner,* Berlin, West Germany, June 26, 1963

7.5   President Lyndon Johnson's Message to Congress on the Tonkin Gulf Incident, August 5, 1964

7.6   President Lyndon Johnson's Speech, "Peace Without Conquest," at Johns Hopkins University, April 7, 1965

7.7   Senator J. William Fulbright on the Johnson Administration's Foreign Policy in Vietnam, May 1966

7.8   "Beyond Vietnam: A Time to Break Silence." Martin Luther King, Jr. Opposes the War, April 4, 1967

7.9   Vo Nguyen Giap on Neo-colonialism and the American War

7.10   Robert McNamara's Memoir of U.S. Involvement in Vietnam

7.11   Mr. McNamara's Other War: A Vietnam Veteran Responds

1961–1968 Timeline

January 1961	1961	John Kennedy becomes president
April 17, 1961		Bay of Pigs invasion
October 22, 1962	1962	Kennedy's address on the Cuban Missile Crisis
June 26, 1963	1963	Kennedy's *"Ich bin ein Berliner"* speech
November 22, 1963		Kennedy is assassinated. Lyndon Johnson becomes president
April 7, 1964	1964	Johnson, "Peace Without Conquest"
August 5, 1964		Johnson on Tonkin Gulf Incident
February 7, 1965	1965	Johnson orders bombing of North Vietnam
March 8, 1965	1966	First U.S. combat troops arrive at Danang
May 1966		Fulbright on Johnson's Vietnam policy
April 4, 1967	1967	Martin Luther King, Jr., "Beyond Vietnam"
January 31, 1968		Tet Offensive
March 1968	1968	Johnson announces that he will not run in November

7.1 **Dean Rusk Recalls the Bay of Pigs Incident, April 17, 1961**

7.2 **E. Howard Hunt Recalls the Bay of Pigs Invasion**

7.3 **President John Kennedy Addresses the Nation on the Cuban Missile Crisis, October 22, 1962**

The cold war reached its most dangerous phase in the early 1960s. Within a three-year period, President John F. Kennedy and Soviet Premier Nikita Khrushchev squared off over issues and incidents that threatened to drag the world into war. Both men needed victories over the other to maintain their positions as national leaders just at the moment when nuclear power and the capability of new delivery systems had reached a new phase. As the arms race intensified, so did the rhetoric from both sides. It was a dangerous time.

When Kennedy came to office in January 1961 he established a foreign policy that deviated drastically from Eisenhower's "New Look." Ike's foreign policy had relied heavily on the inexpensive strategies of covert actions and the threat of a nuclear response, leaving the United States few options beyond not acting or nuclear annihilation of the enemy. Kennedy wanted more options in dealing with the communists. He accepted the viewpoint by his military advisor, General Maxwell Taylor, who believed that the United States should be capable of fighting several types of wars—even several wars at once. Taylor's strategy became known as "flexible response." It allowed the United States to respond to communist insurrections and wars in several different ways. In his first message to Congress on defense, Kennedy, in March 1961, said that the plan was "to deter all wars, general or limited, nuclear or conventional, large or small—to convince all potential aggressors that any attack would be futile. . . ."

As part of flexible response, Kennedy wanted to put out what he called "brush-fires," small wars that threatened U.S. interests. One such brushfire had been raging in Vietnam since, at least, the end of World War II. Throughout the Kennedy administration, and then into Johnson's five years in office that followed, the situation in Vietnam grew from a brushfire to a raging war that divided the nation and finally brought down the Johnson administration.

It was the situation in Cuba, however, that challenged Kennedy the most during his brief three years in office. There, Castro had come to power just two years before Kennedy was inaugurated. By the time Kennedy entered the White House, Castro had thrown his lot with the Soviets. Just ninety miles off the Florida coast, a Soviet-sponsored Cuba promised to be a major threat to the United States, and to American interests in Latin America.

In the closing months of the Eisenhower administration, the CIA had planned an invasion of Cuba using some 1,400 Cuban refugee guerrillas then training in Guatemala. When Kennedy came to office he was faced with the question of whether or not to carry out that invasion. Despite the considerable ambivalence of those around him, the new president gave the order for the invasion to commence. *Document 7.1* is an account of the invasion by Kennedy's secretary of state, Dean Rusk. This recollection comes from a volume entitled *As I Saw It*, a series of interviews given by Rusk to his son Richard. *As I Saw It* serves as Dean Rusk's memoir. *Document 7.2* is E. Howard Hunt's account. Not unlike the CIA action in Guatemala, it was Hunt's job to carry out the dirty work of the administration's covert military policy.

Cuba continued to be a thorn in the side of the Kennedy administration. On October 14, 1962 a U-2 reconnaissance plane photographed several medium range (1,100 mile-capability) missile sites under construction in Cuba. For the next 13 days the United States and the Soviet Union faced each other in the first nuclear confrontation in history. At no time, before or since, were the two superpowers closer to the buttons of nuclear war.

Kennedy took six days to discuss the situation with an informal group of top advisors, including his brother Robert, National Security Advisor McGeorge Bundy, the president's advisor on military affairs General Maxwell Taylor, Secretary of Defense Robert McNamara, Secretary of State Dean Rusk, CIA Director John McCone, Adlai Stevenson, Theodore Sorensen, and others. This ad hoc group soon took the name "ExCom," or the Executive Committee of the National Security Council.

Kennedy's first instincts were to destroy the missiles. Most of the ExCom members agreed, arguing that an air attack was the most obvious solution. But it quickly became clear that the job of removing the sites could not be done completely through air strikes and that eventually a ground invasion of some sort would be necessary. Weighing that, a significant minority, including Robert Kennedy, Rusk, and McNamara, began pushing for a blockade, or "quarantine," of Cuba as an alternative. The ExCom members were also forced to consider such factors as U.S. prestige abroad, especially in Latin America, if the United States attacked Cuba. Quickly, the consensus shifted from an air strike to a blockade, a belligerent act in itself, but one that would give the Soviets an opportunity to back off rather than respond militarily.

At the same time, Kennedy prepared for war. U.S. missile crews were placed on maximum alert, B-52 bombers were loaded with nuclear weapons and sent aloft, the Atlantic fleet of 180 ships steamed toward the Caribbean, and the largest invasion force ever assembled in the United States began forming in Florida. Meanwhile, Allied commanders were briefed, NATO was placed on full alert, congressional leaders were asked to return to Washington, and plans were made to evacuate Guantanamo naval base in Cuba. The world was at the brink.

On October 22, the president went on television to tell the American people of the situation (*Document 7.3*). The United States and the Soviets remained at the brink of war until October 28 when Kennedy and the Soviet Premier Nikita Khrushchev reached a compromise. The Soviets would remove the missiles if the United States would agree not to invade Cuba. That portion of the compromise was made public. However another part of the compromise, agreed to behind the scenes, was that the United States would remove its long-range missiles from Turkey.

DOCUMENT 7.1

DEAN RUSK RECALLS THE BAY OF PIGS INCIDENT, APRIL 17, 1961

On April 17, 1961, a brigade of some fourteen hundred anti-Castro Cuban exiles, organized, trained, armed, transported, and directed by the Central Intelligence Agency, landed at the Bay of Pigs to overthrow Fidel Castro. CIA advisers assured the brigade that Castro's own men would defect, that the landings would inspire a popular uprising against Castro's regime, and that American forces would back them up in case of trouble.

The exile force made it to the beaches, but the landing was opposed. The men fought bravely while their ammunition lasted, but they were quickly surrounded by tanks and twenty thousand Cuban soldiers. Two of their freighters containing vital ammunition, food, and medical supplies were sunk by Castro's planes, and President Kennedy forbade U.S. forces to go to the brigade's assistance. Castro's troops crushed the brigade in less than three days. The general uprising never took place, and Castro arrested two hundred thousand Cubans in Havana alone. Throughout the island he rounded up anyone suspected of underground connections. The circumstances leading to this fiasco are well known. When Castro first seized power in 1959, he was supported by most Americans, relieved that former Cuban dictator Fulgencio Batista's repressive rule had finally ended. Soon afterward Castro even visited Washington and talked about replacing the Batista regime with a constitutional democracy, based upon free elections. Americans at first wanted to work with Castro. In fact, there is some classic television footage of Castro walking out of then Vice President Nixon's office and Nixon putting his arm around Castro and saying, "We're going to work with this man."

However, the relationship soured, and Castro angered Eisenhower even more by demand-

ing that the U.S. Embassy in Havana reduce its staff to eleven people within forty-eight hours. After asking Kennedy and myself through Christian Herter if we wished to advise him on whether to break relations with Cuba (we chose not to), Eisenhower broke off relations on January 3, seventeen days before the Kennedy inauguration.

During the transition State Department briefers warned me there was something I should learn about Cuba as soon as I took office. On January 22 I found out about the Cuban exile brigade training for an invasion of Cuba. Later I learned Kennedy had received a briefing on the brigade in November, but I doubt he ever endorsed it or opposed it. He and I never discussed it before our January 22 meeting.

In subsequent briefings I discovered that the CIA had begun to train the Cuban exiles in Guatemala in 1960. They planned to launch a conventional assault and establish a foothold close to main population centers. The exile group was described as having a broad political base made up of liberal democrats, not just Batista followers. The CIA also believed that defectors from Castro's armed forces and other anti-Castro Cubans would join the brigade after it landed and trigger a popular uprising to overthrow the Castro regime.

If the brigade did not succeed in the invasion, it would fall back into the hills and conduct guerrilla operations.

CIA planners may have remembered that Castro's own movement started small but eventually overthrew Batista. We had heard of widespread disillusionment in Cuba and had seen a steady stream of refugees fleeing the island. This gave us the impression that many Cubans did not like Castro and would do something about him if the opportunity arose.

Within his own administration, President Kennedy received divided advice. White House aide Arthur Schlesinger, Jr., wrote a stiff letter of opposition, and Undersecretary of State Chester Bowles strongly opposed it as well. . . . Vice President Johnson appeared skeptical about the operation, but he didn't attend many

SOURCE: Dean Rusk as Told to Richard Rusk, *As I Saw It* (New York, 1990), 207–12.

of our meetings on it; he seemed to think the invasion was a harebrained scheme that could not succeed. William Fulbright, chairman of the Senate Foreign Relations Committee, also opposed the invasion and told the president so. But other key congressional leaders were not consulted because we feared leaks. Ironically, more congressional consultation might have helped Kennedy avoid a serious mistake.

President Kennedy nevertheless decided to proceed, primarily on the advice of Allen Dulles and Richard Bissell at the CIA. The Joint Chiefs of Staff also supported the operation, but I am convinced they never looked at the plan as professional soldiers. They figured that since the whole show was a CIA operation, they would just approve it and wash their hands of it. Had the Joint Chiefs been responsible for the operation, my guess is they would have expressed serious reservations; for example, they would have spotted the great gap between the brigade's small size and its large operation.

I myself did not serve President Kennedy very well. Personally I was skeptical about the Bay of Pigs plan from the beginning. Most simply, the operation violated international law. There was no way to make a good legal case for an American-supported landing in Cuba. Also, I felt that an operation of this scale could not be conducted covertly. The landing and our involvement would become publicly known the moment the brigade started for the beach. We didn't grapple with that reality at all. Finally, having never seen actual evidence that Cuba was ripe for another revolution, I doubted that an uprising would spring up in support of this operation. . . . I should have pressed Kennedy to ask the Joint Chiefs a question that was never asked. Kennedy should have told the chiefs, "I may want to invade with American forces. How many men would we need to conduct the operation ourselves?" I am sure that the chiefs would have insisted upon sustained preliminary bombing and at least two divisions going ashore in initial landings, with full backup by the Army, Navy, Marines, and Air Force. In looking at the chief's total bill,

Kennedy also would have noted the extraordinary contrast between what our professional military thought was needed and the puny resources of the Cuban brigade. Having been both a colonel of infantry and chief of war plans in the China-Burma-India theater in World War II, I knew that this thin brigade of Cuban exiles did not stand a snowball's chance in hell of success. I didn't relay this military judgment to President Kennedy because I was no longer in the military. . . .

I am not sure which specific arguments convinced Kennedy finally to authorize the invasion. An overriding concern for him might have been the chance to overthrow Castro's regime. Cuba's move toward communism had been a deep shock to the American people, posing a real threat to the stability of other Latin American countries. Thus, Kennedy may have felt the operation worth the risk, if success meant a non-Communist Cuba and a loyal member of the Organization of American State (OAS). Cuba's focus on Marxist revolution was unsettling the hemisphere.

Yet Kennedy was clearly troubled by the operation, and I am sure that he saw the difficulties. His judgment to proceed was very much razor-edge, a closely balanced decision. It would have been very difficult to disband the brigade, already organized and trained.

In retrospect, if I had mounted a campaign within the administration and pulled together Secretary of Defense Robert McNamara and the Joint Chiefs and others, I might have blocked the invasion. But I found that kind of activity distasteful, in terms of the relative positions of the president and his senior advisers and the advice to which he is entitled. To me, such actions would have been like conspiring against my president. Kennedy knew of my doubts. Yet in replaying and rethinking everything, I wished that I had pushed my reticence aside and organized resistance to the invasion or at least insisted that the Joint Chiefs come clean with an honest, professional, military judgment regarding its probability of success.

And so the invasion went on as planned, and it ran into trouble from the beginning. Early Saturday morning, April 15, Cuban exile pilots flying prop-driven B-26's took off from an airfield in Nicaragua and attacked Castro's air force on the ground in Cuba. The raid damaged only a few planes. Equally ominous, the CIA cover story that the raid was the work of defectors from Castro's own air force fell to pieces when one B-26 made an emergency landing in Key West, alerting the American press. Not only did the raid fail to knock out Castro's air force, but it warned him that further action was imminent.

Early Monday morning, April 17, the exile force of fourteen hundred men reached the beaches at the Bay of Pigs after a difficult landing. The brigade met stiff resistance on the ground, and there was no popular uprising. Castro's few T-35's raised havoc during the first two days, strafing the brigade on the beaches and sinking two supply ships. Sometime during this period, with the invasion suffering from inadequate air support, Richard Bissill and Charles Cabell of the CIA came to my office and asked my permission to launch a second B-26 strike against Cuban airfields. They claimed the second strike had already been authorized. My impression was that this had not been part of the plan, although I wasn't sure because I never had a written copy of the plan. I told them I couldn't authorize that strike. They persisted, and I invited them to call President Kennedy and ask him personally. They elected not to do so but later claimed that had that strike gone ahead, Castro's planes would not have hit the landing ships.

That was nonsense. A handful of obsolete B-26's could not have provided air cover for the landing or destroyed Castro's entire air force, as small as it was. Even if American planes had flown the mission, as some were advocating, a sustained and systematic operation would have been required; we didn't even know where Castro had hidden all his planes.

The Bay of Pigs invasion was an obvious blunder. The news of this disaster and the sub-

sequent loss of life hit Kennedy hard. It also shook his confidence in people for whom he had great regard. It increased his tendency to be skeptical of everything he was told, a healthy attitude for any American president. I was especially concerned over what damage it would do to the administration and Kennedy's relations with Congress and our NATO allies.

Kennedy himself refused to deny his responsibility, as some White House aides suggested he do; some even hinted to the press that Kennedy was only carrying out an operation planned and organized by President Eisenhower. This infuriated Kennedy. We had had a full chance to review the operation and make our own judgment, and he wasn't going to dump the failure on Eisenhower. He immediately held a press conference and took full responsibility. . . . He deeply resented any lack of solidarity in his own administration over this debacle. He remarked that "success has many fathers, but failure is an orphan," and he did not like it when some of his own people abandoned ship.

DOCUMENT 7.2

E. HOWARD HUNT RECALLS THE BAY OF PIGS INVASION

Things were getting desperate [in Cuba]; and then suddenly Batista fled, and Castro was in. So I was yanked back from [where I was stationed in] Montevideo, where I would have been content to spend the rest of my life, and told: "What we're doing is reassembling the . . . Guatemala operational team—to take care of Castro, as we did before [in Guatemala]."

Well, of course, this was a much different situation: a much larger body of land, an entrenched, well-trained, devoted communist group of followers of Castro—and the kind of psychological warfare we were able to run

SOURCE: CNN Interview with Howard Hunt (for the program "Cold War"), 1997.

against Castro was insignificant in the long run. Castro was secure, and he was beloved by millions in Cuba, and it was a different situation than Guatemala. So, instead of our having a problem such as we had in Guatemala, of using less than 200 locals to overthrow a government, we were faced with a Cuban army, a Cuban militia, a loyal population—loyal to Castro, that is. He had his own air force, and really his own navy. None of these things [faced us] in the Guatemala situation.

So . . . it just grew and grew and grew. My role was very similar to what it had been in the Guatemalan project; I was located down here in Miami, in Coconut Grove; I was equipped with a safe house. And by that time, several hundred thousand Cuban exiles had come over here and made their homes here. I was told to go over to Havana undercover, and give a personal assessment of the situation. The main object that I was to consider while I was there was the strength of Castro's popularity on the street: in short, if there is an opposition invasion of Cuba, will the populace take up arms against Castro, or will they stay loyal to him? I stayed three or four days in Havana at that time, got out on the street, talked with a lot of people—taxi drivers, naturally, and men and women who ran these small lunch stands down at the waterfront—and all I could find was a lot of enthusiasm for Fidel Castro.

When I came back, I wrote a top secret report, and I had five recommendations, one of which was the one that's always been [attributed to] me: that during or slightly antecedent to an invasion, Castro would have to be neutralized—and we all know what that meant, although I didn't want to say so in a memorandum with my name on it.

Another [recommendation] was that a landing had to be made at such a point in Cuba, presumably by airborne troops, that would quarter the nation; and that was the Trinidad project: cut the communications east to west, and there would be confusion. None of that took place. Once, when I came back from Coconut Grove and said, "Is anybody going after

Castro? Are you going to get rid of him?" "It's in good hands," was the answer I got, which was a great bureaucratic answer. But the long and the short of it was that no attempt that I ever heard of was made against Castro's life specifically.

President Ydigoras Fuentes of Guatemala was good enough to give our Cuban exiles . . . two training areas in his country, one in the mountains, and then at Roberto Alejos' [plantation] we had an unused airstrip that he gave over to us, which we put into first-class condition for our fighter aircraft and our supply aircraft, and we trained Cuban paratroopers there. And the brigade never numbered more than about 1,500, which was ten times more than Castillo Armas commanded [in Guatemala]. . . .

I was instructed by Eisenhower's Office to tell the exile leadership that I dealt with every day that the United States would cover the landing groups, the landing brigade, and that there would be no hostile air [power]. That was a definite commitment made by the Administration to me, and a commitment that I made to the Cuban exiles. So there was no reason to think that anything was going to fail. . . .

Then, in the midst of all that, there was a [U.S.] national election here in November [1960] and the Administration changed. And things were static for a matter of weeks, and our natives there were getting very restless in their training camps, and I was summoned down on one occasion [as I was told] to "put down a mutiny," which was a rather hysterical appreciation of the situation that just simply meant that these men had been told that they were going to be able to get moving soon, and that hadn't happened.

So it was really after Christmas that year before Kennedy's group gave what turned out to be a limited approval, and Dean Rusk insisted on a change in the original plan: he said that an airborne landing at Trinidad, quartering the country, would be too obviously American and it would result in a "big bang"—and he wanted something with a smaller bang. And so despite all of these difficulties and changes and everything, the brigades set off from Nicaragua and from Guatemalan ports headed for southern Cuba. And we had our own fighter aircraft go in and strafe the Cuban airfield to suppress any hostile air. But as it turned out, they didn't get all of the aircraft; they came back to . . . Honduras and Nicaragua to rearm. And at that point, they were told to stand down. Meanwhile, our ships are heading for the Cuban coast, and by then Castro, of course, was alarmed—the planes having gone in and strafed Havana, for Lord's sake—so he was on a high alert and our ships were unprotected. Finally, we got a semi-okay to arm the aircraft and get them moving. By that time, the Cuban air force, [though it] only had, I think, six aircraft left, could fight for awhile and then land, refuel and take off—just the way the Brits did in World War II. It was their home, [but] we had to fly a thousand miles—so that was very difficult for our pilots, many of which were shot down.

So the reason that the Bay of Pigs failed was that the original promise made by Eisenhower was not kept by the subsequent administration. It allowed hostile air to wipe out the approaching invasion force.

DOCUMENT 7.3

PRESIDENT JOHN KENNEDY ADDRESSES THE NATION ON THE CUBAN MISSILE CRISIS, OCTOBER 22, 1962

This government, as promised, has maintained the closest surveillance of the Soviet military buildup on the island of Cuba. Within the past week, unmistakable evidence has established the fact that a series of offensive missile sites is now in preparation on that imprisoned island. The purpose of these bases can be none other than to provide a nuclear strike capability against the Western Hemisphere. . . .

SOURCE: *Public Papers of the Presidents: John F. Kennedy, 1962*, 806–9.

But this secret, swift, and extraordinary buildup of Communist missiles—in an area well known to have a special and historical relationship to the United States and the nations of the Western Hemisphere, in violation of Soviet assurances, and in defiance of American and hemispheric policy—this sudden, clandestine decision to station strategic weapons for the first time outside of Soviet soil—is a deliberately provocative and unjustified change in the *status quo* which cannot be accepted by this country, if our courage and our commitments are ever to be trusted again by either friend or foe.

The 1930s taught us a clear lesson: aggressive conduct, if allowed to go unchecked and unchallenged, ultimately leads to war. This nation is opposed to war. We are also true to our word. Our unswerving objective, therefore, must be to prevent the use of these missiles against this or any other country, and to secure their withdrawal or elimination from the Western Hemisphere.

Our policy has been one of patience and restraint, as benefits a peaceful and powerful nation, which leads a worldwide alliance. We have been determined not to be diverted from our central concerns by mere irritants and fanatics. But now further action is required—and it is under way; and these actions may only be the beginning. We will not prematurely or unnecessarily risk the costs of worldwide nuclear war in which even the fruits of victory would be ashes in our mouth—but neither will we shrink from that risk at any time it must be faced.

Acting, therefore, in the defense of our own security and of the entire Western Hemisphere, and under the authority entrusted to me by the Constitution as endorsed by the resolution of the Congress, I have directed that the following initial steps be taken immediately:

First: To halt this offensive buildup, a strict quarantine on all offensive military equipment under shipment to Cuba is being initiated. All ships of any kind bound for Cuba from whatever nation or port will, if found to contain cargoes of offensive weapons, be turned back.

LAUNCH POSITION

MISSILE-READY TENTS

MISSILE ERECTORS

Aerial photographs taken by U-2 reconnaissance planes flying over Cuba revealed the presence of Russian missile sites under construction on the island. Recently released information about the type and number of Soviet nuclear warheads in Cuba reveals just how imminent was the threat of nuclear war had not the Soviets capitulated to U.S. demands for removal of the missiles. *Archive Photos/Getty Images*

This quarantine will be extended, if needed, to other types of cargo and carriers. We are not at this time, however, denying the necessities of life as the Soviets attempted to do in their Berlin blockade of 1948.

Second: I have directed the continued and increased close surveillance of Cuba and its military buildup. The foreign ministers of the [Organization of American States], in their communique of October 6, rejected secrecy on such matters in this hemisphere. Should these offensive military preparations continue, thus increasing the threat to the hemisphere, further action will be justified. I have directed the Armed Forces to prepare for any eventualities; and I trust that in the interest of both the Cuban people and the Soviet technicians at the sites, the hazards to all concerned of continuing this threat will be recognized.

Third: It shall be the policy of this Nation to regard any nuclear missile launched from Cuba against any nation in the Western Hemisphere as an attack by the Soviet Union on the United States, requiring a full retaliatory response upon the Soviet Union. . . .

Seventh and finally: I call upon Chairman Khrushchev to halt and eliminate this clandestine, reckless, and provocative threat to world peace and to stable relations between our two nations. I call upon him further to abandon this course of world domination, and to join in an historic effort to end the perilous arms race and to transform the history of man. He has an opportunity now to move the world back from the abyss of destruction—by returning to his government's own words that it had no need to station missiles outside its own territory, and withdrawing these weapons from Cuba—by refraining from any action which will widen or deepen the present crisis—and then by participating in a search for peaceful and permanent solutions. . . .

My fellow citizens: let no one doubt that this is a difficult and dangerous effort on which we have set out. No one can foresee precisely what course it will take or what costs or casualties will be incurred. Many months of sacrifice and self-discipline lie ahead—months in which both our patience and our will will be tested— months in which many threats and denunciations will keep us aware of our dangers. But the greatest danger of all would be to do nothing.

The path we have chosen for the present is full of hazards, as all paths are—but it is the one most consistent with our character and courage as a nation and our commitments around the world. The cost of freedom is always high—but Americans have always paid it. And one path we shall never choose is the path of surrender or submission.

Our goal is not the victory of might, but the vindication of right—not peace at the expense of freedom, but both peace and freedom, here in this hemisphere, and, we hope, around the world. God willing, that goal will be achieved.

7.4 President John Kennedy, *Ich bin ein Berliner*, Berlin, West Germany, June 26, 1963

On June 10, 1963 Kennedy gave the commencement address at American University in Washington. It was analyzed at the time as the beginning of a détente with the Soviets, the dawning of an era of conciliation and cooperation following the nuclear confrontation over the missiles in Cuba. Later in the month, the President traveled to Western Europe to assure the Allies that any détente with the Soviets would not come at their expense—that the U.S. would not abandon Western Europe.

Kennedy arrived in Bonn for a four-day tour of Germany. In Cologne, Frankfurt, and other cities, hundreds of thousands of West Germans came out to see the president, shouting at every stop "Ken-ne-dy! Ken-ne-dy!" On Wednesday June 26 the president arrived in the divided city of Berlin, where he was scheduled to speak before a crowd at the city hall to mark the fifteenth anniversary of the 1948 Berlin Airlift. General Lucius Clay, the American commander in charge of the Airlift, was at his side on the podium.

The crowd before him has been estimated at well over a million. It was, William Manchester wrote, an "enormous, swelling, heaving, delirious multitude. . . ." The conciliatory mode of the American University speech was now gone. He let the West Berliners know that the United States was their ally, and, for the first time in his public career, he condemned the Wall—and the Soviets for building it. This "Ich bin ein Berliner speech," (*Document 7.4*) as it has become known, is not among Kennedy's greatest speeches, but it is one of his most memorable.

As a side note, William Bundy, who coached Kennedy on the German phrase, later recalled that Kennedy had no foreign language skills, and on the podium, after a great deal of drilling, Ich bin ein Berliner became a Boston accented "Ich been ine

Bee-leen-ah." In addition, ein Berliner colloquially can mean a donut. A more grammatically correct statement would have been, Ich bin Berliner.

The speech was delivered at Rudolph Wilde Platz, near the Wall. The plaza was renamed John F. Kennedy Platz in 1964. Robert Kennedy attended the dedication.

....

DOCUMENT 7.4

PRESIDENT JOHN KENNEDY, *ICH BIN EIN BERLINER,* BERLIN, WEST GERMANY, JUNE 26, 1963

I am proud to come to this city as the guest of your distinguished mayor, who has symbolized throughout the world the fighting spirit of West Berlin. And I am proud to visit the Federal Republic with your distinguished chancellor, who for so many years has committed Germany to democracy and freedom and progress, and to come here in the company of my fellow American General Clay, who has been in this city during its great moments of crisis and will come again if ever needed.

Two thousand years ago the proudest boast was *Civis Romanus sum.* Today, in the world of freedom, the proudest boast is *Ich bin ein Berliner.*

I appreciate my interpreter translating my German.

There are many people in the world who really don't understand, or say they don't, what is the great issue between the free world and the Communist world. Let them come to Berlin. There are some who say that communism is the wave of the future. Let them come to Berlin. And there are some who say in Europe and elsewhere we can work with the Communists. Let them come to Berlin. And there are even a few who say that it is true that communism is an evil system, but it permits us

SOURCE: *Public Papers of the Presidents, John F. Kennedy, 1963,* 224–25.

to make economic progress. *Lass sie nach Berlin kommen.* Let them come to Berlin.

Freedom has many difficulties and democracy is not perfect, but we have never had to put a wall up to keep our people in, to prevent them from leaving us. I want to say, on behalf of my countrymen, who live many miles away on the other side of the Atlantic, who are far distant from you, that they take the greatest pride that they have been able to share with you, even from a distance, the story of the last eighteen years. I know of no town, no city, that has been besieged for eighteen years that still lives with the vitality and the force, and the hope and the determination of the city of West Berlin. While the wall is the most obvious and vivid demonstration of the failures of the Communist system, for all the world to see, we take no satisfaction in it, for it is, as your mayor has said, an offense not only against history but an offense against humanity, separating families, dividing husbands and wives and brothers and sisters, and dividing a people who wish to be joined together.

What is true of this city is true of Germany—real, lasting peace in Europe can never be assured as long as one German out of four is denied the elementary right of free men, and that is to make a free choice. In eighteen years of peace and good faith, this generation of Germans has earned the right to be free, including the right to unite their families and their nation in lasting peace, with good will to all people. You live in a defended island of freedom, but your life is part of the main. So let me ask you, as I close, to lift your eyes beyond the dangers of today, to the hopes of tomorrow, beyond the freedom merely of this city of Berlin, or your country of Germany, to the advance of freedom everywhere, beyond the wall to the day of peace with justice, beyond yourselves and ourselves to all mankind.

Freedom is indivisible, and when one man is enslaved, all are not free. When all are free, then we can look forward to that day when this city will be joined as one and this country and this great continent of Europe in a peaceful and hopeful globe. When that day finally comes, as it will, the people of West Berlin can take sober satisfaction in the fact that they were in the front lines for almost two decades.

All free men, wherever they may live, are citizens of Berlin, and, therefore, as a free man, I take pride in the words *Ich bin ein Berliner.*

7.5 President Lyndon Johnson's Message to Congress on the Tonkin Gulf Incident, August 5, 1964

Following World War II the United States initiated a foreign policy designed to contain the Soviet Union, and later China. The result was a number of hot spots that included Korea and Southeast Asia. In the late 1940s and early 1950s the French tried in vain to subdue a communist-inspired independence movement in Vietnam. In 1954 that effort failed. The Geneva Conference in July partitioned Vietnam temporarily at the 17th Parallel, with elections to be held two years later to decide on unification. The United States, however, converted the truce line into a national boundary, refused to allow the 1956 elections, and created a separate independent state in the south

In September 1954 the Eisenhower administration created the Southeast Asia Treaty Organization (SEATO) through the Southeast Asia Collective Defense Treaty. The signatories in the region included Thailand, Pakistan, the Philippines, Australia, and New Zealand. South Vietnam, Cambodia, and Laos were forbidden by the Geneva Accords to enter into such a treaty, however the Eisenhower administration created a protocol that extended the protection of the signatories to those countries in the event of an attack.

By 1963 U.S. involvement in Vietnam had deepened significantly, mostly in response to increasing communist insurgency in the South and a growing weakness inside the South Vietnam government. By the fall of that year, South Vietnamese president Ngo Dinh Diem had become a burden to the Washington leadership. He was notoriously corrupt, unpopular with his own people, and an unreliable ally. On November 1, Diem was murdered in a military coup that was encouraged by the Kennedy administration. Diem's fall, however, did not improve the situation in Vietnam. In fact, problems increased dramatically. A succession of military dictators brought serious instability to the Saigon government, while the growing communist incursion in the south threatened to overwhelm the Army of South Vietnam. Following Kennedy's assassination in November 1963, the new president, Lyndon Johnson, responded to the growing problems in Vietnam by increasing aid to the Saigon government.

As the 1964 election approached, Johnson was faced with a political challenge from Senator Barry Goldwater, an arch-conservative who intended to paint Johnson as soft on communism and unwilling to stand up to the communists in Vietnam. Johnson, in turn, hoped to portray Goldwater as a warmonger who might drag the nation into a world-ending global conflict. The president wanted to show voters that he could be firm when it came to dealing with the communists in Vietnam, but that he had a cool head and would not, impulsively, send the nation's sons to fight and die unnecessarily. Two incidents in the Tonkin Gulf in August 1964 gave Johnson just the situation that allowed him to show both firmness and restraint, just three months before the election.

The first incident occurred on the morning of August 2 when the American destroyer *Maddox* came under fire from North Vietnamese torpedo boats. On the night of August 4 the *Maddox* returned to the area, this time accompanied by the destroyer *Turner Joy.* Both boats claimed to have come under attack that night, but since then conflicting accounts have raised doubts as to whether the second attack occurred. Nevertheless, President Johnson ordered an air strike against North Vietnamese coastal batteries and then asked Congress for broad powers to deal with the situation in Vietnam (*Document 7.5*). The result was the Tonkin Gulf Resolution, passed unanimously in the House and with only two dissenting votes in the Senate. The Tonkin Gulf Resolution was the rationale for the U.S. involvement in Vietnam. In June 1970 Congress repealed the resolution in open revolt against the Nixon administration's execution of the war.

....

DOCUMENT 7.5

PRESIDENT LYNDON JOHNSON'S MESSAGE TO CONGRESS ON THE TONKIN GULF INCIDENT, AUGUST 5, 1964

Last night I announced to the American people that the North Vietnamese regime had conducted further deliberate attacks against U.S. naval vessels operating in international waters, and that I had therefore directed air action against gunboats and supporting facilities used in these hostile operations. This air action has now been carried out with substantial damage to the boats and facilities. Two U.S. aircraft were lost in the action.

After consultation with the leaders in both parties in the Congress, I further announced a decision to ask the Congress for a resolution expressing the unity and determination of the United States in supporting freedom and in protecting peace in Southeast Asia.

SOURCE: *Public Papers of the Presidents: Lyndon B. Johnson, 1963–64* (Washington, 1965), 2: 930–32.

These latest actions of the North Vietnamese regime have given a new and grave turn to the already serious situation in Southeast Asia. Our commitments in that area are well known to the Congress. They were first made in 1954 by President Eisenhower. They were further defined in the Southeast Asia Collective Defense Treaty approved by the Senate in February 1955.

This treaty with its accompanying protocol obligates the United States and other members to act in accordance with their constitutional processes to meet Communist aggression against any of the parties or protocol states.

Our policy in Southeast Asia has been consistent and unchanged since 1954. I summarized it on June 2 in four simple propositions:

1. America keeps her word. Here as elsewhere, we must keep and shall honor our commitments.
2. The issue is the future of Southeast Asia as a whole. A threat to any nation in that region is a threat to all, and a threat to us.
3. Our purpose is peace. We have no military, political, or territorial ambitions in the area.

4. This is not just a jungle war, but a struggle for freedom on every front of human activity. Our military and economic assistance to South Vietnam and Laos in particular has the purpose of helping these countries to repel aggression and strengthen their independence.

The threat to the free nations of Southeast Asia has long been clear. The North Vietnamese regime has constantly sought to take over South Vietnam and Laos. This Communist regime has violated the Geneva accords for Vietnam. It has systematically conducted a campaign of subversion, which includes the direction, training, and supply of personnel and arms for the conduct of guerrilla warfare in South Vietnamese territory. In Laos, the North Vietnamese regime has maintained military forces, used in Laotian territory for infiltration into South Vietnam, and most recently carried out combat operations—all in direct violation of the Geneva agreements of 1962.

In recent months, the actions of the North Vietnamese regime have become steadily more threatening. In May, following new acts of Communist aggression in Laos, the United States undertook reconnaissance flights over Laotian territory, at the request of the Government of Laos. These flights had the essential mission of determining the situation in territory where Communist forces were preventing inspection by the International Control Commission. When the Communists attacked these aircraft, I responded by furnishing escort fighters with instructions to fire when fired upon. Thus, these latest North Vietnamese attacks on our naval vessels are not the first direct attack on armed forces of the United States.

As President of the United States I have concluded that I should now ask the Congress, on its part, to join in affirming the national determination that all such attacks will be met, and that the U.S. will continue in its basic policy of assisting the free nations of the area to defend their freedom.

As I have repeatedly made clear, the United States intends no rashness, and seeks no wider war. We must make it clear to all that the United States is united in its determination to bring about the end of Communist subversion and aggression in the area. We seek the full and effective restoration of the international agreements signed in Geneva in 1954, with respect to South Vietnam, and again in Geneva in 1962, with respect to Laos.

I recommend a Resolution expressing the support of the Congress for all necessary action to protect our armed forces and to assist nations covered by the SEATO Treaty. At the same time, I assure the Congress that we shall continue readily to explore any avenues of political solution that will effectively guarantee the removal of Communist subversion and the preservation of the independence of the nations of the area.

The Resolution could well be based upon similar resolutions enacted by the Congress in the past—to meet the threat to Formosa in 1955, to meet the threat to the Middle East in 1957, and to meet the threat of Cuba in 1962. It could state in the simplest terms the resolve and support of the Congress for action to deal appropriately with attacks against our armed forces and to defend freedom and preserve peace in Southeast Asia in accordance with the obligations to the United States under the Southeast Asia Treaty. I urge the Congress to enact such a Resolution promptly and thus to give convincing evidence to the aggressive Communist nations, and to the world as a whole, that our policy in Southeast Asia will be carried forward—and that the peace and security of the area will be preserved.

The events of this week would in any event have made the passage of a Congressional Resolution essential. But there is an additional reason for doing so at a time when we are entering on three months of political campaigning. Hostile nations must understand that in such a position the United States will continue to protect its national interests, and that in these matters there is no division among us.

7.6 President Lyndon Johnson's Speech, "Peace Without Conquest," at Johns Hopkins University, April 7, 1965

7.7 Senator J. William Fulbright on the Johnson Administration's Foreign Policy in Vietnam, May 1966

With the election over, and with a clear mandate in his hands, President Johnson moved to escalate the war in Vietnam. In March 1965, Marines landed at Da Nang, the first combat troops used in the war. In April at Johns Hopkins University, the president asked the question that most Americans seemed to be asking: Why are we in Vietnam? In his most famous war speech, Johnson laid down the various justifications for a major U.S. presence in Vietnam (*Document 7.6*). His answer evoked the main tenets of America's cold war foreign policy, plus the Wilsonian promise of peace without victory. Johnson's Johns Hopkins speech is, unfortunately, remembered only for the president's reasons for escalation and not for his vision of a peaceful world order, or even his simple concept that weapons are a manifestation of man's failures.

A year later, Senator J. William Fulbright, chairman of the Senate Foreign Relations Committee and critic of the administration's Vietnam policy, spoke at Johns Hopkins in what many saw as an answer to Johnson's speech. Fulbright was a Rhodes Scholar and a former president of the University of Arkansas. He was a close friend of the president, and had agreed to push Johnson's Tonkin Gulf Resolution through the Senate in 1964. But by 1965 he had become alarmed over the war and he finally separated from Johnson over the administration's policies. In his Johns Hopkins speech (*Document 7.7*), Fulbright asks many of the questions that much of the nation would soon be asking of their government and its involvement in Vietnam.

....

DOCUMENT 7.6

PRESIDENT LYNDON JOHNSON'S SPEECH, "PEACE WITHOUT CONQUEST," AT JOHNS HOPKINS UNIVERSITY, APRIL 7, 1965

Tonight Americans and Asians are dying for a world where each people may choose its own path to change.

This is the principle for which our ancestors fought in the valleys of Pennsylvania. It is the

SOURCE: *Public Papers of the Presidents: Lyndon B. Johnson, 1965*, 394–99.

principle for which our sons fight tonight in the jungles of Viet-Nam.

Viet-Nam is far away from this quiet campus. We have no territory there. Nor do we seek any. The war is dirty and brutal and difficult. And some too-young men, born into an American that is bursting with opportunity and promise, have ended their lives on Viet-Nam's steaming soil.

Why must we take this painful road?

Why must this nation hazard its ease, its interests, and its power for the sake of a people so far away? We fight because we must fight if we are to live in a world where every country can shape its own destiny, and only in such a world will our own freedom be finally secure.

This kind of world will never be built by bombs or bullets. Yet the infirmities of man are such that force must often precede reason, and the waste of the war, the works of peace.

We wish that this were not so. But we must deal with the world as it is, if it is ever to be as we wish.

The world as it is in Asia is not a serene or peaceful place.

The first reality is that North Viet-Nam has attacked the independent nation of South Viet-Nam. Its object is total conquest.

Of course, some of the people of South Viet-Nam are participating in attacks on their own government. But trained men and supplies, orders and arms, flow in a constant stream from North to South.

This support is the heartbeat of the war.

And it is a war of unparalleled brutality. Simple farmers are the targets of assassination and kidnapping. Women and children are strangled in the night because their men are loyal to their government. And helpless villages are ravaged by sneak attacks. Large-scale raids are conducted on towns, and terror strikes in the heart of cities.

The confused nature of this conflict cannot mask the fact that it is the new face of an old enemy.

Over this war—and all Asia—is another reality: the deepening shadow of Communist China. The rulers in Hanoi are urged on by Peking. This is a regime which has destroyed freedom in Tibet, which has attacked India and has been condemned by the United Nations for aggression in Korea. It is a nation which is helping the forces of violence in almost every continent. The contest in Viet-Nam is part of a wider pattern of aggressive purposes.

Why are these realities our concern? Why are we in South Viet-Nam?

We are there because we have a promise to keep. Since 1954 every American President has offered support to the people of South Viet-Nam. We have helped to build, and we have helped to defend. Thus, over many years, we have made a national pledge to help South Viet-Nam defend its independence.

And I intend to keep that promise.

To dishonor that pledge, to abandon this small and brave nation to its enemies, and to the terror that must follow, would be an unforgivable wrong.

We are also there to strengthen world order. Around the globe from Berlin to Thailand are people whose well-being rests in part on the belief that they can count on us if they are attacked. To leave Viet-Nam to its fate would shake the confidence of all these people in the value of an American commitment and in the value of America's word. The result would be increased unrest and instability, and even wider war.

We are also there because there are great stakes in the balance. Let no one think for a moment that retreat from Viet-Nam would bring an end to conflict. The battle would be renewed in one country and then another. The central lesson of our time is that the appetite of aggression is never satisfied. To withdraw from one battlefield means only to prepare for the next. We must say in Southeast Asia—as we did in Europe—in the words of the Bible: "Hitherto shalt thou come, but no further."

There are those who say that all our effort there will be futile—that China's power is such that it is bound to dominate all Southeast Asia. But there is no end to that argument until all of the nations of Asia are swallowed up.

There are those who wonder why we have a responsibility there. Well, we have it there for the same reason that we have a responsibility for the defense of Europe. World War II was fought in both Europe and Asia and when it ended we found ourselves with continued responsibility for the defense of freedom.

Our objective is the independence of South Viet-Nam and its freedom from attack. We want nothing for ourselves—only that the people of South Viet-Nam be allowed to guide their own country in their own way.

We will do everything necessary to reach that objective and we will do only what is absolutely necessary.

In recent months attacks on South Viet-Nam were stepped up. Thus, it became necessary for us to increase our response and to make attacks by air. This is not a change of purpose. It is a change in what we believe that purpose requires.

We do this in order to slow down aggression.

We do this to increase the confidence of the brave people of South Viet-Nam who have bravely borne this brutal battle for so many years with so many casualties.

And we do this to convince the leaders of North Viet-Nam—and all who seek to share their conquest—of a simple fact:

We will not be defeated.

We will not grow tired

We will not withdraw, either openly or under the cloak of a meaningless agreement.

We know that air attacks alone will not accomplish all of these purposes. But it is our best and prayful judgment that they are a necessary part of the surest road to peace.

We hope that peace will come swiftly. But that is in the hands of others besides ourselves. And we must be prepared for a long continued conflict. It will require patience as well as bravery—the will to endure as well as the will to resist.

I wish it were possible to convince others with words of what we now find it necessary to say with guns and planes: armed hostility is futile—our resources are equal to any challenge—because we fight for values and we fight for principles, rather than territory or colonies, our patience and our determination are unending. Once this is clear, then it should also be clear that the only path for reasonable men is the path of peaceful settlement.

Such peace demands an independent South Viet-Nam securely guaranteed and able to shape its own relationships to all others, free from outside interference, tied to no alliance, a military base for no other country.

These are the essentials of any final settlement.

We will never be second in the search for such a peaceful settlement in Viet-Nam.

There may be many ways to this kind of peace: in discussion or negotiation with the governments concerned; in large groups or in small ones; in the reaffirmation of old agreements or their strengthening with new ones.

We have stated this position over and over again fifty times and more, to friend and foe alike. And we remain ready with this purpose, for unconditional discussions. And until that bright and necessary day of peace we will try to keep the conflict from spreading. We have no desire to see thousands die in battle, Asians or Americans. We have no desire to devastate that which the people of North Viet-Nam have built with toil and sacrifice. We will use our power with restraint and with all the wisdom we can command. But we will use it.

This war, like most wars, is filled with terrible irony. For what do the people of North Viet-Nam want? They want what their neighbors also desire: food for their hungry; health for their bodies; a chance to learn; progress for their country; and an end to the bondage of material misery. And they would find all these things far more readily in peaceful association with others than in the endless course of battle.

These countries of southeast Asia are homes for millions of impoverished people. Each day these people rise at dawn and struggle through until the night to wrestle existence from the soil. They are often wracked by disease, plagued by hunger, and death comes at the early age of 40.

Stability and peace do not come easily in such a land. Neither independence nor human dignity will ever be won, though, by arms alone. It also requires the work of peace. The American people have helped generously in times past in these works. Now there must be a much more massive effort to improve the life of man in that conflict-torn corner of our world.

The first step is for the countries of southeast Asia to associate themselves in a greatly expanded cooperative effort for development. We would hope that North Viet-Nam would take its place in the common effort just as soon as peaceful cooperation is possible.

The United Nations is already actively engaged in development in this area. As far back as 1961 I conferred with our authorities in Viet-Nam in connection with their work there. And I would hope tonight that the Secretary General of the United Nations could use the prestige of his great office, and his deep knowledge of Asia, to initiate, as soon as possible, with the countries of that area, a plan for cooperation in increased development.

For our part I will ask the Congress to join in a billion dollar American investment in this effort as soon as it is underway.

And I would hope that all other industrialized countries, including the Soviet Union, will join in this effort to replace despair with hope, and terror with progress.

The task is nothing less than to enrich the hopes and the existence of more than a hundred million people. And there is much to be done.

The vast Mekong River can provide food and water and power on a scale to dwarf even our own TVA.

The wonders of modern medicine can be spread through villages where thousands die every year from lack of care.

Schools can be established to train people in the skills that are needed to manage the process of development.

And these objectives, and more, are within the reach of a cooperative and determined effort.

I also intend to expand and speed up a program to make available our farm surpluses to assist in feeding and clothing the needy in Asia. We should not allow people to go hungry and wear rags while our own warehouses overflow with an abundance of wheat and corn, rice and cotton.

So I will very shortly name a special team of outstanding, patriotic, distinguished Americans to inaugurate our participation in these programs. This team will be headed by Mr. Eugene Black, the very able former President of the World Bank.

In areas that are still ripped by conflict, of course development will not be easy. Peace will be necessary for final success. But we cannot and must not wait for peace to begin this job.

This will be a disorderly planet for a long time. In Asia, as elsewhere, the forces of the modern world are shaking old ways and uprooting ancient civilizations. There will be turbulence and struggle and even violence. Great

social change—as we see in our own country now—does not always come without conflict.

We must also expect that nations will on occasion be in dispute with us. It may be because we are rich, or powerful; or because we have made some mistakes; or because they honestly fear our intentions. However, no nation need ever fear that we desire their land, or to impose our will, or to dictate their institutions. But we will always oppose the effort of one nation to conquer another nation. We will do this because our own security is at stake.

But there is more to it than that. For our generation has a dream. It is a very old dream. But we have the power and now we have the opportunity to make that dream come true.

For centuries nations have struggled among each other. But we dream of a world where disputes are settled by law and reason. And we will try to make it so.

For most of history men have hated and killed one another in battle. But we dream of an end to war. And we will try to make it so.

For all existence most men have lived in poverty, threatened by hunger. But we dream of a world where all are fed and charged with hope. And we will help to make it so.

The ordinary men and women of North Viet-Nam and South Viet-Nam—of China and India—of Russia and America—are brave people. They are filled with the same proportions of hate and fear, of love and hope. Most of them want the same things for themselves and their families. Most of them do not want their sons to ever die in battle, or to see their homes, or the homes of others, destroyed.

Well, this can be their world yet. Man now has the knowledge—always before denied—to make this planet serve the real needs of the people who live on it.

I know this will not be easy. I know how difficult it is for reason to guide passion, and love to master hate. The complexities of this world do not bow easily to pure and consistent answers.

But the simple truths are there just the same. We must all try to follow them as best we can.

We often say how impressive power is. But I do not find it impressive at all. The guns and the bombs, the rockets and the warships, are all symbols of human failure. They are necessary symbols. They protect what we cherish. But they are witness to human folly.

A dam built across a great river is impressive.

In the countryside where I was born, and where I live, I have seen the night illuminated, and the kitchens warmed, and the homes heated, where once the cheerless night and the ceaseless cold held sway. And all this happened because electricity came to our area along the humming wires of the REA. Electrification of the countryside—yes, that, too, is impressive.

A rich harvest in a hungry land is impressive.

The sight of healthy children in a classroom is impressive.

These—not mighty arms—are the achievements which the American Nation believes to be impressive.

And, if we are steadfast, the time may come when all other nations will also find it so.

Every night before I turn out the lights to sleep I ask myself this question: Have I done everything that I can do to unite this country? Have I done everything I can to help unite the world, to try to bring peace and hope to all the peoples of the world? Have I done enough?

Ask yourselves that question in your homes—and in this hall tonight. Have we, each of us all done all we could? Have we done enough?

We may well be living in the time foretold many years ago when it was said: "I call heaven and earth to record this day against you, that I have set before you life and death, blessing and cursing: therefore choose life, that both thou and thy seed may live."

This generation of the world must choose: destroy or build, kill or aid, hate or understand.

We can do all these things on a scale never dreamed of before.

Well, we will choose life. In so doing we will prevail over the enemies within man, and over the natural enemies of all mankind.

SENATOR J. WILLIAM FULBRIGHT ON THE JOHNSON ADMINISTRATION'S FOREIGN POLICY IN VIETNAM, MAY 1966

We are an extraordinary nation, endowed with rich and productive land and a talented and energetic population. Surely a nation so favored is capable of extraordinary achievement, not only in the area of producing and enjoying great wealth—where our achievements have indeed been extraordinary—but also in the area of human and international relations—in which area, it seems to me, our achievements have fallen short of our capacity and promise. The question that I find intriguing is whether a nation so extraordinarily endowed as the United States can overcome that arrogance of power which has afflicted, weakened and, in some cases, destroyed great nations in the past.

The causes of the malady are a mystery but its recurrence is one of the uniformities of history: Power tends to confuse itself with virtue and a great nation is particularly susceptible to the idea that its power is a sign of God's favor, conferring upon it a special responsibility for other nations—to make them richer and happier and wiser, to remake them, that is, in its own shining image.

Power also tends to take itself for omnipotence. Once imbued with the idea of a mission, a great nation easily assumes that it has the means as well as the duty to do God's work. The Lord, after all, surely would not choose you as His agent and then deny you the sword with which to work His will.

There is a kind of voodoo about American foreign policy. Certain drums have to be beaten regularly to ward off evil spirits—for example, the maledictions which are regularly uttered against North Vietnamese aggression, the "wild men" in Peking, Communism in general. . . . Certainly pledges must be repeated every

SOURCE: *New York Times Magazine,* May 15, 1966.

day lest the whole free world go to rack and ruin—for example, we will never go back on a commitment no matter how unwise; we regard this alliance or that as absolutely "vital" to the free world; and, of course, we will stand stalwart in Berlin from now until Judgment Day.

In recent years the Congress has not fully discharged its obligations in the field of foreign relations. The reduced role of the Congress and the enhanced role of the President in the making of foreign policy are not the result merely of President Johnson's ideas of consensus; they are the culmination of a trend in the constitutional relationship between President and Congress that began in 1940—that is to say, at the beginning of this age of crisis.

In the past twenty-five years, American foreign policy has encountered a shattering series of crises and inevitably—or almost inevitably—the effort to cope with these has been executive effort, while the Congress, inspired by patriotism, importuned by Presidents and deterred by lack of information, has tended to fall in line. The result has been an unhinging of traditional constitutional relationships; the Senate's constitutional powers of advice and consent have atrophied into what is widely regarded—though never asserted—to be a duty to give prompt consent with a minimum of advice.

[O]n August 5, 1964, the Congress received an urgent request from President Johnson for the immediate adoption of a joint resolution regarding Southeast Asia. On August 7, after per-functory committee hearings and a brief debate, the Congress, with only two Senators dissenting, adopted the resolution, authorizing the President "to take all necessary steps, including the use of armed force," against aggression in Southeast Asia.

The joint resolution was a blank check signed by the Congress in an atmosphere of urgency that seemed at the time to preclude debate. Since its adoption, the Administration has converted the Vietnamese conflict from a civil war in which some American advisers were involved to a major international war in which the principal fighting unit is an American army of 250,000 men. Each time that Senators have raised questions about successive escalations of the war, we have had the blank check of August 7, 1964, waved in our faces as supposed evidence of the overwhelming support of the Congress for a policy in Southeast Asia which, in fact, has been radically changed since the summer of 1964.

All this is very frustrating to some of us in the Senate, but we have only ourselves to blame. Had we met our responsibility of careful examination of a Presidential request, had the Senate Foreign Relations Committee held hearings on the resolution before recommending its adoption, had the Senate debated the resolution and considered its implications before giving its overwhelming approval, we might have put limits and qualifications on our endorsement of future uses of force in Southeast Asia. . . .

7.8 "Beyond Vietnam: A Time to Break Silence." Martin Luther King, Jr. Opposes the War, April 4, 1967

For Martin Luther King, Jr., the decision to oppose the war in Vietnam was a difficult one. The Johnson administration had done a great deal to aid the civil rights movement, including the passage of the Civil Rights Act in 1964 and the Voting Rights Act a year later. Just when much of the nation was beginning to abandon Johnson and his Vietnam policy, King, understandably was reluctant to criticize an administration that had, really for the first time in modern history, truly carried the mantle of black America. In addition, King feared for the economic well-being of the movement; his opposition to the war could offend many of his big money supporters. And several of his closest advisors in the Southern Christian Leadership Conference insisted that a foreign policy initiative was not the place of the leader of the nation's modern civil rights movement. Andrew Young agreed with King, but Aaron Henry and Roland Smith did not.

By February 1967 King concluded that he could no longer avoid the issue. In several speeches he voiced his opposition to the war, but it was at the Riverside Church in New York, before a crowd of some 3,000, that King, for the first time, brought his anti-war arguments together. That speech is *Document 7.8*.

Of all King's major speeches, this may well be the least known. It is also one of his most compelling. He lists several reasons for his beliefs, for his journey on "the road from Montgomery to this place," but the most forceful argument—one that had been in the African-American mind for some time—was his assertion that African-American soldiers were fighting and dying for the rights of Southeast Asians—rights that African-Americans did not have in the United States.

By that time, however, King was on the backside of the Vietnam issue. By 1967 the African-American community already stood generally in opposition to the war.

....

DOCUMENT 7.8

"BEYOND VIETNAM: A TIME TO BREAK SILENCE." MARTIN LUTHER KING, JR. OPPOSES THE WAR, APRIL 4, 1967

I come to this magnificent house of worship tonight because my conscience leaves me no other choice. I join with you in this meeting because I am in deepest agreement with the aims and work of the organization which has brought us together: Clergy and Laymen Concerned about Vietnam.

The recent statements of your executive committee are the sentiments of my own heart and I found myself in full accord when I read its opening lines: "A time comes when silence is betrayal." That time has come for us in relation to Vietnam.

The truth of these words is beyond doubt but the mission to which they call us is a most difficult one. Even when pressed by the demands of inner truth, men do not easily assume the task

of opposing their government's policy, especially in time of war. Nor does the human spirit move without great difficulty against all the apathy of conformist thought within one's own bosom and in the surrounding world. Moreover when the issues at hand seem as perplexed as they often do in the case of this dreadful conflict we are always on the verge of being mesmerized by uncertainty; but we must move on.

Some of us who have already begun to break the silence of the night have found that the calling to speak is often a vocation of agony, but we must speak. We must speak with all the humility that is appropriate to our limited vision, but we must speak. And we must rejoice as well, for surely this is the first time in our nation's history that a significant number of its religious leaders have chosen to move beyond the prophesying of smooth patriotism to the high grounds of a firm dissent based upon the mandates of conscience and the reading of history. Perhaps a new spirit is rising among us. If it is, let us trace its movement well and pray that our own inner being may be sensitive to its guidance, for we are deeply in need of a new way beyond the darkness that seems so close around us.

SOURCE: *New York Times*, April 5, 1967.

Over the past two years, as I have moved to break the betrayal of my own silences and to speak from the burnings of my own heart, as I have called for radical departures from the destruction of Vietnam, many persons have questioned me about the wisdom of my path. At the heart of their concerns this query has often loomed large and loud: Why are you speaking about war, Dr. King?

Why are you joining the voices of dissent? Peace and civil rights don't mix, they say. Aren't you hurting the cause of your people, they ask? And when I hear them, though I often understand the source of their concern, I am nevertheless greatly saddened, for such questions mean that the inquirers have not really known me, my commitment or my calling. Indeed, their questions suggest that they do not know the world in which they live. . . .

I come to this platform tonight to make a passionate plea to my beloved nation. This speech is not addressed to Hanoi or to the National Liberation Front. It is not addressed to China or to Russia. Nor is it an attempt to overlook the ambiguity of the total situation and the need for a collective solution to the tragedy of Vietnam. Neither is it an attempt to make North Vietnam or the National Liberation Front paragons of virtue, nor to overlook the role they can play in a successful resolution of the problem. While they both may have justifiable reason to be suspicious of the good faith of the United States, life and history give eloquent testimony to the fact that conflicts are never resolved without trustful give and take on both sides.

Tonight, however, I wish not to speak with Hanoi and the NLF, but rather to my fellow Americans, who, with me, bear the greatest responsibility in ending a conflict that has exacted a heavy price on both continents.

Since I am a preacher by trade, I suppose it is not surprising that I have seven major reasons for bringing Vietnam into the field of my moral vision. There is at the outset a very obvious and almost facile connection between the war in Vietnam and the struggle I, and others, have been waging in America. A few years ago there was a shining moment in that struggle. It seemed as if there was a real promise of hope for the poor—both black and white—through the poverty program. There were experiments, hopes, new beginnings. Then came the buildup in Vietnam and I watched the program broken and eviscerated as if it were some idle political plaything of a society gone mad on war, and I knew that America would never invest the necessary funds or energies in rehabilitation of its poor so long as adventures like Vietnam continued to draw men and skills and money like some demonic destructive suction tube. So I was increasingly compelled to see the war as an enemy of the poor and to attack it as such.

Perhaps the more tragic recognition of reality took place when it became clear to me that the war was doing far more than devastating the hopes of the poor at home. It was sending their sons and their brothers and their husbands to fight and to die in extraordinarily high proportions relative to the rest of the population. We were taking the black young men who had been crippled by our society and sending them eight thousand miles away to guarantee liberties in Southeast Asia which they had not found in southwest Georgia and East Harlem. So we have been repeatedly faced with the cruel irony of watching Negro and white boys on TV screens as they kill and die together for a nation that has been unable to seat them together in the same schools. So we watch them in brutal solidarity burning the huts of a poor village, but we realize that they would never live on the same block in Detroit. I could not be silent in the face of such cruel manipulation of the poor.

My third reason moves to an even deeper level of awareness, for it grows out of my experience in the ghettoes of the North over the last three years—especially the last three summers. As I have walked among the desperate, rejected and angry young men I have told them that Molotov cocktails and rifles would not solve their problems. I have tried to offer them my deepest compassion while maintaining my conviction that social change comes most meaningfully through nonviolent action. But they asked—and rightly so—what about Vietnam? They asked if our own nation wasn't using massive doses of violence to solve its problems, to bring about the changes it wanted. Their questions hit home, and I knew that I could never again raise my voice against the violence of the oppressed in the ghettos without having first spoken clearly to the greatest purveyor of violence in the world today—my own government. For the sake of those boys, for the sake of this government, for the sake of hundreds of thousands trembling under our violence, I cannot be silent.

For those who ask the question, "Aren't you a civil rights leader?" and thereby mean to exclude me from the movement for peace, I have this further answer. In 1957 when a group of us formed the Southern Christian Leadership Conference, we chose as our motto: "To save the soul of America." We were convinced that we could not limit our vision to certain rights for black people, but instead affirmed the conviction that America would never be free or saved from itself unless the descendants of its slaves were loosed completely from the shackles they still wear. In a way we were agreeing with Langston Hughes, that black bard of Harlem, who had written earlier:

O, yes,
I say it plain,
America never was America to me,
And yet I swear this oath—
America will be!

Now, it should be incandescently clear that no one who has any concern for the integrity and life of America today can ignore the present war. If America's soul becomes totally poisoned, part of the autopsy must read Vietnam. It can never be saved so long as it destroys the deepest hopes of men the world over. So it is that those of us who are yet determined that America will be led down the path of protest and dissent, working for the health of our land. . . .

Finally, as I try to delineate for you and for myself the road that leads from Montgomery to this place I would have offered all that was

most valid if I simply said that I must be true to my conviction that I share with all men the calling to be a son of the living God. Beyond the calling of race or nation or creed is this vocation of sonship and brotherhood, and because I believe that the Father is deeply concerned especially for his suffering and helpless and outcast children, I come tonight to speak for them.

This I believe to be the privilege and the burden of all of us who deem ourselves bound by allegiances and loyalties which are broader and deeper than nationalism and which go beyond our nation's self-defined goals and positions. We are called to speak for the weak, for the voiceless, for victims of our nation and for those it calls enemy, for no document from human hands can make these humans any less our brothers.

And as I ponder the madness of Vietnam and search within myself for ways to understand and respond to compassion my mind goes constantly to the people of that peninsula. I speak now not of the soldiers of each side, not of the junta in Saigon, but simply of the people who have been living under the curse of war for almost three continuous decades now. I think of them too because it is clear to me that there will be no meaningful solution there until some attempt is made to know them and hear their broken cries.

They must see Americans as strange liberators. The Vietnamese people proclaimed their own independence in 1945 after a combined French and Japanese occupation, and before the Communist revolution in China. They were led by Ho Chi Minh. Even though they quoted the American Declaration of Independence in their own document of freedom, we refused to recognize them. Instead, we decided to support France in its reconquest of her former colony.

Our government felt then that the Vietnamese people were not "ready" for independence, and we again fell victim to the deadly Western arrogance that has poisoned the international atmosphere for so long. With that tragic decision we rejected a revolutionary government seeking self-determination, and a government that had been established not by

China (for whom the Vietnamese have no great love) but by clearly indigenous forces that included some Communists.

For the peasants this new government meant real land reform, one of the most important needs in their lives.

For nine years following 1945 we denied the people of Vietnam the right of independence. For nine years we vigorously supported the French in their abortive effort to re-colonize Vietnam.

Before the end of the war we were meeting eighty percent of the French war costs. Even before the French were defeated at Dien Bien Phu, they began to despair of the reckless action, but we did not. We encouraged them with our huge financial and military supplies to continue the war even after they had lost the will. Soon we would be paying almost the full costs of this tragic attempt at re-colonization.

After the French were defeated it looked as if independence and land reform would come again through the Geneva agreements. But instead there came the United States, determined that Ho should not unify the temporarily divided nation, and the peasants watched again as we supported one of the most vicious modern dictators—our chosen man, Premier Diem. The peasants watched and cringed as Diem ruthlessly rooted out all opposition, supported their extortionist landlords and refused even to discuss reunification with the north. The peasants watched as all this was presided over by U.S. influence and then by increasing numbers of U.S. troops who came to help quell the insurgency that Diem's methods had aroused. When Diem was overthrown they may have been happy, but the long line of military dictatorships seemed to offer no real change—especially in terms of their need for land and peace.

The only change came from America as we increased our troop commitments in support of governments which were singularly corrupt, inept and without popular support. All the while the people read our leaflets and received regular promises of peace and democracy—and land reform. Now they languish under our

bombs and consider us—not their fellow Vietnamese—the real enemy. They move sadly and apathetically as we herd them off the land of their fathers into concentration camps where minimal social needs are rarely met. They know they must move or be destroyed by our bombs. So they go—primarily women and children and the aged.

They watch as we poison their water, as we kill a million acres of their crops. They must weep as the bulldozers roar through their areas preparing to destroy the precious trees. They wander into the hospitals, with at least twenty casualties from American firepower for one "Vietcong"-inflicted injury. So far we may have killed a million of them—mostly children. They wander into the towns and see thousands of the children, homeless, without clothes, running in packs on the streets like animals. They see the children, degraded by our soldiers as they beg for food. They see the children selling their sisters to our soldiers, soliciting for their mothers.

What do the peasants think as we ally ourselves with the landlords and as we refuse to put any action into our many words concerning land reform? What do they think as we test our latest weapons on them, just as the Germans tested out new medicine and new tortures in the concentration camps of Europe? Where are the roots of the independent Vietnam we claim to be building? Is it among these voiceless ones?

We have destroyed their two most cherished institutions: the family and the village. We have destroyed their land and their crops. We have cooperated in the crushing of the nation's only non-Communist revolutionary political force—the unified Buddhist church. We have supported the enemies of the peasants of Saigon. We have corrupted their women and children and killed their men. What liberators?

Now there is little left to build on—save bitterness. Soon the only solid physical foundations remaining will be found at our military bases and in the concrete of the concentration camps we call fortified hamlets. The peasants may well wonder if we plan to build our new Vietnam on such grounds as these? Could we blame them for such thoughts? We must speak for them and raise the questions they cannot raise. These too are our brothers.

Perhaps the more difficult but no less necessary task is to speak for those who have been designated as our enemies. What of the National Liberation Front—that strangely anonymous group we call VC or Communists? What must they think of us in America when they realize that we permitted the repression and cruelty of Diem which helped to bring them into being as a resistance group in the south? What do they think of our condoning the violence which led to their own taking up of arms? How can they believe in our integrity when now we speak of "aggression from the north" as if there were nothing more essential to the war? How can they trust us when now we charge them with violence after the murderous reign of Diem and charge them with violence while we pour every new weapon of death into their land? Surely we must understand their feelings even if we do not condone their actions. Surely we must see that the men we supported pressed them to their violence. Surely we must see that our own computerized plans of destruction simply dwarf their greatest acts.

How do they judge us when our officials know that their membership is less than twenty-five percent Communist and yet insist on giving them the blanket name? What must they be thinking when they know that we are aware of their control of major sections of Vietnam and yet we appear ready to allow national elections in which this highly organized political parallel government will have no part? They ask how we can speak of free elections when the Saigon press is censored and controlled by the military junta. And they are surely right to wonder what kind of new government we plan to help form without them— the only party in real touch with the peasants. They question our political goals and they deny the reality of a peace settlement from which they will be excluded. Their questions are frighteningly relevant. Is our nation planning to build on political myth again and then shore it up with the power of new violence?

Here is the true meaning and value of compassion and nonviolence when it helps us to see the enemy's point of view, to hear his questions, to know his assessment of ourselves. For from his view we may indeed see the basic weaknesses of our own condition, and if we are mature, we may learn and grow and profit from the wisdom of the brothers who are called the opposition.

So, too, with Hanoi. In the north, where our bombs now pummel the land, and our mines endanger the waterways, we are met by a deep but understandable mistrust. To speak for them is to explain this lack of confidence in Western words, and especially their distrust of American intentions now. In Hanoi are the men who led the nation to independence against the Japanese and the French, the men who sought membership in the French commonwealth and were betrayed by the weakness of Paris and the willfulness of the colonial armies. It was they who led a second struggle against French domination at tremendous costs, and then were persuaded to give up the land they controlled between the thirteenth and seventeenth parallel as a temporary measure at Geneva. After 1954 they watched us conspire with Diem to prevent elections which would have surely brought Ho Chi Minh to power over a united Vietnam, and they realized they had been betrayed again.

When we ask why they do not leap to negotiate, these things must be remembered. Also it must be clear that the leaders of Hanoi considered the presence of American troops in support of the Diem regime to have been the initial military breach of the Geneva agreements concerning foreign troops, and they remind us that they did not begin to send in any large number of supplies or men until American forces had moved into the tens of thousands.

Hanoi remembers how our leaders refused to tell us the truth about the earlier North Vietnamese overtures for peace, how the president claimed that none existed when they had clearly been made. Ho Chi Minh has watched as America has spoken of peace and built up its forces, and now he has surely heard of the increasing international rumors of American plans for an invasion of the north. He knows the bombing and shelling and mining we are doing are part of traditional pre-invasion strategy. Perhaps only his sense of humor and of irony can save him when he hears the most powerful nation of the world speaking of aggression as it drops thousands of bombs on a poor weak nation more than eight thousand miles away from its shores.

At this point I should make it clear that while I have tried in these last few minutes to give a voice to the voiceless on Vietnam and to understand the arguments of those who are called enemy, I am as deeply concerned about our troops there as anything else. For it occurs to me that what we are submitting them to in Vietnam is not simply the brutalizing process that goes on in any war where armies face each other and seek to destroy. We are adding cynicism to the process of death, for they must know after a short period there that none of the things we claim to be fighting for are really involved. Before long they must know that their government has sent them into a struggle among Vietnamese, and the more sophisticated surely realize that we are on the side of the wealthy and the secure while we create hell for the poor.

Somehow this madness must cease. We must stop now. I speak as a child of God and brother to the suffering poor of Vietnam. I speak for those whose land is being laid waste, whose homes are being destroyed, whose culture is being subverted. I speak for the poor of America who are paying the double price of smashed hopes at home and death and corruption in Vietnam. I speak as a citizen of the world, for the world as it stands aghast at the path we have taken. I speak as an American to the leaders of my own nation. The great initiative in this war is ours. The initiative to stop it must be ours.

This is the message of the great Buddhist leaders of Vietnam. Recently one of them wrote these words:

"Each day the war goes on the hatred increases in the heart of the Vietnamese and in the hearts of those of humanitarian instinct. The Americans are forcing even their friends into becoming their enemies. It is curious that the Americans, who calculate so carefully on the possibilities of military victory, do not realize that in the process they are incurring deep psychological and political defeat. The image of America will never again be the image of revolution, freedom and democracy, but the image of violence and militarism."

If we continue, there will be no doubt in my mind and in the mind of the world that we have no honorable intentions in Vietnam. It will become clear that our minimal expectation is to occupy it as an American colony and men will not refrain from thinking that our maximum hope is to goad China into a war so that we may bomb her nuclear installations. If we do not stop our war against the people of Vietnam immediately the world will be left with no other alternative than to see this as some horribly clumsy and deadly game we have decided to play.

The world now demands a maturity of America that we may not be able to achieve. It demands that we admit that we have been wrong from the beginning of our adventure in Vietnam, that we have been detrimental to the life of the Vietnamese people. The situation is one in which we must be ready to turn sharply from our present ways. . . .

Meanwhile we in the churches and synagogues have a continuing task while we urge our government to disengage itself from a disgraceful commitment. We must continue to raise our voices if our nation persists in its perverse ways in Vietnam. We must be prepared to match actions with words by seeking out every creative means of protest possible.

As we counsel young men concerning military service we must clarify for them our nation's role in Vietnam and challenge them with the alternative of conscientious objection. I am pleased to say that this is the path now being chosen by more than seventy students at my own alma mater, Morehouse College, and I recommend it to all who find the American course in Vietnam a dishonorable and unjust one. Moreover I would encourage all ministers of draft age to give up their ministerial exemptions and seek status as conscientious objectors. These are the times for real choices and not false ones. We are at the moment when our lives must be placed on the line if our nation is to survive its own folly. Every man of humane convictions must decide on the protest that best suits his convictions, but we must all protest.

There is something seductively tempting about stopping there and sending us all off on what in some circles has become a popular crusade against the war in Vietnam. I say we must enter the struggle, but I wish to go on now to say something even more disturbing. The war in Vietnam is but a symptom of a far deeper malady within the American spirit, and if we ignore this sobering reality we will find ourselves organizing clergy—and laymen—concerned committees for the next generation. They will be concerned about Guatemala and Peru. They will be concerned about Thailand and Cambodia. They will be concerned about Mozambique and South Africa. We will be marching for these and a dozen other names and attending rallies without end unless there is a significant and profound change in American life and policy. Such thoughts take us beyond Vietnam, but not beyond our calling as sons of the living God.

In 1957 a sensitive American official overseas said that it seemed to him that our nation was on the wrong side of a world revolution. During the past ten years we have seen emerge a pattern of suppression which now has justified the presence of U.S. military "advisors" in Venezuela. This need to maintain social stability for our investments accounts for the counter-revolutionary action of American forces in Guatemala. It tells why American helicopters are being used against guerrillas in Colombia and why American napalm and green beret forces have already been active against rebels in Peru. It is with such activity in mind that the words of the late John F. Kennedy come back to haunt us. Five years ago he said, "Those who make peaceful revolution impossible will make violent revolution inevitable."

Increasingly, by choice or by accident, this is the role our nation has taken—the role of those who make peaceful revolution impossible by refusing to give up the privileges and the pleasures that come from the immense profits of overseas investment.

I am convinced that if we are to get on the right side of the world revolution, we as a nation must undergo a radical revolution of values. We must rapidly begin the shift from a "thing-oriented" society to a "person-oriented" society. When machines and computers, profit motives and property rights are considered more important than people, the giant triplets of racism, materialism, and militarism are incapable of being conquered. . . .

The Western arrogance of feeling that it has everything to teach others and nothing to learn from them is not just. A true revolution of values will lay hands on the world order and say of war: "This way of settling differences is not just." This business of burning human beings with napalm, of filling our nation's homes with orphans and widows, of injecting poisonous drugs of hate into veins of people normally humane, of sending men home from dark and bloody battlefields physically handicapped and psychologically deranged, cannot be reconciled with wisdom, justice and love.

A nation that continues year after year to spend more money on military defense than on programs of social uplift is approaching spiritual death.

America, the richest and most powerful nation in the world, can well lead the way in this revolution of values. There is nothing, except a tragic death wish, to prevent us from reordering our priorities, so that the pursuit of peace will take precedence over the pursuit of war. There is nothing to keep us from molding a recalcitrant status quo with bruised hands until we have fashioned it into a brotherhood.

This kind of positive revolution of values is our best defense against communism. War is not the answer. Communism will never be defeated by the use of atomic bombs or nuclear weapons. Let us not join those who shout war and through their misguided passions urge the United States to relinquish its participation in the United Nations. These are days which demand wise restraint and calm reasonableness. We must not call everyone a Communist or an appeaser who advocates the seating of Red China in the United Nations and who recognizes that hate and hysteria are not the final answers to the problem of these turbulent days. We must not engage in a negative anti-communism, but rather in a positive thrust for democracy, realizing that our greatest defense against communism is to take offensive action in behalf of justice. We must with positive action seek to remove those conditions of poverty, insecurity and injustice which are the fertile soil in which the seed of communism grows and develops.

These are revolutionary times. All over the globe men are revolting against old systems of exploitation and oppression and out of the wombs of a frail world new systems of justice and equality are being born. The shirtless and barefoot people of the land are rising up as never before.

"The people who sat in darkness have seen a great light." We in the West must support these revolutions. It is a sad fact that, because of comfort, complacency, a morbid fear of communism, and our proneness to adjust to injustice, the Western nations that initiated so much of the revolutionary spirit of the modern world have now become the arch anti-revolutionaries. This has driven many to feel that only Marxism has the revolutionary spirit. Therefore, communism is a judgment against our failure to make democracy real and follow through on the revolutions we initiated. Our only hope today lies in our ability to recapture the revolutionary spirit and go out into a sometimes-hostile world declaring eternal hostility to poverty, racism, and militarism. With this powerful commitment we shall boldly challenge the status quo and unjust mores and thereby speed the day when "every valley shall be exalted, and every mountain and hill shall be made low, and the crooked shall be made straight and the rough places plain." . . .

We are now faced with the fact that tomorrow is today. We are confronted with the fierce urgency of now. In this unfolding conundrum of life and history there is such a thing as being too late. Procrastination is still the thief of time. Life often leaves us standing bare, naked and dejected with a lost opportunity. The "tide in the affairs of men" does not remain at the flood; it ebbs. We may cry out desperately for time to pause in her passage, but time is deaf to every plea and rushes on. Over the bleached bones and jumbled residue of numerous civilizations are written the pathetic words: "Too late." There is an invisible book of life that faithfully records our vigilance or our neglect. "The moving finger writes, and having writ moves on . . ." We still have a choice today; nonviolent coexistence or violent co-annihilation.

We must move past indecision to action. We must find new ways to speak for peace in Vietnam and justice throughout the developing world—a world that borders on our doors. If we do not act we shall surely be dragged down the long dark and shameful corridors of time reserved for those who possess power without compassion, might without morality, and strength without sight.

Now let us begin. Now let us rededicate ourselves to the long and bitter—but beautiful—struggle for a new world. This is the calling of the sons of God, and our brothers wait eagerly for our response. Shall we say the odds are too great? Shall we tell them the struggle is too hard? Will our message be that the forces of American life militate against their arrival as full men, and we send our deepest regrets? Or will there be another message, of longing, of hope, of solidarity with their yearnings, of commitment to their cause, whatever the cost? The choice is ours, and though we might prefer it otherwise we must choose in this crucial moment of human history.

7.9   **Vo Nguyen Giap on Neo-colonialism and the American War**
7.10   **Robert McNamara's Memoir of U.S. Involvement in Vietnam**
7.11   **Mr. McNamara's Other War: A Vietnam Veteran Responds**

Greneral Vo Nguyen Giap was the leading military figure in Vietnam's war against the French in the 1950s and then against the Americans after that. Following World War II, Ho Chi Minh named Giap commander-in-chief of the Viet Minh forces fighting French colonial rule, and it was Giap who orchestrated the defeat of the French at Dien Bien Phu in 1954. As minister of defense, Giap was the chief military leader in the war against American forces. In *Document 7.9* Giap explains the Hanoi government's interpretation of U.S. involvement in the war and the nature of American neo-colonialism as an extension of western capitalist imperialism.

Document 7.10 is from Robert S. McNamara's memoir, *In Retrospect,* excerpted in part in *Newsweek* and quoted here. Serving under presidents Kennedy and Johnson as secretary of defense, McNamara was responsible, possibly only less than the two presidents themselves, for America's involvement in Vietnam. Here he explains why the United States became involved in Vietnam and why he now believes that it was a disastrous mistake. McNamara's *mea culpa* did not sit well with many of those who fought the war. *Document 7.11* is a war veteran's response to McNamara's reflections.

....

DOCUMENT 7.9

VO NGUYEN GIAP ON NEO-COLONIALISM AND THE AMERICAN WAR

The present war of national liberation in South Vietnam is directed against the neo-colonialism of the U.S. imperialists and their lackeys, an extremely reactionary and wicked enemy who is materially and technically strong but morally and politically weak.

In the previous resistance war of national salvation, the revolution in South Vietnam as in the rest of our country was directed against the French colonialists and their lackeys assisted by the U.S. interventionists. After peace had been restored in Indochina, U.S. imperialism kicked out defeated French colonialism and set up in South Vietnam the pro-U.S. Ngo Dinh Diem regime. Unlike old-type French colonialism, U.S. imperialism did not build up an administrative machine and bring in an expeditionary corps but nevertheless its control over the South Vietnam regime was complete.

Neo-colonialism is a product of imperialism in the present period. Faced with the powerful influence of the socialist system and the upsurge of the national liberation movement in Asia, Africa and Latin America, the imperialists can no longer use old methods to impose their rule on their colonies; the local reactionary forces, especially the comprador bourgeoisie* and the feudal landlord class feel great fears for their interests and privileges. Neo-colonialism

SOURCE: Vo Nguyen Giap, "The Liberation War in South Vietnam: Its Essential Characteristics," *South Vietnam, 1954–1965; Articles and Documents* (Hanoi, 1966), 5–11.

*Capitalist. Businessman. An Asian representative of a foreign business.

is the result of the collusion and compromise between the foreign imperialists on the one hand and the local comprador bourgeoisie and feudal landlord class on the other, with a view to maintaining colonial rule under new forms and with new methods, and repressing the revolutionary movement of the mass of the people.

The aims of imperialism remain fundamentally the same: enslavement of the weaker nations, grasping of markets and raw materials, ruthless oppression and exploitation of the subjugated peoples. Its principal method remains violence under various forms. It differs from old-type colonialism in only one respect: while old-type colonialism directly takes in hand the enslavement of peoples and uses violence through and administration under its direct control and an army of aggression under its direct command, neo-colonialism carries out enslavement and uses violence in an indirect and more sophisticated manner through a puppet administration and a puppet army camouflaged with the labels of "independence and democracy," and a policy of "aid" or "alliance" in every field. Neo-colonialism, more wily and more dangerous, uses every possible means to conceal its aggressive nature, to blur the contradictions between the enslaved nations and the foreign rulers, thereby paralyzing the people's vigilance and will to wage a revolutionary struggle.

U.S. neo-colonialism has its own specific characteristics. When U.S. capitalism reached the stage of imperialism, the western great powers had already divided among themselves almost all of the important markets in the world. At the end of World War II, when the other imperialist powers had been weakened, the United States became the most powerful and the richest imperialist power. Meanwhile, the world situation was no longer the same: the balance of forces between imperialism, national independence, democracy and socialism had fundamentally changed; imperialism no longer rules over the world, nor does it play a decisive role in the development of the world situation. In the new historical conditions, U.S.

imperialism (which has a long tradition of expansion through trade, different from the classical policy of aggression through missionaries and gunboats) is all the more compelled to follow the path of neo-colonialism. The countries under its domination enjoy nominal political independence, but in fact are dependent on the United States in economic, financial, national defense and foreign relations fields.

At the end of World War II, U.S. imperialism already cast covetous eyes on Vietnam and the other Indochinese countries. In the early fifties, as the situation of the French colonialists was becoming more and more desperate, the U.S. imperialists gradually increased their "aid" and intervention in the Indochina dirty war. When the war ended with the defeat of the French expeditionary corps, they thought that the opportunity had come for them to take the place of the French colonialists. The images of former colonial rule—perfidious and cruel governor-generals and high commissioners, ferocious expeditionary corps—now belonged to the past. The U.S. imperialists could not, even if they wanted to do it, restore to life the decaying corpse of old colonialism. In 1954, when the defeat of the French colonialists was imminent, the U.S. imperialists envisaged the use of "national forces," made up of reactionary forces in the country, in an attempt to give more "dynamism" to the war. And they began to prepare their "special war" against the South Vietnamese people.

U.S. neo-colonialism uses its lackeys in South Vietnam as its main tool to carry out its policy of aggression. Neo-colonialism derives its strength on the one hand from the economic and military potential of the metropolitan country, and on the other hand, from the social, economic and political bases of the native reactionary forces. In the South of our country, the puppet regime was set up by the U.S. imperialists at a moment when our people had just won a brilliant victory against imperialism. That is why since it came into being, it has never shown any vitality, and has borne the seed of internal contradiction, crisis and war.

Its social bases are extremely weak. The feudal landlord class and the comprador bourgeoisie, which had never been very strong under French rule, had become even weaker and more divided in the course of the Revolution and the Resistance. After peace was restored, they became still more divided, as a result of the U.S.-French contradictions. These reactionary classes have long since shown themselves to be traitors to their fatherland, and are hated and opposed by the people. The defeat of the French expeditionary corps was a severe blow to their morals.

Under those circumstances, U.S. imperialism used every possible means to set up a relatively stable administration, camouflaged with the labels of "independence" and "democracy," in an attempt to rally the reactionary forces and at the same time win over and deceive other strata of the population. With this aim in view, they staged the farce of founding the "Republic of Vietnam" in order to perpetuate the partition of our country. Their puppets, claiming to have reconquered "independence" from the French colonialists, proclaimed a "constitution" with provisions on "freedom" and "democracy," and put forth slogans of anticommunism, ordered an "agrarian reform" and noisily publicized a programme for the "elimination of vices" and the "protection of good traditions," etc.

However, the puppet regime could not remain in power if they did not cling to their masters and obey the latter's orders. Outwardly, the "Republic of Vietnam" has all the usual government organs of internal and external affairs, defense, economy and culture, but all these organs, from the central to the local level, are controlled by U.S. "advisers." The latter, who enjoy diplomatic privileges, are not under the jurisdiction of the puppet administration, whose civil and penal codes cannot be applied to them. They are directly under the U.S. ambassador's control. It is U.S. imperialism which determines the fundamental line and policies of the South Vietnam regime. Ngo Dinh Diem, fostered by U.S. imperialism, was "pulled out of Dulles' sleeve" after Dien Bien Phu. The Diem regime, far from springing, as it claimed, from a movement of "national revolution," was only the result of the replacement of French masters by U.S. masters.

Faced with a popular revolutionary upsurge, the puppet regime soon took the road to fascism, and frantically pursued a policy of militarization and war preparation. To gain a reason for existence, it had to bluntly oppose the Geneva Agreements and the deepest aspirations of our people, namely peace, independence, democracy and national reunification. It trampled on the people's most elementary rights and resorted to a most barbarous policy of terror and repression. For these reasons, despite the labels of "independence and democracy" and certain reforms of a demagogic character, the popular masses immediately saw behind the puppet regime the hideous face of U.S. imperialism, that self-styled international gendarme, and that of the inveterate traitor Ngo Dinh Diem. And resolutely the masses rose up against them.

The U.S. imperialists also hurriedly built up and trained an army of mercenaries to be used as a tool for the repression of the revolutionary movement, carrying out their perficious policy of pitting Asians against Asians, Vietnamese against Vietnamese.

With this army of native mercenaries dubbed "national army," the imperialists hope to camouflage their aggression and save American lives. U.S. experts have calculated that expenses for an American mercenary soldier are twenty-four times less than those required for an American soldier.

The South Vietnam "national army" is staffed by puppet officers from the rank of general downwards, but this is coupled with a system of military "advisors" controlling the puppet national defense ministry and extending down to battalion and company level, in the militia as well as the regular forces. U.S. advisors in the puppet army supervise organization, equipment, training and operations. The U.S. imperialists try to camouflage under the labels of "mutual assistance" and "self-defense" the participation of their troops in fighting. With a view to turning South Vietnam into a U.S. military base, they have put under their effective control a large number of strategic points, all the main airfields and military ports.

Economic "aid" is used by the imperialists as a principal means to control South Vietnam's economy. This "aid" is essentially a way of exporting surplus goods and capital to serve their policy of expansion and war preparation. Three-fourths of the amount of yearly "aid" derives from the sale of imported goods. The U.S. aid organs completely ignore both the requests of the puppet regime and the needs of the country, and dump into the South Vietnam market surplus farm products, luxury goods and also consumer goods that could have been produced locally. Furthermore this aid clearly has a military character. It turns South Vietnam's economy into a war economy, eight-tenths of the money being used to cover military expenses of the puppet regime. This "aid" makes this regime totally dependent on the U.S. imperialists.

At first, the U.S. imperialists, thinking that they could rapidly consolidate the puppet regime and stabilize the political and economic situation in South Vietnam, had prepared the ground for the signing of unequal treaties to open the way to a large-scale penetration of U.S. finance capital. But the situation did not develop as they had expected, and so the money they invested in South Vietnam was insignificant, representing hardly two per cent of the total investments in various branches of the economy. In general, U.S. money was invested in joint enterprises, in a very wily economic penetration. Although present conditions are not favourable to the development of the U.S. sector in the South Vietnam economy, U.S. "aid" and the creation of counterpart funds have ensured to U.S.O.M. [United States Operations Mission] complete control over the budget, finances and foreign trade, in fact over the whole economic structure of South Vietnam.

For many years, now the puppet administration and army have been maintained in ex-istence only thanks to the U.S. They relentlessly pursued a policy of violence and war in order to repress the patriotic movement, while granting many privileges to a handful of traitors. The social basis of this regime is made up of the most reactionary elements in the compradore bourgeoisie and the feudal landlord class. . . .

DOCUMENT 7.10

ROBERT McNAMARA'S MEMOIR OF U.S. INVOLVEMENT IN VIETNAM

We of the Kennedy and Johnson administrations who participated in the decisions on Vietnam acted according to what we thought were the principles and traditions of this nation. We made our decisions in light of those values. Yet we were wrong, terribly wrong. We owe it to future generations to explain why.

I truly believe that we made an error not of values and intentions but of judgment and capabilities. I say this warily, since I know that if my comments appear to justify or rationalize what I and others did, they will lack credibility and only increase people's cynicism.

I want Americans to understand why we made the mistakes we did, and learn from them. I hope to say, "Here is something we can take away from Vietnam that is constructive and applicable to the world of today and tomorrow." That is the only way our nation can ever hope to leave the past behind. The ancient Greek dramatist Aeschylus wrote, "The reward of suffering is experience." Let this be the lasting legacy of Vietnam.

Throughout the Kennedy years, we operated on two premises that ultimately proved contradictory. One was that the fall of South Vietnam to Communism would threaten the security of the United States and the Western world. The other was that only the South Vietnamese could defend their nation, and that America

---

SOURCE: *Newsweek*, April 17, 1995.

should limit its role to providing training and logistical support. In line with that latter view, we actually began planning for the phased withdrawal of U.S. forces in 1963, a step adamantly opposed by those who believed it could lead to the loss of South Vietnam and, very likely, all of Asia.

I had never visited Indochina, nor did I understand or appreciate its history, language, culture, or values. The same must be said, to varying degrees, about President Kennedy, Secretary of State Dean Rusk, National Security Advisor McGeorge Bundy, military advisor Maxwell Taylor, and many others. When it came to Vietnam, we found ourselves setting policy for a region that was *terra incognita*.

Worse, our government lacked experts for us to consult to compensate for our ignorance about Southeast Asia. The irony of this gap was that it existed largely because the top East Asian and China experts in the State Department— John Paton Davies Jr., John Stewart Service, and John Carter Vincent—had been purged during the McCarthy hysteria of the 1950s. Without men like these to provide sophisticated, nuanced insights, we—certainly I—badly misread China's objectives and mistook its bellicose rhetoric to imply a drive for regional hegemony. We also totally underestimated the nationalist aspect of Ho Chi Minh's movement. We saw him first as a Communist and only second as a Vietnamese nationalist.

Such ill-founded judgments were accepted without debate by the Kennedy administration, as they had been by its Democratic and Republican predecessors. We failed to analyze our assumptions critically, then or later. The foundations of our decision-making were gravely flawed.

By the fall of 1961, guerrilla infiltration from North Vietnam into South Vietnam had increased substantially, and the Vietcong had intensified their attacks on President Ngo Dinh Diem's government. President Kennedy decided to send Max Taylor and Walt Rostow of the National Security Council staff to South Vietnam. In their report, Max and Walt urged

we substantially boost our support to South Vietnam by sending more advisers, equipment, and even small numbers of combat troops. Such steps, they noted, would mean a fundamental "transition from advice to partnership" in the war.

On November 8, 1961, I submitted a brief memorandum to President Kennedy supporting these recommendations. As soon as I sent the memo, however, I started worrying that we had been too hasty. For the next couple of days, I dug deeper into the Vietnam problem. The more I probed, the more the complexity of the situation and the uncertainties of our ability to deal with it by military means became apparent. I realized that seconding the Taylor-Rostow memo had been a bad idea. Dean Rusk and his advisers came to the same conclusion. On November 11, he and I submitted a joint memorandum to the president advising against sending combat forces. President Kennedy took up both memos in a meeting at the White House later that day. He made clear he did not wish to make an unconditional commitment to prevent the loss of South Vietnam and flatly refused to endorse the introduction of U.S. forces.

The dilemma Dean and I defined was going to haunt us for years. Looking back at the record of those meetings, it is clear our analysis was nowhere near adequate. We failed to ask the five most basic questions: Was it true that the fall of South Vietnam would trigger the fall of Southeast Asia? Would that constitute a grave threat to the West's security? What kind of war—conventional or guerrilla—might develop? Could we win it with U.S. troops fighting alongside the South Vietnamese? Should we not know the answers to all these questions before deciding whether to commit troops?

It seems beyond understanding, incredible, that we did not force ourselves to confront such issues head-on. But then, it is very hard, today, to recapture the innocence and confidence with which we approached Vietnam in the early days of the Kennedy administration. We knew very little about the region. We lacked experience dealing with crises. Other pressing international matters clamored for our attention during that first year: Cuba, Berlin, and the Congo to name but three. Not to mention the civil rights revolution at home. Finally, and perhaps most important, we were confronting problems for which there were no ready, or good, answers. I fear that, in such circumstances, governments—and, indeed, most people—tend to stick their heads in the sand. It may help to explain, but it certainly does not excuse, our behavior.

In spite of the incoherence of our approach to South Vietnam during those early years, many of us—including the president and me—came to believe that the problem was such that only the South Vietnamese could deal with it. This is what President Kennedy said both privately and publicly in the late summer and fall of 1963, when coup plotting against South Vietnamese leader Ngo Dinh Diem began. We could try to help them through training and logistical support, but we could not fight their war. That was our view then. Had we held to it, the whole history of the period would have been different.

I increasingly made Vietnam my personal responsibility. That was only right: it was the one place where Americans were in a shooting war, albeit as advisers. I felt a very heavy responsibility for it. That is what ultimately led people to call Vietnam McNamara's war.

Before authorizing the coup against Diem, whose direction of his nation's war effort was increasingly recognized as inadequate, we had failed to confront the basic issues in Vietnam that ultimately led to his overthrow, and we continued to ignore them after his removal. Looking back, I believe Kennedy and each of his top advisers were at fault:

- I should have forced examination, debate, and discussion on such basic questions as Could we win with Diem? If not, could he be replaced by someone with whom we could do better? If not, should we have considered working towards neutralization? Or alternatively, withdrawing on

the grounds that South Vietnam's political disorder made it impossible for the United States to remain there?
- Max[well Taylor] did not push to resolve the continuing reporting differences surrounding military progress—or the lack thereof—in South Vietnam.
- [Secretary of State] Dean [Rusk]—one of the most selfless, dedicated individuals ever to serve the United States—failed utterly to manage the State Department and to supervise Ambassador Henry Cabot Lodge, Jr. Nor did he participate forceful in presidential meetings.

And President Kennedy—whom I fault least, facing as he did a host of other problems—failed to pull together a divided U.S. government. Confronted with a choice among evils, he remained indecisive far too long.

DOCUMENT 7.11

MR. McNAMARA'S OTHER WAR: A VIETNAM VETERAN RESPONDS

The bitter controversy unleashed by the publication of former defense secretary Robert S. McNamara's Vietnam memoir, *In Retrospect*, gives new meaning to the words "McNamara's war." Having now slogged our way through the book itself, the outpouring of criticism with which it was met at the moment of publication and some of the relevant history of the time, we conclude the following: In a strange way both Mr. McNamara and those who belabor him for not having either resigned or spoken out at a time when he might have hastened the end of the war are saying the same thing. The critics say he should have done one or the other or both. The author provides a devastating case study of a governmental process, which he did much to create and keep running, that all but guaranteed he wouldn't. He and the others

---

SOURCE: *Washington Post*, April 30, 1995.

would instead just keep on improvising, trying one more thing, taking one more step, finding one more reason not to do what both he and his critics now wish he had.

Whatever Mr. McNamara now says about his reasons for not breaking publicly with a policy he believed doomed years and years ago—and while it was still in place and resulting in much destruction, maiming and death—it seems to us that the book itself vividly illustrates and explicitly faults the reasoning that kept him from doing so. Our own misgivings about his position now are different. We think Mr. McNamara goes too far, pushes too much over the side in his *mea culpa*.

Many of the people who have spoken against Mr. McNamara are veterans of the Vietnam political wars who are at pains to reassert the rightness of the position they ended up with. They say little about the very different positions many of them held on the way to that final judgment. But this omission is misleading. For Vietnam was a war in which definitions of right and wrong and success and failure more than once shifted, as events occurred and people learned more. Many who strongly supported the war—or at least went along—when it looked to be a right-minded and manageable enterprise changed their minds when the battle turned uglier, costlier, less winnable and much more destructive than they bargained for.

Mr. McNamara was in that category. So were many of those now heaping obloquy upon him for his role, which they backed at the time, in getting the United States deep into Vietnam and for his later failure to broadcast his change of heart while the men he sent to war were still at risk. . . . Everyone could use a little humility in this argument. But we are not concerned here to defend our several past positions of thirty and twenty years ago, but to offer our judgment on the basis of what can be understood now.

It was McNamara's war in the sense that his Harvard Business School problem-solving methodology soon dominated American policy-making, to the general applause. The results, however, were confounding. The South Vietnamese let the Americans take over the fighting, which led many Americans to the dispiriting view that South Vietnam had not invested amply in its own rescue. Meanwhile, the Americans were justifying their own investment on grounds of Vietnam's indispensability to the overall containment of Communism. To win at acceptable cost was becoming militarily ever more elusive, to lose strategically unthinkable.

Mr. McNamara never resolved this fundamental contradiction. Not that he didn't try. He moved to bombing, to bring Hanoi to the table, and then to bombing pauses, also to bring Hanoi to the table. But North Vietnam kept insisting that the South's internal differences be settled "in accordance with the program of" the South's Communist party. The secretary himself moved toward accepting the idea of a "compromise" or "coalition" solution—in plain talk, a Communist takeover. Lyndon Johnson rejected the idea, and eased his defense adviser out. The American people also rejected the idea, electing a president, Richard Nixon, who promised somehow to pull out but not to abandon South Vietnam.

It is plain in retrospect that the generation in power in the 1960s applied too literally and uncritically the Munich-appeasement analogy and the domino theory and, especially, the patently unhistorical notion that Vietnam was China's pawn. But there is more to it.

McNamara, in dismissing the possibility that America's Vietnam miseries encouraged Soviet adventurism, ignores Afghanistan, Central America, southern Africa and much else. Nor does he examine what happened when Richard Nixon actually consummated his 1968 campaign pledge of withdrawal without abandonment, thereby won landslide reelection in 1972 but then ran afoul of the fierce domestic resistance that his exit escalation tactics (not to speak of Watergate) had generated: Mr. Nixon could not deliver the aid and air support on which his strategy rested, and South Vietnam fell. Nor does Mr. McNamara probe the cost of the war and finally of defeat to the South Vietnamese. They bled, died and finally fled in great numbers from a Communist regime whose totalitarian harshness made South Vietnam's corruption look like an afternoon at the beach.

There was such a thing as communism on the march. It was not a "misunderstanding." It was a threat to what deserved to be called the free world. The American people were indeed denied timely and full awareness of the illusions and evasions of the Kennedy and Johnson teams Mr. McNamara worked with. But Americans, understanding the basics, had for decades committed themselves to meet the challenge and to pay a price for it. For this reason—because it faced an armed takeover by an outside Communist regime—South Vietnam inevitably became a place where the confrontation was played out.

The United States conducted its Vietnam policy unwisely, not well. The result was terrible casualties, terrible human suffering. The McNamara book is an unrelieved narrative of how and why these things happened and its rewards pondering on this score alone. The book provides a cautionary tale that could be useful for people who are prepared to go beyond self-justifying into learning. Mr. McNamara fully earned his remorse. [*In*] *Retrospect* reveals a rich map of roads not taken. But the losses were not futile. They were incurred in a larger, ultimately successful cause worth pursuing, if not in that place and in that fashion. Acknowledging that much is owed those who served.

CHAPTER **8**

....

From Nixon to Carter, 1969–1981

8.1 President Richard Nixon on the Vietnamization of the War, November 3, 1969

8.2 Senator George McGovern and the "Cruel Hoax" of Vietnamization, February 1970

8.3 CIA Operating Guidance Cable on Coup Plotting in Chile, October 16, 1970

8.4 "UN Seats Peking and Expels Taipei," *New York Times,* October 26, 1971

8.5 The Shanghai Communique, February 27, 1972

8.6 Secretary of State Henry Kissinger, Détente, and the Grand Design. Speech Before Senate Foreign Relations Committee, September 1974

8.7 President Jimmy Carter on Human Rights as Foreign Policy. Commencement Address at the University of Notre Dame, May 22, 1977

8.8 President Jimmy Carter Announces the Camp David Accords, September 18, 1978

8.9 *Time's* Report of the Iranian Hostage Crisis, November 19, 1979

1969–1979 Timeline

Date	Year	Event
January 1969	1969	President Richard Nixon becomes president
November 3, 1969		Nixon on the Vietnamization of the War
February 1970	1970	Senator George McGovern on Vietnamization
October 16, 1970	1971	CIA proposed coup on Chile
October 26, 1971		UN seats Peking and expels Taipei
February 1972	1972	Nixon visits China
February 27, 1972	1973	Shanghai Communique
November 1972		Nixon wins re-election
January 27, 1973	1974	Truce signed in Vietnam
August 9, 1974	1975	Nixon resigns. Gerald Ford becomes president
September 1974		Henry Kissinger on détente
April 30, 1975	1976	Saigon falls to North Vietnamese troops
September 1976		Mao Zedong dies
January 1977	1977	Jimmy Carter becomes president
May 22, 1977	1978	Carter on human rights
September 18, 1978		Carter announces the Camp David Accords
November 19, 1979	1979	*Time* reports Iran Hostage Crisis

8.1   **President Richard Nixon on the Vietnamization of the War, November 3, 1969**

8.2   **Senator George McGovern and the "Cruel Hoax" of Vietnamization, February 1970**

From the time of Richard Nixon's election in 1968 until Jimmy Carter left office in 1981, the United States appeared weak and drifting. The period was not without its foreign policy victories and advances, but many Americans saw the 1970s as a time when the United States was unable to work its will in the world, was at odds with its friends, and generally in danger of losing its dominance. The period began with the closing of the war in Vietnam, and it was clear, despite some valiant efforts, that the United States had lost that war. In April 1975 Americans watched as U.S. soldiers and embassy workers fled Saigon in the midst of a panic as North Vietnamese tanks approached the city. It was an agonizing time.

In late 1973 the United States found itself unable to control events in the Middle East. Egypt and Syria invaded Israel in October. U.S. aid to Israel and Soviet aid to Syria threatened to escalate the war into a superpower confrontation. Then, in response to the American support for Israel, the Arab nations shut off the flow of oil to the United States, and that caused long lines at fuel pumps and a drastic rise in U.S. oil prices. Americans had never felt so economically vulnerable. It was a rude awakening. The war in the Middle East ended when Washington and Moscow pressured their client states to agree to a cease-fire later in October, but the oil embargo remained in place until March 1974, keeping prices high and further exposing America's economic vulnerability.

At the end of the period, in early 1979, Americans watched helplessly as Iranian revolutionaries overthrew a U.S.-sponsored government in Iran, and then in October snatch 55 U.S. embassy workers and held them hostage for an agonizing 444 days. A botched rescue attempt in April seemed to expose even further a nation whose power was in decline, whose technological superiority was useless in a great many situations.

But the era was not without its diplomatic highpoints. Détente, the Nixon-Kissinger strategy of limited cooperation with the Soviet Union and China, promised to cool tensions in the world and scale down the dimensions (and the cost) of the cold war. Nixon's trip to China in 1972 had the potential of turning the cold war into a three-sided affair in which the United States could contain both China and Russia by playing the two communist giants off against each another. It also might force Moscow and Beijing to push Hanoi into a compromise and bring an end to the Vietnam War. This Grand Strategy, as it was called, failed to have much impact on the war in Vietnam, but it did open diplomatic and trade relations between the United States and China and paved the way for future engagement with China and the Soviet Union by Nixon's successors.

As Richard Nixon took the oath of office in January 1969 the Vietnam War still dominated the nation's foreign policy. Nixon clearly wanted to end the war quickly. He saw what it had done to the Johnson administration and to the Democrats at a time when their domestic policies were generally popular. In January 1969, just after he took office, Nixon declared to an aide: "I'm not going to end up like LBJ. . . . I'm going to stop that war. Fast."

Just prior to the election, Nixon stated boldly that he had a plan to end the war, and that he would spell it out to the American people when he took office. His plan for "peace with honor," as he called it, revolved mostly around his strategy of "Vietnamization," a plan designed to turn the war over to the Army of South Vietnam as U.S. troops were gradually withdrawn. The South Vietnamese would then carry on the fight using U.S. money and materiel. As one cynical observer at the Pentagon commented, the plan was intended simply to "change the color of the bodies." Nixon also hoped to stifle the antiwar movement by replacing the current draft system with a more equitable lottery.

On November 24, 1969 President Nixon spoke to the American people on the war (*Document 8.1*). The nation was jaundiced and war-weary; nearly 40,000 American soldiers had already been lost in a war that seemed to have no end in sight. Nixon considered the speech one of the most important of his presidency—so important that he wrote it himself. He explained Vietnamization, a plan to reduce (even end) American involvement in the war without surrendering South Vietnam to the communists. It is here also, for the first time, that Nixon identified the "Silent Majority," those Americans supposedly standing in opposition to the vocal minority who opposed the war. This Silent Majority also wanted the war to end, but they wanted it done "honorably." This became the catchword of Nixon's Vietnam policy, and of the Silent Majority during the Nixon years.

Several months after Nixon's Vietnamization speech, Senator George McGovern spoke before the Senate Foreign Relations Committee on Vietnam and the administration's new policy of Vietnamization (*Document 8.2*). McGovern was the leader of a growing anti-war faction in the Senate and was quickly rising to the top of a short list of candidates for the Democratic party's 1972 presidential nomination. His speech rankled conservatives and endeared anti-war advocates.

....

DOCUMENT 8.1

PRESIDENT RICHARD NIXON ON THE VIETNAMIZATION OF THE WAR, NOVEMBER 3, 1969

Good evening, my fellow Americans: Tonight I want to talk to you on a subject of deep concern to all Americans and to many people in all parts of the world—the war in Vietnam.

I believe that one of the reasons for the deep division about Vietnam is that many Americans have lost confidence in what their Government has told them about our policy. The American people cannot and should not be asked to support a policy which involves the overriding issues of war and peace unless they know the truth about that policy.

Tonight, therefore, I would like to answer some of the questions that I know are on the minds of many of you listening to me.

How and why did America get involved in Vietnam in the first place?

How has this administration changed the policy of the previous administration?

What has really happened in the negotiations in Paris and on the battlefront in Vietnam?

What choices do we have if we are to end the war?

What are the prospects for peace?

Let me begin by describing the situation I found when I was inaugurated on January 20.

- The war had been going on for four years.
- 31,000 Americans had been killed in action.

SOURCE: *Public Papers of the Presidents, Richard Nixon, 1969*, 901–9.

- The training program for the South Vietnamese was behind schedule.
- 540,000 Americans were in Vietnam, with no plans to reduce the number.
- No progress had been made at the negotiations in Paris and the United States had not put forth a comprehensive peace proposal.
- The war was causing deep division at home and criticism from many of our friends, as well as our enemies, abroad.

In view of these circumstances there were some who urged that I end the war at once by ordering the immediate withdrawal of all American forces. From a political standpoint this would have been a popular and easy course to follow. After all, we became involved in the war while my predecessor was in office. I could blame the defeat, which would be the result of my action, on him and come out as the peacemakers. Some put it to me quite bluntly: This was the only way to avoid allowing Johnson's war to become Nixon's war.

But I had a greater obligation than to think only of the years of my administration and the next election. I had to think of the effect of my decision on the next generation and on the future of peace and freedom in America and in the world.

Let us all understand that the question before us is not whether some Americans are for peace and some Americans are against peace. The question at issue is not whether Johnson's war becomes Nixon's war.

The great question is: How can we win America's peace?

Let us turn now to the fundamental issue. Why and how did the United States become involved in Vietnam in the first place?

Fifteen years ago North Vietnam, with the logistical support of Communist China and the Soviet Union, launched a campaign to impose a Communist government on South Vietnam by instigating and supporting a revolution.

In response to the request of the Government of South Vietnam, President Eisenhower sent economic aid and military equipment to assist the people of South Vietnam in their efforts to prevent a Communist takeover. Seven years ago President Kennedy sent 16,000 mili-

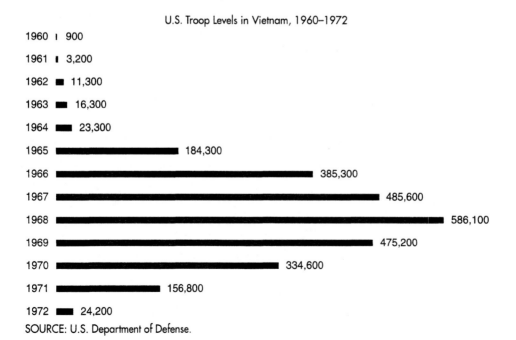

U.S. Troop Levels in Vietnam, 1960–1972

Year	Troops
1960	900
1961	3,200
1962	11,300
1963	16,300
1964	23,300
1965	184,300
1966	385,300
1967	485,600
1968	586,100
1969	475,200
1970	334,600
1971	156,800
1972	24,200

SOURCE: U.S. Department of Defense.

tary personnel to Vietnam as combat advisers. Four years ago President Johnson sent American combat forces to South Vietnam.

Now, many believe that President Johnson's decision to send American combat forces to South Vietnam was wrong. And many others, I among them, have been strongly critical of the way the war has been conducted.

But the question facing us today is: Now that we are in the war, what is the best way to end it?

In January I could only conclude that the precipitate withdrawal of American forces from Vietnam would be a disaster not only for South Vietnam but for the United States and for the cause of peace.

For the South Vietnamese, our precipitate withdrawal would inevitably allow the Communists to repeat the massacres which followed their takeover in the North fifteen years before.

- They then murdered more than 50,000 people, and hundreds of thousands more died in slave labor camps.
- We saw a prelude of what would happen in South Vietnam when the Communists entered the city of Hue last year. During their brief rule there, there was a bloody reign of terror in which 3,000 civilians were clubbed, shot to death, and buried in mass graves.

With the sudden collapse of our support, these atrocities of Hue would become the nightmare of the entire nation—and particularly for the million and a half Catholic refugees who fled to South Vietnam when the Communists took over in the North.

For the United States, this first defeat in our nation's history would result in a collapse of confidence in American leadership not only in Asia but throughout the world.

Three American Presidents have recognized the great stakes involved in Vietnam and understood what had to be done.

In 1963 President Kennedy, with his characteristic eloquence and clarity, said:

. . . we want to see a stable government there, carrying on a struggle to maintain its national independence. We believe strongly in that. We are not going to withdraw from that effort. In my opinion, for us to withdraw from that effort would mean a collapse not only of South Viet-Nam, but Southeast Asia. So we are going to stay there.

President Eisenhower and President Johnson expressed the same conclusion during their terms of office.

For the future of peace, precipitate withdrawal would thus be a disaster of immense magnitude. A nation cannot remain great if it betrays its allies and lets down its friends. Our defeat and humiliation in South Vietnam without question would promote recklessness in the councils of those great powers who have not yet abandoned their goals of world conquest. This would spark violence wherever our commitments help maintain the peace—in the Middle East, in Berlin, eventually even in the Western Hemisphere.

Ultimately, this would cost more lives. It would not bring peace; it would bring more war.

For these reasons I rejected the recommendation that I should end the war by immediately withdrawing all our forces. I chose instead to change American policy on both the negotiating front and the battlefront. . . .

It has become clear that the obstacle in negotiating an end to the war is not the President of the United States. It is not the South Vietnamese Government. The obstacle is the other side's absolute refusal to show the least willingness to join us in seeking a just peace. It will not do so while it is convinced that all it has to do is to wait for our next concession, and our next concession after that one, until it gets everything it wants.

There can now be no longer any question that progress in negotiation depends only on Hanoi's deciding to negotiate, to negotiate seriously.

I realize that this report on our efforts on the diplomatic front is discouraging to the American people, but the American people are entitled to know the truth—the bad news as well as the good news—where the lives of our young men are involved.

Now let me turn, however, to a more encouraging report on another front. At the time we launched our search for peace, I recognized we might not succeed in bringing an end to the war through negotiation. I, therefore, put into effect another plan to bring peace—a plan which will bring the war to an end regardless of what happens on the negotiating front.

It is in line with a major shift in U.S. foreign policy which I described in my press conference at Guam on July 25. Let me briefly explain what has been described as the Nixon doctrine—a policy which not only will help end the war in Vietnam but which is an essential element of our program to prevent future Vietnams.

We Americans are a do-it-yourself people. We are an impatient people. Instead of teaching someone else to do a job, we like to do it ourselves. And this trait has been carried over into our foreign policy.

In Korea and again in Vietnam, the United States furnished most of the money, most of the arms, and most of the men to help the people of those countries defend their freedom against Communist aggression.

Before any American troops were committed to Vietnam, a leader of another Asian country expressed this opinion to me when I was traveling in Asia as a private citizen. He said: "When you are trying to assist another nation defend its freedom, U.S. policy should be to help them fight the war, but not to fight the war for them."

Well, in accordance with this wise counsel, I laid down in Guam three principles as guidelines for future American policy toward Asia:

- First, the United States will keep all of its treaty commitments.
- Second, we shall provide a shield if a nuclear power threatens the freedom of a nation allied with us or of a nation whose survival we consider vital to our security.
- Third, in cases involving other types of aggression, we shall furnish military and

economic assistance when requested in accordance with our treaty commitments.

But we shall look to the nation directly threatened to assume the primary responsibility of providing the manpower for its defense.

After I announced this policy, I found that the leaders of the Philippines, Thailand, Vietnam, South Korea, and other nations which might be threatened by Communist aggression welcomed this new direction in American foreign policy.

The defense of freedom is everybody's business—not just America's business. And it is particularly the responsibility of the people whose freedom is threatened. In the previous administration we Americanized the war in Vietnam. In this administration we are Vietnamizing the search for peace.

The policy of the previous administration not only resulted in our assuming the primary responsibility for fighting the war but, even more significantly, did not adequately stress the goal of strengthening the South Vietnamese so that they could defend themselves when we left.

The Vietnamization plan was launched following Secretary [of Defense Melvin] Laird's visit to Vietnam in March. Under the plan, I ordered first a substantial increase in the training and equipment of South Vietnamese forces.

In July, in my visit to Vietnam, I changed General [Creighton] Abrams' orders so that they were consistent with the objectives of our new policies. Under the new orders, the primary mission of our troops is to enable the South Vietnamese forces to assume the full responsibility for the security of South Vietnam. . . .

We have adopted a plan which we have worked out in cooperation with the South Vietnamese for the complete withdrawal of all U.S. combat ground forces and their replacement by South Vietnamese forces on an orderly scheduled timetable. This withdrawal will be made from strength and not from weakness. As South Vietnamese forces become stronger, the rate of American withdrawal can become greater. . . .

If the level of infiltration or our casualties increase while we are trying to scale down the fighting, it will be the result of a conscious decision by the enemy.

Hanoi could make no greater mistake than to assume that an increase in violence will be to its advantage. If I conclude that increased enemy action jeopardizes our remaining forces in Vietnam, I shall not hesitate to take strong and effective measures to deal with the situation.

This is not a threat. This is a statement of policy which as Commander in Chief of our Armed Forces I am making in meeting my responsibility for the protection of American fighting men wherever they may be.

My fellow Americans, I am sure you can recognize from what I have said that we really only have two choices open to us if we want to end this war:

- I can order an immediate, precipitate withdrawal of all Americans from Vietnam without regard to the effects of that action.
- Or we can persist in our search for a just peace, through a negotiated settlement if possible or through continued implementation of our plan for Vietnamization if necessary—a plan in which we will withdraw all of our forces from Vietnam on a schedule in accordance with our program, as the South Vietnamese become strong enough to defend their own freedom.

I have chosen this second course. It is not the easy way. It is the right way. It is a plan which will end the war and serve the cause of peace, not just in Vietnam but in the Pacific and in the world.

In speaking of the consequences of a precipitate withdrawal, I mentioned that our allies would lose confidence in America.

Far more dangerous, we would lose confidence in ourselves. Oh, the immediate reaction would be a sense of relief that our men were coming home. But as we saw the consequences of what we had done, inevitable remorse and divisive recrimination would scar our spirit as a people. . . .

I have chosen a plan for peace. I believe it will succeed.

If it does succeed, what the critics say now won't matter.

If it does not succeed, anything I say then won't matter.

I know it may not be fashionable to speak of patriotism or national destiny these days. But I feel it is appropriate to do so on this occasion.

Two hundred years ago this nation was weak and poor. But even then, America was the hope of millions in the world. Today we have become the strongest and the richest nation in the world. The wheel of destiny has turned so that any hope the world has for the survival of peace and freedom will be determined by whether the American people have the moral stamina and the courage to meet the challenge of free-world leadership.

Let historians not record that when America was the most powerful nation in the world we passed on the other side of the road and allowed the last hopes for peace and freedom of millions of people to be suffocated by the forces of totalitarianism.

And so tonight—to you, the great silent majority of my fellow Americans—I ask for your support.

I pledged in my campaign for the Presidency to end the war in a way that we could win the peace. I have initiated a plan of action which will enable me to keep that pledge.

The more support I can have from the American people, the sooner that pledge can be redeemed; for the more divided we are at home, the less likely the enemy is to negotiate at Paris.

Let us be united for peace. Let us also be united against defeat. Because let us understand: North Vietnam cannot defeat or humiliate the United States. Only Americans can do that.

DOCUMENT 8.2

SENATOR GEORGE McGOVERN AND THE "CRUEL HOAX" OF VIETNAMIZATION, FEBRUARY 4, 1970

Mr. Chairman and members of the committee, the resolution that I have submitted with the co-sponsorship of Senators Frank Church, Alan Cranston, Charles Goodell, Harold Hughes, Eugene McCarthy, Frank Moss, Gaylord Nelson, Abraham Ribicoff, and Stephen Young of Ohio calls for the withdrawal from Vietnam of all U.S. forces, the pace to be limited only by these three considerations: the safety of our troops during the withdrawal process, the mutual release of prisoners of war, and arrangements for asylum in friendly countries for any Vietnamese who might feel endangered by our disengagement. I have recently been advised by the Department of Defense that the 484,000 men we now have in Vietnam could be transported to the United States at a total cost of $144,519,621.

The process of orderly withdrawal could be completed, I believe, in less that a year's time.

Such policy of purposeful disengagement is the only appropriate response to the blunt truth that there will be no resolution of the war so long as we cling to the Thieu-Ky regime. That government has no dependable political base other than the American military presence and it will never be accepted either by its challengers in South Vietnam or in Hanoi.

We can continue to pour our blood and substance into a never-ending effort to support the Saigon hierarchy or we can have peace, but we cannot have both General Thieu and an end to the war.

Our continued military embrace of the Saigon regime is the major barrier, both to peace in Southeast Asia and to the healing of

our society. It assures that the South Vietnamese generals will take no action to build a truly representative government which can either compete with the NLF [National Liberation Front] or negotiate a settlement of the war. It deadlocks the Paris negotiations and prevents the scheduling of serious discussions on the release and exchange of prisoners of war. It diverts our energies from critical domestic needs. It sends young Americans to be maimed or killed in a war that we cannot win and that will not end so long as our forces are there in support of General Thieu.

I have long believed that there can be no settlement of the Vietnam struggle until some kind of provisional coalition government assumes control in Saigon. But this is precisely what General Thieu will never consider. After the Midway conference in June 1969 he said, "I solemnly declare that there will be no coalition government, no peace cabinet, no transitional government, not even a reconciliatory government."

Although President Nixon has placed General Thieu as one of the two or three greatest statesmen of our age, Thieu has brushed off the suggestion that he broaden his government and has denounced those who advocate or suggest a negotiated peace as pro-Communist racketeers and traitors. A coalition government means death, he has said.

Mr. Chairman, let us not delude ourselves. This is a clear prescription for an endless war, and changing its name to Vietnamization still leaves us tied to a regime that cannot successfully wage war or make peace.

When administration officials expressed the view that American combat forces might be out of Vietnam by the end of 1970, General Thieu called a press conference and insisted that this was an "improbably and impractical goal" and that instead withdrawal "will take many years."

And yet there is wide currency to the view that America's course in Southeast Asia is no longer an issue, that the policy of Vietnamization promises an early end of hostilities. That is a false hope emphatically contradicted not only

SOURCE: *Hearings before the Committee on Foreign Relations, U.S. Senate*, 91st Cong. 2nd sess. (Feb. 4, 1970), 121–40.

by our ally in Saigon but by the tragic lessons of the past decade.

As I understand the proposal, Vietnamization directs the withdrawal of American troops only as the Saigon armed forces demonstrate their ability to take over the war. Yet a preponderance of evidence indicates that the Vietnamese people do not feel the Saigon regime is worth fighting for. Without local support, "Vietnamization" becomes a plan for the permanent deployment of American combat troops, and not a strategy for disengagement. The President has created a fourth branch of the American Government by giving Saigon a veto over American foreign policy.

If we follow our present policy in Vietnam, there will still be an American army, in my opinion of 250,000 or 300,000 men in Southeast Asia fifteen or twenty years hence or perhaps indefinitely. Meanwhile, American firepower and bombardment will have killed more tens of thousands of Vietnamese who want nothing other than an end to the war. All this to save a corrupt, unrepresentative regime in Saigon.

Any military escalation by Hanoi or the Vietcong would pose a challenge to American forces which would require heavier American military action and, therefore, heavier American casualties, or we would be faced with the possibility of a costly, forced withdrawal.

The Vietnamization policy is based on the same false premises which have doomed to failure our previous military efforts in Vietnam. It assumes that the Thieu-Ky regime in Saigon stands for freedom and a popularly backed regime. Actually, the Saigon regime is an oppressive dictatorship which jails its critics and blocks the development of a broadly based government. Last June 20, the Saigon minister for liaison for parliament, Von Huu Thu, confirmed that 34,540 political prisoners were being held and that many of those people were non-Communists who were guilty of nothing more than advocating a neutral peaceful future for their country. In proportion to population the political prisoners held by Saigon would be

equivalent of a half million political prisoners in the United States.

The Thieu-Ky regime is no closer to American ideals than its challenger, the National Liberation Front. Indeed, self-determination and independence are probably far stronger among the Vietnamese guerrillas and their supporters than within the Saigon government camp.

I have never felt that American interests and ideals were represented by the Saigon generals or their corrupt predecessors. We should cease our embrace of this regime now and cease telling the American people that it stands for freedom.

I should like to make clear that I am opposed to both the principle and the practice of the policy of Vietnamization. I am opposed to the policy, whether it works by the standard of its proponents or does not work. I oppose as immoral and self-defeating a policy which gives either American arms or American blood to perpetuate a corrupt and unrepresentative foreign regime. It is not in the interests of either the American or the Vietnamese people to maintain such a government.

I find it morally and politically repugnant for us to create a client group of Vietnamese generals in Saigon and then give them murderous military technology to turn against their own people.

Vietnamization is basically an effort to tranquilize the conscience of the American people while our government wages a cruel and needless war by proxy.

An enlightened American foreign policy would cease trying to dictate the outcome of an essentially local struggle involving various groups of Vietnamese. If we are concerned about a future threat to Southeast Asia from China, let us have the common sense to recognize that a strong independent regime even though organized by the National Liberation Front and Hanoi would provide a more dependable barrier to Chinese imperialism than the weak puppet regime we have kept in power at the cost of 40,000 American lives and hundreds of thousands of Vietnamese lives.

Even if we could remove most of our forces from Vietnam, how could we justify before God and man the use of our massive firepower to continue a slaughter that neither serves our interests nor the interests of the Vietnamese?

The policy of Vietnamization is a cruel hoax designed to screen from the American people the bankruptcy of a needless military involve-ment in the affairs of the Vietnamese people. Instead of Vietnamizing the war let us encourage the Vietnamization of the government of South Vietnam. We can do that by removing the embrace that now prevents other political groups from assuming a leadership role in Saigon, groups that are capable of expressing the desire for peace of the Vietnamese people.

8.3   CIA Operating Guidance Cable on Coup Plotting in Chile, October 16, 1970

In the fall of 1970 Salvador Allende, an avowed Marxist, was about to be elected president of Chile. President Richard Nixon, fearing another Soviet-sponsored state in the Western Hemisphere, gave orders to prevent Allende's election. The CIA planned a coup, hoping to place a retired Chilean general, Roberto Viaux, in power before the election. At the last minute, the CIA canceled the plot, but on October 22, 1970, Viaux attempted a coup on his own and was arrested. Allende was voted into office two days later. The following cable (*Document 8.3*) is from CIA Deputy Director of Plans Thomas Karamessines to Henry Hecksher, the CIA station chief in Santiago. According to the National Security Archives, it contains orders directly from National Security Adviser Henry Kissinger to overthrow Allende. Messages attached to the communication noted that the American ambassador in Chile had not been made aware of the plot. Allende was overthrown (and was either assassinated or committed suicide) on September 11, 1973.

Although the Nixon White House was elated at Allende's downfall, there is little evidence that the Nixon administration had a significant hand in the coup. However, in the three years that Allende was in office in Chile, the CIA engaged in an elaborate and expensive plot to undermine the Allende government and the Chilean economy. Following advice from the White House to "make the economy scream," the CIA pushed American companies to block credit and stop shipments of spare parts to Chile. All sources of economic aid were cut off and Export-Import bank loans were denied. The Nixon administration also spent some $6 million to subsidize newspapers and political parties opposed to Allende. By 1973, Chile was in turmoil and Allende's government was in trouble.

The military government that overthrew Allende suspended freedoms of speech and press, jailed dissenters, and gained worldwide notoriety for torturing and murdering political opponents. For the Nixon administration it was the successful Bay of Pigs that had been denied Kennedy. For critics of U.S. involvement in a sovereign nation and a freely elected government, it was an overreaction to an exaggerated communist threat in the Western Hemisphere.

DOCUMENT 8.3

CIA OPERATING GUIDANCE CABLE ON COUP PLOTTING IN CHILE, OCTOBER 16, 1970

Restricted Handling
Classified Message
CITE Headquarters
Immediate Santiago (Eyes Only)

1. [unintelligible] policy, objectives, and actions were reviewed at high USG level afternoon 15 October. Conclusions, which are to be your operational guide, follow:

2. It is firm and continuing policy that Allende be overthrown by a coup. It would be much preferable to have this transpire prior to 24 October but efforts in this regard will continue vigorously beyond this date. We are to continue to generate maximum pressure toward this end utilizing appropriate resource. It is imperative that these actions be implemented clandestinely and securely so that the USG and American hand will be well hidden. While this imposes on us a high degree of selectivity in making military contacts and dictates that these contacts be made in the most secure manner it definitely does not preclude contacts such as reported in Santiago 544 which was a masterful piece of work.

3. After the most careful consideration it was determined that a Viaux coup attempt carried out by him alone with the forces now at his disposal would fail. Thus, it would be counterproductive to our [blacked out] objectives. It was decided that [CIA] get a message to Viaux warning him against precipitate action. In essence our message is to state, "We have reviewed your plans, and based on your information and ours, we come to the conclusion that your plans for a coup at this time cannot succeed. Failing, they may reduce your capabilities for the future. Preserve your assets. We will stay in touch. The time will come when you together with all your other friends can do something. You will continue to have our support." You are requested to deliver the message to Viaux essentially as noted above. Our objectives are as follows: (a) To advise him of our opinion and discourage him from acting alone; (b) Continue to encourage him to amplify his planning; (c) Encourage him to join forces with other coup planners so that they may act in concert either before or after 24 October. (N.B. six gas masks and six CS canisters are being carried to Santiago by special courier ETD Washington 1100 hours 16 October)

4. There is great and continuing interest in the activities of Tirado, Canales, Valenzuela et al and we wish them optimum good fortune.

5. The above is your operating guidance. No other policy guidance you may receive from [blacked out] or its maximum exponent in Santiago, on his return, are to sway you from your course.

6. Please review all your present and possibly new activities to include propaganda, black operations, surfacing of intelligence or disinformation, personal contacts, or anything else your imagination can conjure which will permit you to continue to press forward toward our [blacked out] objective in a secure manner.

End of message

SOURCE: "Department of State, U.S. Embassy Cables on the Election of Salvador Allende and Efforts to Block his Assumption of the Presidency, September 5-22, 1970" *National Security Archives, Electronic Briefing Books, Chile and the United States.*

8.4   "UN Seats Peking and Expels Taipei," *New York Times*, October 26, 1971
8.5   The Shanghai Communique, February 27, 1972

Since 1949 the United States and the Peoples Republic of China had treated each other as enemies. They had fought a war in Korea. They had accused each other of acts of open aggression, and both had supported the other's enemies in military conflicts. As late as 1970, Washington continued to maintain its position that the Nationalist Chinese on Taiwan represented the only legitimate government of the Chinese people, while Beijing continued its open support of North Vietnam.

In 1970, however, things began to change. The ideological split between China and the Soviet Union had escalated into border clashes along China's northeastern frontier, and China's supreme leader, Mao Zedong, had concluded that a relationship with the United States might stifle Soviet aggressions, while at the same time reduce the U.S. commitment to Taiwan. In January, Chinese officials asked for talks with the Americans, and in December the two nations began a simple dialogue of messages facilitated through Pakistan, a nation friendly to both the U.S. and the P.R.C. In April 1971 the Chinese unexpectedly reached out by inviting an American table tennis team, then on tour in Japan, to China for a series of matches. The Americans were soundly trounced, but within three months Nixon's special envoy, Henry Kissinger, was in Beijing making arrangements for the president's visit. Nixon made the announcement that he would go to China on July 15, 1971.

The issue of Taiwan was, however, still volatile. The "China Lobby" as it was called, was extremely powerful in Washington and it pushed hard for the United States to maintain its recognition of Taiwan as the legitimate government of the Chinese people. A primary aspect of that recognition was Washington's insistence that Taiwan, and not Beijing, be recognized in the United Nations as the representative of all China. When Nixon announced that he would go to China it immediately undermined America's tilt toward Taiwan, and in October a vote in the United Nations removed Taiwan as the representative of the Chinese people and seated the Beijing government. That event is recounted by the *New York Times* in *Document 8.4*. The American ambassador to the UN, George H. W. Bush, was clearly annoyed by the vote that was in defiance of America's will, but it was Nixon's announcement that led to it. Bush would go on to be appointed the first U.S. Liaison Officer to China since the communist takeover in 1949.

Nixon's China trip seemed a bizarre event to most Americans. Nixon, the man who had built a career around anti-communism, was sitting down with Mao, the communist hardliner and theoretician. But in 1972 these two men needed each other. Nixon arrived on February 21 and departed a week later. After much bickering, U.S. and Chinese officials issued the Shanghai Communique, essentially a statement of differences between the two nations (*Document 8.5*). One important aspect of the Communique was the agreement that the United States would recognize one China, governed from Beijing—a China that included Taiwan.

Nixon later said that the United States and China had "agreed to disagree." It was a step toward the normalization of U.S.-Chinese relations that were finally formalized, but not until 1979.

....

DOCUMENT 8.4

"UN SEATS PEKING AND EXPELS TAIPEI," *NEW YORK TIMES,* OCTOBER 26, 1971

In a tense and emotion-filled meeting of more than eight hours, the General Assembly voted overwhelmingly last night to admit Communist China and to expel the Chinese Nationalist Government.

Moments before the vote, Liu Chieh, the Chinese Nationalist representative, announced from the rostrum that his Government would take no further part in the proceedings of the Assembly. He received friendly applause from most delegations, and then led his delegation out of the hall.

The vote, which brought delegates to their feet in wild applause, was 76 in favor, 35 opposed, and 17 abstentions. The vote was on a resolution sponsored by Albania and 20 other nations, calling for the seating of Peking as the only legitimate representative of China and the expulsion of "the representatives of Chiang Kai-shek."

Thus, the United States lost—in the 22d year—its battle to keep Nationalist China in the United Nations. This development, which came with dramatic suddenness, was denounced by the chief American delegate as a "moment of infamy."

The key decision that signaled the United States defeat came an hour and a half earlier, when the Assembly voted, 59 to 55 with 15 absentees, to reject the American draft resolution that would have declared the expulsion of the

SOURCE: Henry Tanner, "UN Seats Peking and Expels Taipei," *New York Times,* October 26, 1971.

Nationalists an "important question" requiring a two-thirds majority for approval.

The United States had successfully used such a resolution since 1961 to keep the Chinese Communists out and the Chinese Nationalists in.

Before that time, a simple majority would have admitted Peking, but no majority could be mustered.

Last night as the electrical tally boards flashed the news that the "important question" proposal had failed, pandemonium broke out on the Assembly floor. Delegates jumped up and applauded.

The American delegation, also in the front row, sat in total dejection. George Bush, the United States delegate, who had been leading the fight for Nationalist China with considerable energy, half turned away from the rostrum, looking silently at the turbulent scene.

An analysis of the voting showed that the abstention of eight nations that had been thought almost to the last to be leaning toward the United States' position had been fatal to the American cause. Had they voted with the United States, the American "important question" resolution would have been adopted, 63 to 59.

The eight nations were Belgium, Cyprus, Laos, Qatar, Senegal, Togo, Trinidad and Tobago, and Tunisia.

However, the 76 members who voted for the Albanian resolution to admit Peking and expel the Nationalists constituted a two-thirds majority of those voting. While this majority would have permitted the admission of mainland China even if the American "important question" motion had won, many observers expressed the opinion that the final vote had been swelled by the pattern of earlier voting.

Meeting with newsmen shortly before midnight at the United States Mission across the street from the United Nations, Bush said he hoped the world organization would "not relive this moment of infamy."

"The United Nations crossed a very dangerous bridge tonight," he said. Expressing surprise at the vote, he added: "I thought we would win and it would be very, very close."

Bush said that he expected a very bad reaction from the American public.

When he was asked when he thought Peking's delegates would be arriving, he said: "It's hard to believe that a few hours ago we didn't think we had anything to worry about."

But Bush said the United States would "cross that bridge when we get to it" as he replied to a question as to how the United States would act regarding Peking's Security Council seat.

During last night's meeting, Adam Malik of Indonesia, who presides as this year's Assembly President, announced that he would notify the Peking Government immediately of its admission.

Communist China had said repeatedly that it would accept a seat in the United Nations only if the Chinese Nationalists were expelled.

The suddenness of the voting came as a surprise to all. As late as the afternoon, as the long China debate was in its final phase, it had been expected that the vote would come sometime in the next day.

Time, many here believed, might have worked in favor of the American position. As late as the morning, it was reported, the 131-member assembly was close to being evenly divided.

Therefore, the Albanian delegation, which for years has sponsored the resolution that would admit Communist China and expel the Nationalists, made it known that it would try to force a quick decision.

This precipitated an attempt by the supporters of Nationalist China to delay the proceedings. Jamil M. Baroody of Saudi Arabia proposed that all voting be postponed for one day, but his proposal lost, 53 to 56, with 19 abstentions.

In the parliamentary maneuvering that ensued, the United States experienced a short-lived victory. By a vote of 61 to 53, with 15 abstentions, the Assembly adopted an American proposal that priority be given to the "important question" resolution.

Earlier in the day, both Saudi Arabia and Tunisia had put forward compromise proposals for settling the China issue. The Saudi proposal included a call for a plebiscite on self-determination for the people on Taiwan.

Baroody, who made many trips to the rostrum during the eight-hour session, made his proposal for a delay in the voting so as to give time for the Assembly to study the American, the Albanian, the Tunisian and the Saudi Arabian resolutions.

The overwhelming vote for the Albanian resolution to seat Communist China and unseat the Nationalists contrasted with last year's bare majority—51 to 49. That was the first majority that advocates of admitting the Communists had obtained since the China item was first taken up by the Assembly in 1950.

DOCUMENT 8.5

THE SHANGHAI COMMUNIQUE, FEBRUARY 27, 1972

President Nixon met with Chairman Mao Tse-tung [Mao Zedong] of the Communist party of China on February 21. The two leaders had a serious and frank exchange of views on Sino-U.S. relations and world affairs.

During the visit, extensive, earnest and frank discussions were held between President Nixon and Premier Chou En-lai on the normalization of relations between the United States of America and the People's Republic of China, as well as on other matters of interest to both sides. . . .

The leaders of the People's Republic of China and the United States found it beneficial to have this opportunity, after so many years

SOURCE: *Public Papers of the Presidents: Richard Nixon, 1972,* 376–79.

without contact, to present candidly to one another their views on a variety of issues. They reviewed the international situation in which important changes and great upheavals are taking place and expounded their respective positions and attitudes.

The U.S. side stated: Peace in Asia and peace in the world requires efforts both to reduce immediate tensions and to eliminate the basic causes of conflict. The United States will work for a just and secure peace: just, because it fulfills the aspirations of peoples and nations for freedom and progress; secure, because it removes the danger of foreign aggression. The United States supports individual freedom and social progress for all the peoples of the world, free of outside pressure or intervention. The United States believes that the effort to reduce tensions is served by improving communication between countries that have different ideologies so as to lessen the risks of confrontation through accident, miscalculation or misunderstanding. Countries should treat each other with mutual respect and be willing to compete peacefully, letting performance be the ultimate judge. No country should claim infallibility and each country should be prepared to re-examine its own attitudes for the common good. The United States stressed that the peoples of Indochina should be allowed to determine their destiny without outside intervention; its constant primary objective has been a negotiated solution; . . . in the absence of a negotiated settlement the United States envisages the ultimate withdrawal of all U.S. forces from the region consistent with the aim of self-determination for each country of Indochina. The United States will maintain its close ties with the support of the Republic of Korea; the United States will support efforts of the Republic of Korea to seek a relaxation of tension and increased communication in the Korean peninsula. The United States places the highest value on its friendly relations with Japan. . . .

The Chinese side stated: Wherever there is oppression, there is resistance. Countries want independence, nations want liberation, and the people want revolution—this has become the irresistible trend of history. All nations, big or small, should be equal; big nations should not bully the small, and strong nations should not bully the weak. China will never be a super-power and it opposes hegemony and power politics of any kind. The Chinese side states that it firmly supports the struggles of all the oppressed people and nations for freedom and liberation and that the people of all countries have the right to choose their social systems according to their own wishes and the right to safeguard the independence, sovereignty and territorial integrity of their own countries and oppose foreign aggression, interference, control and subversion. All foreign troops should be withdrawn to their own countries.

The Chinese side expressed its firm support to the peoples of Vietnam, Laos and Cambodia in their efforts for the attainment of their goal. . . .

There are essential differences between China and the United States in their social systems and foreign policies. However, the two sides agree that countries, regardless of their social systems, should conduct their relations on the principles of respect for the sovereignty and territorial integrity of all states, non-aggression against other states, non-interference in the internal affairs of other states, equality and mutual benefit, and peaceful coexistence. International disputes should be settled on this basis, without resorting to the use or threat of force. The United States and the People's Republic of China are prepared to apply these principles to their mutual relations.

With these principles of international relations in mind the two sides stated that:

- progress toward the normalization of relations between China and the United States is in the interests of all countries;
- both wish to reduce the danger of international military conflict;
- neither should seek hegemony in the Asia-Pacific region and each is opposed to

In January 1972 President Richard Nixon jolted the diplomatic world by going to China and meeting with Chinese Premier Mao Zedong. The meeting exacerbated the Chinese-Soviet split and began the process of U.S. recognition of Mao's China at the expense of Taiwan. It was truly one of the momentous foreign policy events in twentieth century U.S. history. *National Archives/Nixon Presidential Material Staff*

efforts by any other country or group of countries to establish such hegemony. . . .

Both sides are of the view that it would be against the interests of the peoples of the world for any major country to collude with another against other countries, or for major countries to divide up the world into spheres of interest.

The two sides reviewed the long-standing serious disputes between China and the United States. The Chinese side reaffirmed its position: the Taiwan question is the crucial question obstructing the normalization of relations between China and the United States; the Government of the People's Republic of China is the sole legal government of China; Taiwan is a province of China which has long been returned to the motherland; the liberation of Taiwan is China's internal affair in which no other country has the right to interfere; and all U.S.

forces and military installations must be withdrawn from Taiwan. The Chinese Government firmly opposes any activities which aim at the creation of "one China, one Taiwan," "one China, two governments," "two Chinas," an "independent Taiwan," or advocate that "the status of Taiwan remains to be determined."

The U.S. side declared: The United States acknowledges that all Chinese on either side of the Taiwan Strait maintain there is but one China and that Taiwan is part of China. The United States Government does not challenge that position. It reaffirms its interest in a peaceful settlement of the Taiwan question by the Chinese themselves. With this prospect in mind, it affirms the ultimate objective of the withdrawal of all U.S. forces and military installations from Taiwan. In the meantime, it will progressively reduce its forces and military installations on Taiwan as the tension in the area diminishes.

The two sides agreed that it is desirable to broaden the understanding between the two peoples. To this end, they discussed specific areas in such fields as science, technology, culture, sports and journalism, in which people-to-people contacts and exchanges would be mutually beneficial. Each side undertakes to facilitate the further development of such contacts and exchanges.

Both sides view bilateral trade as another area from which mutual benefit can be derived, and agreed that economic relations based on equality and mutual benefit are in the interest of the peoples of the two countries. They agree to facilitate the progressive development of trade between their two countries.

The two sides agreed that they will stay in contact through various channels, including the sending of a senior U.S. representative to Peking from time to time for concrete consultations to further the normalization of relations between the two countries and continue to exchange views on issues of common interest.

The two sides expressed the hope that the gains achieved during this visit would open up new prospects for the relations between the two counties. They believe that the normalization of relations between the two countries is not only in the interest of the Chinese and American peoples but also contributes to the relaxation of tension in Asia and the world.

8.6   Henry Kissinger, Détente, and the Grand Design. Speech Before Senate Foreign Relations Committee, September 1974

It was Henry Kissinger who was the chief architect of America's foreign policy through much of the 1970s. A renowned Harvard political scientist, Kissinger entered the world of politics as an advisor to Nelson Rockefeller in the 1960s. He had written several books, one criticizing the concept of massive retaliation as a limit on U.S. military options, another extolling the virtues of a military balance of power as a means of maintaining peace. He served as Nixon's assistant for national security affairs until 1973 and then as secretary of state through the remainder of Nixon's term and on through the administration of Gerald Ford. Kissinger was the chief originator of the much-celebrated Grand Strategy, a series of foreign policy shifts that promised to change the nature of cold war diplomacy.

The primary aspect of Kissinger's Grand Strategy was détente, or an easing of cold war tensions. Détente, Kissinger argued, would significantly lessen the enormous cost of the cold war while reducing the risk of a civilization-ending nuclear exchange. He also hoped that détente would tame the Soviets, even induce them to scale back their military actions throughout the world—particularly in Vietnam.

Another aspect of the Kissinger-Nixon Grand Strategy grew from Washington's newfound relationship with China. As the Chinese-Soviet alliance soured through the 1960s and into the 1970s, and the two communist powers went from allies, to rivals, to adversaries, Nixon and Kissinger hoped to build a triangular relationship intended to play the Soviets against the Chinese to Washington's advantage. In its most successful form, Nixon and Kissinger intended that the two communist powers would vie for

U.S. support in an economic, ideological, or even military conflict. The plan never quite succeeded to that degree, but it did lead to better relations between all three nations as each tried to lessen tensions in anticipation of conflicts and rivalries. There were other factors that contributed to the success of this strategy, including a strong desire in both the United States and China for renewed trade relations, and a genuine need by the United States and the Soviet Union to reduce the cost of the cold war in a time of worldwide economic recession.

Détente led to a series of talks between the United States and the Soviet Union on the reduction of nuclear armaments and weapons systems. By the time Nixon came to office in 1969 the Dulles-devised concept of "massive retaliation" had evolved into "mutually assured destruction," or MAD. Each of the superpowers had the ability to destroy the other—and take down much of world civilization in the process. In addition, the cost of the arms race was damaging the economies of both the United States and the Soviet Union. Arms reduction seemed to be the answer to lessening the consequences of MAD while cutting down on the enormous cost of the arms race. The result was the Strategic Arms Limitation Talks, or SALT. The SALT talks began in 1969 in Helsinki and Vienna with the intention of freezing the production of additional strategic missiles. SALT-I was signed at the Moscow Summit in May 1972. It limited the number of anti-ballistic missile systems and froze the number of intercontinental ballistic missiles (ICBM), but it did not stop the production of new systems, and thus did not stop the arms race.

By the late 1970s, détente had come to an end, at least in part as a result of the U.S. response to the Soviet invasion of Afghanistan in 1979—leading to a renewed hard-line taken by both Moscow and Washington. SALT-I expired in 1977. SALT-II, although signed in 1979, was never approved by the U.S. Senate.

In 1974, however, Henry Kissinger was riding the successes of détente. Tensions with the Soviets had eased, relations with China showed significant promise, and the war in Vietnam was over. In that atmosphere of triumph, Kissinger appeared before the Senate Foreign Relations Committee to explain the accomplishments of his diplomacy (*Document 8.6*).

....

DOCUMENT 8.6

SECRETARY OF STATE HENRY KISSINGER, DÉTENTE, AND THE GRAND DESIGN. SPEECH BEFORE SENATE FOREIGN RELATIONS COMMITTEE, SEPTEMBER 1974

Since the dawn of the nuclear age the world's fears of holocaust and its hopes for peace have turned on the relationship between the United States and the Soviet Union. . . .

SOURCE: *Department of State Bulletin*, October 14, 1974.

The destructiveness of modern weapons defines the necessity of the task; deep differences in philosophy and interests between the United States and the Soviet Union point up its difficulty. These differences do not spring from misunderstanding or personalities or transitory factors. They are rooted in history and in the way the two countries have developed. They are nourished by conflicting values and opposing ideologies. They are expressed in diverging national interests that produce political and military competition. They are influenced by allies and friends whose association we value and whose interests we will not sacrifice.

Paradox confuses our perception of the problem of peaceful coexistence. If peace is pursued to the exclusion of any other goal, other values will be compromised and perhaps lost; but if unconstrained rivalry leads to nuclear conflict, these values, along with everything, will be destroyed in the resulting holocaust. However competitive they may be at some levels of their relationship, both nuclear powers must base their policies on the premise that neither can expect to impose its will on the other without running an intolerable risk. The challenge of our time is to reconcile the reality of competition with the imperative of coexistence.

There can be no peaceful international order without the constructive relationship between the United States and the Soviet Union. There will be no international stability unless both the Soviet Union and the United States conduct themselves with restraint and unless they use their enormous power for the benefit of mankind.

Thus we must be clear at the outset on what the term "détente" entails. It is the search for a more constructive relationship with the Soviet Union reflecting the realities I have outlined. It is a continuing process, not a final condition that has been or can be realized at any one specific point in time. And it has been pursued by successive American leaders, though the means have varied as have world conditions.

Some fundamental principles guide this policy:

- The United States cannot base its policy solely on Moscow's good intentions. But neither can we insist that all forward movement must await a convergence of American and Soviet purposes. We seek, regardless of Soviet intentions, to serve peace through a systematic resistance to pressure the conciliatory responses to moderate behavior.
- We must oppose aggressive actions and irresponsible behavior. But we must not seek confrontations lightly.
- We must maintain a strong national defense while recognizing that in the nuclear age the relationship between military strength and politically usable power is the most complex in all history.
- Where the age-old antagonism between freedom and tyranny is concerned, we are not neutral. But other imperatives impose limits on our ability to produce internal changes in foreign countries. Consciousness of our limits is recognition of the necessity of peace—not moral callousness. The preservation of human life and human society are moral values, too.
- We must be mature enough to recognize that to be stable a relationship must provide advantages to both sides and that the most constructive international relationships are those in which both parties perceive an element of gain. Moscow will benefit from certain measures, just as we will from others. The balance cannot be struck on each issue every day, but only over the whole range of relations and over a period of time. . . .

America's aspiration for the kind of political environment we now call détente is not new. . . . In the postwar period, repeated efforts were made to improve our relationship with Moscow. The spirits of Geneva, Camp David, and Glassboro were evanescent moments in a quarter century otherwise marked by tensions and by sporadic confrontation. What is new in the current period of relaxation of tensions is its duration, the scope of the relationship which has evolved, and the continuity and intensity of consultation which it has produced.

A number of factors have produced this change in the international environment. By the end of the sixties and the beginning of the seventies the time was propitious—no matter what administration was in office in the United States—for a major attempt to improve U.S.-Soviet relations. Contradictory tendencies contested for preeminence in Soviet policy; events could have tipped the scales either toward increased aggressiveness or toward conciliation.

The fragmentation in the Communist world in the 1960s challenged the leading position of the U.S.S.R. and its claim to be the arbiter of orthodoxy. The U.S.S.R. could have reacted by adopting a more aggressive attitude toward the capitalist world in order to assert its militant vigilance; instead, the changing situation and U.S. policy seem to have encouraged Soviet leaders to cooperate in at least a temporary lessening of tension with the West.

The prospect of achieving a military position of near parity with the United States in strategic forces could have tempted Moscow to use its expanded military capability to strive more determinedly for expansion; in fact, it tempered the militancy of some of its actions and sought to stabilize at least some aspects of the military competition through negotiations.

The very real economic problems of the U.S.S.R. and Eastern Europe could have reinforced autarkic policies and the tendency to create a closed system; in actuality, the Soviet Union and its allies have come closer to acknowledging the reality of an interdependent world economy.

Finally, when faced with the hopes of its own people for greater well-being, the Soviet government could have continued to stimulate the suspicions of the cold war to further isolate Soviet society: in fact, it chose—however inadequately and slowly—to seek to calm its public opinion by joining in a relaxation of tensions.

For the United States the choice was clear: To provide as many incentives as possible for those actions by the Soviet Union most conducive to peace and individual well-being and to overcome the swings between illusionary optimism and harsh antagonism that had characterized most of the postwar period. We could capitalize on the tentative beginnings made in the sixties by taking advantage of the compelling new conditions of the seventies. . . .

The course of détente has not been smooth or even. As late as 1969, the Soviet-American relations were ambiguous and uncertain. To be sure, negotiations on Berlin and SALT had begun. But the tendency toward confrontation appeared dominant.

We were challenged by Soviet conduct in the Middle East ceasefire of August 1970, during the Syrian invasion of Jordan in September 1970, on the question of a possible Soviet submarine base in Cuba, in actions around Berlin, and during the Indo-Pakistani war. Soviet policy seemed directed toward fashioning a détente in bilateral relations with our Western European allies, while challenging the United States.

We demonstrated then, and stand ready to do so again, that America will not yield to pressure or the threat of force. We made clear then, as we do today, that détente cannot be pursued selectively in one area or toward one group of countries only. For us détente is indivisible.

Finally, a breakthrough was made in 1971 on several fronts—in the Berlin settlement, in the SALT talks, in other arms control negotiations—that generated the process of détente. It consists of these elements: An elaboration of principles; political discussions to solve outstanding issues and to reach cooperative agreements; economic relations; and arms control negotiations, particularly those concerning strategic arms. . . .

We cannot expect to relax international tensions or achieve a more stable international system should the two strongest nuclear powers conduct an unrestrained strategic arms race. Thus, perhaps the single most important component of our policy toward the Soviet Union is the effort to limit strategic weapons competition.

The competition in which we now find ourselves is historically unique:

- Each side has the capacity to destroy civilization as we know it.
- Failure to maintain equivalence could jeopardize not only our freedom but our very survival.
- The lead time for technological innovation is so long, yet the pace of change so relentless, that the arms race and strategic policy itself are in danger of being driven by technological necessity.
- When nuclear arsenals reach levels involving thousands of launchers and over 10,000 warheads, and when the characteristics of the weapons of the two sides

are so incommensurable, it becomes difficult to determine what combination of numbers of strategic weapons and performance capabilities would give one side a militarily and politically useful superiority. At a minimum, clear changes in the strategic balance can be achieved only by efforts so enormous and by increments so large that the vary attempts would be highly destabilizing.

- The prospect of a decisive military advantage, even if theoretically possible, is politically intolerable; neither side will passively permit a massive shift in the nuclear balance. Therefore the probable outcome of each succeeding round of competition is the restoration of a strategic equilibrium, but at increasingly higher levels of forces.
- The arms race is driven by political as well as military factors. While a decisive advantage is hard to calculate, the *appearance* of inferiority—whatever its actual significance—can have serious political consequences. With weapons that are unlikely to be used and for which there is no operational experience, the psychological impact can be crucial. Thus each side has a high incentive to achieve not only the reality but the appearance of equality. In a very real sense each side shapes the military establishment of the other.

If we are drive to it, the United States will sustain an arms race. Indeed, it is likely that the United States would emerge from such a competition with an edge over the Soviet Union in most significant categories of strategic arms. But the political or military benefit which would flow from such a situation would remain elusive. Indeed, after such an evolution it might well be that *both* sides would be worse off than before the race began. The enormous destructiveness of weapons and the uncertainties regarding their effects combine to make the massive use of such weapons increasingly incredible. . . .

The SALT agreements already signed represent a major contribution to strategic stability and a significant first step toward a longer term and possible broader agreement. . . .

The agreements signed in 1972 which limited antiballistic missile defenses and froze the level of ballistic missile forces on both sides represented the essential first step toward a less volatile strategic environment. . . .

Some have alleged that the interim agreement, which expires in October 1977, penalizes the United States by permitting the Soviet Union to deploy more strategic missile launchers, both land based and sea based, than the United States. Such a view is misleading. When the agreement was signed in May 1972, the Soviet Union *already* possessed more land-based intercontinental ballistic missiles than the United States and given the pace of its submarine construction program, over the next few years it could have built virtually twice as many nuclear ballistic missile submarines. . . .

The SALT I agreements were the first deliberate attempt by the nuclear superpowers to bring about strategic stability through negotiation. This very process is conducive to further restraint. For example, in the first round of SALT negotiations in 1970-1972, both sides bitterly contested the number of ABM sites permitted by the agreement; two years later both sides gave up the right to build more than one site. In sum, we believed when we signed these agreements—and we believe now—that they have reduced the danger of nuclear war, that both sides have acquired some greater interest in restraint, and that the basis had been created for the present effort to reach a broader agreement. . . .

Détente is admittedly far from a modern equivalent of the kind of stable peace that characterized most of the nineteenth century. But it is a long step away from the bitter and aggressive spirit that has characterized so much of the postwar period. When linked to such broad and unprecedented projects as SALT, détente takes on added meaning and opens prospects of a more stable peace. SALT agreements should be seen as steps in a process leading to progressively greater stability. It is in that light that SALT and related projects will be judged by history.

Where has the process of détente taken us so far? What are the principles that must continue to guide our course?

Major progress has been made:

- Berlin's potential as Europe's perennial flashpoint has been substantially reduced through the quadripartite agreement of 1971. The United States considers strict adherence to the agreement a major test of détente.
- We and our allies are launched on negotiations with the Warsaw Pact and other countries in the conference on European security and cooperation, a conference designed to foster East-West dialogue and cooperation.
- At the same time, NATO and the Warsaw Pact are negotiating the reduction of their forces in Central Europe.
- The honorable termination of America's direct military involvement in Indochina and the substantial lowering of regional conflict were made possible by many factors. But this achievement would have been much more difficult, if not impossible, in an era of Soviet and Chinese hostility toward the United States.
- America's principal alliances have proved their durability in a new era. Many feared that détente would undermine them. Instead, détente has helped to place our alliance ties on a more enduring basis by removing the fear that friendship with the United States involved the risk of unnecessary confrontation with the U.S.S.R.
- Many incipient crises with the Soviet Union have been contained or settled without ever reaching the point of public disagreement. The world has been freer of East-West tensions and conflict than in the fifties and sixties.
- A series of bilateral cooperative agreements has turned the U.S.-Soviet relationship in a far more positive direction. We have achieved unprecedented agreements in arms limitation and measures to avoid accidental war.
- New possibilities for positive U.S.-Soviet cooperation have emerged on issues in which the globe is interdependent: science and technology, environment, energy.

These accomplishments do not guarantee peace. But they have served to lessen the rigidities of the past and offer hope for a better era. Despite fluctuations, a trend has been established; the character of international politics has been markedly changed.

It is too early to judge conclusively whether this change should be ascribed to tactical considerations. But in a sense, that is immaterial. For whether the change is temporary and tactical, or lasting and basic, our task is essentially the same: To transform that change into a permanent condition devoted to the purpose of a secure peace and mankind's aspiration for a better life. A tactical change sufficiently prolonged becomes a lasting transformation.

But the whole process can be jeopardized if it is taken for granted. As the cold war recedes in memory, détente can come to seem so natural that it appears safe to levy progressively greater demands on it. The temptation to combine détente with increasing pressure on the Soviet Union will grow. Such an attitude would be disastrous. We would not accept it from Moscow; Moscow will not accept it from us. We will finally wind up again with the cold war and fail to achieve either peace or any humane goal.

To be sure, the process of détente raises serious issues for many people. Let me deal with these in terms of the principles which underlie our policy.

First, if détente is to endure, both sides must benefit. There is no question that the Soviet Union obtains benefits from détente. On what other grounds would the tough-minded members of the Politburo sustain it? But the essential point surely must be that détente serves American and world interests as well. If these coincide with some Soviet interests, this will only strengthen the durability of the process. . . .

Second, building a new relationship with the Soviet Union does not entail any devaluation of traditional alliance relations. Our approach to relations with the U.S.S.R. has always been, and will continue to be, rooted in the belief that the cohesion of our alliances, and particularly the Atlantic alliance, is a precondition to establishing a more constructive relationship with the U.S.S.R.

Crucial, indeed unique, as may be our concern with the Soviet power, we do not delude ourselves that we should deal with it alone. When we speak of Europe and Japan as representing centers of power and influence, we describe not merely an observable fact but an indispensable element in the equilibrium needed to keep the world at peace. The cooperation and partnerships between us transcend formal agreements; they reflect values and traditions not soon, if ever, to be shared with our adversaries. . . .

Third, the emergence of more normal relations with the Soviet Union must not undermine our resolves to maintain our national defense.

There is a tendency in democratic societies to relax as dangers seem to recede; there is an inclination to view the maintenance of strength as incompatible with relaxation of tensions rather than its precondition. But this is primarily a question of leadership. We shall attempt to be vigilant to the dangers facing America. This administration will not be misled—or mislead—on issues of national defense. At the same time, we do not accept the proposition that we need crises to sustain our defense. A society that needs artificial crises to do what is needed for survival will soon find itself in moral danger.

Fourth, we must know what can and cannot be achieved in changing human conditions in the East.

The question of dealing with Communist governments has troubled the American people and the Congress since 1917. There has always been a fear that by working with a government whose internal policies differ so sharply with our own we are in some manner condoning these policies or encouraging their continuation. Some argue that until there is a genuine "liberation"—or signs of serious progress in that direction—all elements of conciliation in Soviet policy must be regarded as temporary and tactical. In

that view, demands for internal changes must be the precondition for the pursuit of a relaxation of tensions with the Soviet Union.

Our view is different. We shall insist on responsible international behavior by the Soviet Union and use it as the primary index of our relationship. Beyond this we will use our influence to the maximum to alleviate suffering and to respond to humane appeals. We know what we stand for, and we shall leave no doubt about it. . . .

We have accomplished much. But we cannot demand that the Soviet Union, in effect, suddenly reverse five decades of Soviet, and centuries of Russian, history. Such an attempt would be futile and at the same time hazard all that has already occurred, and more will come. But they are most likely to develop through an evolution that can best go forward in an environment of decreasing international tensions. A renewal of the cold war will hardly encourage the Soviet Union to change its emigration policies or adopt a more benevolent attitude toward dissent.

Détente is a process, not a permanent achievement. The agenda is full and continuing. Obviously the main concern must be to reduce the sources of potential conflict. This requires efforts in several interrelated areas:

- The military competition in all its aspects must be subject to increasingly firm restraints by both sides.
- Political competition, especially in moments of crisis, must be guided by the principles of restraint set forth in the documents described earlier. Crises there will be, but the United States and the Soviet Union have a special obligation deriving from the unimaginable military power that they wield and represent. Exploitation of crisis situations for unilateral gain is not acceptable.
- Restraint in crises must be augmented by cooperation in removing the causes of crises. There have been too many instances, notably in the Middle East, which demonstrate that policies of unilateral

advantage sooner or later run out of control and lead to the brink of war, if not beyond.

- The process of negotiations and consultation must be continuous and intense. But no agreement between the nuclear superpowers can be durable if made over the heads of other nations which have a stake in the outcome. We should not seek to impose peace; we can, however, see that our own actions and conduct are conducive to peace. . . .

We have insisted toward the Soviet Union that we cannot have the atmosphere of détente without the substance. It is equally clear that the substance of détente will disappear in an atmosphere of hostility.

We have profound differences with the Soviet Union—in our values, our methods, our vision of the future. But it is these very differences which compel any responsible administration to make a major effort to create a more constructive relationship.

We face an opportunity that was not possible twenty-five years, or even a decade, ago. If that opportunity is lost, its moment will not quickly come again. Indeed, it may not come at all.

As President Kennedy pointed out: "For in the final analysis our most basic common link is that we all inhabit this small planet. We all breathe the same air. We all cherish our children's future. And we are all mortal."

8.7   President Jimmy Carter on Human Rights as Foreign Policy. Commencement Address at University of Notre Dame, May 22, 1977

8.8   President Jimmy Carter Announces the Camp David Accords, September 18, 1978

In the spring of 1977, President Jimmy Carter, speaking at the commencement at the University of Notre Dame, (*Document 8.7*) said he intended to make human rights the basic tenet of the nation's foreign policy. It was important, Carter seemed to be saying, that the United States retake the moral high ground; that the cold war and Vietnam had somehow placed the nation on the wrong path, and it was again time for the United States to be a world leader, at least in a moral sense. The nation would, Carter said, use moral suasion in an attempt to maintain the basic rights of the world's humanity, and thus again become the measure for human rights in the world. To many Americans, Carter's speech was simply another example of the nation's growing weakness in the world, of its willingness to relinquish its role as a world leader—in the military, political, and economic sense—in the face of the Vietnam defeat. But to others, Carter was trying to bring the nation back to its moral center, something America seemed to have lost in the two prior decades.

An important foreign policy bright spot (in this period of few bright spots) was Jimmy Carter's initiatives in bringing an end to the conflict between Israel and Egypt, resulting in the Camp David Accords (*Document 8.8*). The agreement did not end hostilities in the Middle East, but it did bring an end to one of the region's primary conflicts.

PRESIDENT JIMMY CARTER ON HUMAN RIGHTS AS FOREIGN POLICY. COMMENCEMENT ADDRESS AT UNIVERSITY OF NOTRE DAME, MAY 22, 1977

I want to speak to you today about the strands that connect our actions overseas with our essential character as a nation. I believe we can have a foreign policy that is democratic, that is based on fundamental values, and that uses power and influence, which we have, for humane purposes. We can also have a foreign policy that the American people both support and, for a change, know about and understand.

I have quiet confidence in our own political system. Because we know that democracy works, we can reject the arguments of those rulers who deny human rights to their people.

We are confident that democracy's example will be compelling, and so we seek to bring that example closer to those from whom in the past few years we have been separated and who are not yet convinced about the advantages of our kind of life.

We are confident that the democratic methods are the most effective, and so we are not tempted to employ improper tactics here or abroad. . . .

For too many years, we've been willing to adopt the flawed and erroneous principles and tactics of our adversaries, sometimes abandoning our own values for theirs. We've fought fire with fire, never thinking that fire is better quenched with water. This approach failed, with Vietnam the best example of its intellectual and moral poverty. But through failure we have now found our way back to our own principles and values, and we have regained our lost confidence.

By the measure of history, our Nation's 200 years are very brief, and our rise to world emi-

nence is briefer still. It dates from 1945, when Europe and the old international order lay in ruins. Before then, America was largely on the periphery of world affairs. But since then, we have inescapably been at the center of world affairs.

Our policy during this period was guided by two principles: a belief that Soviet expansion was almost inevitable but that it must be contained, and the corresponding belief in the importance of an almost exclusive alliance among non-Communist nations on both sides of the Atlantic. This system could not last forever unchanged. Historical trends have weakened its foundation. The unifying threat of conflict with the Soviet Union has become less intensive, even though the competition has become more extensive.

The Vietnamese war produced a profound moral crisis, sapping worldwide faith in our own policy and our system of life, a crisis of confidence made even more grave by the covert pessimism of some of our leaders.

In less than a generation, we've seen the world change dramatically. The daily lives and aspirations of most human beings have been transformed. Colonialism is nearly gone. A new sense of national identity now exists in almost 100 new countries that have been formed in the last generation. Knowledge has become more widespread. Aspirations are higher. As more people have been freed from traditional constraints, more have been determined to achieve, for the first time in their lives, social justice.

The world is still divided by ideological disputes, dominated by regional conflicts, and threatened by danger that we will not resolve our differences of race and wealth without violence or without drawing into combat the major military powers. We can no longer separate the traditional issues of war and peace from the new global questions of justice, equality, and human rights. . . .

First, we have reaffirmed America's commitment to human rights as a fundamental tenant of our foreign policy. In ancestry, religion, color, place of origin, and cultural background, we Americans are as diverse a nation as the world has ever seen. No common mystique of blood or

SOURCE: *Public Papers of the Presidents: Jimmy Carter, 1977,* 955–62.

soil unites us. What draws us together, perhaps more than anything else, is a belief in human freedom. We want the world to know that our Nation stands for more than financial prosperity.

This does not mean that we can conduct our foreign policy by rigid moral maxims. We live in a world that is imperfect and which will always be imperfect—a world that is complex and confused and which will always be complex and confused.

I understand fully the limits of moral suasion. We have no illusions that changes will come easily or soon. But I also believe that it is a mistake to undervalue the power of words and of the ideas that words embody. In our own history, that power has ranged from Thomas Paine's "Common Sense" to Martin Luther King, Jr.'s "I Have a Dream."

In the life of the human spirit, words are action, much more so than many of us may realize who live in countries where freedom of expression is taken for granted. The leaders of totalitarian nations understand this very well. The proof is that words are precisely the action for which dissidents in those countries are being persecuted.

Nonetheless, we can already see dramatic, world-wide advances in the protection of the individual from the arbitrary power of the state. For us to ignore this trend would be to lose influence and moral authority in the world. To lead it will be to regain the moral stature that we once had.

The great democracies are not free because we are strong and prosperous. I believe we are strong and influential and prosperous because we are free.

Throughout the world today, in free nations and in totalitarian countries as well, there is a preoccupation with the subject of human freedom, human rights. And I believe it is incumbent on us in this country to keep that discussion, that debate, that contention alive. No other country is as well qualified as we to set an example. We have our own shortcomings and faults, and we should strive constantly and with courage to make sure that we are legitimately proud of what we have. . . .

Let me conclude by summarizing: Our policy is based on an historical vision of America's role. Our policy is derived from a larger view of global change. Our policy is rooted in our moral values, which never change. Our policy is reinforced by our material wealth and by our military power. Our policy is designed to serve mankind. And it is a policy that I hope will make you proud to be an American.

DOCUMENT 8.8

PRESIDENT JIMMY CARTER ANNOUNCES THE CAMP DAVID ACCORDS, SEPTEMBER 18, 1978

It's been more than 2,000 years since there was peace between Egypt and a free Jewish nation. If our present expectations are realized, this year we shall see such peace again.

The first thing I would like to do is to give tribute to the two men who made this impossible dream now become a real possibility, the two great leaders with whom I have met for the last two weeks at Camp David: first President Anwar Sadat of Egypt, and the other, of course, is Prime Minister Menachem Begin of the nation of Israel.

I know that all of you would agree that these are two men of great personal courage, representing nations of peoples who are deeply grateful to them for the achievement which they have realized. And I am personally grateful to them for what they have done.

At Camp David, we sought a peace that is not only of vital importance to their own two nations but to all the people of the Middle East, to all the people of the United States, and, indeed, to all the world as well.

The world prayed for the success of our efforts, and I am glad to announce to you that these prayers have been answered.

I've come to discuss with you tonight what these two leaders have accomplished and what this means to all of us.

SOURCE: *Public Papers of the Presidents: Jimmy Carter, 1978*, 1553–57.

The United States has had no choice but to be deeply concerned about the Middle East and to try to use our influence and our efforts to advance the cause of peace. For the last thirty years, through four wars, the people of this troubled region have paid a terrible price in suffering and division and hatred and bloodshed. No two nations have suffered more than Egypt and Israel. But the dangers and the costs of conflicts in this region for our own Nation have been great as well. We have long-standing friendships among the nations there and the peoples of the region, and we have profound moral commitments which are deeply rooted in our values as a people.

The strategic location of these countries and the resources that they possess mean that events in the Middle East directly affect people everywhere. We and our friends could not be indifferent if a hostile power were to establish domination there. In few areas of the world is there a greater risk that a local conflict could spread among other nations adjacent to them and then, perhaps, erupt into a tragic confrontation between us super powers ourselves.

Our people have come to understand that unfamiliar names like Sinai, Aqaba, Sharm el Sheikh, Ras en Naqb, Gaza, the West Bank of Jordan, can have a direct and immediate bearing on our well-being as a nation and our hope for a peaceful world. That is why we in the United States cannot afford to be idle bystanders and why we have been full partners in the search for peace and why it is so vital to our Nation that these meetings at Camp David have been a success.

Through the long years of conflict, four main issues have divided the parties involved.

One is the nature of peace—whether peace will simply mean that the guns are silenced, that the bombs no longer fall, that the tanks cease to roll, or whether it will mean that the nations of the Middle East can deal with each other as neighbors and as equals and as friends, with a full range of diplomatic and cultural and economic and human relations between them. That's been the basic question. The Camp David agreement has defined such relationships, I'm glad to announce to you, between Israel and Egypt.

The second main issue is providing for the security of all the parties involved, including, of course, our friends, the Israelis, so that none of them need fear attack or military threats from one another. When implemented, the Camp David agreement, I'm glad to announce to you, will provide for such mutual security.

Third is the question of agreement on secure and recognized boundaries, the end of military occupation, and the granting of self-government or else the return to other nations of territories which have been occupied by Israel since the 1967 conflict. The Camp David agreement, I'm glad to announce to you, provides for the realization of all these goals.

And finally, there is the painful human question of the fate of the Palestinians who live or who have lived in these disputed regions. The Camp David agreement guarantees that the Palestinian people may participate in the resolution of the Palestinian problem in all its aspects, a commitment that Israel has made in writing and which is supported and appreciated, I'm sure, by all the world. . . .

We all remember the hopes for peace that were inspired by President Sadat's initiative, that great and historic visit to Jerusalem last November that thrilled the world, and by the warm and genuine personal response of Prime Minister Begin and the Israeli people, and by the mutual promise between them, publicly made, that there would be no more war. These hopes were sustained when Prime Minister Begin reciprocated by visiting Ismailia on Christmas Day. That progress continued, but at a slower and slower pace through the early part of the year. And by early summer, the negotiations had come to a standstill once again.

It was this stalemate and the prospect for an even worse future that prompted me to invite both President Sadat and Prime Minister Begin to join me at Camp David. . . .

When this conference began, I said that the prospects for success were remote. Enormous barriers of ancient history and nationalism and suspicion would have to be overcome if we were to meet our objectives. But President Sadat and Prime Minister Begin have overcome these barriers, exceeded our fondest expectations, and have signed two agreements that hold out the possibility of resolving issues that history had taught us could not be resolved.

The first of these documents is entitled "A Framework for Peace in the Middle East Agreed at Camp David." It deals with a comprehensive settlement . . . between Israel and all her neighbors, as well as the difficult question of the Palestinian people and the future of the West Bank and the Gaza area.

The agreement provides a basis for the resolution of issues involving the West Bank and Gaza during the next five years. It outlines a process of change which is in keeping with Arab hopes, while also carefully respecting Israel's vital security.

The Israeli military government over these areas will be withdrawn and will be replaced with a self-government of the Palestinians who live there. And Israel has committed that this government will have full autonomy. Prime Minister Begin said to me several times, not partial autonomy, but full autonomy.

Israeli forces will be withdrawn and redeployed into specified locations to protect Israel's security. The Palestinians will further participate in determining their own future through talks in which their own elected representatives, the inhabitants of the West Bank and Gaza, will negotiate with Egypt and Israel and Jordan to determine the final status of the West Bank and Gaza.

Israel has agreed, has committed themselves, that the legitimate rights of the Palestinian people will be recognized. After the signing of this framework last night, and during the negotiations concerning the establishment of the Palestinian self-government, no new Israeli settlements will be established in this area. The future settlements issue will be decided among the negotiating parties. . . .

Finally, this document also outlines a variety of security arrangements to reinforce peace between Israel and her neighbors. This is, indeed, a comprehensive and fair framework for peace in the Middle East, and I'm glad to report this to you.

The second agreement is entitled "A Framework for the Conclusion of a Peace Treaty Between Egypt and Israel." It returns to Egypt its full exercise of sovereignty over the Sinai Peninsula and establishes several security zones, recognizing . . . sovereignty rights for the protection of all parties. It also provides that Egypt will extend full diplomatic recognition to Israel at the time the Israelis complete an interim withdrawal from most of the Sinai. . . .

None of us should underestimate the historic importance of what has already been done. This is the first time that an Arab and an Israeli leader have signed a comprehensive framework for peace. It contains the seeds of a time when the Middle East, with all its vast potential, may be a land of human richness and fulfillment, rather than a land of bitterness and continued conflict. No region in the world has greater natural and human resources than this one, and nowhere have they been more heavily weighed down by intense hatred and frequent war. These agreements hold out the real possibility that this burden might finally be lifted.

But we must also not forget the magnitude of the obstacles that still remain. The summit exceeded our highest expectations, but we know that it left many difficult issues which are still to be resolved. These issues will require careful negotiation in the months to come. The Egyptian and Israeli people must recognize the tangible benefits that peace will bring and support the decisions their leaders have made, so that a secure and a peaceful future can be achieved for them. The American public, you and I, must also offer our full support to those who have made decisions that are difficult and those who have very difficult decisions still to make. . . .

Finally, let me say that for many years the Middle East has been a textbook for pessimism, a demonstration that diplomatic ingenuity was no match for intractable human conflicts. Today we are privileged to see the chance for one of the sometimes rare, bright moments in human history—a chance that may offer the way to peace. We have a chance for peace, because these two brave leaders found within themselves the willingness to work together to seek these lasting prospects for peace, which we all want so badly. And for that, I hope that you will share my prayer of thanks and my hope that the promise of this moment shall be fully realized.

The prayers at Camp David were the same as those of the shepherd King David, who prayed in the 85th Psalm, "Wilt thou not revive us again: that thy people may rejoice in thee? . . . I will hear what God the Lord will speak: for he will speak peace unto his people, and unto his saints: but let them not return again unto folly."

And I would like to say, as a Christian, to these two friends of mine, the words of Jesus, "Blessed are the peacemakers, for they shall be the children of God."

8.9 *Time's* **Report of the Iranian Hostage Crisis, November 19, 1979**

Americans suffered a great deal of anxiety in the post-Vietnam era. Several events occurred that seemed to portray the United States as a helpless giant, unable to work its will, unable to affect events despite its military power. In Iran, in the fall of 1979, some two hundred "students" in support of the Ayatullah Ruhollah Khomeini stormed the American embassy and took 60 embassy officials and guards hostage. The scenes and stories were reminiscent of the North Vietnamese takeover of the U.S. embassy in Saigon just a few years before. Americans stood helpless as they were forced to watch on their televisions an almost daily routine of Iranian mobs burning American flags and parading American hostages before TV cameras. Many Americans expressed their belief that the incident had occurred precisely because the United States appeared weak and no longer able to use its powers to change world events. It was a painful experience that lasted 444 days.

The Carter administration pursued every avenue of diplomatic and economic pressure in an attempt to gain the release of the hostages, but all failed to achieve results. Finally, in April 1980, in what seemed a desperate act of frustration, the president ordered a military assault on Tehran. The ground commander in charge of the mission was Charles Beckwith, known to his colleagues as "Chargin' Charlie." Just before the event Beckwith remarked: "America needs a win. We need one real, real bad." The mission was a disaster from the beginning. A sandstorm brought down two helicopters, and in the confusion to abort the mission, a C-130 collided with a helicopter, killing eight. Secretary of State Cyrus Vance, who opposed the operation from its inception, resigned, and the press accused Carter of undertaking the mission simply to shore up his sagging approval ratings in the polls. America seemed impotent.

The Iranian Hostage Crisis was instrumental in bringing down the Democratic administration and the rise of Ronald Reagan in 1981. The hostages were finally released the day Reagan was inaugurated. In *Time* magazine's initial report on the incident (*Document 8.9*), the tone is clear. The United States, it seemed, had become a helpless giant in the malaise of the post-Vietnam era.

DOCUMENT 8.9

TIME'S REPORT OF THE IRANIAN HOSTAGE CRISIS, NOVEMBER 19, 1979

It was an ugly, shocking image of innocence and impotence, of tyranny and terror, of madness and mob rule. Blindfolded and bound, employees of the U.S. embassy in Tehran were paraded last week before vengeful crowds while their youthful captors gloated and jeered. On a gray Sunday morning, students invoking the name of Iran's Ayatullah Ruhollah Khomeini invaded the embassy, overwhelmed its Marine Corps guards and took some 60 Americans as hostages. Their demand: surrender the deposed Shah of Iran, currently under treatment in Manhattan for cancer of the lymphatic system and other illnesses, as the price of the Americans' release. While flatly refusing to submit to such outrageous blackmail, the U.S. was all but powerless to free the victims. As the days passed, nerves became more frayed and the crisis deepened. So far as was known, the hostages had been humiliated but not harmed. Yet with demonstrators chanting "Death to America" outside the compound, there was no way to guarantee that the event would not have a violent ending.

In Washington, there were round-the-clock meetings of the National Security Council. At the State Department's operations center, Iranian specialists frantically tried to keep in touch with Tehran and with the few American officials who were not in the students' hands. In New York City, the United Nations Security Council convened in special closed session to search for a solution. Said Jimmy Carter to reporters on Thursday: "These last two days have been the worst I've had." Secretary of State Cyrus Vance counseled the nation grimly and correctly: "It is a time not for rhetoric, but for quiet, careful and firm diplomacy. . . ."

SOURCE: *Time*, November 19, 1979.

The seizure of the embassy and its staff was an ugly permutation of the acts of political terrorism to which the world has grown increasingly accustomed. Most Iranians detest the Shah for the excesses of his regime, and what they feel was his plundering of their country. Many objected to the Carter Administration's decision to admit him to the U.S. under any circumstances. But the students who attacked the U.S. mission were not political adventurers with a lonely, unpopular cause. They were citizens of a state that maintains diplomatic relations with the U.S. Their invasion of the embassy violated a principle of diplomatic immunity that even the most radical and hostile governments have professed to respect. Most important of all, their action was condoned—if not instigated—by Khomeini, Iran's *de facto* head of state and a leader who himself had sought and received political asylum in the West.

For the Administration—and for President Carter personally—the seizure of the embassy was a nightmare. . . . However the crisis ends, it seems likely to enhance the impression of American helplessness. That image is not merely the stuff from which demagoguery is made; it is also the serious preoccupation of political and military analysts who are fearful that an impression of U.S. impotence, however unfair or simplistic, may provoke other probes of the nation's will, other attacks. In the long run, it could create a willingness on the part of the Soviet Union to risk new adventures, ones with serious world implications.

That is the concern of former Secretary of Defense James Schlesinger [in the Nixon administration]. In an interview last week with *Time* Diplomatic Correspondent Strobe Talbott, Schlesinger described the fall of the Shah last January and the rise of Khomeini as "a cataclysm for American foreign policy—the first serious revolution since 1917 in terms of world impact." Said Schlesinger: "It is plain that respect for the U.S. would be higher if we didn't just fumble around continuously and weren't half-apologetic about whatever we do. An image

Iranian demonstrators, atop the U.S. embassy in Tehran, burn an American flag. The violent actions and virulent anti-Americanism of the Iranians shocked U.S. citizens. © *Philippe Ledru/Sygma/Corbis Images*

of weakness is going to elicit this kind of behavior. Wild as the Ayatullah seems to be, he would not dare to touch the Soviet embassy. The point is that the Soviets are in a position, and of a disposition, not to take such events lying down. The fact of the matter is, as Mr. Nixon used to say, if we want to be a pitiful, helpless giant, we're well on the way to seeming to be one."

As for Carter, he knew that the attack in Iran would inevitably worsen his "leadership" problem and make his quest for a second term more difficult. The circumstances required a restrained response and infinite patience; yet this very stance would reinforce the public's perception of the President as a poor leader. Carter must have recognized the potential damage to his candidacy, but concluded that he had little choice but to act as he did.

As frustration about the plight of the hostages increased, there was a sense that the Administration should do something—anything—to free them. The White House, for sound tactical and strategic reasons, rejected the military options. There were demands for the mass deportation of the 50,000 Iranian students in the U.S.—or at least those who had taken advantage of their visas to picket and demonstrate against the U.S. That was also rejected, since it would blatantly violate U.S. immigration laws. Instead, as it has had to do in a number of other recent crises, the Administration decided on restraint. . . .

The decision [to allow the Shah to come to the U.S. for medical treatment] was not taken lightly. Most Iran specialists in the State Department, buttressed by warnings from the embassy in Tehran, were convinced that the Shah should not be allowed into the U.S. even for emergency medical care. They cited explicit threats from members of the Revolutionary Council as well as from the Iranian embassy in Washington. Under Secretary of State for Political Affairs David Newsom, who is in charge of day-to-day U.S. policy toward Iran, agreed with that assessment. He sought to persuade Secretary of State Cyrus Vance that, regardless of political and humanitarian motives, the granting of even a temporary visa to the Shah would have devastating consequences for American interests in Iran. Vance disagreed, and advised the President to grant the Shah a temporary visa. Carter was glad to make the humanitarian gesture. The Tehran government was assured that the Shah was indeed a sick man, that his visit was not a ruse to seek permanent residency and had no political purpose. Iranian authorities warned that the Shah's medical pilgrimage could have "negative consequences. . . . "

After the Shah's arrival in New York in late October, Iranian students in the U.S. launched a series of protests. . . . Far more ominous was the fusillade of anti-American rhetoric launched by Ayatullah Khomeini. Denouncing the U.S. as "the great Satan," he compared the relationship between the U.S. and Iran to "the friendship between a wolf and a lamb. . . . "

On Sunday, Nov. 4, hundreds of protesters gathered in downtown Tehran outside the U.S. embassy, a 27-acre compound surrounded by ten- and twelve-foot brick walls and secured with metal gates. The students, most of whom were unarmed, chanted anti-American slogans and carried banners: DEATH TO AMERICA IS A BEAUTIFUL THOUGHT and GIVE US THE SHAH. At the very hour at which the demonstration was taking place in Tehran, the Ayatullah Khomeini was [telling students] in the holy city of Qum, some 80 miles to the south, that foreign "enemies" were plotting against the Iranian revolution. Repeatedly, he charged that the American embassy in his country's capital was "a nest of spies" and "a center of intrigue."

That was all the inspiration the students needed. Just before 11 a.m., someone with a pair of powerful shears managed to break the chain that held together the gates on Taleghani Street, and the crowd surged through. Once inside the compound, some headed for the ambassador's residence, where the servants offered

no resistance (there has been no U.S. ambassador in Tehran since William Sullivan left in April). Others tried to take over the chancellery but found it protected with armor plating and grillwork. Using bullhorns, they shouted at the occupants: "Give up and you won't be harmed! If you don't give up, you will be killed!" As the attackers struggled to get inside, other protesters and a crowd of curiosity seekers clambered over the embassy walls and swarmed through the compound. . . .

The Carter Administration found itself woefully short of ways to deal with the crisis. It quickly ruled out a Mayaguez- or Entebbe-style attack as impractical under the circumstances. Nor did the Administration have the option of undertaking any kind of covert action inside Iran that might have tempered the situation. When the Shah fell last January, most of the U.S. intelligence apparatus in Iran fell along with him. Confessed one Washington official: "We have reviewed our assets and our options, and they are precious few. . . . "

Late in the week, Carter postponed a scheduled trip to Canada because he wanted to stay in close touch with his foreign policy advisers. He called for the meeting of the U.N. Security Council, at which members adopted a resolution expressing concern over the detention of the American diplomats, and he asked several of Iran's Muslim neighbors, including Pakistan, for help. Fresh offers of assistance poured in. The Shah passed the word that he was willing to leave the U.S., leading Egyptian President Anwar Sadat—who had denounced the seizure of the hostages as "a disgrace to Islam"—to offer to send his private jet to fly the ailing monarch to Cairo. Retired Heavyweight Champion Muhammad Ali announced he would be willing to exchange himself for the prisoners. Said Ali: "I'm a Muslim, and I am known and loved in Iran." Intrigued, State Department officials suggested that Ali try out his offer on the Iranian embassy in Washington. Pope John Paul II dispatched a personal envoy, ProNuncio Annibale Bugnini, to Qum to meet with Khomeini, but the Ayatullah said he could do nothing unless the U.S. extradited the Shah.

Uncertainty and lack of knowledge contributed to the tension. Carter met with relatives of the hostages, tried to reassure them and discussed some of the problems the U.S. was facing. As Scoop Jackson described the dilemma: "Who do you talk to? Who do you deal with? It's a situation of great instability. You don't know what's going to happen from one moment to the next." One White House aide expressed his anxiety in the jargon of the Pentagon's war gamers: "It's a classic case of gaming versus an irrational opponent. As the irrationality approaches 100%, your ability to game nears zero. . . . "

However the embassy affair ends, it is a sharp reminder of the degree to which the traditional rules of international conduct can no longer be taken for granted. The world is changing; the unpredictable is becoming the commonplace.

CHAPTER 9

·····················

The Reagan Era, the Gulf War, and the New World Order

9.1 President Ronald Reagan's "Evil Empire" Speech, March 8, 1983

9.2 President Ronald Reagan's "Star Wars" Speech, March 23, 1983

9.3 Senator Christopher J. Dodd's Opposition to Ronald Reagan's Central American Policy, April 28, 1983

9.4 Pat Buchanan, "How the Gulf Crisis Is Rupturing the Right," August 1990

9.5 Congressman Stephen Solarz, "The Stakes in the Gulf," January 1991

9.6 President George H. W. Bush, "The Challenge of Building Peace: A Renewal of History," September 23, 1991

9.7 U.S. Department of State, Country Reports on Human Rights Practices for 1996

9.8 China Responds, *China Daily,* March 5, 1997

9.9 Secretary of State Madeline Albright on the Legacy of the Marshall Plan, Harvard Commencement Address, June 5, 1997

9.10 President Bill Clinton, "Remarks by the President on Foreign Policy," San Francisco, February 26, 1999

9.11 President George W. Bush, September 11, 2001 Evening Address to the Nation

1981–2001 Timeline

January 1981	1981	Ronald Reagan becomes president
March 8, 1983	1982	Reagan's "Evil Empire" speech
March 23, 1983	1983	Reagan's "Star Wars" speech
	1984	
April 28, 1983	1985	Senator Christopher Dodd opposes Reagan's Central American policy
January 1989	1986	George H. W. Bush becomes president
August 2, 1990	1987	Saddam Hussein invades Kuwait
August 1990	1988	Pat Buchanan, "How the Gulf Crisis Is Rupturing the Right"
October 3, 1990	1989	Reunification of Germany
	1990	
1991	1991	USSR collapses
January 1991	1992	Stephen Solarz, "The Stakes in the Gulf"
January 1993	1993	Bill Clinton becomes president

1996	1994	Department of State reports on human rights practices
March 5, 1997	1995	*China Daily* response
June 5, 1997	1996	Madeline Albright on the Marshall Plan
February 26, 1999	1997	Clinton, foreign policy speech
March 24, 1999	1998	NATO aerial assault on Serbia
January 2001	1999	George W. Bush becomes president
September 11, 2001	2000	Terrorist attacks on US
September 11, 2001	2001	Bush, evening address to the nation

9.1 **President Ronald Reagan's "Evil Empire" Speech, March 8, 1983**

9.2 **President Ronald Reagan's "Star Wars" Speech, March 23, 1983**

9.3 **Senator Christopher J. Dodd's Opposition to Ronald Reagan's Central American Policy, April 28, 1983**

In November 1980, Ronald Reagan rode Carter's troubles to victory. During the election campaign he asked the American people, "Is the United States stronger and more respected than it was three and a half years ago? Is the world today a safer place in which to live?" But Carter's problems were immediately transferred to Reagan's own administration in 1981. The nation's problems, however, were born more from a reticence toward world affairs than any Carter administration policy. The Vietnam experience, still fresh in the nation's collective mind, had made the nation unsure of itself, of its power in certain situations, and of its abilities to work its will in the world. Reagan seemed to understand that. He knew that the nation needed strong leadership. He told a reporter in 1980 that he was certain he would succeed as president "for one simple reason. . . . The American people want somebody in command." In the early 1980s Reagan's strong leadership translated into a new aggressiveness that threatened to open old cold war wounds between the United States and the Soviets, end détente, and begin another dangerous phase in the cold war.

On March 8, 1983 Reagan told the Annual Convention of the National Association of Evangelicals in Orlando, Florida that the Soviet Union continued to act with the "aggressive impulses of an evil empire." He argued that the United States should not enter into any nuclear freeze agreements with the Soviets, and that peace would be attained only through strength. This speech (*Document 9.1*) came to epitomize Reagan's view of the Soviet Union, and it set the tone for the U.S. foreign policy toward the Soviets for the next six years. It also reflected Reagan's long-held view that the Soviet Union would soon collapse. Later that same month, Reagan spoke to the nation again. This time he defended an increase in the military budget, and then, near the end of the speech, explained his plan for a missile defensive shield that would protect the United States from a nuclear attack. By the end of March, Soviet Premier Yuri Andropov was calling Reagan "irresponsible" and "insane."

This plan, called the Strategic Defense Initiative by the administration (but Star Wars by the press and the administration's critics) was a source of controversy through most of the 1980s. Billions of dollars were pumped into what was considered by many to be questionable science that produced very few results. But what most Americans did not understood was that Reagan's Star Wars had forced the Soviets to outlay massive amounts of their financial resources in an attempt to keep up with the new American initiative. By the end of the decade, the Soviet economy began to slip, at least in part because of their attempt to keep up with Star Wars—or at least what they perceived Star Wars to be. Reagan's Star Wars plan undoubtedly contributed to the collapse of the Soviet Union. President Reagan's "Star Wars" speech (as it is commonly called) is *Document 9.2.* President George W. Bush revived the plan after he became president in 2001. At first, Bush said his objective was to deflect attacks from what his administration called "rogue states," such as North Korea or Iran; but following the September 11 attacks, the Bush administration spoke of using a Star Wars-type plan to protect the nation from terrorists.

Reagan's strident language in the early 1980s did a lot to bring an end to détente, but the Soviet invasion of Afghanistan in 1979 was the real beginning of bad U.S.–Soviet relations that lasted through the decade of the 1980s. The Soviets withdrew from Afghanistan, mostly beaten, in 1989. The United States aided the anti-Soviet Mujahedeen rebels, mostly with "Stinger" anti-aircraft weapons that were devastating to Soviet aircraft. The war was damaging to the Soviet economy that further aided in the collapse of the U.S.S.R., and it left behind in Afghanistan a civil war that fostered the emergence of a radical Islamic state that openly harbored terrorists—including Osama Bin Laden.

The nation's insecurity in the post-Vietnam era became abundantly clear when Reagan tried to involve U.S. forces in a situation in Central America that had many of the same characteristics as Vietnam. Fearing another Cuba in the Western Hemisphere, Reagan was determined to overthrow the Sandinista government in Nicaragua and defeat a group of leftist insurgents in El Salvador. The Central American force in opposition to this insurgency was the U.S.-supplied Contras. Reagan called El Salvador the "last domino."

The situation in Central America began to look more and more like the Vietnam quagmire, and in 1982 Congress specifically prohibited the Reagan administration from spending money to overthrow the Nicaraguan government. Two years later, the World Court rebuked the United States for several breaches of international law, and in 1984 Congress banned all aid to the Contras. The Reagan administration, however, continued to funnel money to the Contras, first through right-wing organizations in the United States, and then with funds accumulated from the sale of weapons to Iran. Finally, in February 1988 Congress again banned all military aid to the Contras from all sources. Reagan left office with the Sandinistas still in power in Nicaragua. In 1990 the anti-Sandinista candidate Violeta Barrios de Chamorro defeated the Sandinista candidate Daniel Ortega Saavedra in an election monitored closely by international observers.

Through the early 1980s, Democrats took the Reagan administration to task for exaggerating the situation in Central America, and for even causing many of the problems that existed there. In April 1983, Connecticut Senator Christopher Dodd gave the Democratic party's televised response to one of Reagan's several speeches on the supposed communist insurgency in Central America. According to Dodd, who had served in the Peace Corps in Central America, the problem in that region was poverty and not communism. Dodd's speech is *Document 9.3.*

In several other instances through the 1980s the United States sought to flex its muscles in an attempt to show the world that it remained a formidable power. In October 1983 Reagan invaded the small West Indian island of Grenada to halt what he called a Cuban communist insurgency. The rescue of a few U.S. medical students by 10,000 paratroopers against a few hundred Cuban laborers building an airfield on the vacation island did little to bring back what the nation had lost in Vietnam. Despite the "victory" in Grenada, America's once great power seemed even more in retreat.

Earlier in 1982 the United States sent a peacekeeping force into Lebanon to end a civil war there, fought, essentially, between Israel and Syria. In October, the same month as the Grenada invasion, 241 marines were killed when a terrorist blast destroyed an American barracks. Reagan immediately cut his losses and withdrew the troops. The incident seemed to show the world that the United States was still squeamish about any prolonged military involvement and would not hesitate to withdraw when the going got tough.

In April 1986 U.S. planes attacked Libya in retaliation for what was supposedly Libyan-sponsored terrorism against American soldiers in Europe. And then in December 1989, the United States launched an invasion of Panama to capture Panamanian strongman, Manuel Noriega. The invasion showed only that the U.S. military could overwhelm a Central American police force with stealth technology, massive firepower, and commando operations; it did little to pull the United States out of its post-Vietnam malaise, or raise the nation's esteem on the world stage.

America's fortune, however, changed in the summer of 1989 when communism in Eastern Europe and the Soviet Union collapsed under the weight of a rapidly weakening economy and a disintegrating society. The first hints came from Poland, where the anti-communist Solidarity party won open elections and then claimed power. In October, Hungary and Czechoslovakia overthrew their communist governments, and then Rumania. A month later the Berlin Wall, the very symbol of the cold war, was destroyed and Germany raced toward unification. Then in 1991 the Soviet Union itself broke up into the Commonwealth of Independent States, and the cold war came to an abrupt end with the United States standing alone as the victor. Reagan's evil empire was gone, and there was a New World Order for the first time since 1945.

....

DOCUMENT 9.1

PRESIDENT RONALD REAGAN'S "EVIL EMPIRE" SPEECH, MARCH 8, 1983

There is sin and evil in the world, and we're enjoined by Scripture and the Lord Jesus to oppose it with all our might. Our nation, too, has a legacy of evil with which it must deal.

SOURCE: *Public Papers of the Presidents: Ronald Reagan, 1983,* I, 362–64.

The glory of this land has been its capacity for transcending the moral evils of our past. For example, the long struggle of minority citizens for equal rights, once a source of disunity and civil war, is now a point of pride for all Americans. We must never go back. There is no room for racism, anti-Semitism, or other forms of ethnic and racial hatred in this country.

I know that you've been horrified, as have I, by the resurgence of some hate groups preaching bigotry and prejudice. Use the mighty voice of your pulpits and the powerful standing of your churches to denounce and isolate these hate groups in our midst. The commandment given us is clear and simple: "Thou shalt love thy neighbor as thyself."

But whatever sad episodes exist in our past, any objective observer must hold a positive view of American history, a history that has been the story of hopes fulfilled and dreams made into reality. Especially in this century, America has kept alight the torch of freedom, but not just for ourselves but for millions of others around the world.

And this brings me to my final point today. During my first press conference as President, in answer to a direct question, I pointed out that, as good Marxist-Leninists, the Soviet leaders have openly and publicly declared that the only morality they recognize is that which will further their cause, which is world revolution. I think I should point out I was only quoting Lenin, their guiding spirit, who said in 1920 that they repudiate all morality that proceeds from supernatural ideas—that's their name for religion—or ideas that are outside class conceptions. Morality is entirely subordinate to the interests of class war. And everything is moral that is necessary for the annihilation of the old, exploiting social order and for uniting the proletariat.

Well, I think the refusal of many influential people to accept this elementary fact of Soviet doctrine illustrates an historical reluctance to see totalitarian powers for what they are. We saw this phenomenon in the 1930s. We see it too often today.

This doesn't mean we should isolate ourselves and refuse to seek an understanding with them. I intend to do everything I can to persuade them of our peaceful intent, to remind them that it was the West that refused to use its nuclear monopoly in the forties and fifties for territorial gain and which now proposes a fifty-percent cut in strategic ballistic missiles and the elimination of an entire class of land-based, intermediate-range nuclear missiles.

At the same time, however, they must be made to understand we will never compromise our principles and standards. We will never give away our freedom. We will never abandon our belief in God. And we will never stop searching for a genuine peace. But we can assure none of these things America stands for through the so-called nuclear freeze solutions proposed by some.

The truth is that a freeze now would be a very dangerous fraud, for that is merely the illusion of peace. The reality is that we must find peace through strength.

I would agree to a freeze if only we could freeze the Soviets' global desires. A freeze at current levels of weapons would remove any incentive for the Soviets to negotiate seriously in Geneva and virtually end our chances to achieve the major arms reductions which we have proposed. Instead, they would achieve their objectives through the freeze.

A freeze would reward the Soviet Union for its enormous and unparalleled military buildup. It would prevent the essential and long overdue modernization of the United States and allied defenses and would leave our aging forces increasingly vulnerable. And an honest freeze would require extensive prior negotiations on the systems and numbers to be limited and on the measures to ensure effective verification and compliance. And the kind of a freeze that has been suggested would be virtually impossible to verify. Such a major effort would divert us completely from our current negotiations on achieving substantial reductions.

A number of years ago, I heard a young father, a very prominent young man in the entertainment world, addressing a tremendous gathering in California. It was during the time of the cold war, and communism and our own way of life were very much on people's minds. And he was speaking to that subject. And suddenly, though, I heard him say, "I love my little girls more than anything—"And I said to myself, "Oh, no, you don't. You can't—don't say that." But I had underestimated him. He went on: "I would rather see my little girls die now, still believing in God, than have them grow up under communism and one day die no longer believing in God."

There were thousands of young people in that audience. They came to their feet with shouts of joy. They had instantly recognized the profound truth in what he had said, with regard to the physical and the soul and what was truly important.

Yes, let us pray for the salvation of all those who live in that totalitarian darkness—pray they will discover the joy of knowing God. But until they do, let us be aware that while they preach the supremacy of the state, declare its omnipotence over individual man, and predict its eventual domination of all peoples on the Earth, they are the focus of evil in the modern world.

It was C.S. Lewis who, in his unforgettable "Screwtape Letters," wrote:

> The greatest evil is not done now in those sordid 'dens of crime' that Dickens loved to paint. It is not even done in concentration camps and labor camps. In those we see its final result. But it is conceived and ordered (moved, seconded, carried and minuted) in clear, carpeted, warmed, and well-lighted offices, by quiet men with white collars and cut fingernails and smooth-shaven cheeks who do not need to raise their voice.

Well, because these "quiet men" do not "raise their voices," because they sometimes speak in soothing tones of brotherhood and peace, because like other dictators before them, they're always making "their final territorial demand," some would have us accept them at their word and accommodate ourselves to their aggressive impulses. But if history teaches anything, it teaches that simple-minded appeasement or wishful thinking about our adversaries is folly. It means the betrayal of our past, the squandering of our freedom.

So, I urge you to speak out against those who would place the United States in a position of military and moral inferiority. You know, I've always believed that old Screwtape reserved his best efforts for those of you in the church. So in your discussions of the nuclear freeze proposals, I urge you to beware that temptation of pride—the temptation of blithely declaring yourselves above it all and label both sides equally at fault, to ignore the facts of history and the aggressive impulses of an evil empire, to simply call the arms race a giant misunderstanding and thereby remove yourself from the struggle between right and wrong and good and evil.

I ask you to resist the attempts of those who would have you withhold your support for our efforts, this administration's efforts, to keep America strong and free, while we negotiate real and verifiable reductions in the world's nuclear arsenals and one day, with God's help, their total elimination.

While America's military strength is important, let me add here that I've always maintained that the struggle now going on for the world will never be decided by bombs or rockets, by armies or military might. The real crisis we face today is a spiritual one; at root, it is a test of moral will and faith.

Whittaker Chambers, the man whose own religious conversion made him a witness to one of the terrible traumas of our time, the Hiss-Chambers case, wrote that the crisis of the Western World exists to the degree in which the West is indifferent to God, the degree to which it collaborates in communism's attempt to make man stand alone without God. And then he said, for Marxism-Leninism is actually the second oldest faith, first proclaimed in the Garden of Eden with the words of temptation, "Ye shall be as gods."

The Western World can answer this challenge, he wrote, "but only provided that its faith in God and the freedom He enjoins is as great as communism's faith in Man."

I believe we shall rise to the challenge. I believe that communism is another sad, bizarre chapter in human history whose last pages even now are being written. I believe this because the source of our strength in the quest for human freedom is not material, but spiritual, and because it knows no limitations, it must terrify and ultimately triumph over those who would enslave their fellow man. For in the words of Isaiah: "He giveth power to the faint; and to them that have no might He increased strength. . . . But they that wait upon the Lord shall re- new their strength; they shall mount up with wings as eagles; they shall run, and not be weary. . . ."

One of our Founding Fathers, Thomas Paine, said, "We have it within our power to begin the world over again." We can do it; doing together what no one church could do by itself.

God bless you, and thank you very much.

DOCUMENT 9.2

PRESIDENT RONALD REAGAN'S "STAR WARS" SPEECH, MARCH 23, 1983

My fellow Americans, thank you for shar- ing your time with me tonight.

The subject I want to discuss with you, peace and national security, is both timely and important. Timely, because I've reached a deci- sion which offers anew hope for our children in the 21st century, a decision I'll tell you about in a few minutes. And important because there's a very big decision that you must make for your- selves. This subject involves the most basic duty that any President and any people share, the duty to protect and strengthen the peace.

At the beginning of this year, I submitted to the Congress a defense budget which reflects my best judgment of the best understanding of the experts and specialists who advise me about what we and our allies must do to pro- tect our people in the years ahead. That budget is much more than a long list of numbers, for behind all the numbers lies America's ability to prevent the greatest of human tragedies and preserve our free way of life in a sometimes dangerous world. It is part of a careful, long- term plan to make America strong again after too many years of neglect and mistakes.

Our efforts to rebuild America's defenses and strengthen the peace began 2 years ago when we requested a major increase in the de- fense program. Since then, the amount of those increases we first proposed has been reduced by half, through improvements in management and procurement and other savings.

The budget request that is now before the Congress has been trimmed to the limits of safety. Further deep cuts cannot be made with- out seriously endangering the security of the Nation. The choice is up to the men and women you've elected to Congress, and that means the choice is up to you.

Tonight, I want to explain to you what the defense debate is all about and why I'm con- vinced that the budget now before the Con- gress is necessary, responsible, and deserving of your support. And I want to offer hope for the future. But first, let me say what the defense de- bate is not about. It is not about spending arithmetic. I know that in the last few weeks you've been bombarded with the numbers and percentages. . . .

The defense policy of the United States is based on a simple premise: The United States does not start fights. We will never be an ag- gressor. We maintain our strength in order to deter and defend against aggression—to pre- serve freedom and peace.

Since the dawn of the atomic age, we've sought to reduce the risk of war by maintaining a strong deterrent and by seeking genuine arms control. "Deterrence" means simply this: mak- ing sure any adversary who thinks about at- tacking the United States, or our allies, or our vital interest, concludes that the risks to him outweigh any potential gains. Once he under- stands that, he won't attack. We maintain the peace through our strength; weakness only in- vites aggression.

This strategy of deterrence has not changed. It still works. But what it takes to maintain de- terrence has changed. It took one kind of mili- tary force to deter an attack when, we had far more nuclear weapons than any other power; it takes another kind now that the Soviets, for ex- ample, have enough accurate and powerful nu- clear weapons to destroy virtually all of our missiles on the ground. Now, this is not to say

SOURCE *Public Papers of the Presidents: Ronald Reagan, 1983*, 437–43.

that the Soviet Union is planning to make war on us. Nor do I believe a war is inevitable—quite the contrary. But what must be recognized is that our security is based on being prepared to meet all threats.

There was a time when we depended on coastal forts and artillery batteries, because, with the weaponry of that day, any attack would have had to come by sea. Well, this is a different world, and our defenses must be based on recognition and awareness of the weaponry possessed by other nations in the nuclear age.

We can't afford to believe that we will never be threatened. There have been two world wars in my lifetime. We didn't start them and, indeed, did everything we could to avoid being drawn into them. But we were ill-prepared for both. Had we been better prepared, peace might have been preserved.

For 20 years the Soviet Union has been accumulating enormous military might. They didn't stop when their forces exceeded all requirements of a legitimate defensive capability. And they haven't stopped now. During the past decade and a half, the Soviets have built up a massive arsenal of new strategic nuclear weapons—weapons that can strike directly at the United States.

As an example, the United States introduced its last new intercontinental ballistic missile, the Minute Man III, in 1969, and we're now dismantling our even older Titan missiles. But what has the Soviet Union done in these intervening years? Well, since 1969 the Soviet Union has built five new classes of ICBM's, and upgraded these eight times. As a result, their missiles are much more powerful and accurate than they were several years ago, and they continued to develop more, while ours are increasingly obsolete. . . .

There was a time when we were able to offset superior Soviet numbers with higher quality, but today they are building as sophisticated and modern weapons as our own.

As the Soviets have increased their military power, they've been emboldened to extend that power. They're spreading their military influence in ways that can directly challenge our vital interests and those of our allies. . . .

Some people may still ask: Would the Soviets ever use their formidable military power? Well, again, can we afford to believe they won't? There is Afghanistan. And in Poland, the Soviets denied the will of the people and in so doing demonstrated to the world how their military power could also be used to intimidate. . . .

The Soviet Union is acquiring what can only be considered an offensive military force. They have continued to build far more intercontinental ballistic missiles than they could possible need simply to deter an attack. Their conventional forces are trained and equipped not so much to defend against an attack as they are to permit sudden, surprise offensives of their own.

Our NATO allies have assumed a great defense burden, including the military draft in most countries. We're working with them and our other friends around the world to do more. Our defensive strategy means we need military forces that can move very quickly, forces that are trained and ready to respond to any emergency.

Every item in our defense program—our ships, our tanks, our planes, our funds for training and spare parts — is intended for one all-important purpose: to keep the peace. Unfortunately, a decade of neglecting our military forces has called into question our ability to do that.

When I took office in January 1981, I was appalled by what I found: American planes that couldn't fly and American ships that couldn't sail for lack of spare parts and trained personnel and insufficient fuel and ammunition for essential training. The inevitable result of all this was poor morale in our Armed Forces, difficulty in recruiting the brightest young Americans to wear the uniform, and difficulty in convincing our most experienced military personnel to stay on.

There was a real question then about how well we could meet a crisis. And it was obvious that we had to begin a major modernization program to ensure we could deter aggression and preserve the peace in the years ahead.

We had to move immediately to improve the basic readiness and staying power of our conventional forces, so they could meet—and therefore help deter—a crisis. We had to make up for lost years of investment by moving forward with a long-term plan to prepare our forces to counter the military capabilities our adversaries were developing for the future.

I know that all of you want peace, and so do I. I know too that many of you seriously believe that a nuclear freeze would further the cause of peace. But a freeze now would make us less, not more, secure and would raise, not reduce, the risk of war. It would be largely unverifiable and would seriously undercut our negotiations on arms reduction. It would reward the Soviets for their massive military build up while preventing us from modernizing our aging and increasingly vulnerable forces. With their present margin of superiority, why should they agree to arms reductions knowing that we were prohibited from catching up?

Believe me, it wasn't pleasant for someone who had come to Washington determined to reduce government spending, but we had to move forward with the task of repairing our defenses or we would lose our ability to deter conflict now and in the future. We had to demonstrate to any adversary that aggression could not succeed, and that the only real solution was substantial, equitable, and effectively verifiable arms reduction—the kind we're working for right now in Geneva.

The calls for cutting back the defense budget come in nice, simple arithmetic. They're the same kind of talk that led the democracies to neglect their defenses in the 1930's and invited the tragedy of World War II. We must not let that grim chapter of history repeat itself through apathy or neglect.

This is why I'm speaking to you tonight—to urge you to tell your Senators and Congressmen that you know we must continue to restore our military strength. If we stop in midstream, we will send a signal of decline, of lessened will, to friends and adversaries alike. Free people must voluntarily, through open de-

bate and democratic means, meet the challenge that totalitarians pose by compulsion. It's up to us, in our time, to choose and choose wisely between the hard but necessary task of preserving peace and freedom and the temptation to ignore our duty and blindly hope for the best while the enemies of freedom grow stronger day by day.

The solution is well within our grasp. But to reach it, there is simply no alternative but to continue this year, in this budget, to provide the resources we need to preserve the peace and guarantee our freedom.

Now, thus far tonight I've shared with you my thoughts on the problems of national security we must face together. My predecessors in the Oval Office have appeared before you on other occasions to describe the threat posed by Soviet power and have proposed steps to address that threat. But since the advent of nuclear weapons, those steps have been increasingly directed toward deterrence of aggression through the promise of retaliation.

This approach to stability through offensive threat has worked. We and our allies have succeeded in preventing nuclear war for more than three decades. In recent months, however, my advisers, including in particular the Joint Chiefs of Staff, have underscored the necessity to break out of a future that relies solely on offensive retaliation for our security.

Over the course of these discussions, I've become more and more deeply convinced that the human spirit must be capable of rising above dealing with other nations and human beings by threatening their existence. Feeling this way, I believe we must thoroughly examine every opportunity for reducing tensions and for introducing greater stability into the strategic calculus on both sides.

One of the most important contributions we can make is, of course, to lower the level of all arms, and particularly nuclear arms. We're engaged right now in several negotiations with the Soviet Union to bring about a mutual reduction of weapons. I will report to you a week from tomorrow my thoughts on that score. But let me just say, I'm totally committed to this course.

If the Soviet Union will join with us in our effort to achieve major arms reduction, we will have succeeded in stabilizing the nuclear balance. Nevertheless, it will still be necessary to rely on the specter of retaliation, on mutual threat. And that's a sad commentary on the human condition. Wouldn't it be better to save lives than to avenge them? Are we not capable of demonstrating our peaceful intentions by applying all our abilities and our integrity to achieving a truly lasting stability? I think we are indeed. Indeed, we must.

After careful consultation with my advisers, including the Joint Chiefs of Staff, I believe there is a way. Let me share with you a vision of the future which offers hope. It is that we embark on a program to counter the awesome Soviet missile threat with measures that are defensive. Let us turn to the very strengths in technology that spawned our great industrial base and that have given us the quality of life we enjoy today.

What if free people could live secure in the knowledge that their security did not rest upon the threat of instant U.S. retaliation to deter a Soviet attack, that we could intercept and destroy strategic ballistic missiles before they reach our soil or that of our allies.

I know this is a formidable, technical task, one that may not be accomplished before the end of the century. Yet, current technology has attained a level of sophistication where it's reasonable for us to begin this effort. It will take years, probably decades of efforts on many fronts. There will be failures and setbacks, just as there will be successes and breakthroughs. And as we proceed, we must remain constant in preserving the nuclear deterrent and maintaining a solid capability for flexible response. But isn't it worth every investment necessary to free the world from the threat of nuclear war? We know this.

In the meantime, we will continue to pursue real reductions in nuclear arms, negotiating from a position of strength that can be ensured only by modernizing our strategic forces. At the same time, we must take steps to reduce the risk of a conventional military conflict escalating to nuclear war by improving our nonnuclear capabilities.

America does possess—now—the technologies to attain very significant improvements in the effectiveness of our conventional, nonnuclear forces. Proceeding boldly with these new technologies, we can significantly reduce any incentive that the Soviet Union may have to threaten attack against the United States or its allies.

As we pursue our goal of defensive technologies, we recognize that our allies rely upon our strategic offensive power to deter attacks against them. Their vital interests and ours are inextricably linked. Their safety and ours are one. And no change in technology can or will alter that reality. We must and shall continue to honor our commitments.

I clearly recognize that defensive systems have limitations and raise certain problems and ambiguities. If paired with offensive systems, they can be viewed as fostering an aggressive policy, and no one wants that. But with these considerations firmly in mind, I call upon the scientific community in our country, those who gave us nuclear weapons, to turn their great talents now to the cause of mankind and world peace, to give us the means of rendering these nuclear weapons impotent and obsolete.

Tonight, consistent with our obligations of the ABM [Anti-Ballistic Missile] treaty and recognizing the need for closer consultation with our allies, I'm taking an important first step. I am directing a comprehensive and intensive effort to define a long-term research and development program to begin to achieve our ultimate goal of eliminating the threat posed by strategic nuclear missiles. This could pave the way for arms control measures to eliminate the weapons themselves. We seek neither military superiority nor political advantage. Our only purpose—one all people share—is to search for ways to reduce the danger of nuclear war.

My fellow Americans, tonight we're launching an effort which holds the promise of changing the course of human history. There will be risks, and results take time. But I believe we can do it. As we cross this threshold, I ask for your prayers and your support.

Thank you, good night, and God bless you.

DOCUMENT 9.3

SENATOR CHRISTOPHER J. DODD'S OPPOSITION TO RONALD REAGAN'S CENTRAL AMERICAN POLICY, APRIL 28, 1983

Good evening. I want to thank the networks for an opportunity to offer a different viewpoint. While there's no unanimity in Congress—on either side of the aisle—on Central America, tonight I'm speaking for the many Americans who are concerned about our ever-deepening involvement in the military conflict in that part of the world. . . .

Let me state clearly that on some very important things, all Americans stand in agreement.

We will oppose the establishment of Marxist states in Central America. We will not accept the creation of Soviet military bases in Central America.

And, we will not tolerate the placement of Soviet offensive missiles in Central America—or anywhere in this hemisphere.

Finally, we are fully prepared to defend our security and the security of the Americas, if necessary, by military means. . . .

Those of us who oppose the President's policy believe that he is mistaken in critical ways. To begin with, we believe the Administration fundamentally misunderstands the causes of conflict in Central America. We cannot afford to found so important a policy on ignorance—and the painful truth is that many of our highest officials seem to know as little about Central American in 1983 as we knew about Indochina in 1963.

I've lived with the people in this region. Let me share some facts with you about Central America.

Most of the people there are appallingly poor. They can't afford to feed their families when they're hungry. They can't find a doctor for them when they're sick. They live in rural shacks with dirt floors or city slums without plumbing or clean water. The majority can't read or write; and many of them can't even count.

It takes all five Spanish-speaking countries of Central America more than a year to provide what this nation does . . . in less than three days. Virtually none of even that meager amount ever reaches the bulk of the people. In short, a very few live in isolated splendor while the very many suffer in shantytown squalor. In country after country, dictatorship or military dominance has stifled democracy and destroyed human rights.

If Central America were not racked with poverty, there would be no revolution. If Central America were not racked with hunger, there would be no revolution. If Central America were not racked with injustice, there would be no revolution. In short, there would be nothing for the Soviets to exploit. But unless those oppressive conditions change, the region will continue to seethe with revolution—with or without the Soviets.

Instead of trying to do something about the factions or factors which breed revolution, this Administration has turned to massive military buildups at a cost of hundreds of millions of dollars. Its policy is ever-increasing military assistance, endless military training, and further military involvement. This is a proven prescription for picking a loser. The American people know that we have been down this road before—and that it only leads to a dark tunnel of endless intervention.

Tonight the President himself told us that things were not going well in Central America. But for this, the President cannot blame Congress. We have given him what he has asked for. Seven hundred million in economic and military assistance has been delivered or is on

SOURCE: *New York Times*, April 28, 1983.

its way to El Salvador since Ronald Reagan came to office, all at his request and all with Congressional approval. . . .

Now the President asks for an even greater commitment. His requests for El Salvador alone will bring the total aid to that country during his term to more than $1 billion. . . .

What return have we received for all we have spent? The army of El Salvador has been reluctant to fight—and is led by an officer corps working a nine-to-five shift with weekends off. Land reform has been abandoned. At least 30,000 civilians have been killed and the majority of them have been victims of the Government's own security force. American nuns and labor advisors have been murdered—and the judicial system is so intimidated that it cannot even bring accused murderers to trial.

For those 30,000 murders, confirmed by our own embassy, there have been fewer than 200 convictions.

American dollars alone cannot buy military victory—that is the lesson of the painful past and of this newest conflict in Central America. If we continue down that road, if we continue to ally ourselves with repression, we will not only deny our own most basic values, we will also find ourselves once again on the losing side. It is folly, pure and simple, to pursue a course which is wrong in principle—in order to wage a conflict which cannot be won.

After 30,000 deaths, after hundreds of millions of dollars, with the ante going up, with no end in sight, with no hope for any change, real change, the time has come for a different approach. Yes, we are fully prepared to be involved in Central America. But the question is the nature and quality of our involvement. We must offer an alternative policy that can work.

First, we should use the power and influence of the United States to achieve an immediate cessation of hostilities in both El Salvador and Nicaragua. Already in both countries too many people have died. It is time for the killing to stop.

Second, the United States should use all its power and influence to work for a negotiated political settlement in Central America.

In El Salvador, the rebels have offered to negotiate unconditionally. Let us test their sincerity. We certainly have the leverage to move the Government to the bargaining table. On his recent trip to that very Catholic region, the Pope lent the moral force of his office to such a step. It is practical and realistic to expect, that if we support it, these talks can get underway. And every major ally of ours in the region—Mexico, Panama, Venezuela, and Columbia—is anxious for such a step to be taken and has offered, I might add, to make the arrangements.

Those same nations have volunteered to bring Nicaragua into negotiations—and Nicaragua has agreed to talk. Instead, as we know from the present accounts, press accounts, this Administration is conducting a not-so-secret war inside that country.

No one in Congress or this country is under the delusion that the Sandinista government is a model democracy or a force for stability. But the insurgents we have supported are the remnants of the old Somoza regime—a regime whose corruption, graft, torture, and despotism made it universally despised in Nicaragua. The Sandinistas may not be winners, but right now we are backing sure losers. We are doing for the Sandinista Marxists what they could not do for themselves. We are weakening the very groups inside Nicaragua which believe in a free and democratic society, and that is the sad irony of this Administration's policy.

Third, we must restore America's role as a source of hope and a force for progress in Central America. We must help governments only if they will help their own people. We must hear the cry for bread, and schools, work, and opportunity that comes from campesinos everywhere in this hemisphere. We must make violent revolution preventable by making peaceful revolution possible. Most important, this approach would permit the United States to move with the tide of history rather than stand against it.

For us, the stakes are diplomatic, political, and strategic. But for the people of El Salvador, life itself is on the line. . . .

Two centuries ago our nation raised the light of liberty before the world—and all of this hemisphere looked to us as an example and an inspiration. In this Capitol building, from which I speak tonight, men like Daniel Webster, Henry Clay, Abraham Lincoln once spoke of an America leading the world to progress and human rights—and people everywhere listened with hope to those words. There is no greater or larger ideal than the one which was forged here in the early days of this Republic. That ideal of liberty is our greatest strength as a nation; it is a powerful and peaceful weapon against tyranny of any kind anywhere in this hemisphere.

We can take the road of military escalation. But the real question—what we really don't know—is what the next step will be, where it will lead or how much it will cost.

This much, however, we do know. It will mean greater violence. It will mean greater bloodshed. It will mean greater hostilities. And, inevitably, the day will come when it will mean a regional conflict in Central America.

When that day comes—when the "dogs of war" are loose in Central America, when the cheering has stopped—we will know where the President's appeal for more American money and a deeper American commitment has taken us. Thank you, and good night.

9.4   Pat Buchanan, "How the Gulf Crisis Is Rupturing the Right," August 1990
9.5   Congressman Stephen Solarz, "The Stakes in the Gulf," January 1991

On August 2, 1990 Saddam Hussein invaded Kuwait, and just as the cold war was coming to an end Americans were faced with a new and oppressive enemy. The events over the next seven months would propel the United States back into its self-proclaimed place as the defender of the oppressed against aggressive expansionism—while making it clear that there was only one superpower left in the world. The crushing of the Iraqi war machine, touted as the fourth largest army in the world, brought America out of the funk that was being called the Vietnam Syndrome and into the light of a new era in U.S. foreign policy.

Many Americans, however, could not forget the agony of Vietnam. As the Gulf crisis heated up there was a strong and vocal outcry against the nation's involvement. Many on the left feared another Vietnam, another quagmire of unending involvement on the Asian continent. Others claimed that America's only interests were in the Kuwaiti oil reserves, a resource hardly worthy of American lives. From the right came statements from the likes of Pat Buchanan (*Document 9.4*), who invoked many of the old isolationist arguments that the United States should look only to its affairs at home.

But the case for intervention was loud and strong. There was a New World Order, Democratic congressman Stephen Solarz contended (*Document 9.5*), and the United States could not allow a madman like Saddam Hussein to destroy those great expectations for the future—although no one quite knew what those expectations were. Despite Solarz's discussion of events in a post-cold war context, he invokes all the old cold war concepts of containment, falling dominoes, and rejection of appeasement. As Solarz mentions in his article, he was an anti-Vietnam war advocate. He was also a principal sponsor in Congress of the "Authorization for Use of Military Force Against Iraq Resolution."

The Gulf War victory seemed to give back to America something it had lost in Vietnam. For the first time in decades the United States had a new life, and it was uncontestedly the most powerful nation in the world. Much of this had to do with the simultaneous collapse of the Soviet Union and the end of the cold war, but the victory in the Gulf brought a new confidence in America. America, it seemed, was again on the right side of history.

....

DOCUMENT 9.4

PAT BUCHANAN, "HOW THE GULF CRISIS IS RUPTURING THE RIGHT," AUGUST 1990

The Gulf crisis has brought to the surface of our politics a deep fissure on the Right. On one side: the Old Right, the traditionalists who seized the GOP from the Rockefeller-Eastern Establishment for Barry Goldwater in 1964, and went on to nominate Ronald Reagan in 1980. On the other, the neoconservatives, ex-liberal Democrats who got their baptismal certificates at the Reagan transition office. For the neocons, America is already at war.

New York Times columnist Abe Rosenthal says our duty to our soon-to-be war dead is to castrate Iraq, and kill the Saddam regime. Richard Perle wants a preemptive strike on his nuclear plants. Columnist Charles Krauthammer is virtually drafting a Morgenthau Plan for pastoralization of Iraq. *The Wall Street Journal* says the relevant question is not "whether" to go to war, but "when and how." *The New Republic* urges us to find a pretext—and attack.

Henry Kissinger is point man: "A sharp and short crisis is far more in the interest of all concerned with moderation than a long siege," he writes; the "surgical and progressive destruction of Iraq's military assets" is the way to proceed.

Perhaps, the neocons will get their war. For the Israelis, who have been goading us to attack, are confidently predicting war will break out before this column appears.

Meanwhile, those of us who do not want war are being derided by our old comrades as "chicken hawks" and "isolationists."

It is time to put our cards on the table. The war for which the neocons pant has quagmire written all over it. Should the Iraqis attack, writes General John Odom, ex-head of the National Security Agency, the small U.S. force in Saudi Arabia would have a hellish time. Battles would be lost; U.S. casualties would be heavy. To stop an Iraqi invasion at the Saudi borders could require six U.S. divisions. To dig armored Iraqi troops out of Kuwait could require twelve to eighteen divisions, i.e. the entire U.S. Army. America could find herself in a Korea-style meat grinder. "It is difficult to understand," Odom writes, "the reckless enthusiasm . . . some pundits have for an early attack on Iraq."

Assume U.S. air power destroys the chemical plants of Saddam Hussein. What guarantee have we that such an attack will bring him down? But of one thing we may be sure: A preemptive strike will put the U.S. in the midst of a war producing thousands of casualties.

For what? President Bush not withstanding, it is not our "way of life" that is threatened, but our style of life. Saddam Hussein is not a madman; he is no Adolf Hitler; while a ruthless menace to his neighbors, he is no threat to us.

Mr. Rosenthal talks of Saddam's "power to threaten the world with mass destruction." This is hyperbolic nonsense. All Mr. Bush need

SOURCE: *New York Times*, August 25, 1990.

do is tell Saddam: "Use poison gas on my troops, and I will use atomic bombs on yours."

Have the neocons thought this through?

Could the shiekhs, sultans, emirs, and kings, whose thrones we defend, survive the violent upheavals that would follow a U.S. air strike igniting an American-Arab war? What would we do, if the King of Jordan were overthrown, and his successors opened a "second front?" Invade Jordan? We have been told that Israel is our "strategic asset" in the Middle East. But, when the crisis came, the asset suddenly became a huge liability, use of which would result in the total collapse of our Arab coalition. Is the counsel of people who sold us that bill of goods to be followed into war.

Given U.S. air and naval power and the might of U.S. ground forces, eventually the U.S. could smash Iraq, force withdrawal from Kuwait, declaw Saddam Hussein, if not bring him down. But who would rise from the ruins? Who would fill the power vacuum?

Are we prepared for a NATO-style treaty commitment and a huge troop presence, not only in Saudi Arabia, but Kuwait? That is what it will require to keep Iraq out. And, how would 50 million Shiites in Iran react to 50,000 American troops next door?

The West needs a stable supply of oil at predictable prices, we are told. Indeed, we do. But, war would cost, by one estimate, $1 billion a day, the equivalent, at $40 a barrel, of 25 million barrels of oil a day, or three times what we daily import, only a fraction of which comes from the Gulf. It is not Saddam Hussein who drove the price of oil above $30 a barrel, but our embargo. The Thief of Baghdad stole Kuwait's oil, not to sit on it, but to sell it. He is desperate for cash. If we lifted the embargo tomorrow, the price of oil would fall like a stone.

What is at stake, writes Brother Krauthammer, is "a new world order." Excuse me, but that sounds like the Wilsonian gobbledygook we followed into the trenches of World War I—when, all the time, the hidden agenda was to pull Britain's chestnuts out of the fire.

Before we send thousands of American soldiers to their deaths, let's make damn sure America's vital interests are threatened. That is not 1930s isolationism: it is 1990s Americanism. President Bush should keep his powder dry. Starting wars is not our tradition. Tell Saddam an attack on Saudi Arabia will not only be stopped; it will bring ruin on his country. Tell him we hold him accountable for the interned Americans. Then, let the embargo choke his economy, until he withdraws from Kuwait. It if works, it works; if it fails, it fails. Kuwait is not worth the loss of the 82nd and the 101st Airborne and that's pretty much the asking price.

DOCUMENT 9.5

CONGRESSMAN STEPHEN SOLARZ, "THE STAKES IN THE GULF," JANUARY 1991

Ironies can sometimes be painful. I began my political career in 1966 as the campaign manager for one of the first anti-war congressional candidates in the country. Now, a quarter century later, I find myself supporting a policy in the Persian Gulf that might well lead to a war that many believe could become another Vietnam. Such a position is more and more anomalous, I know, in the Democratic Party, and yet I cannot accept, or be dissuaded by, the analogy with Vietnam.

In Vietnam no vital American interests were at stake. The crisis in the Gulf poses a challenge not only to fundamental American interests, but to essential American values. In Indochina the cost in blood and treasure was out of all proportion to the expected gains from a successful defense of South Vietnam. In the Gulf the potential costs of the American commitment are far outweighed by the benefits of a successful effort to implement the U.N. resolutions calling for the withdrawal of Iraq from Kuwait. The war in Vietnam dragged on for years and ended in an American defeat. A war

SOURCE: *New Republic,* January 7 and 14, 1991.

in the Gulf, if it cannot be avoided, is likely to end with a decisive American victory in months, if not in weeks. Sometimes you are condemned to repeat the past if you do remember it—that is, if you draw the wrong lessons from it, and let the memory of the past distort your view of the present.

The United States clearly has a vital interest in preventing Saddam Hussein from getting away with his invasion and annexation of Kuwait. An aggressive Iraq bent on the absorption of its neighbors represents a serious economic threat to American interests. A hostile Iraq armed with chemical, biological, and eventually nuclear weapons represents a "clear and present danger" to American security. And a lawless Iraq represents a direct challenge to our hopes for a new and more peaceful world order. Any one of these reasons would be sufficient to justify a firm American response to this brutal and unprovoked act of aggression. Together they make a compelling case for doing whatever needs to be done, in concert with our coalition partners, to secure the withdrawal of Iraqi forces from Kuwait and to establish a more stable balance of power in one of the most volatile and strategically important parts of the world.

There is, for a start, the question of oil. If Saddam succeeds in incorporating Kuwait into Iraq, he will be in a position to control, by intimidation or invasion, the oil resources of the entire Gulf. This would enable him, and him alone, to determine not only the price, but also the production levels, of up to half the proven oil reserves in the world. This is not simply a question of the price of gas at the pump. It is a matter of the availability of the essential energy that we and our friends around the world need to heat our homes, fuel our factories, and keep our economies vigorous. . . .

Some have argued that Saddam's control of the oil resources of the Gulf would not pose an unacceptable threat to American interests, since he would presumably wish to sell the oil in order to raise revenues for his benign and malignant purposes. But Saddam would also be in a position to cut back dramatically on pro-

duction, which would give him considerable leverage over the rest of the world, while assuring, through the inflated prices that his reduced production would command, an adequate level of revenue. It would be unthinkable for the United States to permit a rampaging dictator like Saddam to have his hands on the economic jugular of the world.

Far more important than the question of oil, however, is the extent to which, in American constitutional terms, Saddam is a "clear and present danger." This is a man who twice in the last decade has led his country into war, first against Iran in 1980, and then against Kuwait in 1990. Driven by an uncontrollable appetite for power, and by the ideological imperatives of the Baath party, which is committed to unifying the Arab nations under Iraqi control, he is determined to dominate the entire Middle East. President Bush's parallels between Saddam and Hitler are wildly overdrawn. But if there are fundamental differences between Saddam and Hitler, there are also instructive similarities. Like Hitler, Saddam has an unappeasable will to power combined with a ruthless willingness to employ whatever means are necessary to achieve it.

Having stood up to the combined opposition of the superpowers, the Security Council, and the Arab League, Saddam's sense of invincibility will certainly swell—and the stage would be set for more campaigns of conquest and annexation. Moreover, if Saddam prevails in the current crisis, he might eventually pose a direct threat to the United States itself; it would be unacceptable to live in the shadow of an irrational man's nuclear arsenal, even if it is much smaller than our own. . . . Saddam is probably not in a position to produce a nuclear weapon within the next year, but he may well be able to do so in five to ten years. If we do not stop him now, we will almost certainly be obligated to confront him later, when he will be chillingly more formidable.

How, in the context of a political resolution of the Gulf crisis, can we deal with the threat of Iraq's destabilizing weapons of mass destruction?

Ironically, they will pose less of a problem if it should come to war, since Baghdad's chemical, biological, and nuclear facilities would be high-priority targets, and its capacity to use these instruments of demonic destruction would be crippled for a long time to come. There is a real danger, however, that a peaceful resolution of the crisis would leave Saddam with his terrible arsenal intact, and his efforts to acquire nuclear weapons proceeding apace. Such an outcome would buy a Pyrrhic victory. The Bush administration has so far failed to account this problem the priority it deserves. Some will point out that we have lived for many decades with other countries possessing such weapons and have not felt compelled to insist upon their dismantlement. Why should we be any more concerned about the acquisition of nuclear weapons by Iraq than by Pakistan, India, Brazil, Argentina, or South Africa? The answer is that although the nuclear programs of these other countries are a source of legitimate concern, none of them has already used weapons of mass destruction. Apologists for Iraq have argued further that our anxieties are misplaced, inasmuch as Iraq is a signatory to the nuclear Nonproliferation Treaty; but Baghdad used chemical weapons in spite of its signature on the treaty prohibiting their use. In the matter of treaties, Iraq is not exactly to be trusted; and an accomplished sinner like Saddam will not be overly tormented by breaking his own word. . . .

The third reason for thwarting Saddam's ambitions lies in our hopes for the establishment of a new world order. How we resolve the first crisis of the post-Cold War world will have profound historical consequences. Will this be a world in which relations among nations are governed by the rule of law, or will it be a Hobbesian world? Will it be a world in which the strong continue to dominate the weak, or will considerations of justice prevail over realities of force? Had the world responded with collective action when Japan invaded Manchuria, when Italy invaded Abyssinia, and when Hitler occupied the Rhineland, we might have been spared some of history's worst

horrors. If we succeed in our efforts to secure the withdrawal of Iraqi forces and the restoration of the legitimate government of Kuwait through concerted international action, we will have created a powerful precedent for a much more peaceful world in the future. But if Saddam prevails, the word will have gone out to despots around the globe that the old rules still apply, that aggression still pays. . . .

The crisis provides a rare opportunity, perhaps the first since the dawn of the modern age, to create a world order in which the international community upholds the sanctity of existing borders and the principle that nations should not be permitted to invade and to annex their weaker neighbors. The overwhelming votes in the U.N. Security Council demonstrate that there is, at last, an international consensus in favor of this objective. They also suggest that the dream of Franklin Roosevelt and the other founders of the United Nations, that the world organization could be used by the great powers as a mechanism for the preservation of peace, is being realized. . . . For those who believed that there are no differences among nations that cannot be resolved diplomatically, there is always the hope of a negotiated settlement. But we must not generalize from our own fond norms. So far Saddam has not given any indication of a willingness to withdraw entirely and unconditionally from what his propaganda calls the nineteenth province of Iraq. An odd assortment of international itinerants, including Javier Perez de Cuellar and Kurt Waldheim, King Hussein of Jordan and Yasir Arafat, Yevgeny Primakov, Willy Brandt and Yasuhiro Nakasone, Muhammad Ali and Jesse Jackson have all beaten a path to Baghdad, only to return without anything to show for their efforts (except a handful of hostages who would have been released anyway when Saddam concluded that they were no longer valuable to him as a shield against attack). I strongly suspect that James Baker, even if he travels to Baghdad, is no more likely to come home with his pockets full of concessions.

More to the point, what exactly is there to negotiate about? Some have suggested that we offer Bubiyan and Warba, the two Kuwaiti islands that block Saddam's unfettered access to the Persian Gulf, as well as the Rumaila oil fields, just south of the Iraqi border, in exchange for Saddam's withdrawal from the rest of Kuwait. But Kuwait, Saudi Arabia, a majority of the Arab League, the Security Council of the United Nations, and the Bush administration have all rightly rejected this idea, on the grounds that it would be a reward for aggression and set the stage for additional acts of banditry.

Saddam himself has attempted to link the question of an Iraqi withdrawal from Kuwait to an Israeli withdrawal from the West Bank and Gaza, or at least to the convening of an international conference to resolve the Palestinian problem. It should be obvious that this is simply an attempt to sow the seeds of discord among the countries arrayed against him. The two are entirely different issues. Iraq's invasion of Kuwait in 1990 was an unprovoked act of aggression, whereas Israel came into possession of the territories only after it was attacked by a coalition of Arab countries in 1967. Saddam did not invade Kuwait to help the Palestinians, but to maximize his own power. He is not moved by the plight of the Palestinians, or by anybody elses plight. He is merely exploiting it. And the Palestinians seem happy to assist in their own exploitation. . . .

Those who are anxious about the unanticipated consequences of a war have focused attention on the casualties that would result, even from a relatively brief and decisive campaign. I yield to nobody in my concern for American lives; but we must face the hard truth that whatever the casualties we might suffer, they are likely to be far smaller than those that would be inflicted upon us if we postpone the day of reckoning until Saddam has added nuclear weapons to his current arsenal of chemical and biological weapons. Forcefully denying Saddam the instruments of a nuclear war is itself an expression of concern for American lives. And if the maintenance of a large-scale American presence in the Gulf is a source of fiscal and political anxiety, surely we will be obligated to station a

much larger deterrent force in the region if we permit Saddam and his army to remain in Kuwait than if we destroy much of his military and his weapons of mass destruction in the process of liberating Kuwait.

Others have suggested that even if we cannot force Saddam out of Kuwait, we can contain his expansionist tendencies and insulate the rest of the region from his marauding ambitions by permanently stationing American troops in the Gulf. They remind us that we contained Soviet and North Korean expansion for forty years and ask why a policy of containment cannot work in the Middle East. These critics are rather Panglossian about the realities of the Middle East. In Europe and on the Korean peninsula, the presence of American forces contributed to the stability of the countries we were trying to defend. In the Arab world, the long-term presence of many American troops would be almost certainly destabilizing.

It is doubtful, moreover, that Saudi Arabia, which is the most conservative Islamic society in the world, would permit us to maintain a sizable presence in the country for any appreciable period. The Saudis are right: if we keep our troops in the region, we may end up contributing unwittingly to the downfall of the very regimes that we set out to defend. And if we have brought 400,000 American troops to Saudi Arabia to force the Iraqis out of Kuwait, and then accept Baghdad's annexation of Kuwait as a *fait accompli,* the Saudis are unlikely to have much confidence in our willingness to defend them, and will be more likely to seek their security in a vassal relationship with Iraq. Just as we resisted the Finlandization of Europe, we must resist the Saddamization of the Middle East.

If the president concludes that the sanctions are not likely to work, that there is no realistic prospect of an acceptable political settlement, and that we have no alternative but to use force, it will be essential for him to go to war multilaterally rather than unilaterally. The liberation of Kuwait and the elimination of the Iraqi threat is not only an American responsibility. Our Arab and European coalition partners have just as much—indeed, some of them have more—at stake than we do. It is one thing to be the head of an international posse attempting to deprive a criminal state of the rewards of its aggression. It is quite another for the United States to arrogate to itself the role of policeman of the world. The former is a task that the American people can understand and accept. The latter is an assignment that they do not seek. . . .

If the president does decide on the use of force, it will be important for him to have the support not only of our coalition partners, but also of Congress. There is no more fateful decision a nation can make than that of risking the lives of its men and women by going to war. It would be a serious constitutional and political mistake on the part of the president if he were to commit our forces to combat (in the absence of an unexpected provocation, such as a preemptive Iraqi attack) without congressional authorization. And there is another reason why the president should seek the support of Congress. If we go to war and if we win a quick and decisive victory, as is quite probable, the fact that the president did not seek the prior approval of Congress may become a source of debate among historians and columnists, but is not likely to hurt the president seriously with either Congress or the American people. But war is unpredictable, and we may get bogged down in a protracted conflict. Under those circumstances, with casualties beginning to mount, the president's ability to sustain support for the war will be gravely compromised if he fails to secure the authorization of Congress before hostilities begin.

A half century ago, when Hitler invaded Poland, the British House of Commons gathered to debate what course Britain should follow. After a halting defense of government policy by Nevile Chamberlain, one of the opposition MPs rose and began his remarks with the phrase, "Speaking for the Labor Party . . ." Instantly a voice thundered from the back benches: "Speak for England!" It is time to remember this advice. The crisis in the Gulf is not a Democratic issue or a Republican issue. It is an American issue. . . .

If we succeed in blocking Saddam's ambitions and restoring Kuwait's independence, we will have preserved our continued access to a stable supply of oil. The stability of the Arab governments that have joined with us to oppose Saddam will be significantly strengthened. We will have a good chance of eliminating Saddam's weapons of mass destruction and setting back for a substantial period of time, perhaps forever, Iraq's efforts to obtain nuclear weapons. The prospects for progress in the peace process between Israel and the Arabs will be greatly enhanced. We will have reversed a monumental injustice, we will have thwarted one of the most ruthless expansionists in the world, and we will have created the basis for a new international order.

If this isn't worth fighting for, I don't know, as an American and as a Democrat, what is.

9.6 President George H. W. Bush, "The Challenge of Building Peace: A Renewal of History," September 23, 1991

In 1991, fresh from the victory over Saddam Hussein, George Bush addressed the United Nations General Assembly on his vision for the future. To him, the end of the cold war and the checking of Iraqi expansionism had established a new world order, a *Pax Universalis* he called it. And he added that the collapse of the Soviet Union had ushered in a resumption of history—a history held captive by communism for most of the twentieth century. His speech is excerpted in *Document 9.6*.

DOCUMENT 9.6

PRESIDENT GEORGE H. W. BUSH, "THE CHALLENGE OF BUILDING PEACE: A RENEWAL OF HISTORY," SEPTEMBER 23, 1991

My speech today will not sound like any you've heard from a President of the United States. I'm not going to dwell on the superpower competition that defined international politics for half a century. Instead, I will discuss the challenges of building peace and prosperity in a world leavened by the Cold War's end and the resumption of history.

Communism held history captive for years. It suspended ancient disputes; and it suppressed ethnic rivalries, nationalistic aspirations, and old prejudices. As it has been dissolved, suspended hatreds have sprung to life. People who for years have been denied their pasts have begun searching for their own identities—often through peaceful and constructive means, occasionally through factionalism and bloodshed.

This revival of history ushers in a new era, teeming with opportunities and perils. And let's begin by discussing the opportunities.

First, history's renewal enables people to pursue their natural instincts for enterprise. Communism froze that progress until its failures became too much for even its defenders to bear.

And now citizens throughout the world have chosen enterprise over envy; personal responsibility over the enticements of the state; prosperity over the poverty of central planning. . . .

Frankly, ideas and goods will travel around the globe with or without our help. The infor-

mation revolution has destroyed the weapons of enforced isolation and ignorance. In many parts of the world technology has overwhelmed tyranny, proving that the age of information can become the age of liberation if we limit state power wisely and free our people to make the best use of new ideas, inventions and insights.

By the same token, the world has learned that free markets provide levels of prosperity, growth and happiness that centrally planned economies can never offer. Even the most charitable estimates indicate that in recent years the free world's economies have grown at twice the rate of the former communist world. . . .

I cannot stress this enough: Economic progress will play a vital role in the new world. It supplies the soil in which democracy grows best.

People everywhere seek government of and by the people. And they want to enjoy their inalienable rights to freedom and property and person. . . .

The challenge facing the Soviet people now—that of building political systems based upon individual liberty, minority rights, democracy and free markets—mirrors every nation's responsibility for encouraging peaceful, democratic reform. But it also testifies to the extraordinary power of the democratic ideal.

As democracy flourishes, so does the opportunity for a third historical breakthrough: international cooperation. A year ago, the Soviet Union joined the United States and a host of other nations in defending a tiny country against aggression—and opposing Saddam Hussein. For the very first time on the matter of major importance, superpower competition was replaced with international cooperation.

The United Nations, in one of its finest moments, constructed a measured, principled, deliberate and courageous response to Saddam

SOURCE: *Public Papers of the Presidents: George Bush, 1991*, 1199–203.

Hussein. It stood up to an outlaw who invaded Kuwait, who threatened many states within the region, who sought to set a menacing precedent for the post-Cold War World. . . .

We will not revive these ideals if we fail to acknowledge the challenge that the renewal of history presents.

In Europe and Asia, nationalist passions have flared anew, challenging the borders, straining the fabric of international society. At the same time, around the world, many age-old conflicts still fester. You see signs of this tumult right here. The United Nations has mounted more peacekeeping missions in the last 36 months than during the first 43 years. And although we now seem mercifully liberated from the fear of nuclear holocaust, these smaller, virulent conflicts should trouble us all. We must face this challenge squarely: first, by pursuing the peaceful resolution of disputes now in progress; second, and more importantly, by trying to prevent others from erupting.

No one here can promise that today's borders will remain fixed for all time. But we must strive to ensure the peaceful, negotiated settlement of border disputes. We also must promote the cause of international harmony by addressing old feuds. . . .

Government has failed if citizens cannot speak their minds; if they can't form political parties freely and elect governments without coercion; if they can't practice their religion freely; if they can't raise their families in peace; if they can't enjoy just returning from their labor; if they can't live fruitful lives and, at the end of their days, look upon their achievements and their society's progress with pride.

The renewal of history also imposes an obligation to remain vigilant about new threats and old. We must expand our efforts to control nuclear proliferation. We must work to prevent the spread of chemical and biological weapons and the missiles to deliver them.

We can never say with confidence where the next conflict may arise. And we cannot promise eternal peace—not while demagogues peddle false promises to people hungry with hope; not while terrorists use our citizens as pawns, and drug dealers destroy our peoples. We, as a result—we must band together to overwhelm affronts to basic human dignity.

It is no longer acceptable to shrug and say that one man's terrorist is another man's freedom fighter. Let's put the law above the crude and cowardly practice of hostage-holding. . . .

Where institutions of freedom have lain dormant, the United Nations can offer them new life. These institutions play a crucial role in our quest for a new world order, an order in which no nation must surrender one iota of its own sovereignty; an order characterized by the rule of law rather than the resort to force; the cooperative settlement of disputes, rather than anarchy and bloodshed; and an unstinting belief in human rights.

Finally, you may wonder about America's role in the new world that I have described. Let me assure you, the United States has no intention of striving for a *Pax Americana*. However, we will remain engaged. We will not retreat and pull back into isolationism. We will offer friendship and leadership. And in short, we seek a *Pax Universalis* built upon shared responsibilities and aspirations.

To all assembled, we have an opportunity to spare our sons and daughters the sins and errors of the past. We can build a future more satisfying than any our world has ever known. The future lies undefined before us, full of promise; littered with peril. We can choose the kind of world we want; one blistered by the fires of war and subjected to the whims of coercion and chance, or one made more peaceful by reflection and choice. Take this challenge seriously. Inspire future generations to praise and venerate you, to say: On ruins of conflict, these brave men and women built an era of peace and understanding. They inaugurated a new world order, an order worth preserving for the ages.

9.7 U.S. Department of State, Country Reports on Human Rights Practices for 1996

9.8 China Responds, *China Daily*, March 5, 1997

The United States' commitment to human rights went back at least to the Carter administration. Through the 1990s, during Bill Clinton's presidency, that commitment was stepped up considerably with a series of reports on human rights practices throughout the world that singled out various nations for human rights abuses. One such report, issued by the state department in January 1997 (for the year 1996), is excerpted below as *Document 9.7*.

Occasionally, human rights violations have blocked normalized diplomatic and trade relations. That was particularly true of U.S.–Chinese relations through the 1990s. The United States continually blocked China's membership in various international trade organizations—particularly the World Trade Organization—citing human rights abuses, particularly the abuse of Chinese dissidents jailed following the 1989 pro-democracy rallies at Tiananmen Square in Beijing. China continually responded, first, that there were no such abuses; and, second, that such affairs were well beyond the business of the United States. *Document 9.8* is China's response to the state department's 1996 human rights report. The article appeared in the *China Daily*, China's English language newspaper, published by Xinhua, the government-owned news agency in Beijing.

DOCUMENT 9.7

U.S. DEPARTMENT OF STATE, COUNTRY REPORTS ON HUMAN RIGHTS PRACTICES FOR 1996

Half a century ago the building of a global structure of human rights protection was given special urgency by the unprecedented horrors of the Holocaust, of World War II, and of modern totalitarianism. So it was that the close of the war was followed by the Nuremberg Tribunals and the adoption in 1948 of the Universal Declaration of Human

SOURCE: John Shattuck, Assistant Secretary of State, U.S. Department of State, "Overview of Country Reports on Human Rights Practices for 1996," Released by the Bureau of Democracy, Human Rights, and Labor (January 30, 1997).

Rights. This effort has continued to the present day, and while it was given special impetus by the tragic events of our century, its foundations lie deep in the moral values of all humanity and the experience of oppressed people throughout history.

Throughout history, whenever fundamental human values have been assaulted by governments and their leaders, the result has come at horrific human and moral cost. That is what happened over the centuries, in every part of the world, including North America. And that is what happened in this century in the Armenian massacres, in the Nazi concentration camps, in the Soviet Gulag, in the Chinese Cultural Revolution, in the apartheid society of South Africa, in the killing fields of Cambodia, and more recently in the acts of genocide carried out in the former Yugoslavia, Rwanda, and Burundi. These and other massive human horrors, past and present, are a standing affront to civilization and all it stands for. . . .

AUTHORITARIAN REPRESSION

In 1996 patterns of repression and systemic human rights abuse continued in many countries, including some of the world's largest and most influential.

In China, where Marxist ideology has in recent years given way to economic pragmatism and increasingly robust ties of trade and commerce with the United States and many other countries, human rights abuses by a strong central Government persist in the face of legal reform efforts and economic and social change.

The Chinese Government in 1996 continued to commit widespread and well-documented human rights abuses, in violation of internationally accepted norms, stemming from the authorities' intolerance of dissent, fear of unrest, and the continuing absence of laws protecting basic freedoms. All public dissent against party and government was effectively silenced by intimidation, exile, or the imposition of prison terms, administrative detention, or house arrest. No dissidents were known to be active at year's end. Abuses included torture and mistreatment of prisoners, forced confessions, and arbitrary and lengthy incommunicado detention. Severe restrictions were also continued on freedom of speech, the press, assembly, association, religion, privacy (including coercive family planning), and worker rights. In minority areas such as Tibet and Xinjiang, controls on religion and other fundamental freedoms intensified. During 1996, Hong Kong's civil liberties and political institutions were threatened by restrictive measures taken by the Chinese Government in anticipation of Hong Kong's reversion to Chinese sovereignty in July of 1997.

In Nigeria the military council headed by General Sani Abacha, which seized power in 1993, remains in control, and its human rights performance remains dismal. Throughout the year General Abacha's Government regularly relied on arbitrary detention, arrests, and widescale harassment to silence its many critics. Security forces committed extrajudicial killings, tortured and beat suspects and detainees; prison conditions remained life threatening; and security officials continued routinely to harass human rights and democracy activists, labor leaders, environmentalists, and journalists. Nonparty local elections held in March were nullified by the Government, and numerous parliamentarians remain in jail. All these abuses occurred in a climate of infringements of freedom of speech, assembly, association, travel, and workers rights.

Cuba remains a totalitarian anachronism, where human rights deteriorated in 1996, and suppression of dissent worsened.

Despite formally ending Aung San Suu Kyi's house arrest, the military regime in Burma stepped up its "rolling repression" and systematic violation of human rights. North Korea remains an outpost of totalitarian rule.

After more than two decades in power, the Ba'thist regime exercises absolute dictatorial authority in Iraq. Elsewhere in the Middle East, repressive regimes in Iran, Syria, and Libya are responsible for the systematic denial of their citizens' basic human rights.

COUNTRIES IN TRANSITION

The extraordinary democratic revolution of the past decade is as yet unfinished. In many countries, democracy is still fragile, civil-military relations are not properly defined, elections are subject to manipulation, women cannot fully participate, and the institutions of justice and civil society that guarantee human rights over the long term have not yet fully emerged.

The picture in Russia is mixed. It continues to undergo profound transformations as its as yet unfinished democratic institutions and practices continue to evolve. July 1996 saw Russia's first-ever presidential election, and in December 1995 its second multiparty parliamentary elections. Human rights NGO's [Non-Governmental Organizations] were generally free to operate. However, prison conditions—always harsh—have worsened, and lengthy pretrial detention continued. . . .

One genuine bright spot at year's end was the withdrawal of Russian forces from Chechnya, where conflict had claimed tens of thousands of lives.

Bosnia and Herzegovina enjoyed a year of comparative peace in 1996 as implementation of the 1995 Dayton Accords proceeded. The September elections for major offices were, despite their shortcomings, an important step in solidifying the foundations of peace and establishing representative institutions.

The largest challenge facing Bosnia has been to overcome the staggering effects of three years of warfare. In 1996 the international community sought to promote reconciliation. Yet political authorities continued, in varying degrees, to violate basic human rights. Members of the security forces mistreated citizens. Judicial institutions did not function effectively, freedom of movement was restricted, refugees were not able to return to their homes, freedom of the press and expression were curtailed, and ethnic discrimination was widespread. In the Serb entity and the Croat parts of the Federation, war criminals remained at large. . . .

There was marked progress in Guatemala, where a peace accord between the Government and guerrillas ended a 36-year civil war. Some serious abuses did continue, although the Government demonstrated the political will to combat impunity, and courts have, in marked contrast to past years, convicted some members of the security services.

Haiti continued the democratic advances begun in 1994, although abuses and the poor condition of its judicial system remain issues of concern.

In the Middle East, the peace process suffered setbacks in 1996, which had negative effects on human rights in both the Occupied Territories and the areas administered by the Palestinian Authority. Terrorist acts had a deeply chilling affect on both diplomacy and human rights observance. The successful completion of elections for the Palestinian Council in March of 1996 marked a significant step in the development of Palestinian institutions; and

there was some progress towards year's end in the easing of some aspects of Israel's closure of the Territories, in increased cooperation on the ground between Israeli and Palestinian authorities, and in the talks on Israeli redeployment within Hebron, which then reached a successful conclusion in January of 1997. . . .

RELIGION

A disturbing aspect of the post-Cold War world has been the persistence, and in some cases the intensification, of religious intolerance, religious persecution, and the exploitation of religious and ethnic differences for narrow and violent ends. In 1996 many religious groups around the world continued to face persecution and other difficulties in practicing their faiths and maintaining their cultural loyalties.

In China the Government intensified its policy of severely restricting and bringing under official control all religious groups, including Christians, Muslims, and Buddhists.

Christians are subject to difficulties ranging from interference to outright persecution in many countries, including Iraq, Pakistan, and the Sudan. In Cuba persecution continues, despite the easing of some of the harsher measures.

Non-Muslims are prohibited from public worship in Saudi Arabia, while elsewhere in the Middle East anti-Semitic materials regularly appear in government-controlled media. The Government of Iran continued its repressive practices against members of the Baha'i faith. In Vietnam both Buddhists and Christians suffer from government restrictions. . . .

THE RIGHTS OF WOMEN

Discrimination reached new heights of severity in Afghanistan with the rise to power of the Taliban.

Violence against women, both in and outside the home, a particularly widespread and entrenched violation of women's rights, is either legally permitted or simply allowed to continue in many countries and is by no means restricted to the developing world. In a number of countries, the continued practice of female genital mutilation is a particularly egregious form of violence against women. Rape has been a particularly cruel tool of warfare in a number of conflicts. Despite the enormous strides of recent years, there is much that remains to be done. . . .

WORKER RIGHTS AND CHILD LABOR

Failure to respect basic worker rights as defined in several key International Labor Organization Conventions continues to be a problem in many countries. These core worker rights include freedom of association, which is the foundation on which workers can form trade unions and defend their interests; the right to organize and bargain collectively; freedom from discrimination in employment; and freedom from child and forced labor. . . .

CONCLUSION

In conclusion, let us remember on whose behalf we labor in the field of human rights and on whose behalf a global structure of protection is being built. This structure belongs to all of us, and it is being built for all of humanity. In building this structure the world is responding to the pain and need of men and women and children on all continents and to the historical conscience of mankind. . . .

It is true that human rights find their realization in a highly imperfect world. But that does not free us from responsibility to support respect for human rights in the processes of government and law and does not permit us to shirk this responsibility by invoking national sovereignty, or claims of social stability, economic development, or cultural difference.

As we near the dawn of a new century, the international community has an unprecedented opportunity to engage in respectful dialog on how best to promote human rights, freedom, and dignity. Every culture, tradition, and civilization brings its own genius to

bear on this monumental effort, and that moral responsibility rests with every man and woman on this planet, calling us to a modern-day pursuit of an age-old quest for justice. In the words of the Talmudic sage Hillel: "If I am not for myself, who will be for me? If I am only for myself what am I? And if not now, when?"

John Shattuck
Assistant Secretary of State
Democracy, Human Rights, and Labor

DOCUMENT 9.8

CHINA RESPONDS, *CHINA DAILY,* MARCH 5, 1997

The State Department of the United States recently released its own state-of-the-world verdict on human rights around the globe.

The lengthy "Country Reports on Human Rights Practices for 1996" once again distorted and attacked at length the state of human rights in China and more than 190 other countries and regions.

The U.S. Government, posing as a self-appointed "human rights judge of the world," turned a blind eye yet again to the serious human rights problems it has in its own country. It did not utter a single word about them in the report.

Indeed, it is the United States, the self-declared "global human rights authority," that has a very poor human rights record in the world. . . .

The United States always portrays itself as the incarnation of the "model of international human rights." However the level of constitutional rights granted to its citizens is far below internationally accepted standards.

MONEYBAG DEMOCRACY

The United States, which boasts about being the model of democracy, has been peddling its democratic system throughout the world with

---

SOURCE: Ren Yanshi, "USA, A Country in Need of Human Rights," *China Daily*, March 5, 1997.

wishful thinking. But everyone knows that the 200-year-old American democracy remains a democracy for the rich. . . .

In presidential elections, which are cited as a major political event in the country, the highest ever voter turnout was only 65 per cent. Since a presidential candidate needs only a simple majority of votes to win the election, U.S. presidents can be elected by a very small proportion of the electorate, often less than 35 per cent, of eligible voters. According to statistics, voter turnout in the 1996 presidential election was only 49 per cent, the lowest since 1924. That means the president had the support of only around 25 per cent of eligible voters. It is obvious that the results of the so-called general election reflect neither the will of the people as a whole nor the majority. . . .

Political democracy in the United States has always been the game of the rich. Since the early days of the republic, the overwhelming majority of high public officeholders, including presidents, vice presidents, members of the cabinet and the Supreme Court, have come from among the richest five per cent of families in the U.S.

LAND OF TERROR

Terrifying bomb explosions in the United States in recent years have stunned the world. In February 1993, a 1,500 pound car bomb damaged the underground garage of the 110-story World Trade Centre in the financial district of Manhattan, New York, killing six people and injuring more than 1,000 others, and forcing 50,000 employees and tourists to flee the building.

In April 1995, a powerful 1,200 pound car bomb destroyed a federal office building in Oklahoma City, Oklahoma, killing 168 people and injuring 850 others. Among the victims were 19 children in a day-care centre in the building. In July 1996, a bomb explosion in the Centennial Olympic Park in Atlanta, Georgia, killed two people and injured more than 110 others during the Olympic Games, a sports event that attracted world-wide attention.

It is not accidental that terrorist bomb attacks continuously occur in the United States, an excessively violent country where terrorism is deeply rooted in society.

The United States has the highest rate of violent crime in the world. An average of two million violent crimes occur annually with six million victims, of whom 24,000 are murdered. . . .

The United States has one of the world's largest police forces relative to its population and the largest prison population. A report released by the U.S. Justice Department on June 30, 1996 revealed that the number of people serving a prison sentence in the country was 5.36 million, three in every 100 adults.

POVERTY, HUNGER AND THE HOMELESS

The United States is the richest country in the world, but because of the serious polarization between the rich and poor, the issues of poverty, hunger and the homeless have always been an inherent malady in its society. The gap between the haves and have-nots in the United States is one of the widest in the western world. According to statistics, the richest 1 per cent of families today possess 40 per cent of the nation's wealth. . . .

In May 1994, in a "strategic plan" on the homeless, the US Government estimated there were 9.52 million homeless people in the country, of whom 43 per cent were drug users, 26 per cent had mental disorders, eight per cent were Aids patients or HIV positive, and 40 per cent were alcoholics. . . .

DEEP-ROOTED RACIAL DISCRIMINATION

The world is well aware of racial discrimination in the United States. The racial genocide of native Americans and the bloody enslavement of black people based on the slave trade are two indelible blemishes on American history. . . .

In the United States, blacks and other ethnic minorities have always been second-class citizens. Black people, who account for 12 per cent of the American population, occupy only 5 per cent of elected positions at various levels and 1 per cent of the seats in the Senate.

A 1995 U.S. Government survey indicated that although women and ethnic minorities accounted for two-thirds of the total population and 57 per cent of the total workforce, 97 per cent of the high-level executives in big businesses were white males. In contrast, the unemployment rate among black people was twice as high as that among whites.

In 1994, while the national unemployment rate was 5.6 per cent, 15.9 per cent of black adults, 40 per cent of black youth and 46 per cent of native Americans were out of work. The poverty rate among blacks, Hispanics and Indians was more than 30 per cent, three times that for whites, and the chances of black children living in poverty were four times greater than for white children. . . .

Statistics in 1991 in the U.S. showed that the country had the highest number of juveniles sentenced to death and that all juveniles condemned to death in the country were black.

A US national drug addiction research group reported that although 80 per cent of drug users in the country were whites, only 7 per cent of those arrested for taking drugs were whites while 28 per cent were blacks. Blacks accounted for 98 per cent of those receiving life sentences for cocaine addiction. . . .

Discrimination against blacks and ethnic people is an inherent evil in the U.S. and this tragic problem continues to plague American society.

Sex discrimination is a long-standing problem which still dogs American society today. . . .

The majority of American women work in the low-paid service sector. A 1995 survey by the magazine *Fortune* reported that women accounted for only 5 per cent of top-level executives in U.S. companies.

Moreover, men and women do not receive equal pay for equal work. Waitresses in restaurants are paid the equivalent of only 75 per cent of the wages paid to their male counterparts, and the incomes of male scientists are generally 24 to 35 per cent higher than their female counterparts. Female civil servants at different levels earn only about half of the salaries of their male counterparts. . . .

The United States is the only country in the world which has actually used nuclear weapons. It has conducted more nuclear tests than any other country and possesses the largest nuclear arsenal. A 1995 report said that America had 25,000 nuclear weapons. Since the explosion of its first atomic bomb in 1945, America has conducted 1,030 nuclear tests, accounting for more than half of the world's total of 2,037 tests.

Its military spending is also the largest in the world. In 1994, it amounted to $274.3 billion, more than twice as much as the combined spending of eight other countries including Russia, China and India. Currently, its average daily spending on nuclear weapons is $80 million. From 1940 to 1995, America's total nuclear weapons spending added up to $4 trillion. Its nuclear weapons spending in 1995 alone was $27 billion. If this money was used to solve the poverty problem in Third World countries, it would relieve hundreds of millions of people from poverty. . . .

America is the world's largest arms dealer. Its overseas arms sales since 1989, according to a December 12, 1994 *Time* magazine article, hit $82.4 billion, more than the combined total ($66.8 billion) of all other countries in the world, and now its share of the world's arms sales market has reached 70 per cent.

The German magazine *Der Stern* reported in 1995 that America had captured three quarters of the post-Cold War world weapons market, reaching 146 countries and regions. More and more American weapons have been used to trigger wars and unrest, said *Der Stern*. *USA Today* also reported in 1994 that warring parties in 39 of the 48 ethnic conflicts around the world in the previous year obtained weapons from the United States. No wonder the U.S. has been dubbed "the world's largest exporter of death. . . ."

While U.S. human rights reports rattle on about human rights violations in other countries, it has been refusing to join the major international conventions on human rights adopted by the United Nations. They include the International Covenant on Economic, Social and Cultural Rights; the International Convention on the Suppression and Punishment of the Crime of Apartheid; the Covenant on the Elimination of All Forms of Discrimination against Women; and the Convention on the Rights of the Child.

As for the International Covenant on Civil and Political Rights, the United States reluctantly ratified it only in 1992, 26 years after it was adopted by the United Nations. And it restricted the covenant's implementation strictly within the framework of its constitution by adding a string of reservations, understandings, statements and agreements so that the document would apply only to the federation, not to individual states, and could not come into force automatically. These preconditions make the document not worth the paper it is written on.

The United States' hegemonic acts of refusing to accept international norms and frequently infringing on the sovereignty of other countries and human rights have earned it the notoriety of being the most condemned country in the world at the end of this century.

As a popular saying goes, one should first correct oneself before trying to correct others. It is bizarre that the United States, with such a poor human rights record of its own, should act as the world's human rights judge and concoct human rights reports year after year, mounting "crusades" against other countries.

If the United States insists on having its own way, it will inevitably provoke more counterattacks from other countries. In the end, it will only hurt itself with the very stick it has been brandishing against others. The U.S. Government would be strongly advised to put its own house in order before pointing its finger at other countries.

9.9   Secretary of State Madeline Albright on the Legacy of the Marshall Plan, Harvard Commencement Address, June 5, 1997
9.10   President Bill Clinton, "Remarks by the President on Foreign Policy," San Francisco, February 26, 1999

In December 1996, Madeline Albright was nominated by President Bill Clinton to serve as his secretary of state. Confirmed a month later, Albright became the first woman in the nation's history to hold that post. She continued as secretary of state through the remainder of the Clinton administration, leading the nation's diplomatic corps in the Kosovo crisis, the NATO bombardment of Serbia, Clinton's visit to China, and the ongoing Mideast peace talks.

Born Madeline Korbel in 1937 in Prague, she escaped Czechoslovakia with her family following the 1939 Nazi takeover, and then again following the 1948 communist coup. The Korbels came to America, settling in Denver. Madeline was 11. Her father, Josef Kobel, an important figure in the Czech diplomatic corps, founded a graduate school in international relations at the University of Denver.

In June 1997, just months following her Senate confirmation, Secretary of State Albright delivered the commencement address at Harvard (*Document 9.9*). It was the 50th anniversary of George Marshall's Harvard commencement speech, and Albright took the occasion to celebrate America's postwar leadership in the world, while using the lessons of the past to condemn those who would draw the U.S. back from international engagement. It is clear from her statements here that she believes strongly in the lessons of World War II—and the lessons of her life as a child in Europe during the tumultuous decades of the 1930s and 1940s.

One of the primary lessons of World War II (one that Albright clearly endorses) has been that force must be met with force—that unchecked aggression will only breed further aggressions. That lesson was played out in the Clinton administration's pursuit of Serbian leader Slobodan Milosevic, the man Clinton called "Europe's last dictator." In July 1998, Serbian police and the Yugoslav army, under Milosevic's direction, launched a massive attack against the Muslim Albanian majority in the Serbian province of Kosovo. Milosevic's objective (although he later denied it) was to remove the Kosovar Albanians from the province, a process known as ethnic cleansing. It soon became apparent that "ethnic cleansing" was a euphemism for a combination of expulsion, extermination, and murder. In September, NATO intervened to stabilize the region. In San Francisco, in February 1999, President Clinton spoke on the situation in Kosovo and the growing problems in the Balkans (*Document 9.10*). Just a month later, Milosevic continued his ethnic cleansing in Kosovo despite repeated demands from NATO to cease and desist. In March, NATO responded to Milosevic's intransigence by launching an around-the-clock air attack on Serb positions in Kosovo, and then finally on Serbia itself. It was the first use of NATO forces in battle. Defiant, Milosevic refused to surrender. He also refused to recognize the outcome of a general election in Serbia that voted him out of power. Finally, in April 2001 he was arrested and charged with war crimes against humanity. He was tried before an international war crimes tribunal at The Hague.

America's action in Kosovo raised a question that has plagued the nation at least since Woodrow Wilson's proposal of the League of Nations. Should the United States be an international policeman? Should the United States be responsible for stopping regional clashes? Using a number of historical references, Clinton, here, addresses the question of globalism and the need for American involvement in world affairs. He also states, in Wilsonian language, that democracy will solve many of the world's problems.

DOCUMENT 9.9

SECRETARY OF STATE MADELINE ALBRIGHT ON THE LEGACY OF THE MARSHALL PLAN, HARVARD COMMENCEMENT ADDRESS, JUNE 5, 1997

Graduations are unique among the milestones of our lives, because they celebrate past accomplishments, while also anticipating

SOURCE: U.S. Department of State Press Release, June 6, 1997.

the future. That is true for each of the graduates today, and it is true for the United States. During the past few years, we seem to have observed the fiftieth anniversary of everything. Through media and memory, we have again been witness to paratroopers filling the skies over Normandy; the liberation of Buchenwald; a sailor's kiss in Times Square; and Iron Curtain descending; and Jackie Robinson sliding home.

Today, we recall another turning point in that era. For on this day fifty years ago, Secretary of State George Marshall addressed the graduating students of this great university. He spoke to a class enriched by many who had fought for freedom, and deprived of many who had fought for freedom and died. The Secretary's words were plain; but his message reached far beyond the audience assembled in this yard to an American people weary of war and wary of new commitments, and to a Europe where life-giving connections between farm and market, enterprise and capital, hope and future had been severed.

Secretary Marshall did not adorn his rhetoric with high-flown phrases, saying only that it would be logical for America to help restore normal economic health to the world, without which there could be no political stability and no assured peace. He did not attach to his plan the label, Made in America; but rather invited European ideas and required European countries to do all they could to help themselves. His vision was inclusive, leaving the door open to participation by all, including the Soviet Union—and so there would be no repetition of the punitive peace of Versailles—also to Germany.

British Foreign Secretary Ernest Bevin called the Marshall Plan a "lifeline to sinking men," and it was—although I expect some women in Europe were equally appreciative.

By extending that lifeline, America helped unify Europe's west around democratic principles, and planted seeds of a transatlantic partnership that would soon blossom in the form of NATO and the cooperative institutions of a new Europe. Just as important was the expression of American leadership that the Marshall Plan conveyed.

After World War I, America had withdrawn from the world, shunning responsibility and avoiding risk. Others did the same. The result in the heart of Europe was the rise of great evil. After the devastation of World War II and the soul-withering horror of the Holocaust, it was not enough to say that the enemy had been vanquished, that what we were against had failed.

The generation of Marshall, Truman and Vandenberg was determined to build a lasting peace. And the message that generation conveyed, from the White House, from both parties on Capitol Hill, and from people across our country who donated millions in relief cash, clothing and food was that this time,

America would not turn inward; America would lead.

Today, in the wake of the Cold War, it is not enough for us to say that Communism has failed. We, too, must heed the lessons of the past, accept responsibility and lead. Because we are entering a century in which there will be many interconnected centers of population, power and wealth, we cannot limit our focus, as Marshall did in his speech to the devastated battleground of a prior war. Our vision must encompass not one, but every continent.

Unlike Marshall's generation, we face no single galvanizing threat. The dangers we confront are less visible and more diverse—some as old as ethnic conflict, some as new as letter bombs, some as subtle as climate change, and some as deadly as nuclear weapons falling into the wrong hands. To defend against these threats, we must take advantage of the historic opportunity that now exists to bring the world together in an international system based on democracy, open markets, law and a commitment to peace.

We know that not every nation is yet willing or able to play its full part in this system. One group is still in transition from centralized planning and totalitarian rule. Another has only begun to dip its toes into economic and political reform. Some nations are still too weak to participate in a meaningful way. And a few countries have regimes that actively oppose the premises upon which this system is based.

Because the situation we face today is different from that confronted by Marshall's generation, we cannot always use the same means. But we can summon the same spirit. We can strive for the same sense of bipartisanship that allowed America in Marshall's day to present to both allies and adversaries a united front. We can invest resources needed to keep America strong economically, militarily and diplomatically—recognizing, as did Marshall, that these strengths reinforce each other. We can act with the same knowledge that in our era, American security and prosperity are linked to economic and political health abroad. And we can recognize, even as we pay homage to the heroes of history, that we have our own duty to be authors of history.

Let every nation acknowledge today the opportunity to be part of an international system based on democratic principles is available to all. This was not the case fifty years ago.

Then, my father's boss, Jan Masaryk—foreign minister of what was then Czechoslovakia—was told by Stalin in Moscow that his country must not participate in the Marshall Plan, despite its national interest in doing so. Upon his return to Prague, Masaryk said it was at that moment, he understood he was employed by a government no longer sovereign in its own land.

Today, there is no Stalin to give orders. If a nation is isolated from the international community now, it is either because the country is simply too weak to meet international standards, or because its leaders have chosen willfully to disregard those standards.

Last week in the Netherlands, President Clinton said that no democratic nation in Europe would be left out of the transatlantic community. Today I say that no nation in the world need be left out of the global system we are constructing. And every nation that seeks to participate and is willing to do all it can to help itself will have America's help in finding the right path.

In Africa, poverty, disease, disorder and misrule have cut off millions from the international system. But Africa is a continent rich both in human and natural resources. And today, its best new leaders are pursuing reforms that are helping private enterprise and democratic institutions to gain a foothold. Working with others, we must lend momentum by maintaining our assistance, encouraging investment, lowering the burden of debt and striving to create successful models for others to follow.

In Latin America and the Caribbean, integration is much further advanced. Nations throughout our hemisphere are expanding commercial ties, fighting crime, working to raise living standards and cooperating to ensure that economic and political systems endure.

In Asia and the Pacific, we see a region that has not only joined the international system, but has become a driving force behind it—a region that is home to eight of the ten fastest growing economies in the world.

With our allies, we have worked to ease the threat posed by North Korea's nuclear program, and invited that country to end its self-imposed isolation. We have encouraged China to expand participation in the international system and to observe international norms on everything from human rights to export of arms-related technologies.

Finally, in Europe, we are striving to fulfill the vision Marshall proclaimed but the Cold War prevented—the vision of a Europe, whole and free, united—as President Clinton said this past week, "not by the force of arms, but by possibilities of peace."

Where half a century ago, American leadership helped lift Western Europe to prosperity and democracy, so today the entire transatlantic community is helping Europe's newly free nations fix their economies and cement the rule of law.

Next month in Madrid, NATO will invite new members from among the democracies of Central and Eastern Europe, while keeping the door to future membership open to others. This will not, as some fear, create a new source of division within Europe. On the contrary, it is erasing the unfair and unnatural line imposed half a century ago; and it is giving nations an added incentive to settle territorial disputes, respect minority and human rights and complete the process of reform.

NATO is a defensive alliance that harbors no territorial ambitions. It does not regard any state as its adversary, certainly not a democratic and reforming Russia that is intent on integrating with the West, and with which it has forged an historic partnership, signed in Paris just nine days ago.

Today, from Ukraine to the United States, and from Reykjavik to Ankara, we are demonstrating that the quest for European security is no longer a zero-sum game. NATO has new allies and partners. The nations of Central and

Eastern Europe are rejoining in practice the community of values they never left in spirit. And the Russian people will have something they have not had in centuries—a genuine and sustainable peace with the nations to their west.

The Cold War's shadow no longer darkens Europe. But one specter from the past does remain. History teaches us that there is no natural geographic or political endpoint to conflict in the Balkans, where World War I began and where the worst European violence of the past half-century occurred in this decade. That is why the peaceful integration of Europe will not be complete until the Dayton Peace Accords in Bosnia are fulfilled.

When defending the boldness of the Marshall Plan fifty years ago, Senator Arthur Vandenberg* observed that it does little good to extend a fifteen-foot rope to a man drowning twenty feet away. Similarly, we cannot achieve our objectives in Bosnia by doing just enough to avoid immediate war. We must do all we can to help the people of Bosnia to achieve permanent peace.

In recent days, President Clinton has approved steps to make the peace process irreversible, and give each party a clear stake in its success. This past weekend, I went to the region to deliver in person the message that if the parties want international acceptance or our aid, they must meet their commitments—including full cooperation with the international war crimes tribunal.

That tribunal represents a choice not only for Bosnia and Rwanda, but for the world. We can accept atrocities as inevitable, or we can strive for a higher standard. We can presume to forget what only God and the victims have standing to forgive, or we can heed the most searing lesson of this century which is that evil, when unopposed, will spawn more evil.

The majority of Bosnia killings occurred not in battle, but in markets, streets and play-grounds, where men and women like you and me, and boys and girls like those we know, were abused or murdered—not because of anything they had done, but simply for who they were.

We all have a stake in establishing a precedent that will deter future atrocities, in helping the tribunal make a lasting peace easier by separating the innocent from the guilty; in holding accountable the perpetrators of ethnic cleansing; and in seeing that those who consider rape just another tactic of war answer for their crimes.

Since George Marshall's time, the United States has played the leading role within the international system—not as sole arbiter of right and wrong, for that is a responsibility widely shared, but as pathfinder—as the nation able to show the way when others cannot.

In the years immediately after World War II, America demonstrated that leadership not only through the Marshall Plan, but through the Truman Doctrine, the Berlin airlift and the response to Communist aggression in Korea.

In this decade, America led in defeating Saddam Hussein; encouraging nuclear stability in the Korean Peninsula and in the former Soviet Union; restoring elected leaders to Haiti; negotiating the Dayton Accords; and supporting the peacemakers over the bomb throwers in the Middle East and other strategic regions.

We welcome this leadership role, not in Teddy Roosevelt's phrase, because we wish to be "an international Meddlesome Matty," but because we know from experience that our interests and those of our allies may be affected by regional or civil wars, power vacuums that create opportunities for criminals and terrorists and threats to democracy.

But America cannot do the job alone. We can point the way and find the path, but others must be willing to come along and take responsibility for their own affairs. Others must be willing to act within the bounds of their own resources and capabilities to join in building a world in which shared economic growth is possible, violent conflicts are constrained, and those who abide by the law are progressively more secure.

---

*Arthur Vandeburg was a Republican senator from Michigan who embraced isolationism through the 1930s, but following Pearl Harbor became one of the Senate's leading internationalists.

While in Sarajevo, I visited a playground in the area once known as "sniper's alley," where many Bosnians had earlier been killed because of ethnic hate. But this past weekend, the children were playing there without regard to whether the child in the next swing was Muslim, Serb or Croat. They thanked America for helping to fix their swings, and asked me to place in the soil a plant which they promised to nourish and tend.

It struck me then that this was an apt metaphor for America's role fifty years ago, when we planted the seeds of renewed prosperity and true democracy in Europe; and a metaphor as well for America's role during the remaining years of this century and into the next.

As this great university has recognized, in the foreign students it has attracted, the research it conducts, the courses it offers, and the sensibility it conveys, those of you who have graduated today will live global lives. You will compete in a world marketplace; travel further and more often than any previous generation; share ideas, tastes and experiences with counterparts from every culture; and recognize that to have a full and rewarding future, you will have to look outwards.

As you do, and as our country does, we must aspire to set high standards set by Marshall, using means adapted to our time, based on values that endure for all time; and never forgetting that America belongs on the side of freedom. I say this to you as Secretary of State. I say it also as one of the many people whose lives have been shaped by the turbulence of Europe during the middle of this century, and by the leadership of America throughout this century.

I can still remember in England during the war, sitting in the bomb shelter, singing away the fear and thanking God for American help. I can still remember, after the war and after the Communist takeover in Prague, arriving here in the United States, where I wanted only to be accepted and to make my parents and my new country proud.

Because my parents fled in time, I escaped Hitler. To our shared and constant sorrow, millions did not. Because of America's generosity, I escaped Stalin. Millions did not. Because of the vision of the Truman-Marshall generation, I have been privileged to live my life in freedom. Millions have still never had that opportunity. It may be hard for you, who have no memory of that time fifty years ago, to understand. But it is necessary that you try to understand.

Over the years, many have come to think of World War II as the last good war, for if ever a cause was just, that was it. And if ever the future of humanity stood in the balance, it was then.

Two full generations of Americans have grown up since that war—first mine, now yours; two generation of boys and girls, who have seen the veterans at picnics and parades and fireworks saluting with medals and ribbons on their chests; seeing the pride in their bearing and thinking, perhaps, what a fine thing it must have been—to be tested in a great cause and to have prevailed.

But today of all days, let us not forget that behind each medal and ribbon, there is a story of heroism yes, but also profound sadness; for World War II was not a good war. From North Africa to Solerno, from Normandy to the Bulge to Berlin, an entire continent lost to Fascism had to be taken back, village-by-village, hill-by-hill. And further eastward, from Tarawa to Okinawa, the death struggle for Asia was an assault against dug-in positions, surmounted only by unbelievable courage at unbearable loss.

Today, the greatest danger to America is not some foreign enemy. It is the possibility that we will fail to hear the example of that generation; that we will allow the momentum towards democracy to stall; take for granted the institutions and principles upon which our own freedom is based; and forget what the history of this century reminds us—that problems abroad, if left unattended, will all too often come home to America.

A decade or two from now, we will be known as neo-isolationists who allowed tyranny and lawlessness to rise again; or as the generation that solidified the global triumph of democratic principles. We will be known as the neo-protectionists, whose lack of vision produced financial meltdown; or as the generation that laid the groundwork for rising prosperity around the world. We will be known as the world-class ditherers, who stood by while the seeds of renewed global conflict were sown; or as the generation that took strong measures to forge alliances, deter aggression and keep the peace.

There is no certain road map to success, either for individuals or for generations. Ultimately, it is a matter of judgment, a question of choice. In making that choice, let us remember that there is not a page of American history, of which we are proud, that was authored by a chronic complainer or prophet of despair. We are doers. We have a responsibility, as others have had in theirs, not to be prisoners of history, but to shape history; a responsibility to fill the role of pathfinder, and to build with others a global network of purpose and law that will protect our citizens, defend our interests, preserve our values, and bequeath to future generations a legacy as proud as the one we honor today.

To that mission, I pledge my own best efforts and summon yours. Thank you very, very much.

DOCUMENT 9.10

PRESIDENT BILL CLINTON, "REMARKS BY THE PRESIDENT ON FOREIGN POLICY," SAN FRANCISCO, FEBRUARY 26, 1999

I very much appreciate this opportunity to speak with all of you, to be joined with Secretary Albright and Mr. Berger, to talk about America's role in that century to come; to talk about what we must do to realize the promise of this extraordinary moment in the history of the world. For the first time since before the rise of fascism early in this century, there is no overriding threat to our survival or our freedom. Perhaps for the first time in history, the

SOURCE: *Public Papers of the Presidents: William Jefferson Clinton, 1999,* 271–79

world's leading nations are not engaged in a struggle with each other for security or territory. The world clearly is coming together.

Since 1945, global trade has grown fifteenfold, raising living standards on every continent. Freedom is expanding; for the first time in history, more than half the world's people elect their own leaders. Access to information by ordinary people the world over is literally exploding.

Because of these developments, and the dramatic increase in our own prosperity and confidence in this, the longest peacetime economic expansion in our history, the United States has the opportunity and, I would argue, the solemn responsibility to shape a more peaceful, prosperous, democratic world in the twenty-first century.

We must, however, begin this discussion with a little history and a little humility. Listen to this quote by another American leader, at the dawn of a new century: "The world's products are exchanged as never before, and with increasing transportation comes increasing knowledge and larger trade. We travel greater distances in a shorter space of time, and with more ease, than was ever dreamed of. The same important news is read, though in different languages, the same day, in all the world. Isolation is no longer possible. No nation can longer be indifferent to any other."

That was said by President William McKinley a hundred years ago. What we now call globalization was well underway even then. We, in fact, had more diplomatic posts in the world than we have today, and foreign investment actually played a larger role in our own economy then than it does today.

The optimism being expressed about the twentieth century by President McKinley and others at that time was not all that much different from the hopes commonly expressed today about the twenty-first. The rising global trade and communications did lift countless lives then, just as it does today. But it did not stop the world's wealthiest nations from waging World War I and World War II. It did not stop the Depression, or the Holocaust, or communism. Had leading nations acted decisively then, perhaps these disasters might have been prevented. But the League of Nations failed, and America—well, our principal involvement in the world was commercial and cultural, unless and until we were attacked.

After World War II, our leaders took a different course. Harry Truman . . . said that to change the world away from a world in which might makes right, "words are not enough. We must once and for all prove by our acts conclusively that right has might." He and his allies and their successors built a network of security alliances to preserve the peace, and a global financial system to preserve prosperity.

Over the last six years, we have been striving to renew those arrangements and to create new ones for the challenges of the next fifty years. We have made progress, but there is so very much more to do. We cannot assume today that globalization alone will wash away the forces of destruction at the dawn of the twenty-first century, any more than it did at the dawn of the twentieth century. We cannot assume it will bring freedom and prosperity to ordinary citizens around the world who long for them. We cannot assume it will avoid environmental and public health disasters. We cannot assume that because we are now secure, we Americans do not need military strength or alliances, or that because we are prosperous, we are not vulnerable to financial turmoil half a world away.

The world we want to leave our children and grandchildren requires us to make the right choices, and some of them will be difficult. America has always risen to great causes, yet we have a tendency, still, to believe that we can go back to minding our own business when we're done. Today we must embrace the inexorable logic of globalization—that everything, from the strength of our economy to the safety of our cities, to the health of our people, depends on events not only within our borders, but half a world away. We must see the opportunities and the dangers of the interdependent world in which we are clearly fated to live.

There is still the potential for major regional wars that would threaten our security. The arms race between India and Pakistan reminds us that the next big war could still be nuclear. There is a risk that our former adversaries will not succeed in their transitions to freedom and free markets. There is a danger that deadly weapons will fall into the hands of a terrorist group or an outlaw nation, and that those weapons could be chemical or biological.

There is a danger of deadly alliances among terrorists, narco-traffickers, and organized criminal groups. There is a danger of global environmental crises and the spread of deadly diseases. There is a danger that global financial turmoil will undermine open markets, overwhelm open societies, and undercut our own prosperity.

We must avoid both the temptation to minimize these dangers, and the illusion that the proper response to them is to batten down the hatches and protect America against the world. The promise of our future lies in the world. Therefore, we must work hard with the world—to defeat the dangers we face together and to build this hopeful moment together, into a generation of peace, prosperity, and freedom. Because of our unique position, America must lead with confidence in our strengths and with a clear vision of what we seek to avoid and what we seek to advance.

Our first challenge is to build a more peaceful 21st century world. . . . That is why I have pushed hard for NATO's enlargement and why we must keep NATO's doors open to new democratic members, so that other nations will have an incentive to deepen their democracies. That is why we must forge a partnership between NATO and Russia, between NATO and Ukraine; why we are building a NATO capable not only of deterring aggression against its own territory, but of meeting challenges to our security beyond its territory—the kind of NATO we must advance at the Fiftieth Anniversary Summit in Washington this April. . . .

It's easy . . . to say that we really have no interests in who lives in this or that valley in Bosnia, or who owns a strip of brushland in the Horn of Africa, or some piece of parched earth by the Jordan River. But the true measure of our interests lies not in how small or distant these places are, or in whether we have trouble pronouncing their names. The question we must ask is, what are the consequences to our security of letting conflicts fester and spread. We cannot, indeed, we should not, do everything or be everywhere. But where our values and our interests are at stake, and where we can make a difference, we must be prepared to do so. And we must remember that the real challenge of foreign policy is to deal with problems before they harm our national interests. . . .

It is in our interest to be a peacemaker, not because we think we can make all these differences go away, but because, in over 200 years of hard effort here at home, and with bitter and good experiences around the world, we have learned that the world works better when differences are resolved by the force of argument rather than the force of arms. . . .

We will also keep working with our allies to build peace in the Balkans. Three years ago, we helped to end the war in Bosnia. A lot of doubters then thought it would soon start again. But Bosnia is on a steady path toward renewal and democracy. We've been able to reduce our troops there by 75 percent as peace has taken hold, and we will continue to bring them home.

The biggest remaining danger to this progress has been the fighting and the repression in Kosovo. Kosovo is, after all, where the violence in the former Yugoslavia began, over a decade ago, when they lost the autonomy guaranteed under Yugoslav law. We have a clear national interest in ensuring that Kosovo is where this trouble ends. If it continues, it almost certainly will draw in Albania and Macedonia, which share borders with Kosovo, and on which clashes have already occurred.

Potentially, it could affect our allies, Greece and Turkey. It could spark tensions in Bosnia itself, jeopardizing the gains made there. If the conflict continues, there will certainly be more atrocities, more refugees, more victims crying out for justice and seeking out revenge. Last fall, a quarter of a million displaced people in Bosnia were facing cold and hunger in the hills. Using diplomacy backed by force, we brought them home and slowed the fighting.

Here's where we are. Kosovar Albanian leaders have agreed in principle to a plan that would protect the rights of their people and give them substantial self-government. Serbia has agreed to much, but not all, of the conditions of autonomy, and has so far not agreed to the necessity of a NATO-led international force to maintain the peace there.

Serbia's leaders must now accept that only by allowing people in Kosovo control over their day-to-day lives—as, after all, they have been promised under Yugoslav law—it is only by doing that can they keep their country intact. Both sides must return to the negotiations on March 15, with clear mandate for peace. In the meantime, President Milosevic should understand that this is a time for restraint, not repression. And if he does not, NATO is prepared to act.

Now, if there is a peace agreement that is effective, NATO must also be ready to deploy to Kosovo to give both sides the confidence to lay down their arms. Europeans would provide the great bulk of such a force, roughly 85 percent. But if there is a real peace, America must do its part as well.

Kosovo is not an easy problem. But if we don't stop the conflict now, it clearly will spread. And then we will not be able to stop it, except at far greater cost and risk.

A second challenge we face is to bring our former adversaries, Russia and China, into the international system as open, prosperous, stable nations. The way both countries develop in the coming century will have a lot to do with the future of our planet.

For fifty years, we confronted the challenge of Russia's strength. Today, we must confront the risk of a Russia weakened by the legacy of communism and also by its inability at the moment to maintain prosperity at home or control the flow of its money, weapons and technology across its borders.

The dimensions of this problem are truly enormous. Eight years after the Soviet collapse, the Russian people are hurting. The economy is shrinking, making the future uncertain. Yet, we have as much of a stake today in Russia overcoming these challenges as we did in checking its expansion during the Cold War. This is not a time for complacency or self-fulfilling pessimism. Let's not forget that Russia's people have overcome enormous obstacles before. And just this decade, with no living memory of democracy or freedom to guide them, they have built a country more open to the world than ever; a country with a free press and a robust, even raucous debate; a country that should see in the first year of the new millennium the first peaceful democratic transfer of power in its thousand-year history. . . .

The question China faces is how best to assure its stability and progress. Will it choose openness and engagement? Or will it choose to limit the aspirations of its people without fully embracing the global rules of the road? In my judgment, only the first path can really answer the challenges China faces.

We cannot minimize them. China has made incredible progress in lifting people out of poverty, and building a new economy. But now its rate of economic growth is declining—just as it is needed to create jobs for a growing, and increasingly more mobile, population. Most of China's economy is still stifled by state control. We can see in China the kinds of problems a society faces when it is moving away from the rule of fear, but is not yet rooted in the rule of law.

China's leaders know more economic reform is needed, and they know reform will cause more unemployment, and they know that can cause unrest. At the same time, and perhaps for those reasons, they remain unwilling to open up their political system, to give people a peaceful outlet for dissent.

Now, we Americans know that dissent is not always comfortable, not always easy, and often raucous. But I believe that the fact that we have peaceful, orderly outlets for dissent is one of the principal reasons we're still around here as the longest-lasting freely elected government in the world. And I believe, sooner or later, China will have to come to understand that a society, in the world we're living in—particularly a country as great and old and rich and full of potential as China—simply cannot purchase stability at the expense of freedom.

On the other hand, we have to ask ourselves, what is the best thing to do to try to maximize the chance that China will take the right course, and that, because of that, the world will be freer, more peaceful, more prosperous in the twenty-first century? I do not believe we can hope to bring change to China if we isolate China from the forces of change. Of course, we have our differences, and we must press them. But we can do that, and expand our cooperation, through principled and purposeful engagement with China, its government, and its people. . . .

[It has also been our challenge] to keep freedom as a top goal for the world of the twenty-first century. Countries like South Korea and Thailand have proven in this financial crisis that open societies are more resilient, that elected governments have a legitimacy to make hard choices in hard times. But if democracies over the long run aren't able to deliver for their people, to take them out of economic turmoil, the pendulum that swung so decisively toward freedom over the last few years could swing back, and the next century could begin in as badly as this one began in that regard.

Therefore, beyond economics, beyond the transformation of the great countries to economic security—Russia and China—beyond many of our security concerns, we also have to recognize that we can have no greater purpose than to support the right of other people to live in freedom and shape their own destiny. If that right could be universally exercised, virtually every goal I have outlined today would be advanced. . . .

For our nation to be strong, we must maintain a consensus that seemingly distant problems can come home if they are not addressed, and addressed promptly. We must recognize we cannot lift ourselves to the heights to which we aspire if the world is not rising with us. I say again, the inexorable logic of globalization is the genuine recognition of interdependence. We cannot wish into being the world we seek. Talk is cheap; decisions are not. . . .

I hope all of you, as citizens, believe that we have to seize the responsibilities that we have today with confidence—to keep taking risks for peace; to keep forging opportunities for our people, and seeking them for others as well; to seek to put a genuinely human face on the global economy; to keep faith with all those around the world who struggle for human rights, the rule of law, a better life; to look on our leadership not as a burden, but as a welcome opportunity; to build the future we dream for our children in these, the final days of the twentieth century, and the coming dawn of the next.

The story of the twenty-first century can be quite a wonderful story. But we have to write the first chapter.

Thank you very much.

9.11   President George W. Bush, September 11, 2001 Evening Address to the Nation

On the morning of September 11, 2001 radical Muslim terrorists attacked the United States. The events amounted to an unspeakable horror that the nation had not seen since the assassination of John F. Kennedy or (as most compared it) the attack on Pearl Harbor in 1941. President George W. Bush called for war, built up a Gulf War-style coalition, and mobilized the military. The enemy was terrorism. The face of the enemy was Osama bin Laden, a Saudi national hiding out in Afghanistan and reportedly the head of a large, well-funded international terrorist organization devoted to terrorizing the United States for its support of Israel and its role in the Gulf War. *Document 9.11* is President George W. Bush's words to a stunned nation, delivered on the evening of the attack.

....

DOCUMENT 9.11

PRESIDENT GEORGE W. BUSH, SEPTEMBER 11, 2001 EVENING ADDRESS TO THE NATION

Good Evening.

Today, our fellow citizens, our way of life, our very freedom came under attack in a series of deliberate and deadly terrorist acts. The victims were in airplanes, or in their offices, secretaries, businessmen and women, military and federal workers, moms and dads, friends and neighbors. Thousands of lives were suddenly ended by evil, despicable acts of terror.

The pictures of airplanes flying into buildings, fires burning, huge structures collapsing, have filled us with disbelief, terrible sadness, and a quiet, unyielding anger. These acts of mass murder were intended to frighten our

SOURCE: White House Press Release, Sept. 12, 2001.

nation into chaos and retreat. But they have failed; our country is strong.

A great people has been moved to defend a great nation. Terrorist attacks can shake the foundations of our biggest buildings, but they cannot touch the foundation of America. These acts shattered steel, but they cannot dent the steel of American resolve.

America was targeted for attack because we're the brightest beacon for freedom and opportunity in the world. And no one will keep that light from shining.

Today our nation saw evil, the very worst of human nature. And we responded with the best of America—with the daring of our rescue workers, with the caring for strangers and neighbors who came to give blood and help in any way they could.

Immediately following the attack, I implemented our government's emergency response plans. Our military is powerful, and it's prepared. Our emergency teams are working in New York City and Washington, D.C. to help with local rescue efforts.

Our first priority is to get help to those who have been injured, and to take every precaution to protect our citizens at home and around the world from further attacks.

The functions of our government continue without interruption. Federal agencies in Washington which had to be evacuated today are reopening for essential personnel tonight, and will be open for business tomorrow. Our financial institutions remain strong, and the American economy will be open for business, as well.

The search is underway for those who are behind these evil acts. I've directed the full resources of our intelligence and law enforcement communities to find those responsible and to bring them to justice. We will make no distinction between the terrorists who committed these acts and those who harbor them.

I appreciate so very much the members of Congress who have joined me in strongly condemning these attacks. And on behalf of the American people, I thank the many world leaders who have called to offer their condolences and assistance. America and our friends and allies join with all those who want peace and security in the world, and we stand together to win the war against terrorism.

Tonight, I ask for your prayers for all those who grieve, for the children whose worlds have been shattered, for all whose sense of safety and security has been threatened. And I pray they will be comforted by a power greater than any of us, spoken through the ages in Psalm 23: "Even though I walk through the valley of the shadow of death, I fear no evil, for You are with me."

This is a day when all Americans from all walks of life unite in our resolve for justice and peace. America has stood down enemies before, and we will do so this time. None of us will ever forget this day. Yet, we go forward to defend freedom and all that is good and just in our world.

Thank you. Good night, and God bless America.